Brooklyn Ethical Association

Factors in American Civilization

Studies in Applied Sociology

Brooklyn Ethical Association

Factors in American Civilization
Studies in Applied Sociology

ISBN/EAN: 9783743388949

Manufactured in Europe, USA, Canada, Australia, Japa

Cover: Foto ©Suzi / pixelio.de

Manufactured and distributed by brebook publishing software (www.brebook.com)

Brooklyn Ethical Association

Factors in American Civilization

FACTORS IN AMERICAN CIVILIZATION

STUDIES IN APPLIED SOCIOLOGY

POPULAR LECTURES AND DISCUSSIONS
BEFORE THE
BROOKLYN ETHICAL ASSOCIATION

NEW YORK
D. APPLETON AND COMPANY
1893

COPYRIGHT, 1893,
BY THE BROOKLYN ETHICAL ASSOCIATION.

PREFACE.

THE consideration of the general topics of current political and economic importance in Man and the State led naturally to the discussion of those special circumstances and conditions—physical, sociological, and economic—which have entered as factors into the growth of our American civilization. In both these courses of lectures the aim and effort has been to apply to the study of the topics therein treated the sound scientific and evolutionary principles outlined and exemplified in the previous works issued by the Brooklyn Ethical Association—Evolution, Sociology, and Evolution in Science, Philosophy, and Art.

That every lecture in these volumes constitutes a wholly satisfactory and final application of evolutionary principles to the problems treated is by no means to be assumed. The social and economic philosophy implied in the doctrine of evolution is nowhere yet completely formulated. Mr. Spencer has given the world an admirable statement and argument of general principles in his epoch-making Synthetic Philosophy, but he has left to others the application of these principles to the detailed problems of social and economic science, as well as to those of physics and theology.

Many able writers in Europe and America are to-day contributing to the growth of these yet inchoate sciences. To this end these lectures may be regarded as an humble contribution. The concentration of the thought of many able minds upon a limited and definite field of research and investigation gives it, we believe, a cumulative value which seldom results from isolated study, and justifies the careful consideration of these lectures by students of political and economic science.

In the arrangement of topics, and the assignment thereof to their chosen exponents, as well as in the discussion following each lecture, the aim has been, as heretofore, to avoid all partisan bias, and to secure a fair representation of both sides of all disputed questions. The only condition expressly urged and emphasized has been that all disputants should endeavor to sustain their views by appeal to sound scientific and evolutionary principles.

The present situation in America furnishes evidence, at least, of the imperative need of a closer and more scientific study of the social and economic principles underlying our national life. The American people have followed the empirical captains of opposing partisan hosts— blind leaders of the blind—to the verge of political and economic anarchy and disaster. To avert or cure such and even more serious impending disasters we have been taught to rely on the lip salve of *a priori* political theories and the rose water of a mechanical system of superficial intellectual culture. Is it not time to recognize the fact that both national and individual prosperity depend upon the recognition of and obedience to physical, biological, social, and ethical laws which are inherent in the nature of things, and the violation of which brings certain destruction to men and nations?

To diffuse sound principles, based on the dynamic laws of evolution rather than upon the static assumptions of metaphysical and *a priori* reasoning, should be the object of all wise and patriotic instruction, in pulpit, school, university, scientific or ethical society or political club. To teachers in such organizations, as well as to the thoughtful and patriotic American citizen, of whatever school or partisan predilection, we commend the perusal and consideration of these lectures.

CONTENTS.

Preface, ... v

THE NATION: ITS PLACE IN CIVILIZATION, . . . 3
Inadequacy of the police idea of the State; its growth out of man's social nature and its necessities; spiritual conception of the nation advocated.
BY CHARLES DE GARMO, PH. D.

NATURAL FACTORS IN AMERICAN CIVILIZATION, . 23
Geology, geography, virgin soil, territorial size; relation to water courses and climatic conditions; natural scenery and the human factor.
BY REV. JOHN C. KIMBALL.

WHAT AMERICA OWES TO THE OLD WORLD, . . . 55
Its discovery; the Puritan spirit; community of language and institutions; the town meeting; popular education; religious freedom.
BY A. EMERSON PALMER.

WAR AND PROGRESS, ... 85
Early uses of conflict; when it becomes injurious; militant and industrial types; our American wars; war and crime; cost of the military establishment; international amity a practicable ideal.
BY DR. LEWIS G. JANES.

INTERSTATE COMMERCE, ... 119
Economic nature of transportation; its evolution; natural and artificial highways; enormous volume of our internal commerce; the railway problem and Interstate Commerce act.
BY ROBERT W. TAYLER.

PAGE

FOREIGN COMMERCE, ... 147
Its beginnings and evolution; England's commercial influence; modern methods; subsidies and tariffs; reciprocity treaties; ethical value of commercial intercourse.

BY HON. WILLIAM J. COOMBS.

THE SOCIAL AND POLITICAL STATUS OF WOMAN, . 173
Her industrial advancement and higher education; her place in the professions; her claims for equal suffrage; social leverage of the ballot; equal suffrage a logical necessity.

BY REV. JOHN W. CHADWICK.

THE ECONOMIC POSITION OF WOMAN, ... 199
How her progress illustrates evolution's law; statistics of her work in America; influence of the factory system and the sewing machine; how her work affects her own character, the family and society.

BY CAROLINE B. LE ROW.

EVOLUTION OF PENAL METHODS AND INSTITUTIONS, 227
Primitive penal methods; growth of prison science; improvements in America; flagrant abuses of our county jails; advances in criminal anthropology; ethical aspects of the problem.

BY JAMES MCKEEN.

EVOLUTION OF CHARITIES AND CHARITABLE INSTITUTIONS, ... 255
Characteristics of natural and human selection; utility of the charitable impulse; almsgiving; the Church and State as almoners; public and private relief work in the United States.

BY PROF. AMOS G. WARNER, PH. D.

THE DRINK PROBLEM, ... 279
Origin and growth of the drink habit: its change with increasing brain development; indiscriminate marriages as influencing its growth; heredity; inebriety an inherited disease; psychological factors; isolation and classification of patients demanded.

BY DR. T. D. CROTHERS.

THE LABOR PROBLEM, ... 307
Slavery and the wages system; working on shares; the factory system; co-operative production and profit-sharing; just

distribution of earnings; profit-sharing an evolutionary method.

BY NICHOLAS PAINE GILMAN.

POLITICAL ASPECTS OF THE LABOR PROBLEM, ... 331

Where labor's strength lies; a type of trade organizations; their democratic character; direct legislation; condition of the laboring classes in England and America; poverty recently intensified; the question of personal freedom; not charity, but justice.

BY J. W. SULLIVAN.

THE PHILOSOPHY OF HISTORY, ... 363

History an evolution of the family; clans, tribes, cities, states; the family in America; the town and individual; our federal system; Church and State; history a real progress; the laws of progress; writers of history; importance of historical studies.

BY EDWARD P. POWELL.

THE NATION:
ITS PLACE IN CIVILIZATION

BY
CHARLES De GARMO, Ph. D.
PRESIDENT OF SWARTHMORE COLLEGE

COLLATERAL READINGS SUGGESTED:

Spencer's Principles of Sociology, Social Statics (revised edition), and Justice; Mulford's The Nation; Bryce's The American Commonwealth; Maine's Ancient Law, Early Law and Customs, and Popular Government; Lubbock's Origin of Civilization; Woodrow Wilson's The State; Freeman's Comparative Politics; Woolsey's Political Science; Humboldt's The Sphere and Duties of Government; Draper's Intellectual Development of Europe.

THE NATION'S PLACE IN CIVILIZATION.

BY CHARLES DE GARMO, PH. D.

WHAT constitutes a state? There are two answers—one defining it as a negation, the other as an affirmation. As a negation the state is a necessary evil; as an affirmation it is a necessary good. If the nation is regarded negatively, the man must go down as the state goes up; if it is positive, the man rises or falls with his country, for their destinies constitute a pre-established harmony. The first is a mechanical, the second an organic conception; the first regards the state as taking away freedom from the individual, the second as conferring and confirming it.

The high standing of the men who maintain that the state is merely a system of police surveillance for the suppression of violence, and hence a necessary evil, a thing to be regretted, and therefore repressed to the greatest possible extent, gives warrant, perhaps, for a brief examination of this theory, which must in the end be rejected as unethical and hence untenable.

Mr. Spencer says in Social Statics, p. 230: "Nay, indeed, have we not seen that government is essentially immoral? Is it not the offspring of evil, bearing about it all the marks of its parentage? Does it not exist because crime exists? Is it not strong, or, as we say, despotic when crime is great? Is there not more liberty—that is, less government—as crime diminishes? And must not government cease when crime ceases, for very lack of objects on which to perform its functions? Morality can not recognize it." "Government," he says again (p. 25), "is a necessary evil, to terminate with the evil which is assumed as the ground of its existence; it is a mistake to assume that government must last forever." This theory finds a momentary assent, for it expresses a phase of truth. Crime and other evils are undoubtedly bad things, and their suppression causes much anxiety and labor, yet surely their repression is not the only or even the chief function of the nation. The family governs, so does the tribe, so indeed does Nature, but these are not nations. There is so much truth that this formula does not express that we are warranted in neglecting it as an inadequate statement of the functions of the nation. Even if requital of deeds were the only ethical principle in the world, this view of the state covers but one half of that, for good may be requited as well as evil. Is there no common welfare in moral, political, social, or economic realms that the nation may create, or, if created, cherish and maintain? Could each of an aggregate of discrete atoms, as men would be without the nation, develop for himself such an ethical world as is now possible to him through the institutions of the nation? This is a new doctrine of monadology in which the separate monads are expected to reach in the short span of a human life a development such as in the theory of Leibnitz has taken all the time since creation to the present. Such a view as this assumes that man has by nature, before ever he becomes a social being, all the blessings, powers, privileges, and rights that now belong to him, plus those that he has surrendered to the state, the necessary evil, without which he would not enjoy the little good he may now claim as his own. That sober men could imagine a state of things in which uncivilized man is such a reservoir of unadulterated blessings is another proof of the fertility of the human imagination.

A corollary of this theory is found in Rousseau's favorite conception of the social contract, in which a bargain between sovereign individuals, existing in some impossible, antenational condition, gives rise to the sovereign state. These doctrines, founded on a partial view of the functions of the nation, or invented to make plausible some desired social or political condition, as was the case on the eve of the French Revolution, all assume that the "natural rights" of man include those he has acquired as a citizen as well as those he may be presumed to yield for the common good. The truth is, however, that all civil rights either enjoyed or surrendered are still civil rights. They are founded not in "Nature" but in society. Their genesis is in the nation itself, and not in some unimaginable situation in which men are together bodily, but apart spiritually.

As a natural or non-social being, a man would be only an intelligent animal. He would owe no allegiance to any authority save his own will—his caprice would be his constant warrant for his conduct; no one could call him to account, for he would be responsible to nobody. His "natural rights" would be to get what he could find and to enjoy what he could hold by physical force. One might just as well carry the argument to its logical conclusion, and take the man out of all relations to his fellow-beings, when he becomes simply an animal. He ceases to be an end in himself and may be utilized by any stronger power. When a man enters the civilized life, therefore, the only "natural rights" he surrenders are those that belong to him as a being of caprice or instinct; not a vestige of civil right is surrendered in such a case, for civil rights belong to a man only as a citizen, not as a natural man.

Such doctrines, though intending to be concrete and practical, are in reality founded on partial facts, or else they assume in the premises the results that are to appear in the conclusion. They wholly ignore the most potent facts in modern civilization. They fail to see that it is to the nation that we owe most of our dignity as men; that through the nation we work out the moral ends for which men exist; that the nation is the source and conserver of our freedom; that, instead of surrendering any rights of value for our spiritual or industrial development, we have made inestimable gains on every side.

How, then, must the nation be thought of if these conceptions are inadequate? A much truer idea is conveyed in the lines of Sir William Jones:

> "What constitutes a state?
> Not high-raised battlement or labored mound,
>   Thick wall or moated gate;
> Not cities proud with spires and turrets crowned;
>   Not bays and broad-armed ports,
> Where, laughing at the storm, rich navies ride;
>   Not starred and spangled courts,
> Where low-browed baseness wafts perfume to pride.
>   No: men, high-minded men,
> With powers as far above dull brutes endued
>   In forest, brake, or den,
> As beasts excel cold rocks and brambles rude:
>   Men who their duties know,
> But know their rights, and, knowing, dare maintain,
>   Prevent the long-aimed blow,
> And crush the tyrant while they rend the chain:
>   These constitute a state,
> And sovereign Law, that state's collected will
>   O'er thrones and globes elate,
> Sits empress, crowning good, repressing ill."

Over against the police idea of the state stands the spiritual conception, which regards the nation as an organism for the realization of the ethical ends of man, or for the establishment and maintenance of freedom in the broad sense. That the full significance of this idea may be seen, it will be well to examine somewhat in detail the forces that are at work to make the nation.

Aristotle boldly asserts that man is by nature a political being. The notion that he is a "natural being," having civil rights to surrender before he ever becomes a citizen, is a modern invention. If, however, Aristotle is right, there must be a set of forces at work in the nature of man or in the nature of things, or both, that tend everywhere to create and sustain the nation. Among the important forces tending to this end we may distinguish first the institutional instinct. By this is meant the impulse for the organized effort of individuals working together, through certain regulations or systems of written or unwritten laws, for common ends. The family, even among savages, is such an institution; so are all organized efforts for worship, whether to a fetich, an oracle, or a god. These elementary stages of the religious institution find their most complete development as organisms in the Roman Catholic Church. In the same way, institutions for the furtherance of economic welfare, or for political freedom, or for the administering of charity, grow up. The Anglo-Saxon race furnishes the finest example of the instinct for institutional organization. A party of half a dozen persons can hardly come together to do a common work, even of a transient nature, without formulating at once a constitution and by-laws. A social club, a reading circle, a literary society, a temperance band, a political club, a charity aid society—all must have written constitutional forms, and transact their business according to Cushing's Manual or Roberts's Rules of Order.

But behind this institutional instinct, its occasion, if not its cause, lies a logical necessity. It is that of having some objective standard of ethical order to which the good may and the bad must conform. Such a standard can be found only in the nation or some equivalent organization. Were there no common agreement, and were the consensus of opinion not embodied in some legal or constitutional form, we should still be in that much-lauded but very undesirable "state of nature" in which each acts for himself, with only his caprice for a guide. Without such institutional aids the race could never have advanced. However far up the hill individuals may have succeeded in rolling the stone of progress, it would have rolled back to the bottom again when they were gone. But with a mechanism for recording, fixing, and transmitting the ethical gains, it is possible for the children to continue the advance from where their fathers left off. Individual conscience is indeed a thing to be cherished, for out of it are the issues of life for the individual; but it may become a monstrous thing if it is not in substantial conformity with the ethical insight of the race. An insane man might obey the dictates of his conscience, yet work untold mischief both to himself and others. The same is true of others who, though not regarded as demented, still magnify an incident into a ruling principle, and then for the sake of conscience do great evil for the sake of a little good. There come times in the life of every nation where the question must be answered by some of its citizens: "Which will you obey, conscience or the constitution?" But these are the great periods of ethical advance in the nation, when transition must be made from a lower to a higher plane. Sometimes, especially in these later years, it may be made wholly by peaceful methods, but sometimes also the shock of war is necessary. In the days before our late war every Northern man had to settle with himself between his conscience and the laws of his country. But now, when this new advance in ethical state has been made, if the conscience of any individual commands him to re-enslave an emancipated race, the organized ethical sense of the nation brushes him aside like an intruding cobweb. The nation, then, is a logical necessity for the highest ethical advance of the race. Instead of being a necessary evil, it is therefore a necessary good.

However evident it may be that the social or institutional instinct is strong in man, and that only through organization in such institutions as the state can freedom be attained or preserved, we need not on this account assert that these high ethical results have been consciously sought from the beginning. It may be that the very passions and selfish desires of men have been the immediate occasion of their developing political organizations, which in the end control the very passions that occasioned their existence. Thus when fire is employed in melting the iron that is to be cast into a stove, the fire itself is used to create an instrument for directing its own future power into more useful channels. So the very wrath of man may lead to the establishment of rules of conduct that will control wrath, even making it serve the good. The desire to preserve personal property may lead to the establishment of such a system that even those who would steal have helped to erect a bulwark against theft, such as they themselves are unable to overthrow when temptation to steal assails them. In his desire to be protected from the results of ignorance in his neighbors, a man may help to set up a system of compulsory education which in the end will apply to his own children. Thus the daily passions and selfish desires of men are at work busily, even if unconsciously, erecting the structure of the state, which in the end shall protect them even against themselves. The latent ethical force in a people is like the latent electric force that exists in every wind that blows, in every babbling stream, in every ton of coal. The institutional devices of the nation are the instruments through which this force can manifest itself. If the falling water turns no wheel, its power runs away unused; if the burning coal has no machinery to utilize its force, no electric current will ever arise from it; if the wind is arrested by no windmill, its latent energy can never find a useful manifestation. Just so with the ethical capacities of a people; without the machinery of the nation, its power would pass unheeded. From these arguments it would appear that the development of the nation rests, first, upon an inherent institutional instinct in men; second, in the logical necessity that makes organization the essential condition of advance from the irrational freedom of caprice found in the "natural man," to the rational institutional freedom enjoyed only by the citizen of the enlightened state; and, third, in the fact that the ordinary passions and desires of men lead, perhaps unconsciously, to the establishment of a national system that protects men from the irrational exercise of the very forces that occasioned the organizations.

Besides all these internal forces that have been active in developing the nation, there is another set of external influences that have also contributed to the final result. Physiography as a scientific basis for the study of history is now being taught in many German universities; it has also gained a foothold in England. Some authors, notably Buckle and Draper, have indeed sought to find the adequate explanation of the development of nations in the physical environment; but no amount of mechanical force, however favorable, will enable a pebble to sprout and become an oak. The living organism of the acorn is alone capable of such development. In the same way, unless the germs of national life exist already in the people, environment can have no potency in unfolding them. Climate, land, water, contour, relief, immigration, migration, incursion, conquest, are all factors that help to determine the form in which the national life shall be embodied. They may decide its rate of development, the limits to which it shall reach, and may even cause its destruction or total transformation. In other words, they furnish the conditions to which the nation must conform, and which may further or retard its growth. If the acorn gets the right conditions of temperature, moisture, and soil, it will grow; otherwise not. It is in this manner that we must regard the forces of the environment of a nation. Spiritual development is always occasioned or influenced by Nature, but never caused by it.

The mechanical theory of civilization implies that man is determined by Nature, granting that he does contribute the spiritual germ; but even this is only a half-truth, for man determines Nature quite as much as he is determined by it. Invention of tools, clothing, shelter, transportation facilities, and the like enable men to live in comfort where the natural man would have perished or have dragged out an unprogressive existence. The whole modern age of mechanical invention is witness to the fact that man determines, and within certain limits even creates, his environment. On the other hand, it is equally evident that certain unchangeable elements of climate, soil, water, and relief, as well as the proximity of other people, invariably have an unquestionable influence in fixing the rate of progress as well as the general character of the national life. Nature and man work together—man furnishes the idea and its institutional mechanism, Nature the external means for realizing the idea.

The evolution of the nation, therefore, is the evolution of the idea of rational freedom, together with the legal or institutional means for its realization.

"Yet I doubt not through the ages one increasing purpose runs,
And the thoughts of men are widened with the process of the suns."

The Oriental thought of freedom is that one, the absolute ruler, should be free; the Greek made some free, the Roman made all free in some things, while the Anglo-Saxon makes all free in all things. The conception of a nation in which each individual shall attain a consistent rational freedom in all things has been a constantly widening one through the ages. Caprice of the individual as the typical freedom of the natural man has constantly yielded to the ethical freedom that can be attained only through political organization.

If, now, we ask what relation the individual bears to the nation, we must answer, An organic, not a mechanical one. His relations to the nation are vital. He is a part of the life of the nation, and in a much larger sense the nation is a part of his life. Without the individual the nation would not exist; without the nation the individual could never become really free. The nation is the ethical macrocosm of which the individual is the microcosm. Just as in education the student seeks to reproduce in little all the knowledge that man has acquired in the past, or as the creature mirrors in his little world of mind all that the Creator has developed in his great universe, so the individual re-enforces a thousand fold his tiny ethical might in the larger life of the nation. A few years of school training put a man into possession of the intellectual life of the race, thus vastly enlarging his individual worth, dignity, and usefulness, making him "the heir of all the ages in the foremost files of time." In the same way participation in the national life raises him from Lear's condition of a "forked animal" to that of a citizen who bears within his bosom the magnificent worthiness of a mighty nation. Why does the American tread the pavements of the Old World with so exalted a spirit? Because he is an American. As an individual he is nothing. As a citizen of this great nation, he is ready to sit down unabashed in the presence of kings and emperors. In his tiny self he implies and reflects the great self; he is the microcosm of which his country is the macrocosm. Were his nation nothing but a police department, his patriotism would have only an exchange value; but if his fatherland is his own larger self, if in his nation he sees the source of his true freedom, the hope of his posterity, the glory of his manhood, then he may deliberately lay down his life in her behalf, assured that he is performing the act of a rational man, not that of a fool. My friends, as the Church is more than a fire-insurance society, so is our country more than a police department. Its flag has more than a commercial value, its citizens are more than an aggregate of separate atoms. The nation is that larger political and ethical self in which we live and move and have our being.

The relation of the family to the nation must be somewhat similarly conceived. The nation is not a large family, whose leaders stand in a paternal relation to the citizens, but is a larger organism for the further development of the ethical functions of the family. The latter secures to the child a certain growth in freedom. It preserves him from the evil consequences that would otherwise follow from his physical and moral helplessness; it surrounds him with an air of love and helpfulness such as the state could not render. But the subordinate relation of child to parent does not suffice for the adult. Only in the state, as we have seen, does he find his larger self, only here does he realize freedom. The nation must look to the family for the beginnings of that rational life of freedom of which it forms the culminating condition. The family must look to the nation for the maintenance of its integrity, hence it is eminently fitting that the state should establish laws for marriage and divorce, for the protection and support of wife and children.

Having established our ideal of the nation as that of a great ethical and political organism through which the race has recorded its progress, and in which alone the individual finds his real freedom, we shall have no difficulty in discovering the difference between a nation and a confederacy. Taking the mechanical view of the nation simply as a police organism for the suppression of disorder, it is difficult to see why a confederation of the colonies would not have been as good as the nation which was finally established, except that it did not work well in practice. But with our present idea of the nation the matter is easy to understand. A confederation is a mechanical, not an organic union; there is reciprocity in trade, but none in moral and political rights and duties. In a confederacy there is simply a league of sovereign states, so that we have to do with an external union of little nations, among which there can, in the nature of the case, be no community of duties and rights. Had we carried out the idea of the confederation in this country we should simply have repeated on a larger scale the experience of Germany and Italy, where every petty prince became the nucleus of a still more petty state. Instead of having as now a mighty nation, capable of determining the destinies of half the world, we should have had an apotheosis of provincialism, which would have dwarfed the growth of freedom, and have reduced the citizen of to-day to a Lilliputian. The primary impulse of provincialism arises from the desire to control domestic affairs in accordance with local desires. Under the Roman imperial ideas of government this was impossible. Every province had to submit to foreign dictation in important domestic affairs unless able to sustain a successful rebellion. The Anglo-Saxon contribution to the nation is one that precisely meets this difficulty—namely, that of local self-government. This device enables men to dispense with the former need for provincialism, thus making it possible for all people to unite into a single nation, who are fitted for such a union by circumstances of geography, race, education, and common purposes. Indeed, England has shown us that by the aid of this new principle geographical position may be largely ignored. The old familiar doctrine of State Rights or State Sovereignty was a remnant of the provincial idea. It was fostered by the presence of the local institution of slavery. That being out of the way, the device of local self-government meets all our needs for communal control of domestic affairs, so that the doctrine of State Sovereignty has already become a historical reminiscence. The adjustment between national and local affairs is now so perfect that only an extraordinary condition of the country can ever again give rise to serious efforts to sacrifice this nation to the provincial idea. The Greeks ultimately sacrificed everything to the independence of small communities or to the greatness of a few men; Rome sacrificed the special wants of the provinces to an all-powerful central government; but Anglo-Saxons have discovered how to preserve both the nation and the community, through the invention of representative government and local self-control of domestic affairs. This makes it possible for us to have at the same time federal union and true nationality. The instincts of the people were right, therefore, when they preferred to suffer any loss rather than sacrifice the national to the provincial spirit, even though the province should include a third of the dominion. We are one people, having a common ancestry, a common language, a common moral destiny. It was better for the South to sacrifice all her slaves, the North all her treasure, and both their best blood, rather than allow the nation to be rent in twain, for this would mean not only a division of ethical force, but the hostility of the two parts. It would have been a relapse into the provincial condition that it cost

Italy and Germany so much blood and treasure to emerge from. For an enlightened people, one capable of self-government, it would appear, therefore, that with the aid of this Anglo-Saxon contribution to liberty, and with the consequent decline of the old provincial need, the chief factors of the nation are the ideal ones already mentioned, viz., substantial unity of institutional instincts, similar ideas of ethical and political freedom, and impulses for economic progress. Given these agreements, there is room for variety in the means for the realization of a higher national life. England has shown that democracy can get along very well with a queen and a house of noblemen; France has demonstrated that the ministry may be changed every few months without bringing the nation to ruin; Germany, that a free nation can get along with a tyrannical emperor; and Italy, that the Church, even where strongest, is not an insurmountable barrier to a free and united nation.

The question is asked, "When is the sentiment of nationality a help, when a hindrance, to universal human brotherhood?" It can hardly be a hindrance when the nation is conceived as an organism for directing, recording, preserving, transmitting the ethical forces active among a people. When it is regarded as a supreme instrument for developing the most sacred rational freedom of men, it is inconceivable that the nation should generate hatred of men. Universal human brotherhood implies divine fatherhood, and a love for the most potent influence in the world for realizing the decrees of Providence can hardly be in conflict with a brotherly love for God's creatures. It may be that improper tests of brotherhood are sometimes applied. Because I love my neighbor as myself, it does not follow that I am to receive him into my family, or into my business, for such a proceeding might injure me without helping him. Because the citizens of the United States are in substantial accord regarding the exclusion of the Chinese, it does not therefore follow that this is from a lack of brotherly sympathy. To sacrifice everything to a mistaken idea of brotherhood would be in the end to sacrifice the conditions of making brotherhood helpful. We have a certain standard of civilization to maintain, and the claims of our fellow-men do not extend so far as to render our efforts futile. This would be to sacrifice the greater to the lesser good. Only devotion to an inadequate national ideal could ever be in conflict with a true ideal of human brotherhood.

It has been the dream of the philanthropist and socialist to break down the national barriers, and to place all mankind in one political state in which strife should be swallowed up in universal love. Peace, prosperity and progress, brotherly love and mutual helpfulness, are to be the characteristics of this new federation of the world. This natural desire of the man who loves his neighbor as himself was greatly augmented by the abnormal development of the provincial spirit during the eighteenth century, in which mutual jealousy often led to useless wars between those who by culture, language, and general moral aim should have been one people. But now that the provincial spirit has merged into the national, we are beginning to see that, for long periods to come, the road to the progress of all is through the unhampered development of the separate nations.

It is perhaps natural for us to pity the Germans on account of their feeble democracy, their love of a strong, centralized, and even bureaucratic government. But it is very evident that any attempt to graft our democratic notions upon the stock of their imperial ones would ruin both stock and graft. The German nation must have the opportunity of self-evolution, untrammeled by well-meant but futile efforts to force a premature growth. In the same way, every nation has a strong basis of national ideals; it is dominated by common sentiments that may be entirely out of harmony with those of other nations; its physical environment may determine it to a line of growth very different from that of other nations with other surroundings; its natural resources may be such that one form of civilization would thrive where another would not. A common religion is much more likely to make all men brothers than common political organization, yet this does not, and perhaps can not, exist. Those states of civilization that make one set of men Mohammedans and another Christians preclude the idea that their political progress can be best attained by amalgamation. The strong would be retarded, checked, and hindered, and the weak unduly hurried. Cosmopolitanism in government is undesirable, even if not impossible. A nation can best help the world to an advance in civilization by developing her own as rapidly as her natural conditions will admit. Through her isolation as a nation, England was able not only to develop the industrial spirit within her own narrow borders, but to transmit it by example to the whole world.

Because of her isolation from Europe, this country has been able to raise a mighty people to the stage at which self-government appears to be a permanent success. Had either of these nations been under the dominating influence of the continent of Europe during the periods of their national development, the European conditions of the seventeenth and eighteenth centuries might still prevail. As it was, both nations fully developed the best that was in them, then transmitted their demonstrated excellence to the rest of the world.

Our own nation now has the greatest opportunity of realizing the ethical ends for which men exist that has ever been granted to any people in any age. With the choicest natural heritage that has ever fallen to any race; with the conscious possession of all the knowledge that the labor of the past has stored up for us; with the accumulated freedom that has been secured since men began to shed their blood to preserve their liberty; and with a marvelously perfected political organization, we are, above all other nations, endowed with the means of making righteousness prevail. If the forces of life are in us, we shall proceed along our destined way, always standing like Liberty enlightening the world, ready to send the rays of freedom to the farthest bounds of the earth, but steadily resisting every influence that would fetter our fleet limbs by making them keep step with antagonistic or less worthy nations. I conclude, therefore, that, so far as our vision will reach, the nation, conceived in its broad sense, is the ultimate unit of civilization.

ABSTRACT OF THE DISCUSSION.

Mr. WILLIAM POTTS:

While I have been greatly interested in the lecture to which we have listened, it seems to me that one or two fallacies have run through Dr. De Garmo's paper which vitiate some of his conclusions. The first is the confusion of the nation with social relations in general. Also there is a certain not unnatural confusion of the terms organic and organization. The general trend of the discourse seems to imply that the nation is more important than the individual. I should contend that the individual is of the first importance. The nation or any other factor of civilization is of importance simply as it serves the individual. I do not exist for the purpose of making a nation; the nation exists in order that I may be strengthened and improved. I think the nation is by no means a permanent institution. I agree that it is useful for the time being, but merely as an instrument which a body of persons uses in assisting its own development.

I can not think that national development is a good when it is at the expense of another nation or people. The speaker seemed to assume that the nation is an aid to the individual in all cases. He lost sight of the fact that the nation is a machine, and that the machine can not be run without an engineer. The nation, being a machine, can never do the best kind of work; that can only be done by a free agent. I have had to do with a movement (civil-service reform) the success of which people from the outside think would make everybody happy. We have had two objects: first, to obtain a body of men to operate the machine so that it may be as well worked as possible; second, which is more important, to relieve the people at large of the tremendous crushing power of the machine which hampers their development. But when we accomplish these objects, all that we shall do is to secure the best methods of running the machine. With our form of government we can never expect to get governmental positions in the hands of the men best fitted to perform their functions. We are therefore, of necessity, forced to officer the machine with such as can be obtained, and then to fight all the time the men we have in. I doubt whether we shall ever see a different state of affairs. The nation is created by the individual, to do what can best be done by an organized body of people to promote the development of individuals;

it is not an end in itself, to which the welfare of individuals should be sacrificed.

PROF. GEORGE GUNTON:

When Dr. De Garmo had finished his address, I thought there was little more to be said. It was such a concise and rational exposition of the subject that it should have produced conviction in all minds. But the last speaker differs from me. The point of the lecture was to present the nation as a permanent factor in civilization, not a mere police function to disappear in the future evolution of the race. The nation is an organic force in civilization. Now, government, of which Mr. Potts complains, seems to me a very different thing from the nation. I was glad that the speaker commenced with a criticism of Herbert Spencer, because Mr. Spencer stands out conspicuously as an advocate of the doctrine enunciated by Mr. Potts—that the nation is finally to disappear. My definition of the nation is that it is the social environment of the individual. The nation is a social aggregate; not only like the stove, to conduct and control the fire, but it is the creative genius in the environment from which individuality is constantly developed. Instead of regarding the nation as inimical to the individual, I think of it as indispensable to him. As Mr. Spencer has elsewhere said, "It is a question of the development of character." The characters of individuals are drawn from the nation, developed by the environment which the social solidarity of the people creates. The nation, therefore, seems to be socially indispensable, not merely as a machine, but as an environment for the creation of the individual. It is a mistake to think that national lines will finally be obliterated. The nations develop differentiated types of character, and it is as important for the advancement of the race that we should have all types of social environment developed, in which individuals can live and attain the highest evolution of their own natures, as that we should have a diversity of occupations and industries. Mr. Potts says that whenever a nation grows at the expense of another people it is wrong. But the true function of the nation is to develop the character of its own citizens without injuring others. The development of a national type of character and civilization is the best possible contribution to the advancement of all. We can advance the civilization of Africa most quickly by developing that of America. I was pleased with Dr. De Garmo's remark that we could not manage German affairs better than they do. The character of German freedom is best developed in Germany. We can do more for Russia by sending our machinery there for their own use than by abolishing the national lines and inviting Russians to come here. This pooling of issues and abolishing national lines would be most detrimental to human advancement. It is most important for Americans to learn the true place of the nation in civilization. We are prone to the conceit that we must take the world in our arms all at once. If we insist that the lowest elements in civilization be brought in juxtaposition with the highest, we prevent the progress of both. Society naturally differentiates into groups whose members are harmonious in their aims. Mr. Potts does more good in the Civil-Service Reform Association and the Ethical Association than he would by working in the uncongenial society of Mott Street. The nation is a grouping of the human race according to the social, industrial, and political affinities of its members. It is the necessary road to human advancement. Every practical gain in liberty for the individual has been made by erecting barriers. The savage has fewest legal and institutional obstructions to his action and least freedom. Obstacles promote freedom when they shut out what is inimical to freedom. Freedom is not merely negative permission to act, but it also implies power. No man is free to do anything unless he has the power to do it. Poverty is never free. The nation is the first condition to the increase of wealth and power and safety; and these are the very source of freedom.

DR. ROBERT G. ECCLES:

I think there has been a misunderstanding all around this evening. Certainly the attitude of the speaker toward Mr. Spencer is different from my own; either he or I must have misunderstood Mr. Spencer. So far as the question of the freedom of the will enters into this problem, the Gordian knot is cut when we stop to think that all progress is by the survival of the fittest—the killing off of those who go in the wrong direction. The wills in the past which went wrong were killed off, and as progress goes on we become nearer and nearer alike, and more free because we all will to move nearly alike. I think there is no way in which a nation can advance except by hurting others. We can not even improve ourselves except by hurting ourselves. One man clashes with another, and whips the other or is whipped by him, and both are improved by the encounter. So it is with nations. The governmental function of the nation has been characterized as a police function by Prof. Huxley and others, because the English idea of a police is different from ours. Mr. Spencer says it is the duty of government to see that justice is done between man and man and nation and nation; that is the meaning of "police function" in Great Britain. The duty of government is simply to prevent one man or nation from interfering with the progress of others. The speaker's distinction between a vital and a mechanical force is remarkable in this last decade of the nineteenth century. The notion of a "vital" force has been obliterated by modern science. Everything vital is also mechanical. As against the democratic doctrine of "State Rights" I believe in the nation as a power superior to the individual. As Mr. Spencer says: Society must take the precedence of the individual because it is essential to the progress of the individual. There must be an equilibrium of the centralizing and localizing forces in our government. Let each party hold fast to its doctrine and fight for it. It will be a sad day when either idea gains a complete supremacy, whichever it may be.

DR. LEWIS G. JANES:

I wish to protest again in this place against judging Mr. Spencer by quotations from Social Statics, unless in recent times he has repeated the opinions therein expressed. He long ago repudiated a large part of that book, and in the latest edition about two thirds of the original is stricken out. In his most recent work on Justice he sets forth his mature thought on the powers of the state. I doubt whether the language quoted by Dr. De Garmo would now correctly represent his ideas. What he does believe and teach is that government as a coercive force over the individual has decreased and will continue to decrease in the future as individuals gain in intelligence and morality. As thus stated, the truth of his doctrine seems to me to be self-evident; all history demonstrates and illustrates it. I do not think that Mr. Spencer anticipates the cessation of all the internal and non-aggressive functions of government. He admits that there are certain things which people can do better in their collective than in their individual capacities. He teaches that it is the duty of the state to secure justice and equal opportunity to individuals, and will be so long as these are endangered by the encroachments of others. As the average intelligence and morality of a community rise, the coercive functions of government decrease. Laws which interfere with individual liberty are either repealed or become "dead letters" on our statute books, because they no longer apply to existing facts. What has thus taken place in the past is sure to take place in the future. Many things will be done by the voluntary action of individuals which have hitherto been done by governmental coercion. In this sense the state will be a constantly diminishing factor in civilization. Prof. Gunton defines the nation as "the social environment of the individual," and then accuses Mr. Spencer of being a conspicuous advocate of the doctrine that it will finally disappear. This is a manifest absurdity. Mr. Spencer never taught any such doctrine. What he believes will disappear is the government in its coercive functions; and that only as the growing intelligence and ethical character of the people render it unnecessary. Nor does Mr. Spencer look for the abolition of the coercive functions of government in order to resolve society into its "discrete atoms"; but rather as a condition for more perfect social union, based on the voluntary consent and co-operation of individuals instead of governmental coercion. Thus only, he believes, can society reach a condition of stable equilibrium, consistent with the functions of a permanent progressive civilization.

Dr. De Garmo, in reply:

I suspect that when we find out where we are, we are really not very far apart. The exposition of Herbert Spencer's views has been to me the greatest gain in the discussion. As thus explained, they are perfectly rational. I suspect that my opposition to Mr. Spencer is based upon psychological rather than sociological grounds. I do not belong to the company who can not distinguish themselves from their nervous systems. One speaker regards it as an astounding fact that in the nineteenth century one should conceive of anything in the universe superior to mechanics. I used to quarrel with such statements, but the gentleman included in mechanism all that I mean by spiritualism. I have no quarrel with those who put life and spirit into the lowest atom. The human race is not merely a race of fighting animals. The law of the survival of the fittest does hold good in a mechanical way among the beasts of the field; but the human race has developed a system of mutual helpfulness—and that is just what the nation is. I have endeavored to set forth what I regard as the spiritual view of the nation as a permanent force in civilization. If I have not succeeded in making it clear that the individual is the microcosm of which the nation is the macrocosm, and that the individual is dignified by his relations with the nation, my labor has been in vain. Without society man is only an animal; it is only by society as organized in the nation that he makes any progress.

NATURAL FACTORS IN AMERICAN CIVILIZATION

BY
JOHN C. KIMBALL
AUTHOR OF EVOLUTION OF ARMS AND ARMOR, MORAL QUESTIONS IN POLITICS, ETC.

COLLATERAL READINGS SUGGESTED:

Bryce's The American Commonwealth; Carey's Principles of Social Science, Past, Present, and Future, and Harmony of Interests; Marsh's Man and Nature; Guyot's Earth and Man, and Physical Geography; Huxley's Physiography; Shaler's Man and Nature in America; Payne's History of the New World called America; Introductory Chapters in Buckle's History of Civilization; Hutchinson's History of Massachusetts Bay; Capt. John Smith's Generall Historie; Edward Everett's Orations on The First Settlement of New England and on The Pilgrim Fathers.

NATURAL FACTORS IN AMERICAN CIVILIZATION.

BY JOHN C. KIMBALL.

> How many subtlest influences unite
> With spiritual touch of joy or pain,
> Invisible as air and soft as light,
> To body forth that image of the brain
> We call our country:
> Mountain and river, forest, prairie, sea,
> A hill, a rock, a homestead, field, or tree,
> The casual gleanings of unreckoned years,
> Take goddess shape at last, and there is she.—LOWELL.

HOW NATURE IS RELATED TO CIVILIZATION.

FOUR hundred years ago this past week Columbus and his fellow-voyagers were having their first thrilling sensations over the discovery of what is now known as the New World; and, remembering the immeasurable difficulties and uncertainties of their great enterprise, the ridicule and stupidity in the midst of which it was begun, the slenderness of its outfit, the long voyage of its participants off into the ocean's dread unknown, the dependence of the whole thing, idea and deed, steering amid shallow brains and over soundless seas, on its single cranky leader—

> "One faith against a whole earth's unbelief,
> One soul against the flesh of all mankind,"

and the blossoming at last of its flower of success out of the sea's awful waste at the very moment when its stem of means had been stretched to its utmost limit—remembering all these things as a background, whose fancy can picture too vividly the delight and wonder with which, in those morning hours of history's new day, they must have scanned the strange scenes its light revealed?

But, impressive as the discovery was even with their limited view of its nature, what would have been their emotions if they could have seen it stretching out in time as well as space, and in its moral as well as in its material significance? It was not only so many millions of square miles added to the earth's geography and so many new species of animals and plants to its natural history, not only the opening of a new realm over which to extend the government, civilization, and society of the Old World, but the addition of a new horizon to its mind, the starting-point of a new type of government, civilization, and society for its hopes, the opening of a new environment with which to shape into nobler forms all the attainments of the past. We know now under evolution, as we never could before, that man is not a mere fiat being created by a let-him-exist decree outside of the earth, and dropped by a Dr. Deity independent of any earthly parentage into his mundane cradle, but the product all through of our own terrestrial sphere— know how largely not only animals and plants, but races, nations, institutions, religions, souls, are shaped from age to age by their visible material surroundings. If the correspondence between character and condition, between the world's political and natural divisions, is not always directly manifest, if meanness seems sometimes to be nourished by the mountains and grandeur by the plains, and heathenism to hold its widest sway—

> "Where every prospect pleases,
> And only man is vile,"—

it is because we look at the exceptions and not the rule, at one of the factors instead of the whole, at the surface of things rather than at their root. It is not by any mere accident that the larger half of the world's enlightenment is in its northern hemisphere and that the mercury of its civilization has climbed highest in its temperate zones, but from the fact that the physical elements on which they depend, the light of suns and the warmth of skies which enter into them, are there the best adapted to their growth. Where but on a soil fenced in by the desert and fertilized by the Nile could Egypt and the pyramids have been built up? Where the Greece of art and song have arisen but from the Greece of Olympic mount and Tempean vale? How Rome have set its foot on the neck of the world without having it incased in its wonderful Italian boot? It was not the barren Palestine of to-day out of which ever could have come the wealth and beauty of Hebrew faith and Christian grace, but only the old one of Eschol grapes, the cedars of Lebanon, and Galilean corn; and the strongest argument against the Asiatic origin of the great Aryan race is that no scenery along the Caspian shore could have nursed a tree whose branches have covered such breadths of continent and borne such fruits of soul. Many and mighty, and often old and far-reaching, are the hands with which Nature has shaped and is still shaping our modern life. Before the beginnings of human beings are the beginnings of human history. The geology of the continents is the embryology of the nations; inspecting their rocky entrails the scientific way of knowing their destiny. Not in Saxon bone or Norman blood, but in Silurian shale and carboniferous strata, were laid the deeper foundations of England's greatness. Battles have been fought between the elements as decisive of all after-events as any of the fifteen between armies Mr. Creesy has so graphically described. And on the eastern coast of South America there is a single cape determining the hemisphere of the Gulf Stream, a change in whose location a hundred miles would have changed the course of European history more profoundly than has been done by the wars of all its Napoleons and Cæsars; the earthquake which made it failing to come to time a mishap that might have lost the world not a Waterloo, but a civilization.

Ascribing to Nature such an immense part in the drama of history is very far from making history, as is sometimes charged, a mere fatalistic development exclusive of all will power, either human or Divine. The Nature it compels us to recognize as its factor is not a mere dead mechanism, not the carpenter and chemist Nature that Mr. Buckle and others have made so much of in the past, but the Nature of evolution, the Nature that, even in its most physical and material parts, is alive with the indwelling God, the Nature out of which man comes not as a vase does from the potter's wheel, but as the child does out of the mother's body and the father's love. So far, indeed, as the individual man is concerned, this Nature was doubtless to begin with his exclusive factor, made him body and mind, color, form, structure, senses, and soul, with as little reference to his own will as the mother does her babe. But that part of her work has for ages been done. Climate, food, scenery, soil, the mountain's grandeur, and the ocean's wonder make now only the slightest impression on his stature, shape, complexion, character, or anything about him which is bodily and individual. The negro of Africa remains as black amid Northern snows as under tropic suns, and the Tennyson of England becomes in all lands the poet of human hearts.

What Nature is at work upon to-day and all through the historic ages is society—the building up of the individual man into nations, institutions, civilizations. And it is here, without at all going out of the business herself, that she has taken man in as a partner; here that the factors of climate, soil, site, scenery, and that inward life-spirit of hers which no outward term can describe, unite with those of will and soul. And what the great poet of England, recognizing both factors, has put in song is equally the truth of science—that

> "Life is not an idle ore,
> But iron dug from central gloom,
> And heated hot with burning fears,
> And dipped in baths of hissing tears,
> And battered with the shocks of doom
> To shape and use."

AMERICA'S SPECIAL INDEBTEDNESS TO NATURE.

Pre-eminently has Nature thus interpreted been an agent in shaping our American life—has done it and is still doing it with a beauty, a distinctness, and in some cases with a dramatic skill that have been equaled in no other land; and, while its human agencies are not to be forgotten, no one can thoroughly understand our country's civilization, act in harmony with it and be its helper, who does not begin with the study of its great natural factors.

GEOLOGY.

First among them are its geological treasures—not only their variety, abundance, and accessibility, but their peculiar adaptation to such human needs as our country has since developed. As in every crawling caterpillar are the skeleton and wings folded up of an air-sweeping butterfly, and as it is at these rather than at its outside feet and fur that we must look to find the kind of life it was meant finally to shape itself to, so beneath the caterpillar Indian civilization, which was merely crawling over America when Columbus discovered it, and which has seemed to some its only natural product, there were folded up in its rocks and mines the skeleton-and-wings indications all the time of an estate meant for it eventually to reach that was to be as different from its Indian feet and fur as a life that flies is from a life that crawls. Looked at in even the most cursory manner, who can deny the immense influence of these geological agents in feeding and shaping its civilized life? What has sent the millions of its white inhabitants trooping over the great West, dragging behind them homes, churches, schools, workshops, but its wealth-giving minerals and its wheat-growing soils? Where would have been its railroads, its steamboats, its factories, without its vast deposits of coal? Who shall measure the multiplied civil uses, from cannon loaded with shot to pens loaded with thought, that its vast stores of iron have been put to? How wonderfully its veins of silver and gold have shaped themselves into wings which have borne its commerce from sea to sea, and, alas! into weights which have dragged its souls from crime to crime! And what truths of science, what revelations of the earth's history in the mighty past, what revolutions in theology and overturnings of creeds, have the strange stony teachers that it has sent into our colleges and schools, not by any means their most fossilized ones, joined with those of other lands in bringing about!

Then, apart from the special work of these factors, how largely has the exceeding abundance of their products contributed, not only to the country's luxury and stupid display, but to its business, art, taste, culture, comfort, and even religion! For, say what we will about the corrupting influence of mere wealth—the poverty, vice, crime, and degradation it leads to—it is out of it also that comes all that is best in civilization. No wealth, no worth; no coin, no conscience—that is the law, ignoble as it seems, that we have to recognize as true, if not of the individual, yet of society. Take the single matter of its food-supply. Not in any blind materialism did Jesus make the petition for bread a prominent part of Christianity's unending prayer. Why, more religions and more civilizations have been starved by the lack of it than by the lack of truth. Its abundance is the mighty stream pouring out of the earth which drives the great nation factories from whose looms and hammers come the webs of character and the goods of soul. And it is because America has the fountain-head of such a stream stored up for it in the mighty past, as no other nation ever did, that it has before it the possibility of a social state such as no other ever reached.

And behind these immediate agents entering into our civilization, how many are the other remoter ones, makers of the makers, that must be reckoned as its factors? Dr.

Holmes, when asked how early the training of a child should begin, replied: "A hundred years before it is born." Nature, wiser than that, began the training of her American child millions of years before its birth. Earthquakes laid the foundations of its stability, and its culture is rooted in furrows that were made with glacier plows. Its homes are warmed with fuels that carboniferous ages stored away, and are lighted with wicks and pipes that go down into Silurian lamps and Devonian tanks. Starfish paved the way for its star of empire. And a crinoid and labyrinthodont took the first steps of a progress in which a Columbus and a Cabot, a Washington and a Lincoln, a Whittier and a Lowell have taken the last.

How subtle and far-reaching the influence of its geological factors has been, sometimes up into the very heart of its civilization, is curiously illustrated by the relation of its Cretacean limestone to our recent civil war.* Deposited in one of the old Mesozoic ages, and cropping out on the surface in the Southern and border states, it gave their soil a special richness which made the raising of cotton and the use of slave labor profitable to their inhabitants as they never could be in the more sandy and clayey North—rallied them, too, as nothing else could have done, to the defense of their peculiar institution. The line of separation between the two parts of the country was very closely the dividing line of their two soils, cleaving sometimes, as in the case of Kentucky, even the states themselves into halves whose geology was also their politics. The cultivators of the Cretacean soil flocked instinctively to the standard of the Confederacy, the dwellers on the sand and clay to that of the Union; and if the strata of that old Mesozoic era had extended up North a few miles farther, dividing the two sections a little more evenly, the result of the struggle might have been entirely the other way, and our civilization to-day been that of the slaveholder rather than that of the freeman. Darwin's famous chain of connection between cats and clover is not more certain directly than is inversely our American one between lime and liberty. The rhizopods that helped make those old cretaceous deposits—too small for eye to see—shaped the policy of States, modified the Church's interpretation of Scripture, twisted the conscience of a great nation out of shape, and set five hundred thou-

* Shaler's Man and Nature in America.

sand human beings to fighting each other for four years on bloody battle-fields.

It is only one of many cases, found in all forms, that go to show how little of death there is in a thing's being dead. Science is obliged continually to confess an article of religion that theology is giving up—its belief in a resurrection; and everywhere the ghosts of the mighty past, even its animal ones, are stalking out of their graves to take part, more actively, I often think, than some living men, in settling the problems of our civilized age. While cruising this last summer up among the Thousand Islands, the only stepping stones left by which the great Laurentian formation of geology crosses over into the United States, I saw one day a typical summer girl, dainty in dress, delicate in form, and radiant all over with the nameless charm of maidenhood, sitting on a spur of the rock that jutted out into the river—she the fairest flower, if not the richest fruit, of our American civilization, the rock the abode once of America's, and perhaps of the world's, oldest inhabitant. What a contrast of attainments! What millions of years and myriads of changes between the two! And yet they were related, if not as parent and child, yet as cause and condition. The rock and the rhizopod were factors, humble but real, in the long line of agencies out of which had come not indeed her blood, but the wealth, home, culture, country in which alone her blood could have reached its special fineness. And as the father dwelling in the city likes now and then to take his children back to the humble country home from which he started out in life, and to show them by contrast how low down his fortunes began, so in civilization's larger family there seemed a like dramatic fitness in having the maiden of its meridian splendor return to spend a summer day at the home of its Eozoon dawn.

GEOGRAPHY.

But with such factors as these beneath the soil and an antiquity at least equal to that of the Old World for them to act in, the question arises, Why did not the country develop a civilization on its own native stock parallel with that of Europe? Why did its Indian tribes reach at the highest only their mound-building estate, and fall back even from that? Why have we had no American Greece and Rome? Why no Indian Columbus meeting the Italian one half way across the sea? And why are we not celebrating to-day America's discovery of Europe instead of Europe's discovery of us—we who geologically are the Old World and mineralogically the rich one?

Part of the reason may be a defect in the stock itself, Nature not being able to make her race children any more than her family children all equally perfect; and a part the lack of that stimulus to development which comes from immigration. into new climates and new scenes; but the chief cause seems to have been the geographical one that Guyot and Shaler and others have set forth. In raising an infant civilization to maturity, the same as in raising an infant child, there is needed a cradle in which it can be put and a state of peace in which to begin. Nature, in building America, built a magnificent house for adults, but omitted to build in it a cradle for children. Its parts, otherwise favorable, have no sheltered peninsulas like those of Greece and Italy, no sea-girt isles like those of Great Britain, no mountain-defended valleys like those of Switzerland, no partitioned-off corner like that of Spain, in which their inhabitants, secure from foreign invasion, could cultivate the soil, develop the arts of peace, and knit together the bones and muscles of an adult civilization. Its wide-apart Appalachian and Cordilleran walls made it a grand inclosure for animals and plants, but left it for infant nations all out of doors. The moment that any one made a step forward in agriculture and wealth, it offered a temptation all the more for the inroads of its neighbors. And the very abundance of its natural productions, those especially in the way of game, served to encourage a nomadic hunting life that is everywhere incompatible with a highly organized social state.* What the country needed was a race raised elsewhere to such manly strength as could resist assault to come in and be its possessor. This was what Columbus pioneered. The civilization of America had of necessity to be rocked in the cradles of Europe. The wisdom of Providence in having America remain so long in a barbarous state is sometimes wondered at. It was not discovered one hour too late. Europe in the tenth century, when probably it was first visited, was not strong enough, as the event proved, for its permanent occupation. It was a question for two hundred years even in the sixteenth and seventeenth

---

* See Shaler's Man and Nature in America for a full elaboration of these points.

centuries as to whether its colonies could resist the assaults of the wilderness and the savage. And then it was only by repeated influxes of new life from its parent states that the question received its triumphant answer.

Nature, however, is never so good a friend as when it is a conquered foe. The very thing which had been such an obstacle to its development under savagery, its want of small natural divisions, when once overcome, has proved its civilization's greatest helper, has made it not a nest of quarreling States, but a great united nation. On one occasion during our civil war—a war in which this very thing was tried—while the Federal army under General Rosecrans was marching through a border town of Kentucky just escaped from rebel rule, all of whose loyal inhabitants, full of enthusiasm, were flinging out the Stars and Stripes from every window, roof, and flagstaff as a symbol of their sentiments, a beautiful rainbow appeared suddenly in the eastern sky, and a little boy, observing it, ran to his home, exclaiming, "O mother, mother, come and see! God, too, is a Union man! he has hung out his red and white and blue away up in the sky where everybody can see it and know for a certainty the side he is on!" The boy was right. God from the country's very birth has been its Union man. Not only in the blended hues of its rainbows, but in its mountain passes, its river veins, its valley slopes, its mighty prairies, and its circling sea he has written out that he is on the side of its being one united, civilized nation. Its mountain-chains are the walls that hem it in, not the fences which divide it up. Who can believe that the mouth of the Mississippi was meant to be in the control of one nationality and its springs in the control of another? Who fail to see that its multiplied watery arms clasp together its North and South, its East and West, with a strength mightier than that of cannon and more unanswerable than that of logic? If the noble St. Lawrence, running the other way, has been made a divider of the country, it is only for a while, only by a force contrary to that of Nature. Its waters, rushing to the sea at the rate of a million cubic feet a minute, are bound sooner or later to wash out all enmity between the people on its shores, bound to make them as the highway of their commerce to the sea, if not one nation, yet one civilization. Even the country's very diversities, those especially of climate and soil, are but factors in its higher unity, giving each of its parts a set of products the others want it for, and binding them together with all the multiplied ties of trade and social intercourse. As a matter of mere selfish interest, the liver secreting bile, the mouth secreting saliva, and the brain secreting thought could as naturally be the parts of two different bodies as the South secreting cotton, the West secreting wheat, New England secreting schoolma'ams, and New York secreting—Presidents could be the parts of two separate nations. And thus the geographical unity of the country, that was so long the stumbling block of its savagery, has become one of the chief stepping stones in the progress of its civilization.

VIRGIN SOIL.

The long withholding of America from the knowledge of Europe gave its civilization, when at last it came here, not only the strength needed for its occupancy, but also a new and virgin soil on which to plant itself. All the great upward movements of humanity have been made through immigrations. Nature seems to have the same object in the birth and death of nations and civilizations that it does in the birth and death of individuals—that of allowing the diseases and conservatisms and bondages of habit that years have accumulated to be shuffled off, and the good they have gained to be carried over in a fresh seed whose unfolding, untrammeled by the past, shall be nourished and shaped by a new environment. And the newer and more distinct from the old one the environment is, the more powerfully it acts to bring forth in the seed all that is highest and best in its latent qualities.

Never in all history did the seed of an old civilization find a more virgin soil than that of Europe did when it first crossed over to America. The Indian races which it found here were too distinct from it to endanger its blending with them to more than a limited degree. It was isolated by three thousand miles of ocean from the agedness of its old home. There were no social traditions of the hoary past, no aristocracies of an early day that had lost everything of the best out of them but its hardened shell, no ecclesiastical yokes still rough with their pagan hewing, no "bygone ages in their palls," and

"Titan shapes, with faces blank and dun,"

to hamper its young life. Everything that was noble and needed in the institutions of the past had a chance to unfold in accordance with its own true nature. The town idea, the people's getting together and managing their own local affairs, originating in the forests of Germany two thousand years ago, bruised and trampled into the earth again and again by the monarchies and imperialisms of continental Europe, transplanted to England and there growing to be only a stunted scrub, brought to these shores, developed into a tall tree, out of which has come our whole governmental structure. Religion, obliged, amid the overcrowding institutions of the Old World, to reach upward almost exclusively in the form of piety, has been enabled in our broader spaces to spread out laterally as also fraternity. Labor, applied directly to the wilderness, enabled each workman to carve out of it his own fortune, independent of what his fathers had handed down; made each one of them an eldest son in the great family of humanity. And Nature, who hitherto had been obliged to make her hero out of slaughter and military ability and after the crude ideals of barbarous ages, coming to these shores,

> "For him her Old-World molds aside she threw,
> And choosing sweet clay from the breast
>   Of the unexhausted West,
> With stuff untainted shaped a hero new,
> Wise, steadfast in the strength of God, and true."

Territorial Size.

Size of territory taken by itself is very far from meaning civilized greatness, but, taken in connection with geographical unity, natural wealth, and a virgin soil, it has been a wonderful factor, not only in the degree, but also very curiously in the kind and complexity of our country's civilization.

To begin with, it brought about inevitably its political independence from the Old World. The little territories of Europe with their parental protection were, indeed, all-important as the cradles of its civilization. But when the civilization had grown to its early manhood and had a continent to occupy, like all other manhood, it felt instinctively the impulse to self-control and to the management of its own affairs; and when Europe's cradle governments were sent over to these shores and the effort was made to rock the man in their littleness, the man whose chest was already fifteen hundred miles broad and his single foot larger than the whole body of his old homes, he very naturally rebelled, and, declaring his independence of them, kicked the cradles back again three thousand miles across the seas.

The same factor, however—its size—that made America's independence of the mother countries a necessity, made its independence of itself, made the personal liberty of its citizens and a government and civilization which should be the embodiment of their liberty, a necessity also; made it just as impossible for it when free to get into their grown-up clothes of government as it had been for it to remain in their infant cradles. The countries of the Old World were either small and compact like Greece, which was hardly larger than a single modern city—well adapted, therefore, to a social organization in which the state was everything and the individual nothing; or else like Rome, vast in territory, but with forms like that of the octopus, centrally small, and with only their long colonial arms reaching out to the ends of the earth—naturally adapted, therefore, to monarchies at home and satraps abroad. But with America's immense size and at the same time absence of any natural head there was no possibility of centering its settlements all in one section, or bringing them all under one monarchical rule. They had to be scattered here and there in its vastness, and had each one to take care of itself. The scattering gave them elbow room, "space for the body and space for the soul," and accustomed them from the start to the administration of their own local affairs. The poorest man in them counted a full one, and had his own special worth—had often lands assigned him that a prince at home would have envied. Individuality came to the front—

> "Called to solve
> On the rough edges of society
> Problems long sacred to the choicer few,
> And improvise what elsewhere men receive
> As gifts from Deity,"

each citizen was made "king by mere manhood." The doctrine set forth in its declaration of independence was taught in the woods, and sung in the winds, and opened up to in the fields, and writ out large on the hills. And so, when the territorial spaces were closed up and the settlers came together for the making of a general government, it was as sovereigns and not as subjects; and they naturally made one in which the individual, and not the state, was the unit—exactly the opposite of how it was with the civilizations of the Old World.

Equally potent has been its size as a factor in developing arts and inventions, those especially which relate to its social and commercial intercourse. With its immense distances, rendering the old methods of communication utterly inadequate, railroads, canals, steamboats, mails, telegraphs, telephones, electric motors, palace cars have had of necessity to come in and take their place. Distance has become nearness; separation, union. Boston is closer to Chicago than Athens was to Sparta. It is safer to go from New York to New Orleans than it was to go from Jerusalem to Jericho. The great social body has its nerves and arteries. The country's natural bonds are supplemented with those of art. And the smallest village of the Old World, four hundred years ago, did not pulse more completely with one life than this whole nation does to-day, whose sides are two oceans and two zones, and which four hundred years ago was a howling wilderness.

Nor is this all. It is a well-known principle of zoölogical evolution that the larger the territory in which animals live, the more varied will be their species, the more animated their struggles for existence, and the more elevated their forms that survive. Australia and New Zealand have developed nothing higher in the scale of life than marsupials, animals like the opossum and kangaroo that carry their young in a pouch on their bodies, because their territory is not extended enough for those diversities of environment which give rise to competing varieties; and it is only when we go to the full-sized continents like Europe, Asia, and the Americas, where the competitors are innumerable, that we find such highly organized animals as the lion, horse, elephant, bear, monkey, and man—species that, while not neglecting to feed and shelter their young, give them at birth a more distinct and independent existence.

It is a law which holds equally good in the evolution of industries, institutions, civilizations. The larger their field the more will be their varieties and competitions, and the finer and more complex the forms that survive. Territories that are small in themselves, like the South Sea Islands, or that shut themselves up from others, like China and Africa, develop only marsupial civilizations, those that are low down in the scale of organization, and that timidly carry their offspring of ideas, employments, religions, and the like in a pouch next to their own bodies, afraid to trust them even to a natural cradle. So far as the outside world is concerned, American statesmanship, alas! has adopted the non-competing, narrow principle with regard to our American civilization—treated it as if it were only an opossum or kangaroo, built around its business a wall of duties and tariffs, and tried to shut it out from competition with the rest of mankind. What is the entire system of "protection to our infant industries" that we hear so much about but the marsupial way of dealing with them, an arrested commercial development? And if we wish ever to become high-grade mammals, wish ever to rise to be the man-species of the world's civilization, what surer way is there than for us to obey the great natural law through which all past progress has been made, abolish all artificial barriers, and let our business compete freely with the world's whole continent?*

It is this larger principle, thanks to the country's size, that we have adopted with regard to our internal trade. Our forty-four States, differing from each other in climate, soil, productions and interests as widely as most nations do, have established the completest free trade with each other that ever scholar dreamed of or politician dreaded; have set down their infant industries as soon as born to run about of themselves, so far as our own land is concerned, utterly unprotected. What is the result? The same here as in Nature everywhere. Each State, each city, each village, each man being brought into sharp competition with every other, is on the constant lookout for some invention, some improvement, some science, that will give it some special advantage in the struggle for success. No one can adopt a new light, a new motor, a new method of voting, or even a new paving stone, but all the rest have to do the same. It is one of the most powerful of all the stimulants that our country is under for the development of its industrial civilization; is spreading out its civilization, also, into its remotest borders. And at the same time it is giving all other lands a lesson that even our own falsity to it in dealing with them can hardly counteract; is the prototype of

---

* This is not inconsistent with the explanation given on page 30 as to why America did not develop its native tribes into a civilized condition. The competition which kept them from it was the militant one which destroyed goods, not the industrial one of exchanging them and seeing which tribe could make them cheapest and best. It is not to be denied, however, that Nature, as interpreted by evolution, favors to some extent both protection and free trade, each for a special social stage; and the real question of statesmanship is which form of protection—that of the pouch, or that of the cradle—shall be used at first, and how soon both shall be laid aside.

that coming civilization in which there shall be a United States of earth, a race without a tariff, and a world without a fort.

TRADE WINDS AND THE ST. LAWRENCE RIVER.

One of the most interesting questions connected with our civilization is what gave the best parts of America—the central parts of its northern half—to the predominance in it of the Protestant religion and of the Anglo-Saxon race. Nature contributed two great primary factors to its answer—one the trade winds, the other the St. Lawrence River. It was the necessity of using the trade winds, with their aërial currents blowing forever westward, the embodiments of destiny itself, that carried Columbus down into the tropics for his ocean voyage, the only way with his frail barks that it could ever have been made, brought him to tropical America rather than to what is now the United States as its first discovered point, and, as other voyagers from Spain naturally followed in his path, gave tropical America to Spain's colonies and Spain's religion as the center from which to spread over South America and along the coast up into the great Mississippi Valley of North America. On the other hand, when France, the second great European power to feel imperatively the breath of that world-exploring age, started out on its voyages, obliged to take a more northern course so as not to infringe on the rights of its predecessor, the St. Lawrence River was the first opening to which it came large enough to promise a passage through to the long-sought Indies; and the result was that it gave Canada, and then, farther along, the northern half of the rich Mississippi Valley, to French explorers and again to the Roman Catholic faith.

Hemmed in thus by its two great rivals, England, on waking up to the spirit of the age, had only the narrow Atlantic coast that it could fairly take possession of by right of discovery—a most hopeless state of things, apparently, for its future continental supremacy. But when Nature starts to bring about the survival of the fittest, it never makes any mistakes. The trade winds had given Spain, after all, a part of the country that was too hot, and the St. Lawrence River a part of it to France that was too cold, for the nurture of really first-class civilizations—opened to them regions where the search for gold led away the one and the trade in furs the other from the culture of the soil; brought them in contact with Indian races they could convert and mingle their blood with to the weakening of its native vigor; and yet farther had pushed them into the great Mississippi Valley at a time when, in trying to occupy it, they were tempted to spread themselves over it too far and too thin for its permanent possession.

Exactly opposite to these drawbacks, the climate to which the English colonies had been driven proved, with its alternations of heat and cold, to be the very best stimulant for keeping up and developing their native energies. Hopeless of gold and fur, they went to digging for tobacco and corn. The ocean on their one side and the great Appalachian Mountains on the other, backed with the forts of France and Spain, while holding them in contact across the water with the civilization of their old home, kept them from dissipating their strength by spreading it out into the tempting Mississippi Valley. Most important of all, the fiercer Indian tribes they had come in contact with on the Atlantic coast preferred fight to faith—insisted on shedding the white man's blood in hate rather than mingling it with theirs in love. And the result was that when the times were ripe for such a movement, the unenervated English forces broke through their mountain barriers into the garden riches of the Mississippi Valley, trampled down the weakened blood of France and Spain, and established on this continent forever the supremacy of the Protestant faith and of the Anglo-Saxon race.* It is a long and terrible history. There is nothing in the annals of wrong more cruel and unjust than that part of it especially which covers our dealings with the Indian—nothing, as the experience of Williams and Penn shows, which might apparently have been more easily avoided and which ought in itself to be more severely condemned. And yet with all its horrors it has been our civilization's salvation, the shedding of their blood by the English whites keeping it from a mongrel offspring which, like those of Mexico and South America, would have been forever shedding it among themselves. It is one of the countless illustrations history is full of that evil is evil only close at hand. The wrongs of to-day are the rights of

---

* Of course this is written only in outline. The part of Holland in the settlement of New York and of the great Hudson River opening is not to be forgotten. And, in spite of Washington Irving, it may well be a question whether the interests of liberty alike in government and religion would not have been equally served, to begin with, at any rate, by Dutch rather than English supremacy.

to-morrow; the cruelties of the hour, the kindnesses of the ages; and, like the crags and gorges and pitfalls of mountain scenery, so difficult to travel when the feet are among them, so grand to view when we are far away, their most awful forms, looked at through the long corridors of time, become, equally with those of goodness, the features, shadowy though they be, of one complete and glorious picture—make from the eternal standpoint, the same as from that of Venus or Mars,

"The globe we grow in fairest of the evening stars." *

WIND AND WATER.

There are other ways, if less unique yet not less beneficial, in which wind and water have been the factors of our civilization. Where the rains and dews end, no matter how rich the soil may be, there ends its food supply. When I was out in Kansas I asked a man who had been the agent of a great loaning association, where he drew the line at which he refused to recommend land as good security for Eastern investments. He answered that when he came to a farm where the owner had to dig down a hundred and fifty feet for water, it was as far as he could get his conscience to stretch. Nature's conscience is not any more elastic. A civilization to flourish needs its convenient drink as much as an animal or plant or schoolboy. And not in the mythology of ancient Greece alone, but in the sober experience of all lands, the goddess of beauty, the beauty of hills and plains first, and then the beauty of art and soul, rises as a mist out of the sea.

America, besides its great ocean tanks on either side, and that wonderful apparatus of sun-pump and cloud-cart for taking it up and carrying it inland, which all countries to some extent enjoy, has some special arrangements for its own special needs. The Gulf of Mexico is in itself one of the most unpoetic and disagreeable sheets of water on the globe; and yet there is probably no other of its size which is the agent of more good. The great problem with a vast compact country like America is to provide its interior parts with a sufficient supply of rain. When I was a boy and had to take my turn going round the school-room in the hot summer days with a dipper and a bucket of water, the thirsty

* See Edward Everett's eloquent oration on The Battle of Bloody Brook for an admirable presentation of both sides of the Indian controversy.

urchins near the door always managed to get their full supply; but when I reached the middle of the room the pail was very apt to be empty and the seats there got only half their need. It is so with the thirsty States near the ocean when the summer clouds go around with their buckets. Their ten thousand uplifted lips drain the carriers dry before they can get inland. And if the great Mississippi Valley had to depend on the bounty of its two oceans for moisture, it is safe to say that what is now the country's very garden would be indeed " the great American desert," and that the consciences of Western farm loan agencies would have to stretch everywhere more than their accustomed hundred and fifty feet, or else give up the business.

In this state of things the Gulf of Mexico comes in to solve the problem. It is a huge kettle of water kept boiling with tropical suns and refilled by ocean currents, one part of which is sent off in the Gulf Stream to make all northern Europe glad, and the other, rising up as vapor, is seized by the upward strata of returning trade winds, prevented from going farther west by the lofty Cordilleran mountains, and carried all over the Mississippi Valley, the entrance to which on the south has been very conveniently left open, to make what would otherwise be a desert bring forth its twenty, thirty, and fifty fold.* Of course, under evolution it does not do, at least in some quarters, to talk of design. But if the best plumber that city ever saw had been given the job, and had worked with all the light of science and all the resources of art, it is difficult to see how he could have arranged tank, heat, mountain walls, air pipes, and valley opening more skillfully to accomplish the desired result than Nature has—putting them in, too, not apparently as an after-thought, but laying the foundations for them in that far-off Laurentian age when the country was begun. And Nature never yet has sent us in a plumber's bill.

LAKES AND RIVERS, SEAS AND SHORES.

Water is good, however, not only to make things grow, but as the medium by which to carry them about afterward to human markets and human mouths. Never was a system of lakes and rivers better fitted for this service than that of America. The Mississippi Valley has fifteen thousand miles of navigable streams. Huge vessels can load at Duluth, and

* Shaler and Guyot.

Natural Factors in American Civilization. 41

without breaking bulk go down the St. Lawrence to any part of the world. The Sierras reach out their mighty Columbian arm to connect themselves with the sea on the west; and plowers of the prairie and plowers of the ocean's plains meet each other in the streets of Chicago at the country's heart.

Its marine borders and bays and inlets are less in proportion to its whole size than those of Europe, but they have acted a most honorable part in its civilization. The ocean which once meant separation now means union. It is its own bridge, with a span three thousand miles long to Europe and ten thousand miles long to China and Japan. It is not only commerce and trade, but letters, liberalism, ideas, humanities, that pass for us back and forth over its blue arch. The question was raised a few years ago why it was that all the seaport towns of New England, though settled by Puritans and standing at the very heart of Calvinism, were studded with the churches of a liberal religion. It was found to be through their sea-captains, and merchant citizens, whose ships, trading with a hundred heathen lands, had found such honesty and high principle and gracious manhood among them that they could but believe that they and their religions were all alike the offspring of one Eternal Father.

Nor is this all. Palates can not drink the salt sea, but characters can. It has been the nurse on our shores, as everywhere, of generosity, courage, hardihood. There were no grander deeds done in our civil war than those of the Kearsarge on the coast of France and of the Hartford in Mobile Bay; no steps on shore that marched truer to the music of the Union than its web-feet on the sea. And amid all the vice and folly and effeminacy that characterize the pleasures of our land, it is a most hopeful sign that so many of its golden youth are finding their best sport in the swift canoe and in the sea-battling, race-winning pleasure yacht.

CLIMATE.

The energizing influence which a climate with a fair proportion of cold weather exerts on business is felt in America the same as in all other lands; and so is its power in building up the home and in developing that factor which is such an important element in all high civilization—its domestic life. But there is another form in which it acts that to some extent is peculiar to America. It is that of mingling its different classes of people socially together—the people of the South with those of the North, and those of the city with those of the hills. Not more surely does the moon set the great tides of ocean sweeping from east to west than does the sun set the great tides of humanity in motion between New England and Florida, the sea-bordering States and the mountain-crowned inlands. And who shall measure the value of the better knowledge of each other, the refining influence, the mingling of country strength with city grace, and the removal of alienations and distrusts, that are thus brought about—the city girl in her summer surroundings of whom Whittier has so sweetly sung,

> "The coarseness of a ruder time
> Her finer mirth displaces;
> A subtler sense of pleasure fills
> Each rustic sport she graces";

and the country boy who gives to her

> "The steady force of will whereby
> Her flexile grace seems sweeter,
> The sturdy counterpoise which makes
> Her woman's life completer";

and the union of the two in a relation

> "Where more and more we find the troth
> Of fact and fancy plighted,
> And cultured charm and labor's strength
> In rural homes united."

NATURE WEDDED TO ART.

Nature is usually regarded as a factor in civilization only when it acts on man in its own untrammeled state, and is counted as losing itself in art when it is guided by human wills and enabled through inventions and machinery to do its higher work. It is a distinction, however, for which there seems to be no good reason. When a river turns the wheels of a factory, it does it by its own strength and in obedience to its own laws just as truly as when it carves the channel of a Mississippi to the sea, or fertilizes an Egypt with its flood; and the electricity which drives a street-car and delivers a message of love is the same fluid that leaps from cloud to cloud in the live lightning and terrifies a city with its thunder crash.

It is through its union with art that Nature enters most powerfully into our modern and especially into our American civilization—the revolution which in this respect has taken place in man's relation to it, the most significant and far-reaching that earth has ever known. There is nothing in the civilizations of antiquity which is more conspicuous than the way in which Nature dominated man. He lived for ages in the most abject terror of its phenomena. No tyrant sitting on a throne ever had a more unquestioned sovereignty, no Nero striking down his victims wherever whim prompted, a more hideous reputation. Absolutely nothing was known of its interior laws and forces. And though a person might now and then avail himself of its milder forms as aid in his work—the sailor trim his sail to its winds and the miller turn his wheel with its waters—it was very much as he might harness a tiger to his cart, uncertain whether it would draw him home or eat him up.

How utterly in our modern age has all this changed! It is man now that dominates Nature. He has torn open its rocky breast, set its mighty forests up at auction, put asunder in his crucible the elements that its God had joined together, tortured the secret out of its lightning, learned the trick of its earthquakes, and harnessed its mighty forces—tandem, single, and abreast—to draw his cars, drive his mills, run his errands, take his pictures, print his thoughts, do his killing, and be his mercy. What fall of monarchies, what triumph of democracy has the world ever known that is equal to this? In Europe an exiled prince may be your coachman and a wandering king do your chores; but in America it is the prince in his own home that is our helper, and the king with his kingdom that is placed at our service.

The danger is now that the country will go to the other extreme—abuse and waste, not use and cherish, its natural gifts. Other lands have experienced to their sorrow that such treasures are not inexhaustible or indestructible; and already we, too, are finding that our people have been too prodigal with some of their abundance, too reckless in cutting off forests, digging up coal, and exhausting soils—spending in a day what frugal ages have toiled to produce. We need to learn that it is not as overwrought and downtrodden slaves, but only as harnessed kings, that Nature's factors will do their work. With all our domination over them through art, it is Nature still, not man, that makes the laws under which they act—obeying these laws, not overriding them, that is the condition of our supremacy in their use. The forces behind them have an alliance with each other older and closer than that with art, an *esprit du corps* that does not always include man. And the moment one of them is ill-treated, even though it be through ignorance, its associates have a way of turning and rending their abuser—blasting him with lightnings, poisoning him with miasmas, starving him with droughts, drowning him with floods, and dazing him with cyclones—whose savagery even a Homestead laborer dealing with a Pinkerton policeman could hardly match. Nature weds art, but has the bridegroom repeat the word "obey" in the ceremony; endows him with all her worldly goods, but only on condition that he does not use them like a spendthrift or a fool; and bears him civilized children only so long as he keeps his marriage vow to obey.

NATURAL SCENERY.

Closely connected with the change which has come over natural force as a factor in our civilization is that which has taken place with natural scenery as its shaping influence. Nature of old was to man not only a tyrant but a monster. Its passive face, hardly less than its active force, was looked upon with dread. All that man had of the higher life had been won from it by a desperate fight, was held against it only by unremitting vigilance. It was the synonym of what was wild and barbarous, was supposed to have an intrinsic tendency to drag man back from what was cultivated and refined; and to have spoken of its scenery as in any way a factor of civilization would have seemed as incongruous as to have spoken of darkness as a factor of light or of ugliness as a maker of beauty.

There can be no question that in the mighty past, lasting almost down to our day, it did have this depressing influence. When our ancestors came to America its wilderness aspect was itself, apart from all its other dangers, one of the very worst foes they had to contend against. Its wood, in whose shadows superstition has always loved to linger, stretching around them in a sea more unbroken than the watery one they had sailed across, pressed upon them with all the gloom of unmeasured years as well as space. Fancy peopled it with all manner of strange monsters. Not even the bravest man liked to be caught out alone in its depths. Contact with it added a new somberness to their religion.

Their very stock showed its depressing results in the lowered tone of its second and third generations. Out of it, intensified by what the forests of northern Europe had already put into their Anglo-Saxon blood, came the horrors of the Salem witchcraft delusion. And it is not too much to say that New England's early civilization was nearer being wiped out by savage trees than by savage men.

There is a strain of the same influence appearing in our blood now and then even to this day. But with the subjugation of the wilderness, the influx of fresh life from the Old World, and the coming in of modern science, the same change has taken place in our feeling toward the woods and toward all natural objects that has taken place in our use of their indwelling forces—a change from dread to love, from being overpowered by their gloom to being uplifted by their grace.

It shows itself in the daily life of our people, in their fondness for getting out of doors, in their many visits to special points of natural beauty, and in their efforts to give all the places they are in something of Nature's charm. Though the country has many scenes of pre-eminent beauty—its Yosemite Valley, Yellowstone Park, Niagara Falls, White Mountains, Garden of the Gods, and leagues of seashore—yet, owing to its immense size, only a small proportion of its people can live, as two thirds of those in Europe do, within daily sight of magnificent natural scenery. But what they can not have as common food they go all the more to feast upon now and then as a luxury. There is notoriously hardly a lovely view point in the land which does not have its cluster of hotels and cottages built especially for the accommodation of summer visitors, hardly a railroad which does not find the travel to them a large element of its business. And though all their visitors are very far from being drawn to their beauty by natural taste, though the advertiser of pills makes a palimpsest of sublimity's scroll, and the tunes of the dance and the garishness of fashion mingle too often with the tinkle of rills and the grandeur of the mountains, nevertheless the presence even of such triflers indicates how the popular tide sets. Nature has become to America what art was to Greece and Rome, the minister to taste and the food to its æsthetic wants. We have indeed some human artists not to be despised; but, after all, as factors in our civilization, the lawn-mower is for us the painter's brush, the gardener's hoe the sculptor's chisel.

The Yosemite is our Vatican, Colorado our Egypt. And when we want a gallery of home paintings—

> "Touched by a light that hath no name,
> A glory never sung,
> Aloft on sky and mountain wall
> Are God's great pictures hung."

It is an influence that shows itself conspicuously in our literature. Bryant, Cooper, Hawthorne, Lowell, Longfellow, Emerson, Whittier—our favorite authors; Thanatopsis, The Leather-stocking Tales, The Blithedale Romance, The Vision of Sir Launfal, Evangeline, Each for All, Maud Müller—our favorite books, are all rilled, prairied, mountain-peaked, flower-decked, honey-beed, and hay-scented with the objects and scenes of our American natural world. And it is not merely their outward beauty that is sung and brought out, but, most satisfying of all, their inner meanings, their music for the soul's ear, and their colors for the mind's eye—

> "Not fair alone in curve and line,
> But something more and better,
> The secret charm eluding art,
> Its spirit, not its letter."

Pre-eminently does Nature show itself in our day as a factor in the country's religion, a factor that comes in part from science and in part from scenery—the one making it a truth, the other a worship. It is at this point that the difference between the ancient and modern view of it culminates. Christianity for ages looked on the natural world as not only dreadful but devilish, the antagonist of God, and a snare and delusion to the soul. "Lord, turn away mine eyes from beholding vanity," prayed the theological student at Andover, only fifty years ago, as his attention was called one June morning to the lovely scenery around that now heretical hill. And when Science began its interpretations of natural scripture, it was the Church, notoriously, that did all it could to argue and ridicule and persecute them down. Yet this very Nature to our modern civilized thought has become filled not only with beauty, poetry, truth, love, but, marvel of marvels, has become to us the very robe of Deity. It is a change not by any means complete, but one that runs in America to some extent through all denominations. The most pronounced professors of a biblical and church religion like to go out again into "God's first temples" for their summer worship. The natural has taken the place of the supernatural, the scientific of the scriptural. The autumn wood is the burning bush out of which God speaks to us, the harvest field our miracle of the multiplied bread. The æsthetic element that Protestantism on leaving Catholicism lost for a while is being refound by it in the music of sea waves, the pomp and ceremony of the seasons, the paintings of sunset cloud, and in the architecture of the universe; and the truth that was fast disappearing under the touch of criticisms and translations is returning re-enforced out of crucibles and telescopes. Christianity has come around in the great upward spiral of progress to where fetichism began. And to our civilized thought, not indeed gods many, but the one Eternal God, is in every object of Nature, in every stump and stone even,

"And faith has still its Galilee
And love its Olivet."

WHAT THEN?

Recognizing thus the great natural forces which have been concerned so largely in the shaping of our country's civilized life, it needs perhaps to be doubly emphasized as a closing thought that what they have done is very far from making it a finished work, and that their greatness calls for something on man's part widely different from the mere Fourth-of-July boastfulness to which it has sometimes given rise. Looked at soberly, there is no denying that the factory as yet is finer than the cloth—the field richer than the grain; no denying that however complete America may be geologically and geographically, there are many respects in which humanly it is far back in a Paleozoic age—that society has its Silurian strata yet at the top, the industrial world its Dinichthyian corporations and Megalosaurian trusts, as huge and ravenous as ever their prototypes were in the eons of old, and that, mingled with all the liberties, riches, and refinements of its civilization, are oppressions, poverties, and degradations that even barbarism would be ashamed of. Instead of its being a finished work,

"The rudiments of empire here are plastic yet and warm;
The chaos of a mighty world is rounding into form."

And in such a state of things what are all its magnificent natural endowments but a challenge to us, their human possessors, not to rest in any optimistic idleness, but to bring up our part of the work, our aspirations, our ideals, our patriotism, our deeds, to a level with what they are doing? And at the same time, while challenged to do our best, conscious of our limitations even then, and of the immensity of the work that is yet before us, not only the unfinished old but the opening new—problems to be solved such as no other people ever faced, social forces to be dealt with in comparison with which the earthquake and the cyclone are children's play, garments of liberty and life to be adjusted to what will soon be six hundred millions of human beings—is it not also a satisfaction to feel, a cause not of spread-eagle boasting, but of energizing confidence, that underneath the nation's workshop of human will and wisdom, supplying forever the motive power for turning its wheels, is this mighty, rushing mountain stream of civilization's natural factors?

ABSTRACT OF THE DISCUSSION.

DR. MARTIN L. HOLBROOK:

It seems to me that there ought to be more emphasis put upon the following natural factors which promote civilization:

1. Good harbors and rivers and lakes for the promotion of travel, commerce, and intercommunication among the inhabitants. We do not adequately realize how much trade and commerce favor and stimulate intellectual growth and moral culture. I include morality because trade can never be profitably carried on to any extent except upon principles of mutual justice. Indirectly, trade promotes civilization by securing the means to satisfy wants and leisure to cultivate all the sciences and arts in greater or less degree. If commerce and intercourse are prevented by natural or artificial barriers, civilization will languish proportionately. Our country has these natural conditions which favor intercourse in its rivers, lakes, and harbors. Even without railroads communication is easy.

2. Another natural advantage which promotes civilization is the possession of a soil which will yield abundant vegetable food. Though overeating and gluttony may be evils, they harm comparatively few. A good soil yielding rich harvests benefits the masses and gives them well-nourished, fully developed bodies, capable of endurance and hard work. A poor soil uses up the energies of those who cultivate it and gives them no time for culture. We have vast regions of productive soil, and our products are easily sent to places where the soil is poor in exchange for manufactured articles.

3. A temperate climate, giving both heat and cold in the right proportion to stimulate activity. Our bravest and strongest men and highest civilizations are always developed in this climate.

Finally, abundant cheap land to attract immigrants from every part of the world. Many as are the evils of immigration, its benefits far outweigh them. Isolated regions out of the way of immigration suffer. Our Southern States suffer for want of fresh blood and varied intellects to promote enterprise and effort.

DR. DUREN J. H. WARD:

I wish to say a word first about the Ethical Association. Some years ago, in the last part of my college course, I became interested in scientific study and inspired by the scientific spirit. I came to the conclusion that science was likely to become the basis of a new faith, and I hoped that a church might ultimately be founded on such a basis. When I read the constitution of this association I said: This is the thing I wish to see, for the Ethical Association comes very near to being a church. The discoveries which science has made by its method of verification are the soundest, stablest, and safest truths man has ever had presented to him. To have this fact preached regularly institutes an order of progress such as the world has never before seen.

As I listened to the able lecture of Mr. Kimball I wished that the word "natural" had not been used in its limited sense, for men, too, are a part of Nature. But I suppose the subject was meant to be limited to the physical factors. It struck me that the first natural factor in our civilization was the discovery of America, which was to modify all the people who came to inhabit it. Before, Europeans did not believe there was another world; they were self-centered, regarded themselves as the most important part of the universe. I sympathize with what the lecturer said as to the strength of the natural environment and its effect in making civilization. But scientists are apt to think that the strength of physical nature is the only noteworthy element, and forget that man reacts upon Nature by the exercise of his intelligence and will. They forget the human factor, and think that Nature has done all the work—that it is not necessary for us to do anything. This attitude hinders the progress of the new view which science has brought about. The apostles of science need more enthusiasm, more anxiety to stimulate the human race to rational efforts in behalf of a progressive civilization.

The Edinburgh Review once asked the sneering question, "Who reads an American book?" But now our literature is read and respected all over the world. In four hundred years people have been pouring into this country, bringing with them their Old-World ideas of the earth and human society. But here was an opportunity to shake off those ideas and put on broader and grander ones. We possess advantages superior to those of any other country. In many ways we have achieved great success. But we are too easily satisfied. We have stultified ourselves by self-praise. We are too apt to think that progress begins and ends with ourselves. Our very supremacy on this continent tends to give our thought an insular limitation, which we must correct by cultivating broader sympathies and a closer scientific study of man and society.

Dr. Lewis G. Janes:

I think no member of this association will accuse me of pessimism; but I confess that I find Mr. Kimball in some respects more op-

Natural Factors in American Civilization. 51

timistic than I am. His lecture seems to carry the implication that everything in our past experience and present circumstances tends toward advancement in civilization. I am not so sure of this. If we look down the lines of history we shall see that civilizations have not only grown up out of barbarism, but that some in process of time have become static, fallen into decay, and finally become extinct. We should closely watch our own civilization for retrogressive tendencies in the light of the experience of other nations.

I thought the speaker was too optimistic in his treatment of our Indian wars. I am unable to see that we have in any way profited by these conflicts. I believe it can be shown that, instead of "insisting on shedding the white man's blood in hate," the Indian tribes with which our forefathers came in contact seldom, if ever, attacked the whites without abundant provocation, or unless they became involved as allies in the white man's quarrels, as during the French and Indian War. Roger Williams and William Penn had to deal with very much the same sort of Indians as the Puritans of Massachusetts and Connecticut; but, by a juster and more humane policy, they avoided conflicts that were destructive and injurious, both physically and morally, to both parties. No nation can thrive by doing injustice either to its own or to an alien people; and neither our colonial nor our national prosperity has been favored by our treatment of the Indians.

In the main, however, I agree with the positions taken by Mr. Kimball in his able lecture. Whether we consent or not to all his conclusions, we must all recognize the mental stimulus derived from his thoughtful and original treatment of his topic.

Respecting free trade, which the speaker has so eloquently eulogized, I am not quite sure that the time has come when we can safely let down all the barriers and open our doors to absolutely free competition. I believe in ultimate freedom of trade between nations, but we must approach it wisely, along the lines of evolution, not by violent revolutionary changes in our financial policy. We must apply the principle of relativity, consider just what our present conditions are, how best we can do justice to all classes and interests involved, and adjust our policy accordingly. I believe we are now ready for a forward step; but if we attempt too much, if we exceed the degree of progress indicative of natural, healthful growth, an injurious reaction will surely follow.

MR. KIMBALL replied briefly with a humorous story, defending himself against the charge of too great optimism.

WHAT AMERICA OWES TO THE OLD WORLD

BY
A. EMERSON PALMER

COLLATERAL READINGS SUGGESTED:

Bryce's The American Commonwealth; Fiske's Discovery of America, The Beginnings of New England, The American Revolution, The Critical Period in American History, American Political Ideas, and Civil Government in the United States; Campbell's Puritan in Holland, England, and America; Maine's Popular Government; Freeman's An Introduction to American Institutional History, J. H. U. Studies, vol. i; Eggleston's The Planting of New England, and Migrations of American colonists, Century, vol. xxv; Adams's The Germanic Origin of New England Towns, J. H. U. Studies, vol. i; Von Holst's Constitutional and Political History of the United States.

WHAT AMERICA OWES TO THE OLD WORLD.

By A. Emerson Palmer.

The consideration of the question of America's debt to what we are in the habit of calling the Old World has a certain timeliness at this short remove from the date of the festivities in remembrance of that great event in modern history which a kindly calendar has permitted us to celebrate on at least two days, with an interval of a week and more between. We are still in the Columbian era, and thoughts of the discovery and the discoverer are frequently in the minds of all of us. It is well, therefore, at this time to ask what Columbus accomplished in our behalf; to inquire what the Old World has done for the New; and to endeavor to sum up, however inadequately, some results of the event which, beyond doubt, renders the year 1492 the most epoch-making year in history.

What does America owe to the Old World? The query could be more briefly answered if we should ask, What does America *not* owe to the Old World? To the main question the answer might be briefly and comprehensively given in a single word—*Everything*. But such an answer would by no means be satisfactory, even if it be accepted as literally true. We do not owe everything to Europe, intimate as are the ties which bind us to the earlier civilization from which we sprang. I need do no more on this point than simply to call your attention to the mighty work done by Nature for America, so eloquently and graphically described in the preceding lecture.

Let me say here that by America I mean the United States; and when I speak of what America owes to the Old World I mean the debt due to the Eastern Hemisphere from the principal nation of the Western. It is, perhaps, regrettable that we are compelled to use the words America and Americans in a restricted sense as relating to the United States and its people. There appears, however, to be no alternative. The United States is a magnificent fact, but there is no denying that it is not a good name; and everybody knows that such a derivative as *United-Statesian* is an utter impossibility. The incongruity, even the absurdity, of speaking of Canadians and Americans, or of Mexicans and Americans, or of the relations between Chile and America, is self-evident; yet this form of speech seems to be an actual necessity. Especially it is wise to make use of the term America when an inhabitant of this country goes abroad. In England, for example, America, meaning the United States, is an easily understood fact, whereas to say that you come from the United States does not, to certain classes of people at all events, convey a very definite idea.

Not all foreigners are as intelligent as the keeper of a little inn in Paris at which a friend of mine once spent a few days. When my friend informed his landlord that he was from the United States, the hotel man put on his wisest air and with the utmost gravity inquired: "Do you mean ze United States of North America, or ze United States of South America?"

And that brings to mind a good story which Mr. Fiske has told in print, and which will bear retelling—even with a variation. It is of a company of Americans who were dining in Paris about the time of the close of our civil war, when a favorite topic with Americans everywhere was the bigness of their country. "Here's to the United States," said the first speaker, in proposing a toast, "—the United States, bounded on the north by British America, on the south by the Gulf of Mexico, on the east by the Atlantic Ocean, and on the west by the Pacific." Needless to say that this was accepted as correct, but evoked a very moderate amount of applause. Then arose a second speaker. "Gentlemen," said he, "the view of the United States which has just been given is far too limited. Let us consider the manifest destiny of our country. So I say, Here's to the United States of the future—bounded on the north by the North Pole, bounded on the south by the South Pole, bounded on the east by the Rising Sun, and bounded on the west by the Star of Empire." But the limits of "spread-eagleism" had not been reached. A third speaker rose to his feet. "Mr. President and gentlemen," he began, "the definitions of the boundaries of the United States which have already been given do not satisfy me. I can be content with no such pent-up Utica. I make bold to peer into the mighty future, and with my mind's eye I behold the United States bounded on the north, sir, by the Aurora

Borealis, bounded on the south by the Precession of the Equinoxes, bounded on the east by the Primeval Chaos, and bounded on the west, sir, by the Day of Judgment!"

The United States—the America—composed of forty-four splendid commonwealths, some of them more than Old-World empires in extent, in population, in wealth, in resources, is, however, sufficient for us; and it is this America which we have in mind when we ask the question, What does America owe to the Old World?

THE DISCOVERY OF AMERICA.—OUR DEBT TO COLUMBUS.

First and foremost, in taking account of stock in order to determine how large is the balance on the debit side of the ledger, we must mention the discovery of the Western world. To this, of course, I shall make only the briefest reference. But it is the foundation fact which can not be overlooked. If there had been no Europe, there would be no America—at all events, no such America as we know and enjoy. That America would soon have been discovered if Columbus had not made his memorable voyage there is the strongest reason for believing. None the less is Christopher Columbus entitled to full credit for his great achievement. Nor does it detract in the slightest degree from the splendor of his fame that he was all unaware of the true significance of what he had accomplished when, as Mr. Lowell says, " seeking the back door of Asia, he found himself knocking at the front door of America." But, in fact, he did not so find himself, and when he died, in 1506, it was in the full belief that what he had discovered was the outcroppings of Asia. Of America proper, of the mainland of the continent, he caught but one glimpse, and his eyes were holden so that he did not know what he had seen. Nevertheless, Columbus discovered America. And no one can stand on the deck of a steamship in mid-ocean and gaze out upon the seemingly limitless reaches of water without feeling a new admiration for the indomitable courage and the lofty faith which carried that intrepid navigator, in spite of all opposition, across the dark and unknown Atlantic.

> " How, in God's name, did Columbus get over,
> Is a pure wonder to me, I protest,
> Cabot, and Raleigh too, that well-read rover,
> Frobisher, Dampier, Drake, and the rest.

> Bad enough, all the same,
> For them that after came,
> But, in great heaven's name,
> How *he* should ever think
> That on the other brink
> Of this wild waste terra firma should be,
> Is a pure wonder, I must say, to me."

Columbus discovered America. This is the first item to be set down on the credit-sheet of Europe. He did not discover the United States—our America—but he made our America a possibility. But America's debt to Europe is not all positive; there are some negative factors of immense importance. My predecessor in this course has dwelt on the fortunate disposition of events whereby the trade winds carried Columbus to the West Indies, and thus set the tide of Spanish occupation toward tropical America; while when France set out to possess itself of new territory across the Atlantic, it entered the then unknown new world by the St. Lawrence River, thinking thus to find a short cut to China—a historic fact which is preserved for us in the name of the Lachine Rapids, near Montreal. Thus was the truly temperate part of the Atlantic coast region reserved for occupation by the sturdy English race. They did not discover our America, but they planted it; and what a superb harvest has come from that planting! We owe something to Spain; something to France; something to Germany; not a little to the Netherlands; something to the rest of continental Europe: our debt to England is prodigious. In the international ledger it is England which fills the largest number of pages by far.

Our Kinship with England.—Community of Language.

Of all the names ever applied to England I like Hawthorne's best. *Our Old Home* he called it—a name as full of truth as of felicitousness. This happy phrase has a fellow, if not an equal, in Mr. Gladstone's *Kin Beyond Sea*. The question "Do Americans hate England?" has been discussed in one of our magazines. To me it seems passing strange that the occasion for the asking of such a question could ever have arisen. Why should Americans hate the country out of whose loins they sprang, with whose people they have so much in common, whose language they speak, as to which, indeed, their foremost feeling should be a feeling of kinship and sympathy? It is true that we have had two wars with Great Britain, but the first, at least, was not an unmixed evil, since it led to the independence of the American colonies and the development of this incomparable republic. Our revolutionary forefathers had good cause to resent and refuse to submit to the exactions and tyrannies of the British Government; but every student of our early history knows that it was with no glad hilarity that the sober-minded colonists rent asunder the ties that bound them to the mother land. The attitude of England toward the United States during our civil war—the attitude, at any rate, of not a few Englishmen—was not precisely what we would have wished to have it, but still, in view of the triumph of the Union cause, we can afford to be magnanimous. There should be no room in our hearts for such a thing as Anglophobia. We are their *Kin Beyond Sea*. England is of a truth *Our Old Home*. Let us not be content to accept these facts simply in their historic bearings. Let us do our part toward making them actual, living realities.

In counting up the sum of our inheritance from England, should not the first place be given to the imperial language which we have in common with our kin beyond the sea? The English tongue is our tongue. All English literature is our literature. All American literature is English literature. Who is wise enough to draw the mystic line rightly severing theirs from ours? In reality there is no such line. Not without reason has Hawthorne been included in the series of English Men of Letters. But not Hawthorne alone is entitled to a place there. The sixty-five millions of Americans share and speak the English language, and it is as truly their language as it is England's own. Curiously enough, too, not a few of the so-called "Americanisms" to which some of our English cousins object have been found to be simply survivals; that is to say, words which were in common use in England before the planting of the colonies in America have been retained here while becoming obsolete there, so that now to English ears they seem to have been first brought to light on this side of the Atlantic.

Who can estimate the influence of the English language in making the United States what it is to-day? Our common speech is indeed a mighty legacy from the little island which is "roughly set" amid "blown seas and storming showers." Whether the English tongue is ever to become the universal language, who is far-seeing enough to predict? Certainly it seems more likely to become such than any other language of the present day; and infinitely more likely than a manufactured thing like Volapük. If English ever does achieve this pre-eminence, it will be owing in great part to the influence of the American branch of the English-speaking race.

THE PURITAN SPIRIT.—ORIGIN OF AMERICAN INSTITUTIONS.

In the second place, though possibly it should have been mentioned first, we owe to England the Puritan spirit and all that that implies. We are wont nowadays to speak lightly, if not scoffingly, of Puritanism. We are too prone to underestimate the influence of the Puritans, despite the annually recurring dinners of our New England Societies, and to think that, on the whole, we are well rid of them at this stage of our development. As a corrective of this tendency let me quote a sentence or two from Prof. Fiske. "No loftier ideal," he says, "has ever been conceived than that of the Puritan who would fain have made of the world a City of God. If we could sum up all that England owes to Puritanism, the story would be a great one indeed. As regards the United States, we may safely say that what is noblest in our history to-day, and of happiest augury for our social and political future, is the impress left upon the character of our people by the heroic men who came to New England early in the seventeenth century."*

What these heroic men brought with them across the Atlantic was the democratic spirit. "Without having any profound or fine-spun theories, the Pilgrims put in force the divine right of common sense. Republican institutions in America were merely the result of the application, first and last, of practical shrewdness to the wants and circumstances of the people." †

Within the last few years the origins of American institutions have been studied as never before, and a large amount of new and valuable light has been cast upon this most interesting subject. It used to be the commonly accepted opinion that our institutions were either brought

* American Political Ideas, p. 27.
† The Planting of New England. Edward Eggleston, Century, vol. xxv, p. 858.

bodily from England, being subject, as a matter of course, to certain enlargement and modification on the new soil, or else that in some mysterious way théy were evolved or invented by the English colonists and their descendants, who must, in this point of view, be regarded as the possessors of almost superhuman wisdom and political sagacity.

Mr. Freeman takes a broader and more philosophic view, though it may be charged that his view is somewhat vague. He says: "The institutions of Massachusetts or Maryland . . . are a part of the general institutions of the English people, as these are again part of the general institutions of the Teutonic race, and these are again part of the general institutions of the whole Aryan family. . . . The institutions of England are the general institutions of the Teutonic race, modified, as they could not fail to be, by settlement in a great European island, and by the events which have taken place since that settlement. The institutions of the American States are the institutions of England, modified, as they could not fail to be, by settlement in a greater American continent, and by the events which have taken place since that settlement."*

In seeking to determine to how great an extent we are indebted to the mother country for our institutions, let us inquire what institutions we have in common with England, and what we possess which have no prototypes in that country, and then we shall be ready to ascertain, if possible, from what source the latter were derived.

On this head a valuable contribution has recently been made by Mr. Douglas Campbell, of New York, in his book entitled The Puritan in Holland, England, and America. The work shows careful research and exhaustive inquiry, but, while gladly acknowledging my obligations to Mr. Campbell, I can not help feeling that he has not, in his investigations and conclusions, been always animated by the impartial, judicial, and scientific spirit of the true historian. The following statement, for example, can hardly be read without a feeling of surprise and dissent: "Instead of those [the institutions] of the United States being derived from England, it is a curious fact that, while we have in the main English social customs and traits of character, we have scarcely a legal or political institution of importance which is of English origin, and but few which

* An Introduction to American Institutional History. E. A. Freeman, Johns Hopkins University Studies, vol. i, No. 1, pp. 13, 15.

have come to us by the way of England." * At the same time, it is not to be denied that Mr. Campbell's book is an important and suggestive addition to the literature of this subject.

Now let us consider the cardinal differences and likenesses between the institutions of the United States and those of the mother country, and endeavor to trace the origin of those factors in our nation's life which have exerted the greatest influence.

THE CHURCH IN ENGLAND AND THE UNITED STATES.

First, England has its established church, while in America there is no such thing as a state religious establishment. The difference is immense. Not only is the state church in England supported by taxes levied upon all the people, irrespective of their own religious preferences, but it fills a part in the common life which it is difficult for those not closely familiar with it to appreciate. The parish in England is the center of everything. Even the street watering-carts in London are marked as belonging to such and such parishes; and parish there means simply an ecclesiastical district.

In our own country, on the other hand, it is prescribed the in our fundamental law (Article VI) that "no religious test shall ever be required as a qualification to any office or public trust under the United States," and the first amendment to the Constitution, proposed by the very first Congress, in 1789, provides that "Congress shall make no law respecting an establishment of religion, or prohibiting the free exercise thereof."

Whence came the absolute separation of church and state in the United States? "Of all the differences between the Old World and the New," says Mr. Bryce, "this is perhaps the most salient"; and there is a note of surprise—the surprise that his English readers will feel—in the opening sentence of his chapter on The Churches and the Clergy: "In examining the National Government and the State governments we have never once had occasion to advert to any ecclesiastical body or question, because with such matters government has in the United States absolutely nothing to do." † Provisions similar to those already quoted from the Federal Constitution and the first amendment are to be found in the

* Vol. i, p. 11.   † The American Commonwealth, vol. ii, p. 570.

constitutions of all our States, though with some variations and qualifications, so that, in the opinion of Mr. Bryce, the "neutrality of the State [in America] can not be said to be theoretically complete." *

For all practical purposes, however, there are entire religious freedom and religious equality throughout the United States. But it was not so from the beginning. Church establishments were the rule during the colonial period. In Massachusetts the Puritan theocracy long held undisputed sway. The earlier constitutions of several of our States virtually recognized a state church. It was not so in Pennsylvania, where no church was ever legally established. In New York, although first the Dutch Reformed and afterward the Anglican Church enjoyed a special degree of favor, the first constitution, adopted in 1777, repealed all such parts of the common law and all such statutes as could "be construed to establish or maintain any particular denomination of Christians or their ministers." † Virginia followed in 1785. It was not till 1818, however, that Connecticut placed all religious bodies on a level; and in Massachusetts a tax for the support of the Congregationalist churches was, up till 1811, imposed on all citizens not belonging to some other incorporated religious body, and full religious equality was first recognized in that State by a constitutional amendment in 1833.‡ Prof. Bryce comments upon the remarkable fact that the "disestablishment," if it may be so called, in the several States was "accomplished with no great effort, and left very little rancor behind. In the South it seemed a natural outcome of the Revolution. In New England it came more gradually, as the necessary result of the political development of each commonwealth." # Religious freedom in America seems, accordingly, to have been the normal outgrowth of what may be termed the American spirit, although Holland

---
* "Vermont and Delaware declare that every sect ought to maintain some form of religious worship, and Vermont adds that it ought to observe the Lord's Day. Six Southern States exclude from office any one who denies the existence of a Supreme Being. Besides these six, Pennsylvania and Tennessee pronounce a man ineligible for office who does not believe in God and in a future state of rewards and punishments. Maryland and Arkansas even make such a person incompetent as a juror or witness. Religious freedom has been generally thought of in America in the form of freedom and equality as between different sorts of Christians, or at any rate different sorts of theists; persons opposed to religion altogether have till recently been extremely few everywhere, and practically unknown in the South."—Idem, p. 571.
† Schaff's Church and State in the United States, quoted in Campbell's Puritan, vol. i, p. 15.
‡ American Commonwealth. Bryce, vol. ii, p. 572.   # Idem.

undoubtedly exerted much influence in this regard upon the founders of New England. If the example of the Dutch had been more sedulously followed, the dark chapters which record the persecution of witches and the proscription of Quakers and Baptists could be omitted from the annals of Massachusetts.

In England to-day there are almost complete religious toleration and equality, save that a Roman Catholic can not sit on the throne, nor can one of that faith hold the office of Lord Chancellor of England or that of Lord Lieutenant of Ireland. But in these matters America has been the leader of the mother country. "In 1689 a partial Act of Toleration was enacted [in England], but it was not extended to Unitarians until 1813, to Roman Catholics until 1829, and to Jews until 1858. Until such respective dates the members of these proscribed religious bodies were excluded from public office, while it was not until 1871 that all religious tests were abolished in the universities of Oxford and Cambridge, so as to open those institutions equally to students of all religious denominations."*

THE BRITISH AND AMERICAN CONSTITUTIONS.

In the next place, the United States has a written Constitution, whereas what is called the constitution of England is merely a mass of precedents, traditions, usages, and understandings. Our Constitution is our glory and our pride. It is a wonderful piece of work, and it was framed under difficulties which most of us are not accustomed to appreciate. Mr. Gladstone paid it a splendid tribute when he said: "The American Constitution is, so far as I can see, the most wonderful work ever struck off at a given time by the brain and purpose of man." But, as a matter of fact, it was not thus "struck off." It does not contravene the law that what is of real and permanent value must be of slow growth. The Constitution of the United States was the product of evolution in a very real sense. Prof. Bryce takes a deeper view than the English Prime Minister. "The American Constitution," he says, "is no exception to the rule that everything which has power to win the obedience and respect of men must have its roots deep in the past, and that the more slowly every institution has grown, so much the more enduring is it likely to prove. There is

* Campbell's Puritan, vol. i, p. 47.

little in this Constitution that is absolutely new. There is much that is as old as Magna Charta." *

Sir Henry Maine observes that " the Constitution of the United States was the fruit of signal sagacity and pre-science " † on the part of its framers. This is undeniably true ; but it is not underrating that sagacity and prescience to point out that those wise and far-sighted men had valuable models for their work in the various State constitutions which had been in existence for some ten years previous to the meeting of the memorable convention of 1787. These instruments varied widely, showing the great diversity of views entertained by the men who framed them, but not a few of their most important provisions found a place in the Federal Constitution. But there had been written constitutions long before. The earliest was that adopted in Connecticut in 1639; and if a precedent be sought for this, it may be found in the Union of Utrecht, which was the written constitution of the Netherland Republic.

In spite of the fact that England was then, as now, without a written constitution, it was from England and from what had been developed through the relations of the colonies with the home government that the framers of the American Constitution drew many of the principles that give stability and strength to the bond which united the thirteen States into one, and which has sufficed, with little change, for the development and orderly control of a Union of States of which the founders of the republic could never have dreamed in their wildest imaginings.

No reader of the Federalist can fail to note the influence of Montesquieu upon Hamilton and Madison. Montesquieu's Spirit of Laws, published in 1748, is placed by Prof. Bryce in that "small class of books which permanently turn the course of human thought." This famous book emphasized the separation of the executive, legislative, and judicial powers as the most remarkable and admirable feature of the British system. It is evident enough now that the views of Montesquieu and Blackstone on this point were mistaken, and that no such separation does exist in the British constitution, where the executive has become the merest figurehead and Parliament has become absolutely supreme. Nevertheless, Hamilton and his coadjutors accepted implicitly the teachings of the great French writer on this matter; and hence the rigid separation of the executive, legislative,

* American Commonwealth, vol. i, p. 25.   † Popular Government, p. 109.

and judicial branches of government which was embodied in our Constitution, and which remains unaltered. It was derived in a roundabout way from England, although in reality it did not exist there.

Of the difference between the executive in England and the United States it is needless to speak. The nominal executive in England is, as I have said, no more than a figurehead; the real executive is the Prime Minister, together with the committee of the House of Commons which is known as the Cabinet. In America the President is a real executive. Besides being the commander of the army and navy and having power to appoint judges and a large number of other officers, including the members of the Cabinet, he possesses a substantial veto power. The members of our Cabinet have no voice in legislation, and, with the exception of the veto power of the President, the separation of the executive from the legislative department is complete.

More important still is the separation of the judiciary from both. The creation of the Supreme Court was the crowning act of the immortal Constitutional Convention. "There is no exact precedent for it either in the ancient or the modern world."* " This is the most noble as it is the most distinctive feature of the Government of the United States. It constitutes a difference between the American and British systems more fundamental than the separation of the executive from the legislative department."† In its sphere the Supreme Court is precisely what its name implies—supreme. Not only does it construe and determine the constitutionality of acts of Congress, but it is charged with interpreting the Constitution itself. There is no mystery about this to the American mind. But to the English mind it seems almost incomprehensible, for in England there is nothing corresponding with our court of final resort. The Englishman's difficulty in understanding this feature of our Government arises from the radical difference between the constitutions of the two countries. In England Parliament is omnipotent. According to Prof. Bryce, even Magna Charta and the Bill of Rights are no more than " ordinary laws, which could be repealed by Parliament at any moment in exactly the same way as it can repeal a highway act or lower the duty on tobacco."‡ Our

---
* Popular Government. Maine, p. 218.
† Critical Period of American History. Fiske, pp. 300, 301.
‡ American Commonwealth, vol. I, p. 237.

fixed Constitution, and the Supreme Court with power to interpret it, are the two most distinctive features of our Government, and have had the greatest influence in forming and preserving the American republic. Yet neither of them was borrowed directly from the mother country.

In the make-up of our national legislature, it is true, we have copied the English in providing two houses, but the resemblance between our Senate and the House of Lords is a surface resemblance only. The House of Lords is a hereditary assembly and represents the aristocracy. More than that, at the present day its functions are merely nominal, and it may be said to exist solely by sufferance of the House of Commons, whereas, in the opinion of so clearsighted an observer as Matthew Arnold, the United States Senate is perhaps, of all our institutions, "the most happily devised and the most successful in its working."* For all practical purposes the House of Commons is the English Parliament; but the House of Representatives is by no means the American Congress. Our House of Representatives stands for the people, while the Senate represents the States as so many separate units. This arrangement was the result of a famous compromise in the convention of 1787, and it has proved a most beneficent one.

LOCAL GOVERNMENT.—THE TOWN MEETING.

The question of local government in the United States is one of the most interesting of all questions to the student of our history and politics. Of all our local institutions, the town meeting has been the most distinctive and important. The "Aryan mark" it has been happily called by a writer in one of the recent magazines. It is in New England that the town meeting has had the largest sway and the greatest development, but it was in no sense indigenous on New England soil. Prof. Herbert B. Adams has clearly pointed out the Germanic origin of the New England town, and the subject has of late been thoroughly dealt with by Prof. Fiske and other writers. Mr. Freeman says that "a New England town meeting is essentially the same thing as the Homeric ἀγορή, the Athenian ἐκκλησία, the Roman *comitia*, the Swiss *Landesgemeinde*, the English folk-moot"; and

* Nineteenth Century, February, 1885.

that it is "the survival, or rather revival, of the old Teutonic assembly on the soil of a third England."* In the forest valleys of Germany, says Prof. Adams, the ancient Teutons came together and "talked over, in village-moot, the lowly affairs of husbandry and the management of their common fields. Here were planted the seeds of Parliamentary or Self - Government, of Commons and Congresses. Here lay the germs of religious reformations and of popular revolutions, the ideas which have formed Germany and Holland, England and New England, the *United States* in the broadest sense of that old Germanic institution." †

It has been found that in principle the town meeting is the oldest form of government known to man. It really antedated Athens and Rome. Research has shown that the first town was the stationary home of a clan, or a group of people united by family ties. This home was called a *tun*, which is equivalent to our word town. The old English town had its *tungemot*, or town meeting, at which by-laws were made and various business transacted. (It is an interesting fact that our word by-law originally meant simply town law, the old word *by*, signifying *town*, existing now only in certain combinations, such as Derby, Whitby, and the like.) Originally, as far as can be ascertained, the officers of these primitive town meetings were elected by the people, but when great landowners came to exercise large power the lord's steward and bailiff appear to have taken the place of the elected officials. After the Conquest the towns in England became manors, in which the officers were responsible to the neighboring lord, but they did not lose their self-government altogether. As the clans formed towns, so the uniting of clans into tribes formed shires or counties, and ultimately by the union of the shires the English nation came into being. Very early there came to be shire motes, or county meetings, to which each town sent representatives. Here was the beginning of representative government, which is such a familiar fact to us to-day. From the shire motes of England came the House of Commons, the glory of establishing which, in 1265, belongs to Simon de Montfort, although the first Parliament in which

---

* Introduction to American Institutional History. J. H. U. Studies, vol. i, No. 1, pp. 16, 38.
† The Germanic Origin of New England Towns. J. H. U. Studies, vol. i, No. 2, p. 5.

the people were fully represented did not assemble until thirty years later.*

Thus we trace the beginnings of the town and the town meeting, which have had such a vital share in the making of New England, and, in fact, of the greater part of the United States. The town meeting has been very truly called the "primordial cell" out of which a great portion of our national life has come. Although in England the town had fallen from its high estate by the seventeenth century, and although during the last five hundred years the county has sunk there into a mere administrative district, the settlers of New England had been accustomed to the discussing of local affairs in public meetings—that is, parish meetings—and it was for the very purpose of self-government, more particularly in church matters, that they had left their homes and crossed the ocean. In New England the meeting-house was from the beginning the center of the settlement, and town government there was neither more nor less than parish government adapted to the new conditions of life. Here was the very essence of democracy, although in an important sense the early government of New England was a theocracy. But as far as outward forms were concerned, it was emphatically government of the people, by the people, and for the people.

In Virginia and the Southern colonies generally there was a somewhat different condition of things, and there the county was the political unit. The county, however, has had far less influence than the town in the development of the nation, and does not call for special consideration. The idea of town government has been carried from New England throughout most, if not all, of our new West; and it is significant that where the town and the county have come into competition, as has been the case in Illinois especially, the superiority of the town has slowly but certainly brought it to the front. Roughly speaking, the lower half of Illinois was settled by people with Southern ideas and the northern half by pioneers of New England blood. The former were the first comers, and brought in the county system; the New Englanders strongly favored township organization, and through their influence four fifths of the counties in the State have since adopted the township sys-

* Most of what is said here about the town meeting is condensed from John Fiske's Civil Government in the United States, pp. 34 et seq.

tem. This experience is highly significant of the vitality and value of the town in America.*

The town meeting—that is, a primary assembly of all the voters in a town for the discussion and settlement of questions of local government—has, of course, never prevailed over a large extent of the country; but there is no doubt of the general tendency toward a spread of township government. For a small community the town meeting affords an ideal method for the control and adjustment of local affairs, but with the growth of population representative government becomes a necessity. Boston remained a town until at its town meetings not less than seven thousand men came together, making an intelligent interchange or expression of opinions impossible. Not the least of Samuel Adams's titles to fame is the fact that he was " the man of the town meeting"; and the importance of the town was clearly recognized by Thomas Jefferson, who urgently desired its adoption in his own Virginia. " Those wards called townships in New England," he said, " are the vital principle of their governments, and have proved themselves the wisest invention ever devised by the wit of man for the perfect exercise of self-government, and for its preservation." †

GROWTH AND SPREAD OF POPULAR EDUCATION.

Popular education has been one of the most prominent and distinctive features in the growth and development of the United States. In our free-school system we easily lead the world, and there can be no question that the average of education, superficial though the education may be, is higher in America than in any other country. The idea of general education may be said to have come over in the Mayflower. At any rate, as early as 1647 a law was enacted in Massachusetts providing that every town with fifty householders should establish a school in which children could be taught to read and write, and that every town with one hundred families of householders should have a school in which boys could be fitted for Harvard College. Before this, however, several towns had begun to appropriate money for free schools, and Harvard College had been founded in 1636. By 1665 every

---

* It is scarcely necessary to point out that *town* and *township* are two words for one thing, *town* alone being used in New England, while in the rest of the country *township* is more common. Some confusion is almost inevitable, since *town* is also used as meaning village, and sometimes even city.

† Works, vol. ii, p. 13.

town in Massachusetts had a common school, and all with over one hundred families a grammar school. In this matter Massachusetts was the leader of the other colonies, but they followed not far behind. I am speaking now only of those of New England, although the Dutch early established free schools in New York. The spirit of education was slow to penetrate the South. In 1671 the Governor of Virginia wrote to the English Commissioners for Foreign Plantations: "I thank God there are no free schools or printing-presses, and I hope we shall not have any these hundred years." Is it not a most suggestive fact that at this very time the Governor of Connecticut wrote to these very Commissioners: "One fourth of the annual revenue of the colony is laid out in maintaining free schools for the education of our children"?

This striking difference is "significant of much." How did it come about that popular education was from the first fostered in New England and frowned on in Virginia? These colonies were all settled by English men and women. What caused such a world-wide difference in them on this most important subject? It seems perfectly clear that the idea of popular education was not brought to this country directly from England. In the first place, there was no such thing in England at the time of the American settlements, nor, indeed, until nearly two centuries and a half afterward. How the free-school system has spread over the United States is well known; and it is equally well known that its progress has been slower in the South than elsewhere. In England it was not until as late a date as 1832 that the Government took a hand in the matter of education at all. In that year it made an appropriation for educational purposes of £20,000. The appropriation was gradually increased until 1869, when it amounted to half a million pounds. In 1870 England first adopted a system of general education by establishing common schools for the people. But these were not at that time wholly free; in truth, they have only just become so. Instead of leading the United States in this vital matter, it is plain that England has followed a long, long way after us.

We must look elsewhere for the origin of our common-school system. It would be easy to say, with Lowell, that it was the invention of the Puritan settlers in Massachusetts; or with Bancroft, that it "was derived from Geneva, the work of John Calvin; introduced by Luther into Germany, by John Knox into Scotland, and so became the property of the English-speaking nations." But Lowell's remark is a mere guess, and Bancroft's is a palpable *non sequitur*. Mr. Campbell insists that the idea of a school supported by the state, in which instruction should be given to all desirous of obtaining it, was not the creature of the Reformation. There were free schools in Rome, according to Pliny, and the Moors in Spain established many such schools nine or ten centuries ago. No doubt the Reformers did good work in spreading abroad the idea of popular education. At all events, it took firm hold upon a number of European countries in the century following the Reformation. In 1637 there was not a single peasant child in Sweden who was unable to read or write. In the Netherlands, even before the war with Spain, there is good evidence that the peasants could read and write well; and in 1609, when the first migration of the Pilgrims to Leyden took place, that was a land where, according to Motley, "every child went to school, where almost every individual inhabitant could read or write, where even the middle classes were proficient in mathematics and the classics, and could speak two or more modern languages." * It can hardly be doubted that this was the source from which was derived the first idea of popular education in the newly established colonies, even though the first schools in New England were not, like those of the Dutch Republic, absolutely free.

Here, too, we see why it was that education was favored in New England and repressed in Virginia. New England was settled by Puritans, not a few of whom had been in the Netherlands, and all of whom were familiar with its institutions, while the people who founded Virginia were of a different class, and were devoted to the Church of England and opposed to innovations of all kinds. Sir William Berkeley, whose famous assertion I have quoted,† may be regarded as typical of this class. It is sometimes said that the New England colonists represent the Roundheads of England, and those of Virginia the Cavaliers, but this I take to be a partial and superficial view. Still it is certain that the two sets of colonists were composed of very different classes of people, and the impress which they made upon the soil was lasting. In no respect, perhaps, is this difference shown more strikingly than in the disregard for public education

---

* United Netherlands, vol. iv, p. 432.   † Page 71.

which is still very evident throughout our Southern States, although the condition of things there is continually improving.

The schoolmaster has been abroad in our land as a whole, and the sum of the good done by him is immeasurable, even though many of the species have believed, as Mr. Lowell has suggested regarding the founders of Harvard, that whipping was "a wild benefit of nature," and, if they could have had their way, would have substituted "birchen" for "vernal" in the well-known stanza of Wordsworth, and so made it read:

> "One impulse from a *birchen* wood
> Can teach you more of man,
> Of moral evil and of good,
> Than all the sages can."

OTHER FACTORS IN OUR NATIONAL LIFE.

Two or three other potent factors in our national life press for consideration, but must be disposed of briefly. One of these is the freedom of the press; another is the written ballot; a third, ease in the transfer of land; and a fourth, the amelioration and perfection of the forms of legal procedure.

There was a rigid censorship of the press in England at the time the first American settlements were made and for many years afterward; and something of the same spirit found a place in the colonies. In Holland, however, more liberal ideas prevailed, and doubtless from that source they were carried across the Atlantic, to bear abundant fruit in later times. In the matter of the law of libel America has pointed the way for England, where the preposterous doctrine that "the greater the truth the greater the libel" prevailed until 1845. Our Constitution affirmed the freedom of speech and of the press; but these are elastic phrases. More to the point was the action of Pennsylvania in 1790, when there was inserted in its second constitution a provision that in actions for libel "the truth thereof may be given in evidence"; and the same principle speedily found a place in the law and practice of the other States.

Nothing is more essential to the safety and permanence of republican institutions than the secret ballot. The written or printed ballot is so familiar to us that we are apt to forget that it has not always been equally familiar in other countries where a system of voting prevails. It is the fact, however, that the ballot was not used in Great Britain until the year 1872. Previous to that time all voting had been done *viva voce* or by a show of hands. Plainly enough, America borrowed nothing from the mother country in this regard; and it is a suggestive fact that when England wanted a model ballot law, it turned for it, not to the United States, but to Australia. The Greeks had a primitive form of balloting by means of shells or stones, and in the Roman republic magistrates were voted for by means of wooden tablets. In the thirteenth century the written ballot was adopted by the Roman cardinals in choosing popes. In America the written ballot was first used in electing a minister for the Salem church in 1629. There can be no question that it was brought hither from the Netherlands, where it was the custom to choose both ministers and magistrates, at least in some towns, by ballot. In 1634 Thomas Dudley was elected Governor of Massachusetts, over John Winthrop, by means of " voting papers." The written ballot was embodied in the Connecticut constitution of 1639; Rhode Island followed in 1647, and West Jersey and Pennsylvania a few years later. In the first constitutions adopted by five of the thirteen original States it was provided that all elections should be by ballot. New York was not one of them, but the advantages of this system soon came to be recognized here. At present the use of the ballot is universal in the United States; but it has remained for us, in the last three or four years, to borrow from England the state-printed ballot, which England in turn had borrowed from Australia. The so-called Australian system, with modifications more or less marked, has now been established in three quarters of our States, and will in all probability, in spite of the opposition of unscrupulous politicians, soon be in general use throughout the country. Many of the existing laws on this subject are far from perfect, but, as a whole, they mark a very long stride in the right direction. We are also beginning to learn from England the wisdom of requiring from candidates an account of their expenditures. Soon, let us hope, we shall require the same from our political committees, and, furthermore, place a rigid limit upon the amount of money which a candidate may spend to secure his election—or defeat.

Our forefathers builded wisely when they refused to establish an aristocracy on American soil, and wisely, too, when they threw aside the law of primogeniture, which still prevails in the mother country and permits almost all its land to remain in the hands of a few owners. Here, again, the good example of the Dutch Republic was followed in America. So also in the matter of the recording of deeds, as to which England lags far behind us, but which has, beyond doubt, had a vast influence in promoting the prosperity of our people as a whole by making the transfer of land from one owner to another an easy and simple matter.

It is needless for me to do more than mention our great inheritance from England in trial by jury, and time would fail me should I undertake to trace in its fullness the history of this important factor in our social organization. Only in Great Britain and America is this institution, if it may be so termed, found in its completeness; and it is more closely woven into the texture of the state here than there.

Of one important difference between our criminal procedure and that in England, however, I must speak. Our public prosecutor, or district attorney, is one of our most important officials. It is almost impossible for us to think of enforcing the laws and punishing criminals without such an officer for every county; and, moreover, for offenses against the laws of the United States a Federal district attorney everywhere stands ready to prosecute. It seems wonderful to us that no such officers are known in England even to this day, in spite of numerous and eloquent appeals on the subject.* In 1855 Lord Brougham, in a striking speech in the House of Lords, called attention most emphatically to the evils resulting from a state of things in which the criminal procedure of England was "left to shift for itself, its execution being everybody's business in theory, and so nobody's in fact." † By an act of 1884, it is true, the Solicitor of the Treasury in England was made director of public prosecutions, to act in important cases; but it is easy to see that appointing one officer of this kind for the entire kingdom is a very different thing from having a district attorney for each county, as in the United States. Let us be thankful to the Netherland Republic for this factor in the enforcement of our criminal laws.

The English and the Americans are indeed kin, but to find the common stock we must in most cases go back two centuries or more. During this long lapse of time the English characteristics have been wonderfully preserved on

---

* The Puritan in Holland, England, and America, vol. ii, pp. 441-444.
† Speech on criminal law procedure, March 23, 1855.

American soil. The likenesses between the average Englishman and the average American are a thousand times more salient than the unlikenesses. The American is quicker in his movements and his thoughts, more restless, more energetic, more enterprising, more self-reliant, less conservative, ever ready to hear or ask some new thing. This difference in national type is easy to understand. It was, very naturally, the restless, unquiet spirits in the England of the seventeenth century who desired to leave their homes and cross the ocean, and this quality was transmitted to their descendants without stint. Almost inevitably it was increased by the new and strange conditions of life in the new country. "The mental alertness which comes of changed circumstances, new scenes, and unexpected difficulties was early remarked by travelers as a characteristic of the native of the colonies."* From this point of view it is not hard to understand the distinctive Yankee spirit and the wonderful fecundity of America in mechanical invention. All has come as an orderly development and a normal growth.

IMMIGRATION.—THE CHINESE.—THE NEGRO PROBLEM.

But not all of the American nation is of English origin. Some of our best and soundest ingredients have come from Germany, from Ireland, from the Scandinavian countries, from Scotland, from Switzerland. Until recently America opened wide her doors to all comers, and was proud to be known as an asylum for the oppressed of all nations—

"She of the open soul and open door,
With room about her hearth for all mankind."

In a high sense we would have it so. But it is plain that we should welcome immigration no faster than we can assimilate the immigrants; and it is also plain that we want none to come who are unwilling to make common lot with us in developing and maintaining our institutions. I heartily indorse what Mr. Depew said on this subject in a recent address: "Unwatched and unhealthy immigration can no longer be permitted to our shores. We must have a national quarantine against disease, pauperism, and crime. We do not want candidates for our hospitals, our poor-

---

* Migrations of American Colonists. Edward Eggleston, Century, vol. xxv, p. 74.

houses, or our jails. We can not admit those who come to undermine our institutions and subvert our laws. But we will gladly throw wide our gates for, and receive with open arms, those who by intelligence and virtue, thrift and loyalty, are worthy of receiving the equal advantages of the priceless gift of American citizenship." * As for the Chinese, ample experience has shown us that they can not be assimilated, and I have no doubt that the great majority of Americans are convinced that we are doing right in excluding them from our shores, even though we are unable to approve in all points the treatment of the Chinese either by our Government or by the people on our Pacific coast.

Another element has come into our life as a contribution from the Old World—an involuntary element: I mean the negro. The negro problem is still a problem, although it can hardly be doubted that, in the opinion of the wisest minds among us, it is slowly but surely solving itself, and the best thing to do about it is to keep hands off. What has been done regarding the treatment of the negro can not be undone, and, having been raised to the dignity of American citizenship, he must be left to work out his own political and social salvation.

THE DUTY OF THE HOUR.

"The past, at least, is secure." In this necessarily hurried and incomplete survey of the origin of some of the potent factors in the life of the American Republic, in endeavoring to cast up the sum of What America Owes to the Old World, has it not been plainly shown that we are, in very truth, "the heirs of all the ages"? Our America, our republican institutions, our free schools, our wide liberty of thought, our splendid national life, our restless, inventive, self-reliant spirit—what are they all—what, indeed,

"but the rushing and expanding stream
Of thought, of feeling, fed by all the past"?

What a duty, what a responsibility, then, are ours! Advantages are obligations: they are likewise opportunities. Let us not by absorption in contemplation of the past miss the lesson of the present and the alluring promise of the future. We have been warned to "look forward and not backward"; and I do not forget that some one has wittily

* Columbian Oration at Chicago, October 21, 1892.

said, as an illustration of the inequality of the sexes, that Lot's wife looked back and was turned into a pillar of salt, while Mr. Edward Bellamy looked back and made sixty thousand dollars. However that may be, there has of late been a vast deal of looking backward in this country. We have been doing this ever since the first of our long series of centennial celebrations began—the series that has just ended with the observance of the quadricentenary of the discovery. No survey of what has been can be complete without a glance forward toward what is to be. But our duty lies in the immediate *now*.

> "Future or Past no richer secret folds,
> O friendless Present! than thy bosom holds."

Let us be worthy of our great inheritance. If we act our part wisely in the present—no longer the "friendless Present"—we shall build strong and sure the foundations of the future. That other nations have fallen into decay is no reason for believing that the United States is to perish in like manner. It has been suggested by a recent writer that what has been evolved in America by a century of republican institutions is "government of the people, for the people, by 'the best people.'" Do not let us believe it. Rather are we in danger of government by the worst people—that is, by the ignorant, the degraded, the corrupt. "We can not expect the nature of the aggregate to be much better than the average natures of the units." Are we really justified in expecting it to be any better? Most certainly not, if a large number of the units voluntarily turn themselves into ciphers. The dignity and the responsibility of American citizenship need to be emphasized. No man in all the land should be able to omit the duty of voting, with a clear and approving conscience. Patriotism ought to be a part of every school and college curriculum, and history should be made the teacher and inspirer of patriotism. In reviewing the past and tracing the evolution of the things that make America what it is, we shall miss the finest lesson if we fail to see that our obligations, in view of all that we have received, are many and great. Shall we not accept them willingly and gladly, and front the future with courageous hearts, inspired by the "high faith that fails not by the way"?

ABSTRACT OF THE DISCUSSION.

REV. JOHN W. CHADWICK:

I have little more to say to Mr. Palmer's paper than just a loud Amen. First of all, of course, we owe our discovery to Europe; then our exploration, and that we owe in much larger degree to France than to England. How great a debt this is we can find by reading the histories of Parkman. It is interesting to study the influence of the discovery of America on the Old World. Two great events occurred very nearly together—the discovery of America and the Protestant Reformation. Though there were several hundred voyages to America within a few years after its discovery, yet Europe was so much engaged with the Reformation that it seemed to have little time to give to the New World. After a while the Reformation seems to have spent itself, and then comes in the newly discovered world. Five nations were chiefly engaged in its exploration and settlement—Portugal, Spain, France, Holland, and England—and it had the effect of making them world powers or oceanic civilizations. England was not a maritime power until the time of Drake and Frobisher and Elizabeth's other great captains. The struggle for the possession of America became the determining influence in European wars. England was the final conqueror, and so we owe to England the making of our America. The fight was in Europe, but also here, and France enlisted the Indian on her side. The struggle was long and bitter; but in it England hardened the fiber of the colonists so that they might in time break the yoke of her own power. Hardly had the echoes of the victory of Wolfe over Montcalm at Quebec died away when the first sounds of the Revolution began to be heard. I think we owe it to England largely that we asserted our independence.

In regard to our written Constitution, I sympathize with Mr. Palmer's admiration of Mr. Campbell's book, and also with his criticism. I felt in reading the book that the temper of the man was extremely bad—often that of a campaign document. I felt that the author had taken a brief for his theory, and put his telescope to his blind eye when the facts did not help his inverted Anglomania. In Australia the development of institutions is more radically different from that of England than is that of this country; but no one contends that Australia owes anything to Dutch influence.

Washington was inaugurated in April, 1789, and in May of the same year the States General met in France. From that time on our politics was biased by French and European politics. Sympathy with France and sympathy with England were the determining factors in our first political divisions. French influence dominated the old Republican party (opposed to the Federal), and gave our development its right direction—quite different from the idea of Alexander Hamilton.

The influence of Africa has been enormous. But for Africa, no slavery; but for slavery, no civil war; but for the war, no such nationality as we now have. Dr. Hall, of Trinity Church, who knows a great deal of the South, assured me that, in his opinion, the Southern people had taken those graces of gentleness and suavity so characteristic of them largely from the negro. It was the contact of the Southern gentleman with his slaves that gave him the pleasantest traits of his character. The opinion is unique and interesting, whether it is sound or not.

MR. JAMES A. SKILTON:

I am much pleased with the presentation of the subject by Mr. Palmer. It was as full as time permitted. But to me, as an evolutionist, there was an important omission. It was perhaps necessary, to fill in the details, to get near the subject, but to my mind he got too near. We ought to consider more fully the influences acting upon American civilization from abroad that tend to survival or non-survival. The lecture should have in it more of Ionic perspective—more of a distant look. The question should be whether from the Old World we have derived laws and institutions that insure perpetuation and advancement on lines pointed out by the evolution philosophy. Treating the topic thus, we would begin with Asia and inquire into the conditions there in the past. The main characteristic there would be the domination of law. The Asiatic people are an obedient, docile people. They have the capacity to wait long enough to work out the problems put upon them. The question is, Has England or Europe furnished us with the elements of perpetuity such as might be furnished by the Asiatic? When we take Asia as an example, one of the difficulties is that there obedience to law has produced stagnation. Asia does not show progress, development. Looking at Africa, we see nothing but darkness. Considering Europe as related to Asia, is it not true that the reign of law in Asia has acted like a hydraulic press, forcing men out of Asia into Europe to seek the freedom and opportunity which they did not find at home? How have they used their opportunity in Europe? There they have not developed the same obedience to law and willingness to endure. I hold that the civilization of Europe is akin to barbarism, and I deny that it has in it the elements of perpetuity. These elements were found in the Hebrew civilization: there was law, firm and rigid, its origin professedly divine. The Hebrew civilization worked wonders, yet it was imperfect. The man who has affected our civilization more than any other declared that he came not to destroy the law, but to fulfill. That man's teaching furnishes the material wherein lies the salvation of our civilization. He did not undertake to destroy the civilization that had gone before, but to develop it. He proposed that man be governed by the laws of the kingdom of Heaven—that is, by the laws of eternal justice—by means of the human intellect, by which we have discovered the principle of development in Nature. We must apply the same principle intelligently in the solution of our own social and political problems if we wish our civilization to endure.

MR. Z. SIDNEY SAMPSON:

It seems to me that the basic principle in English character—that to which we owe the most—is the principle of individualism. The English have inherited this principle from their Teutonic and Norman ancestors; it has never been lost, but we are indebted to the insularity of England for its intensity; the centripetal character of the continental civilization might have destroyed it entirely. The imperial idea of continental Europe was directly opposed to individualism, and their people have been submissive to authority. When the English came to America they brought with them a desire for strong government, and also the flexibility induced by individualism. They brought steadfastness—they came to stay. They overcame adverse circumstances. They came for a purpose. This steadfastness was not characteristic of the French, or the Spanish, or the Dutch. They lacked staying qualities. They had ulterior motives—ties to the old country. The centrifugal tendencies kept the bonds to the old country so strong that they never felt that they were here for a definite purpose. Some things are due to accident: for instance, the English settled in the best part of the new territory. With the natural fastness of the Appalachian Mountains on the west and the sea on the east, they had an opportunity to consolidate and develop national characteristics.

MR. PALMER, in reply: There is scarcely anything in the way of criticism to answer. Mr. Skilton is right in saying that it is impossible in an hour to treat this subject in full. I am glad Mr. Chadwick said a word in favor of the Dutch. The Dutch did a great work in New York, on which I did not have time to dwell. An interesting line of discussion is suggested by the conflict between the English, French, and Spanish, which proved that the English were superior from the start. I can not agree altogether with Mr. Chadwick's denunciation of Mr. Campbell's book. I have heard of a reviewer of books who said that the best way to criticise a book was to do so before reading it; and I fear Mr. Chadwick has not read this book carefully. I do not indorse it *in toto,* but I have found it very suggestive indeed, and I warmly recommend it; but it should be read with the corrective of other histories, in order that one may not get a partial or incomplete view.

WAR AND PROGRESS

BY
LEWIS G. JANES
AUTHOR OF A STUDY OF PRIMITIVE CHRISTIANITY, LIFE AS A FINE ART,
THE PROBLEM OF CITY GOVERNMENT, ETC.

COLLATERAL READINGS SUGGESTED:

Spencer's Principles of Sociology, Principles of Ethics, vol. i, and Justice; Sheldon Amos's Political and Legal Remedies for War; Maine's Ancient Law, Early History of Institutions, and International Law; Field's Outlines of an International Code; Sumner's The True Grandeur of Nations; Channing's Discourse on War; Palm's Capital Punishment, with a Chapter on War; Fiske's Beginnings of New England, and American Revolution; Arnold's History of Rhode Island; Greene's Short History of Rhode Island; Krapotkin's War, Law, and Authority; Tolstoi's War and Peace.

WAR AND PROGRESS.

By Lewis G. Janes.

The New Historical Standpoint.

In considering the part which war has played in the advancement of civilization the modern student of social science is compelled to deviate widely from the sentimental method in vogue during the early part of the present century. The doctrine of evolution as applied to sociological questions has transformed and reconstructed our method of writing and teaching history, and enabled us to estimate more correctly the character and place of those phenomena which appear morally inexplicable when judged by the absolute standards of an advanced ethical and intellectual stage of human development. Thus our sympathies are greatly broadened, and we can repeat with a new and significant emphasis the noble sentence of Terence: "I am a man, and nothing human is indifferent to me."

It is no longer sufficient for the historical student to perceive certain leading facts relating to the sequence of dynasties, the conquest of nations, and the deeds of martial heroes, in their proper time relations; he must see them as vitally related to the totality of their environing conditions. He must study the life of peoples, the development of industries, and the laws of social growth; he must know man as a progressive being, tracing him from the rude animalism of the childhood of the human race up through savagery and barbarism and the various ethnic stages of a progressive civilization as he slowly and painfully struggles onward toward the millennial era of the future, which, transcending the boundaries of race and nationality, shall unite mankind in a universal brotherhood.

Early Uses of Conflict.

The original condition of men in this world of ours was one of perpetual warfare—warfare with the forces of Nature, with beasts of prey, and with their fellow-men, struggling like themselves to maintain a foothold on the planet.

Wild men, like wild animals, were unsocial and unprogressive. Savage races, and even some that we call civilized, are unprogressive at the present time. The problem before us is to ascertain how human societies first became progressive —how the wild man of the earliest ages has been tamed and civilized. In this process conflict has played an important and, in many respects, a beneficial part. As Mr. Bagehot has shown, "civilization begins because the beginning of civilization is a military advantage." * That which enables one tribe or incipient tribe of savage men to triumph over its competitors is its relatively superior faculty of coherence—the disposition and ability of its members to live together, work together, and fight together for common ends and against the common enemy. In this earliest stage of human progress, even the slightest symptom of social coherence, to quote again from Mr. Bagehot, "the least indication of a military bond, is sufficient to turn the scale; the compact tribes win, and the compact tribes are the tamest." Those tribes and individuals which do not prove susceptible of cultivating co-operative habits—the disposition to work and fight in common—are gradually swept away. The same principle holds good all along the line of human progress; it is thus that the family, clan, hundred, and tribe of the earlier stages of social evolution have been gradually supplanted by the compact city, the cohesive state, the triumphant unified nationality. The law of natural selection has been the dominant factor in the initiation and original advancement of human progress, operating almost as unrestrainedly as in the evolution of the various forms of vegetal and animal life. In remote regions of the world where savage tribes have been protected from this conflict, where subsistence has been easy, and the soil has not even required to be tickled with a hoe to laugh with an abundant harvest, there humanity has not progressed. Man has remained in a state of arrested development, a child of Nature, "a powerless, pulpy soul," a being of purely negative virtues, without distinct individuality of character, possessed of neither physical nor moral stamina.

The important fact to note in connection with this brief survey of the period of man's earlier social evolution is that the effect of these early conflicts was to develop certain fundamental virtues in human character essential to progress

---

* Physics and Politics. By Walter Bagehot.

and success in life in all subsequent generations. Primitive man was not only weak and plastic by reason of his undeveloped powers, but his mind was filled with vague and overpowering fears of the universe which surrounded him. His religions were religions of fear. His home training rested upon fear as a motive, inculcating absolute submission to arbitrary and often unreasonable commands. The patriarchal ruler of the earliest communities was a tyrant, to whom his subjects rendered abject and submissive allegiance. One influence of the perpetual conflicts of the earlier ages was to develop what are termed the manly virtues; to measurably dissipate irrational fears, to stimulate courage, fortitude, energy, endurance, perseverance; to induce habits of discipline which led to greater economy of strength; and these virtues in turn became the very points of variability and superior fitness on which the law of natural selection operated to secure the survival of the community in which they had reached the highest development; so that, in the long run, that which has given the race success in the struggle for existence has been of permanent advantage, moral as well as intellectual and physical, in its subsequent career. Conquest has been "the missionary of valor, and the hard impact of military virtues has beaten meanness out of the world." *

HOW WAR SOMETIMES PROMOTES PROGRESS.

In yet another way war has not infrequently exerted a beneficial influence on the welfare of mankind—in breaking up that "cake of custom" which, too strongly solidified, renders nations sessile and unprogressive. This end has indeed been effected largely by the arts of peace, the progress of industries and inventions, and the advancement of education; but conquest has done its part in liberating the human mind from the bondage of convention and breaking up those ethnic barriers that have often been detrimental to human progress. The most striking instance of this sort in human history is exemplified in the fact that the spread of Christianity and the wonderful civilization of which it forms a component part has been limited almost absolutely to the boundaries of the Roman Empire at the time of its advent and to the colonies since peopled by nations contained within its limits. The Christian religion

* Bagehot. Physics and Politics.

has obtained only a nominal and transient foothold in other parts of the world. England's long occupation of India has made scarcely an impression in converting the natives to Christianity, and China and the nations of eastern and central Asia as well as the peoples of Africa have been alike impervious to the principles and methods of our Christian civilization. The conquests of Rome had broken up the ethnic barriers of the conquered peoples, brought alien religions into contact, sown the seeds of mutual toleration, and prepared the way for a universal faith. But for the military achievements of the Roman Empire, Christianity would probably have remained an insignificant Jewish sect, and long since have ceased to exert an appreciable influence on the thought and destinies of the world. Other noticeable examples of a similar character are found in the history of the crusades of the middle ages, and of the conquests of Napoleon, which destroyed the last remaining traces of feudalism in Europe and prepared the way for the unity of the nations based upon the natural lines of race, language, industrial interests, and community of ideas and institutions. Thus even those virtues which work for peace and brotherhood—the domestic virtues and finer graces of character, that are directly opposed to the cultivation of the warlike spirit—indirectly owe much of their opportunity for development to the conflicts and conquests of the earlier ages.

WHEN CONFLICT BECOMES INJURIOUS.

When the causes which originally impelled men to physical conflict no longer exist, when communities are secure from the assaults of the savage and semi-civilized races, when nations are consolidated by internal cohesion, along natural lines of race and language and the physical conformation of the continents, instead of by external compulsion, then aggressive war becomes a scourge and an injury instead of an advantage in human evolution. The higher virtues of magnanimity, concession and brotherly affection, should thereafter control and direct the lower warlike faculties, and impel men to attack the evils of their own nature and of contemporary society, to overcome the inertia and opposition of natural forces, and thus to make a nobler conquest of the world for the advantage of all mankind. " The military habit," says one of the ablest philosophical writers upon this subject, " makes man think far too much of definite action and far too little of brooding meditation; life is not a set campaign, but an irregular work, and the main forces in it are not overt resolutions, but latent and half-voluntary promptings. Military morals can direct the axe to cut down the tree, but it knows nothing of the quiet force by which the forest grows."* The ultimate human character is the product of long eras, both of conflict and of peace. In the making of a man all things finally work together for good.

> "Let war and trade and creeds and song
> Blend, ripen race on race,
> The sunburnt world a man shall breed
> Of all the zones and countless days."

Since the higher virtues which come to fruition latest grow out of the friendly and peaceable intercourse of man with man, war serves mankind only when it favors, encourages, and affords superior conditions for such intercourse. When it creates permanent antagonisms between men and nations and destroys progressive civilizations, it is always, even when unavoidable, a tremendous evil. Among the higher races of mankind and the more advanced civilizations of the present day, even defensive wars are admittedly followed by a long train of injurious effects. Wars of conquest and of glory, wars for the settlement of petty disputes about national boundaries, or for the recompense of offended national honor, can find no justification when judged by evolutionary tests.

MILITANT AND INDUSTRIAL TYPES OF SOCIETY.

Still less is it justifiable for the modern civilized community to cultivate voluntarily that militant type of society which results from the habitual exercise and stimulation of the warlike spirit. This type of society as described by Mr. Spencer implies a strong centralized government, the loss of individuality in the citizen by the rigid restraint of his self-prompted actions, the decay of local self-government and consequent distrust of man's capacity for self-government, the devotion of a considerable portion of the able-bodied citizens to warlike pursuits and their withdrawal from productive occupations, necessitating their support by

---

* Bagehot.

the rest of the community, the institution of castes and ranks in society, the antagonization of capital and labor, the repression of voluntary organizations among the people, and the extension of the functions of the state to a degree inconsistent with individual liberty; the evolution of the state as a self-sustaining organization, and the consequent discouragement of commerce and intercourse with other nations; all of these influences tending to the ultimate establishment and perpetuation of a rigid and permanent national type of character, self-complacent of its own attainments, inimical to progress, and which can only become progressive through violent disruption or revolution. This type of society results in the production of a small number of so-called great men, distinguished for military prowess or ability in the arts of aggressive statesmanship, and in the repression and atrophy of individual character and distinction among the masses of the people. It is therefore an essentially aristocratic and anti-democratic type of society.*

The whole beneficent tendency of our modern industrial progress has been toward the repression of the militant and the development of the industrial type of social organization. By a slow process of evolution, the manual laborer, who was originally a captive taken in war, owned like a beast of burden and subject to the tyrannical caprice of his master, first became a serf, with some measure of personal freedom, but still attached to the soil by the militant power of the nation, then a wage laborer, with an assured certainty of income which favored peace of mind and social advancement, and finally a man and a citizen, having recognized rights guaranteed by the fundamental law and alienated only by crime, " totally detached from master, soil, and locality, free to work anywhere and for any one," and to become master, if competent and worthy, of his own concerns. Barter and trade, instead of a mutual exchange of presents, under the compulsion of custom and with little regard for their reciprocal worth, has become a recognized rendering of equivalent values under contract of equity, expressed or implied. For the external protection of the citizen by means of standing armies, expensive fortifications, Chinese walls, and prohibitory tariffs, is substituted the internal protection afforded by just laws, executed by the civil authorities and guaranteeing the equal opportunity of all, the universally

* See Spencer's Principles of Sociology, Principles of Ethics, The Man vs. The State, and Justice.

diffused blessings of education, just methods of taxation, tariffs no higher than is necessary to equalize the wage level with competing nations, and thus afford opportunity for free and fair competition, and the influence of a worldwide commerce, the beneficent agent for carrying to the remotest quarters of the earth the blessings of civil liberty and an advanced civilization. This type of society has become a recognized ideal in the minds of thinking and intelligent men the world over. It is an ideal not yet perfectly realized by any nation or people; but it is the ideal of evolution, and all the fingers of prophecy point thitherward as the ultimate goal of human progress.

THE NATION'S PLACE IN SOCIAL EVOLUTION.

That all distinctions of race and nationality will disappear when the sword is beaten into the plowshare and the spear into the pruning-hook is by no means a necessary deduction from the application of evolutionary principles to the great problems of associated human life. On the contrary, it will doubtless happen that the nation as well as the individual will find its highest and most characteristic development under freedom. The compulsion of the militant system is essentially inimical to this free development of national types, and is only justifiable at all among civilized nations to repel those assaults from without which interfere with the freedom of internal evolution. When such assaults are no longer to be feared, militancy will have no further *raison d'être*. Races will then seek their natural habitats, and perform voluntarily the particular functions in the world's work for which they are best fitted. Those racial types and governmental forms which preserve and add something to the world's store of social virtues will survive and flourish; those which prove static and retrogressive or inimical to progress will gradually be eliminated. Nations will develop each an internal structure adapted to its physical, intellectual, and industrial environment, and thus be enabled to contribute the most useful service to advance the civilization of the world. The enormous energy and treasure now wasted in the support of the enginery of war will be diverted to the arts and industries of peace, thus adding to the wealth and happiness of the masses of the people. The *régime* of status, characteristic of the militant type of society, will be fully supplanted by that of contract, wherein the worker will freely choose his occupation, in which he will obtain an equitable compensation for his labor, and in the development of which he will have a direct personal interest in proportion to the intelligence, faithfulness, and skill which he puts into his work. Voluntary co-operation will take the place of socialistic compulsion, and the arbitrary regulation of labor, either by capitalistic employers or the iron rule of the trades union, will be a thing of the past. Under this freer system benefits will be automatically adjusted to efforts, and that correct apportioning of reward to merit will be secured which the requirements of justice demand and which stimulates progress by insuring the greater prosperity of the superior and more industrious workman.

WHITHER IS AMERICA TENDING?

Having thus briefly outlined the part which militancy has played in the upbuilding of past civilizations, noted its diminishing efficacy for good with the advance of our modern industrial system, and hastily sketched the evolutionary ideal of an industrial civilization not impossible of ultimate realization in the future progress of the race, it now remains to inquire, Whither is our own America tending? Are we looking forward or looking backward; toward a higher evolution of industrial civilization, or toward a revival of reactionary militantism in our social and political life? What part has war played in our past history? What should be our attitude toward militant methods in the present? What may and ought our nation to do in the future toward advancing the civilization of the world?

OUR INDIAN WARS.

That the bloody struggles of our forefathers with the aborigines were justified either by good policy or by necessity is an assumption which seems to be unwarranted by the facts of history. I believe them to have been, in the main, unnecessary. I by no means idealize the American Indian. He was a savage, too long isolated from contact with civilization to be susceptible of great progress or advancement. His destiny in any event was probably to disappear before a superior race. But the Indian, like most savage peoples, was in many respects like a child. He knew when he was treated justly, and injustice filled his mind with a desire for vengeance. He would sell his lands for a song, and if well treated he always proved a steadfast friend. He was prone, however, to visit the wrongs done him by any white settler upon the entire community, as is the custom of all savage peoples. The chief conflicts into which the settlers of New England were precipitated grew out of their own militant and bigoted spirit, or were incidents of the contests between France and England for supremacy on this continent, as even the narrative of Mr. Fiske, whose attitude is generally apologetic, abundantly proves.* Take, for example, the infamous treachery of the Massachusetts authorities which resulted in the slaughter of the Narragansett sachem Miantonomo, and which rivals that of the worst of the so-called "treacherous" natives. Miantonomo was charged with the crime of selling a tract of land on the western shore of Narragansett Bay, beyond the jurisdiction of the Massachusetts colony,† to Samuel Gorton—the ancestor, I believe, of my friend Dr. Gorton of this city, and, like him, an independent in politics and religion—and condemned by the committee of a synod of clergymen then in session to be put to death by his rival and captor, Uncas, chief of the Mohegans. At a signal from Uncas, and in the presence of a committee of the colonists, a warrior, who was walking behind the unarmed friend of Gorton and Roger Williams, sank his tomahawk into the skull of the victim, killing him by a single blow. "Uncas cut a warm slice of flesh from his shoulder and greedily devoured it, declaring that it was the sweetest of meats and gave strength to his heart." ‡

Mr. Gorton, who, whatever his eccentricities of opinion, seems at least to have possessed the spirit of a civilized white man, and whose claim to his purchase was subsequently confirmed by the British Government through the mediation of the Puritan Earl of Warwick, endeavored in vain to save the life of Miantonomo. He was himself condemned to death by the clerical synod and the Governor's Council, and only escaped alive after a term of imprisonment through lack of concurrence by the representatives of the people. The natural outcome of Miantonomo's murder was a long period of smothered ill-feeling and the sympathy of the Narragansetts with King Philip, the chief of the

---

* The Beginnings of New England. By John Fiske.
† This section is specifically included in the grant to the colony of Rhode Island by the terms of its charter.
‡ *Vide* Fiske. Beginnings of New England.

Wampanoags, in the subsequent war which bears his name. The immediate incentive to that war seems to have been the death of Philip's brother, Alexander, or Wamsutta, who, on a frivolous charge, was marched through the forests in the torrid heat of summer to appear before the General Court of the colony, but who died in the house of his captor of exhaustion and fever—his brother and followers naturally enough imagining by poison. He had with him some eighty followers—men, women, and children—on foot, while the military guard of white men, under Major Winslow, were on horseback. When about to sink from fatigue, even the stern heart of the Puritan warrior was touched, and he asked Wamsutta to take his horse. The reply of the chief was worthy of a Sir Philip Sidney: "No! there are no horses for my wife and the other women." Massachusetts chroniclers naturally ignore this incident; it was left for the historians of the colony of Roger Williams, the steadfast friend of the Indians until his death, to preserve it to this generation.* The Sunday massacre of the Narragansetts in their fortress at South Kingston, R. I., was an episode of the King Philip War. They were charged with no overt act of warfare, but merely with sheltering some stray followers of Philip. This outrage, perpetrated by the Puritan hosts of Massachusetts, Plymouth, and Connecticut, was not only an uncalled-for insult to humanity, but also a violation of an express provision of the charter of the colony of Rhode Island, within the jurisdiction of which the tribe was located. The charter of King Charles II provided that "It shall not be lawful to or for the rest of the colonies to invade or molest the native Indians or any other inhabitants . . . (they having subjected themselves to us, and being by us taken into our special protection) without the knowledge and consent of the Governor and Company of our Colony of Rhode Island and Providence Plantations." Prof. George Washington Greene, the able historian of Rhode Island, says of this assault: "Volunteers from Rhode Island joined them [the attacking party] on the way, *but Rhode Island as a colony was not consulted.*" † Thus did Massachusetts repay the noble service of Roger Williams, whom she had banished for his opinions, but called upon for succor in her dire extremity at the time of

---

* See A Short History of Rhode Island. By George Washington Greene, LL. D., late Non-resident Professor of American History in Cornell University.
† Ibid.

the previous Pequot War. Alone and unarmed, returning good for evil in her behalf, he traveled more than twenty miles through swamp and wilderness to the fastness of the Narragansetts, and at the risk of his life prevailed upon them not to join the Pequots in their assault upon the whites. We shudder with horror at the barbarism which scalps the fallen foe, but, in the person of our ablest historian, we have no word of reproach for the Puritan "braves" who quartered the body of King Philip and set his head upon a pole before the gates of Plymouth, where it testified to their tender mercies and æsthetic sensibilities for twenty years after his death. Mr. Fiske's only comment is the obvious one that "It may be supposed that . . . at this time a Christian feeling of charity and forgiveness was not uppermost." One of Philip's hands was sent to Boston, where it was welcomed as a trophy, and the other was given to the renegade who shot him, who exhibited it for money. Verily, all the barbarism was not on the part of the Indians.

The experience of William Penn and Roger Williams, who were never molested by the natives, seems to sustain my conviction that the struggling settlements were subjected to a waste of life and treasure which a little humanity and common sense might easily have prevented. I recognize the sterling virtues of the Puritan character and the great force for good which it has been in the history of our country. Tracing my own ancestry to the Mayflower, I at least have no inherited anti-Puritan bias. But as a native of Rhode Island I also clearly perceive that without the broader and more humane spirit of Roger Williams to modify its narrowness and severity Puritanism could never have become a permanent and beneficent influence in our national life. The Puritans took for their model the story of the triumphs of Israel in Canaan, and whom they could not convert they had little conscience in destroying. When the Miles Standishes and the Benjamin Churches and the John Masons drew the sword of the Lord and Gideon, little mercy could be expected by their heathen enemies. Mr. Fiske assumes that political reasons will account for the immunity of Pennsylvania from Indian disturbances, but this explanation certainly did not hold good in Rhode Island, where such influences were all adverse to the little colony. Nor can I accept the optimistic *ex post facto* view of this question which Mr. Kimball presented in his recent lecture.* I

* Natural Factors in American Civilization. By Rev. John C. Kimball.

do not believe that these conflicts were necessary to prevent the amalgamation of the races in our Anglo-Saxon settlements. No such mingling occurred in Pennsylvania or Rhode Island any more than in Massachusetts and Connecticut; and in Mexico and Central America, where the amalgamation has been most complete, the early conflicts were most barbarous and destructive. The same is also measurably true in Canada. Indeed, our entire dealings with the Indians, not only in the colonial period but since we became an independent nationality, have been of such a character that we have reason to regret that that chapter can not be blotted from our nation's history. Our Indian wars have always been a curse and never a blessing, and can find no philosophical justification at the hand of the impartial historian. Except for a few shining individual instances of justice in our dealings with him, like those already cited, and some of later days, the red man would be abundantly justified in reversing the dictum of General Sherman and concluding that "the only good white man is a dead white man."

THE REVOLUTIONARY CONFLICT.

To the conflict with Great Britain, however, we manifestly owe our present status as an independent, self-regulated nationality. That our revolutionary struggle for independence was worth all it cost I can not doubt, seeing that local self-government is the goal which evolution indicates in the development of political institutions under a *régime* of freedom, and that this right was denied us by the mother country. Nor would England's habitually indefensible treatment of her colonies serve to do aught but strengthen this conclusion. The Revolutionary War was not fought on account of a threepenny tax on tea, but for a principle—a fundamental principle of self-government; and in securing our autonomy as a nation, an end indeed not originally sought or contemplated, our fathers builded better than they knew. Yet at what cost of life and treasure was this right of self-government achieved—leaving us at last with a worthless currency, a dishonored credit, and thousands of sad homes bereft of husbands, sons, and fathers sacrificed in fratricidal strife. We can hardly be surprised that one of our wisest counselors in this time of trial, one of the truest patriots and ablest men that America has ever produced, Benjamin

Franklin, wrote to Josiah Quincy within eight days after he had placed his name to the treaty of peace which secured the independence of his country: "May we never see another war! for, in my opinion, there never was a good war or a bad peace."*

THE SECOND WAR WITH ENGLAND.

The War of 1812, waged by us against Great Britain for the protection of our seamen on the decks of American vessels, was a contest honorable to neither of the contesting parties. It was concluded by a treaty in which Great Britain expressly refused to have inserted a clause against impressment, and to which we finally assented, though Secretary Monroe had previously written to our commissioners that the omission of such a clause would constitute a confession of our failure. It left us with our national capital in ruins and our national dishonor mitigated, but by no means fully redeemed, by the triumphs of Perry on Lake Erie and Jackson at New Orleans. Subsequently, in the exaggerated phraseology of our Fourth of July oratory, we have made the most of these local successes; but the fact remains that this contest reflected credit neither on our statesmanship nor on our arms.†

THE MEXICAN WAR.

Nor can the war with Mexico be justified save upon the ethically unsafe plea that the end sanctifies the means, and that by the consequent enlargement of our national domains to the Golden Gates of the Pacific we were fulfilling the manifest destiny of the American republic. Obviously, at the time of its occurrence, the Mexican War was a contest waged in the interest and at the behest of the Southern slave system. Some obvious results of the Mexican War were the immediate intensification of the slavery agitation, the encouragement of the South by the acquisition of Texas to hold on to slavery, the onslaught on the Territories, the refusal to listen to overtures for the purchase of the slaves for manumission, the bequest of Taylor, Fillmore, and the Fugitive Slave Law to the nation, and the subsequent hor-

---

* Franklin's Works, vol. x, p. 11.
† The cessation of impressment in subsequent years, without special treaty stipulation, was an indication of good sense on the part of Great Britain, which may have been stimulated, in part, by our naval successes. Patriotism, at least, urges us to cherish this opinion.

rors of the civil war. The cession of territory to our country by France, Spain, and Russia through peaceful purchase was surely a better bargain for us, besides being ethically justifiable, which the Mexican War was not.

THE CIVIL CONFLICT.

The War of the Rebellion was apparently one of those offenses which, owing to the ignorance and folly of the people, must needs come. In its defense even the lyrics of our Quaker poet took on a martial tone, and cheered on the armies of Union and Liberty to their final triumph.* It is easy now to look back and see that every slave might have been purchased at his full value and set free by the United States Government at one third the cost in money of the war, and with the saving of a million lives of home-makers and wealth-producers. But on the one hand the slaveholders, profiting as they thought by the institution and educated to regard it as divinely sanctioned, absolutely refused to sell their human chattels, while, on the other hand, the aroused antislavery sentiment of the North denied the right of property in slaves *in toto*, and refused to entertain propositions to pay their masters for them, saying, with Emerson:

" Who is the owner? The slave is owner,
And ever was: *Pay him!* "

Goaded to madness by the gods who sought its destruction, Slavery struck a deadly blow at its only reliable guerdon of defense, the union of the States, and perished in the resulting conflict. On the part of the Government the war was one of defense, in the interest of freedom and a higher civilization, and therefore ethically justifiable. The South could not truthfully interpose the plea of the right of local self-government in defense of her attempted secession —leaving the constitutionality of the act entirely in abeyance—for millions of black men had no opportunity to express their desires upon the question, while other millions of white men were dragooned into secession by force and false pretenses and against their sober will and judgment. The war is over, however, and far be it from me to stir its ashes anew.

* *Vide* Whittier's In War Time, etc.

REVIVAL OF THE MILITANT SPIRIT.

Justifiable though I regard the war of the Union on the part of our own Government, it was inevitable that two millions of men in arms for four years in defense of country and liberty on one side and of their homes and what they deemed their rights on the other, should bring about a marked revival of the militant spirit in our country. This has been manifested by a decided tendency toward the centralization of our government; efforts for the governmental control of elections; a marked increase in the crimes of violence, as shown by our State prison records; the introduction of a legalized espionage of the mails in the avowed interest of protecting the public against the circulation of vicious literature; the persistent adhesion to the unscientific war tariff in the avowed interest of domestic manufactures; repeated efforts to govern cities by the establishment of a police and commissions appointed under the authority of the State; the development of corporations, trusts, and combines on the part of capital; the growth of trade unions among the wage laborers, exercising a militant control over their members, and assuming also to exercise it over their employers and non-union men; the growth of the pension list to proportions equivalent to the expense of maintaining a large standing army; the employment of subsidized armed bodies of private citizens, not enrolled in the police force or militia of the State, in defense of private corporations; and many other equally obvious, if less important, facts.

These encroachments of the militant spirit, naturally following our great civil war, have not been unobserved or unopposed by large numbers of our thinking citizens. In defense of local self-government appeal has been taken to the wise safeguards of our fundamental law, and when brought by legitimate procedure to the bar of our Supreme Court, its decisions have uniformly sustained the rights of the people and the legitimate authority of the States, and opposed the encroachments of militant centralization. The recent uprising against the war tariff and national control over elections, whatever our partisan predilections, must be recognized as one of the most impressive demonstrations of the popular will in our nation's history. In recent years a strong reaction has been manifested against the tendency to deprive cities of their privilege of local self-government, and further discussion of the municipal problem will doubtless intensify and confirm this tendency. Our citizens are generally alive to the dangers of our industrial situation, though they may not be agreed as to the best way to relieve its evils.

BENEFICENT INFLUENCE OF OUR ERAS OF PEACE.

The prevalence of peace tends as surely to the discouragement of the militant spirit as that of war does to its stimulation and extension. All of our eras of peace have been fraught with manifold blessings to the republic. From the close of the Revolution to the War of 1812 our financial credit was restored under the wise statesmanship of Hamilton and his successors, and industrial enterprises sprung up in all directions, in spite of the shortsighted and malevolent efforts of England to "protect" her own industries by preventing the introduction of machinery and skilled operatives into this country. In Pawtucket, R. I., Samuel Slater started the first cotton mill December 21, 1790,* and in 1816 there were nearly half as many operatives employed in cotton manufacture as are so employed at the present time. Everywhere the industrial spirit extended its beneficent sway, except in the southern portion of our country, where slavery, the offspring and dependent of militantism, demanded the supremacy of the militant spirit, and denounced the free mechanic and wage laborer as a "mudsill" of society.

From the close of the Mexican War to the beginning of the great rebellion, except for the encroachments of slavery and consequent local paralysis of free industries, was in some respects the most fortunate period of our history. During this time deposits in our savings banks showed a larger percentage of increase than in any similar period of our history, before or since; a fact strikingly indicative of the rapidly improving condition of our working people. Farmers were generally prosperous, though their farms were usually without that modern improvement, the mortgage. Manufactures showed a steady and healthy development without the artificial stimulation of high tariffs, the tendency being toward the inauguration and success of many small factories and workshops under individual ownership, rather than toward

---

* Slater came to Rhode Island by the urgent invitation of Moses Brown, whose capital and faith sustained him in his enterprise. Moses Brown, in a published letter, declares: "No encouragement has been given by any laws of this State, nor by any donations of any society or individuals, but cotton manufacture has been wholly begun, carried on, and thus far perfected by private enterprise." Such was the beginning of one of our "infant industries," shaming the subsequent demand for prohibitory tariffs. See "Moses Brown: a Monograph," by Augustine Jones, LL. B., Principal of Friends' Seminary, Providence, R. I.

the concentration of such enterprises into the hands of a
few. The condition of the wage laborer was steadily improving, and the mechanic classes were generally content.
The army of nomadic tramps which sprang up after our
civil war and still infests large portions of our country was
wholly unknown in this period. The street beggar was a
picturesque and sporadic figure upon our streets: begging
had not then become a fine art and a recognized means of
support to large numbers of people. The financial panic of
1857, which I well remember, caused by wild speculation
and the universal distrust in the wild-cat currency of our
State banks, created great stringency and distress for a time,
but was followed by a speedy and beneficent reaction. The
essential soundness of our financial condition as a people
was demonstrated by our splendid response to the unprece-
dented demands upon our resources during the earlier stages
of the civil conflict.

Effect of Militant Methods on our Industries.

In spite of the tremendous drain upon our resources and
productive population incident upon this struggle, wealth
has increased marvelously in recent years, and the condition
of our people, including our wage laborers, ought accordingly to be better to-day than at any previous period in our
history. The feeling, however, that there has been a growing tendency to the unequal distribution of wealth in recent
years is not wholly without warrant. This was the inevitable result of the application of militant methods in the
development of our industries. The concentration of capital and industrial enterprises in a few hands, the growth
of great corporations and trusts, due in part to the artificial
stimulation of our war tariff and the revival of the militant
spirit, have certainly not been favorable to the success of
independent individual investments in such enterprises, and
have favored the concentration of large fortunes into a few
hands. Undoubtedly a larger proportion of our population
are hired laborers, and a smaller proportion independent
managers of their own business interests, than ever before in
the history of our country. This is true not only in our
manufacturing industries, but also throughout our agricultural districts. Here the tendency has also been toward the
accumulation of large properties by a few wealthy proprietors. Thirty years ago the most of our farms were unen-

cumbered by mortgages, the interest on which is now often a serious consideration for their owners, to say nothing of the remote prospects of their final extinction. These tendencies are too suggestive of the era deprecated by the poet,

"When wealth accumulates and men decay";

for these facts are incidental to an undoubted increase in the wealth of the nation relatively more rapid than the increase in population. This is not the time to discuss the rationale of these phenomena or the prospect of their continuance. I desire merely to call attention to them as concomitants of the revival of militant tendencies following our civil war.

COST OF OUR MILITARY ESTABLISHMENT.

Let us now contemplate for a moment the actual drain which the military establishment is annually making upon the productive resources of our country. For the year ending June 30, 1892, the aggregate expenditures of the United States Government for the War and Navy Departments, pensions, Indian service, and interest on war debt, was $245,181,321.97 out of a total expenditure of $415,953,-806.56, or about sixty per cent of the entire expenditure of the national Government. Nor is this all the tribute which we paid to Mars during that year; for in the same period we also paid the sum of $40,570,467.98 in liquidation of a portion of the war debt—the whole amounting to the enormous sum of $285,751,789.95.* According to the latest report of Commissioner Raum, in the fiscal year ending June 30, 1892, the single item of pensions reached the princely sum total of $140,847,417. Though it is now twenty-seven years since our civil war closed, this item has steadily grown from $16,348,000 in 1865 to $28,340,000 in 1870, $29,346,000 in 1875, $56,777,000 in 1880, dropping to $56,102,265.49 in 1885, rising to $106,936,855.07 in 1890, and to the figures already named in 1892.† No one more than I honors the brave volunteers of the republic who risked or lost their lives in behalf of the unity and freedom of their country; but it may well be questioned whether these or their descendants are the men who are now the advocates of service pensions, and in whose inter-

---

* See report of Secretary Foster.
† It is estimated that this item will reach $188,000,000 by June 30, 1894. See Message of President Harrison. This increase is in part offset by a reduced payment on the principal of the national debt.

est our pension list has grown to the enormous figures which I have set before you. Every instinct of patriotism and justice demands that the widows and dependent families of those who fell in battle, and those soldiers whose health was undermined or ability impaired by wounds or sickness incurred in the military service of their country, shall be generously cared for by the republic. But not to discriminate between these and the ones who returned with health unimpaired, sound in limb and body, is to put a premium on patriotism "for revenue only"; still more so when we remember the numbers of drafted patriots, hired substitutes, and bounty-jumpers who filled the depleted ranks of our regiments in the last years of the war, and the bounty-brokers who are now the chief instigators and plethoric beneficiaries of the enormous pension list. It is an execrable policy and most mistaken generosity for any government to create a class of pensioned dependents from among those who are able to work and take care of themselves. Remarking upon the neglected appearance of a fine farm to a citizen of the neighborhood as I was walking through Vermont last summer, I inquired who was the owner. "Oh! it is John Blank," was the reply; "probably you saw him back in the village, hanging around the store." "But why doesn't he cultivate it and keep it in order? Is the land exhausted? Doesn't it pay?" "Oh, yes," was the answer, "it pays as well as ever it did. It's as good land as there is in this county. The trouble is, he's got a pension, and doesn't have to work." On further inquiry, I was informed that the pension disease was quite prevalent—that the people were numerous in the community who neglected their farms because the Government supplied them with ready money, and constituted a heavy tax upon the consciences of law-abiding innkeepers in that "prohibitory" State.*

WAR AND CRIME.

"Every war," says a popular German proverb, born out of the long experience of the people with a militant civilization, "leaves three armies—an army of heroes, an army of cripples, and an army of thieves."

---

* The number of people now in receipt of pensions (876,604 for the year ending June 30, 1892) exceeds the number in actual service at any one time during our civil war, in spite of the inroads of death—a most remarkable circumstance. Doubtless the number will reach 1,000,000 before the close of the present fiscal year. Some of these are, however, the widows and families of deceased soldiers.

Immediately following our civil war a report of the inspectors of the Eastern District Penitentiary of Pennsylvania—I select a State which has been steadily under Republican rule, that there may be no suspicion of partisan prejudices—declared: "There is in our social condition a predisposition to crimes of the higher grades which is easily comprehended. The crime cause arises from the demoralization which ever attends on wars and armies. Familiarity with deeds of destruction and violence, thus induced, leaves its impression after the one is over and the other disbanded. We find all over the country the most distressing evidence of this fact. Crimes against persons are daily committed, and crimes against property are equally frequent." Of the 250 prisoners received in the Eastern Penitentiary in 1866, 153, or sixty per cent, had served in the army. Of 364 received in 1867, 165, or forty-five per cent, had been in the army. In 1868, of 291, 113, or forty per cent, had served in the army. In 1869, the number received was 253, of whom 137, or fifty-four per cent, had been soldiers. In 1874, forty-seven per cent had served in the army. In the Western Penitentiary in 1879, out of 312, 265, or eighty-five per cent, had served in the army or navy. These percentages far exceed the normal ratio of returned soldiers to the population. The National Conference of Charities, in its report for 1887, says: "The ultimate relation between crime and pauperism has naturally led every State prison board to take notice, more or less constantly, of the startling increase of crime since the civil war." *

WAR EXPENSES IN EUROPE AND AMERICA.

A brief comparison will further illustrate the enormous tribute which we yearly pay to the God of War. Taking the latest figures at my command, it appears that England pays annually for the support of her standing army of 133,375 men and navy of 54,400 men the sum of £27,114,100, or about $135,572,500. Our expenditure, not counting the amount paid for the interest or principal of our public debt, is more than fifty per cent greater, though our army, including the retired list, comprises only 29,719 officers and men. Germany pays annually for her army and navy, invalid fund, and military pensions, $22,871,105, or about $114,355,525—but little more than half of the amount which

* Palm. The Death Penalty, with a Chapter on War.

we pay for the same items. The German army, on a peace footing, numbers about 500,000 men.* Ours numbers less than one sixteenth of this number. Germany's war expenses constitute about four fifths of the entire expenditures of her Government. France, in time of peace, supports an army of 440,000 men,† at an annual expense of 717,770,952 francs, or about $123,554,190—a little more than half our own expenses, and nearly one third of the total cost of her Government. The standing army of Russia in time of peace comprises (including the navy) 713,144 men,‡ and is supported at a cost to the nation of 436,000,000 roubles, or about $325,000,000. The expenses of this great militant nation are always in excess of her income, whether in peace or in war, and the taxes are paid chiefly by her peasantry. The taxes necessary to support the military arm of the Government comprise more than four sevenths of the entire income of the nation. Thus we see that America stands first, relative to her population, among the leading nations of the world in its annual war expenses to-day, first absolutely except in the case of Russia, though our standing army is relatively small, and our remoteness from powerful neighbors is a surer protection than any military defenses. And in making this estimate I take no account of the expense of sustaining our State militia, now aggregating 106,269 men, according to the last official army register, which is no inconsiderable drain upon the private and public purse in the several States. Inasmuch as the common people—the wage-earners of every country—are the severest sufferers, both in purse and in person, from the scourge of militancy, does it not behoove them, and all philosophical thinkers, to consider whether all this really pays—whether we are not prepared to take the next step toward the triumph of industrial civilization, and reduce armaments and preparations for war to a minimum throughout all our civilized communities?

* In 1878, 498,735 (Encyclopædia Britannica). Later figures place the total number at 511,657 (1892).
† Encyclopædia Britannica (for 1878). More recent figures indicate an increase to 525,259 men (1892).
‡ Later figures, 843,000 men. This includes only troops actually under arms. The entire population of military age is enrolled and liable to service, as likewise in France and Germany. A large force is also maintained for police purposes.

Is International Amity a Practicable Ideal?

To the philosophical evolutionist there can be but one question in deciding upon the utility of present striving for this beneficent end. What are the actual status and effect of militant methods as related to our present social and industrial situation and needs? Where do we now stand in the onward march toward a higher civilization? Are we yet barbarians, or are we a decent civilized people, endowed with a modicum of common sense? Already there are indications of a growing popular demand for the ways that make for peace and brotherhood among the nations. The working man is naturally an internationalist. His "fatherland" is the land which guarantees to him equity and justice, and the opportunity of earning an honest livelihood. If born in a nation like Germany or Russia, where military service is compulsory to every able-bodied citizen, he seizes his first opportunity to escape to the freer social atmosphere of England or America. It is from precisely these countries that our predominant immigration comes to-day. Nor will the poorer classes on either side of the Atlantic long remain ignorant of the fact that militancy attacks their pockets as well as their persons. Instead of discussing methods of taxation, single tax, tariff, or what not, the burning question will soon be whether by far the greatest item of public expense may not, by the mutual comity of the law of nations, be obliterated mainly or entirely. The present century has seen the practical annihilation of slavery in civilized communities. It is not unreasonable to hope that the coming century will see the practical cessation of international strife.

Treaties of Arbitration.

Happily, it has been the honorable office of our own nation to take the initiative in this direction by proposing the formation of general treaties of arbitration between the United States and such nations as are willing to make such treaties. This proposition, originating in the recent Pan-American Congress and commended to the nations by Secretary Blaine in behalf of President Harrison, was heartily indorsed by the Inter-parliamentary Peace Conference which met in Berne, Switzerland, on the closing days of last summer. This conference had in attendance about one hundred members of the parliaments of some twelve European states, including England, Germany, Austria, Switzerland, France, Italy, Spain, Denmark, Holland, Portugal, and Roumania. Its president was Dr. Gobat, a deputy of the National Council of Switzerland. After thorough and able discussion, it was voted to recommend to governments—

1. To recognize as a principle of international law the inviolability of private property upon the sea in time of war.*

2. To insert clauses favoring arbitration in all treaties concerning commerce, navigation, and the protection of industrial, literary, and artistic property.

3. To accept the proposition of the United States relative to the formation of treaties of arbitration as before described.

These propositions look toward the final establishment, in no distant millennial era, of an international court, for which our Supreme Court furnishes an admirable model, for the arbitration and final settlement of disputes between nations. They are moderate and rational in their tone, not the product of long-haired fanatics and wild theorists, but of some of the ablest, sanest, and most philosophical minds in public life in Europe at the present day.

A few days before the meeting of the International Parliamentary Conference, a Universal Peace Congress was also held in Berne, presided over by M. Louis Rochonnet, who has been twice elected president of the Swiss republic. Here also questions of arbitration and nationality were ably discussed, and the excellent and practical suggestion was made that school histories should hereafter be written so as to emphasize and exalt the men and deeds of peace instead of war. Histories of the life of peoples, of the great industrial movements in society, embodying the principles of evolutionary sociology, are demanded at the present time. It was also recommended that constitutions should be so amended that no declaration of war can be made by any nation save by a vote of the representatives of the people—a proposition which, if carried out, would do much toward the abolition of war among civilized nations.

* Great Britain, which would seem likely to be the principal gainer from such an agreement, is to-day the chief obstacle to its adoption by the nations of Europe. See Political and Legal Remedies for War. By Sheldon Amos, M. A., late Professor of Jurisprudence in University College, London.

THE EXAMPLE OF SWITZERLAND.

The little republic of Switzerland to-day presents a most encouraging object lesson to the nations, illustrating the possibility of the substitution of a well-organized militia for a standing army, and of maintaining a federal union transcending the limitations of language, religion, and race. For more than five hundred years it has constituted an independent federation of free states, environed by a cordon of nations in arms. It is the only country in the world which does not now maintain a standing army. By the constitution of 1848, the maintenance of such an army is expressly forbidden. Its entire male population, of suitable age, is, however, enrolled in the militia, and thoroughly trained in military service, being subjected to camp discipline several weeks in every year; and each separate canton is permitted to maintain a permanent force of three hundred armed men. Its twenty-two cantons are sectionally divided among people of the Teutonic and Latin races, speaking four different languages—German, French, Italian, and Romansch—some of them stalwart Protestants and Freethinkers, and others Roman Catholics, but held together by a sympathetic belief in certain advanced political ideas and by a compact industrial civilization. In Switzerland we find the most perfect system of local self-government which the world to-day affords—a system which, by means of its peculiar features, the initiative and referendum, is more truly democratic even than our own, and brings home the privileges and responsibilities of citizenship to every individual citizen. With a tariff limited by constitutional provision to the revenue necessities of the country, compelled by like limitations to place its severest burdens on articles of luxury and to lighten as far as possible the tax on articles necessary to supply the daily wants of the people,* in close contact and competition with the great manufacturing centers of Germany, France, and Italy, Switzerland is a very hive of manufacturing industry, sending its products to every quarter of the world. No people are more universally educated than the citizens of the Swiss republic. No people are more tolerant of diverse opinions. No people are more cosmopolitan in their modes of thought. No people are more

---

* The "protectionist" wave which has recently passed over Europe resulted in raising the tariff of Switzerland as a retaliatory measure; but it is still limited by the above-named constitutional provisions.

earnest in their advocacy of the principle of international arbitration, though their advocacy is based on practical rather than sentimental reasons. Though there are doubtless many cases of suffering from poverty, as in all thickly populated countries, no European nation is less afflicted with official pauperism. With Switzerland to illustrate the possibilities of a federal union based upon broad principles of tolerance and a democratic political system, and with the United States to illustrate the possibility of the expansion of this principle to a continental scope and domain, the people of Europe can hardly fail before many decades to make strenuous and concerted efforts for the recognition of the principle of arbitration by the law of nations, the consequent disarmament of Europe, and the liberation of its military serfs for the advancement of industrial enterprise.

WAR TO CEASE THROUGH INDUSTRIAL PROGRESS.

Looking at this question from the standpoint of the evolutionary sociologist and political economist no less than from that of the humanitarian reformer, the conclusion can not be avoided that war between civilized nations, in this last half of the nineteenth Christian century, is a monstrous anomaly of unreason, a relic of barbarism which reasonable men should no longer tolerate. In this great beneficent industrial civilization, which is the noblest product of our century, built up by the united efforts of the common people, international strife can have no legitimate part or lot. By the very progress of industrialism war is gradually being eliminated from the world.* Commerce, which has been the world's great civilizing agent; science, whose discoveries are for the healing and salvation of the race; ethics, which is no respecter of persons or nationalities, but preaches the equal obligation of all to the performance of equity and justice; evolution, which has brought man up out of animalism to the high estate of a citizen in the republic of the world; religion, which, in the person of its loftiest representatives, has always transcended ethnic and racial limitations and proclaimed the brotherhood of the human race—alike exhort us to submit to peaceful arbitration all questions of international dispute. The maintenance of a well-disciplined militia, as in Switzerland, instead of a standing army

* *Vide* Political and Legal Remedies for War. By Sheldon Amos, M. A. See also The Principles of Social Economics, by George Gunton.

depleting the ranks of wealth producers, should hereafter suffice for the protection of civilized peoples against foreign or domestic foes. In regard to civil conflicts there is but one way in which they can be avoided hereafter, thus indicated by Prof. Le Conte: "If revolutions are to be prevented in future, it must be by the use of more rational methods, by understanding the laws of sociology, and the wise application of these laws to politics." This is measurably true of international politics as well. Wars will not cease by mere legislative fiat, but by the gradual adoption of the better methods of an industrial civilization which makes for international comity and amity. Unless we can trust that such better methods will be adopted, unless upon the rude stalk of war through the rational volition of man shall speedily blossom the white flower of peace, the long struggle for existence through which man and his brute ancestors have passed can have no final warrant at the bar of the human conscience and reason. In the industrial civilization which is to dominate the world in the future, the beneficent beginnings and marvelous progress of which it has been our privilege to witness and experience, as Mr. Spencer has well affirmed: "With war come all the vices and with peace come all the virtues. The suppression of international antagonisms is the one reform which will bring all the other moral reforms."

Let the watchword of Science and Humanity be then, henceforward, the noble exordium of the Great Captain of the Union armies—which shall live in the memories of men when his sword has rusted in its scabbard and the story of his victories has faded into the nebulous haze of the past—"*Let us have peace!*"

> "O men and brothers! let that voice be heard.
> War fails, try peace: put up the useless sword!
> Fear not the end. There is a story told
> In Eastern tents, when autumn nights grow cold,
> And round the fire the Mongol shepherds sit
> With grave responses listening unto it:
> Once, on the errands of his mercy bent,
> Buddha, the holy and benevolent,
> Met a fell monster, huge and fierce of look,
> Whose awful voice the hills and forests shook.
> 'O son of Peace!' the giant cried, 'thy fate
> Is sealed at last, and love shall yield to hate.'
> The unarmed Buddha, looking, with no trace
> Of fear or anger, in the monster's face,

In pity said: 'Poor fiend, even thee I love.'
Lo! as he spake the sky-tall terror sank
To hand-breadth size; the huge abhorrence shrank
Into the form and fashion of a dove;
And where the thunder of its rage was heard
Circling above him sweetly sang the bird:
'Hate hath no harm for love,' so ran the song;
'And peace unweaponed conquers every wrong.'"

ABSTRACT OF THE DISCUSSION.

Mr. Thaddeus B. Wakeman:

My first duty is to give expression to the thankfulness we all feel for the able and beautiful lecture to which we have listened, so rich in illustrations and so wise in its conclusions; and to congratulate the lecturer, regarding his result as the expression of one of the leading ethical bodies of our country. To me it has been a most agreeable surprise. I did not expect that he would present the subject in just this way, judging from his past record. My learned friend is like the lawyer who forgot on which side he was retained. He has come completely over to my side. I thought as I listened, "O Inconsistency, what a jewel thou must be!" For years back, the lecturer has said, with Herbert Spencer, that natural selection is the controlling power in all human progress; that all attempts of man to better himself, all artificial selection, is an obstruction to progress. That is the position of Herbert Spencer, and has been that of my learned friend hitherto. Consistency would make him an advocate of war. If natural selection applies to labor, trade, politics, it applies just as much to the rivalry of nations. Applying it thus, his position would be strong; for it can be shown that all progress of the human race is founded on war. War has been the universal rule between nations. All peace has been but breathing spells between wars. The Greeks warred each other out of existence. Rome was continually at war. Christianity is not a religion of peace, but of blood. "Not peace, but a sword," is what its founder declared he came to bring. "Peace and good will to men" is a wrong interpretation. In the original it means "Peace to men of good will"—that is, to men who agree with us; those who are not with us are damned already. De Quincy, in his essay on war, which the speaker apparently has not read, gives us the straight doctrine; he shows that we must always have war, and asserts that it is a positive good. There is the doctrine of Herbert Spencer, and of my learned friend when he is consistent. If we are not free to fight we are not free to do anything. In our system of government we expressly reserve the right of revolution. The Puritans had to fight the Indians—they couldn't help it. The Penn story, by the way, is sheer nonsense. The Quakers used wiliness; they cheated the Indians out of their territory instead of fighting them out The account of it is the record of a most amusing piece of swindling. The Indian knows nothing about selling land; he doesn't know what it means. The Indians were all socialists; they were willing to share their land, but had no idea of selling it. Against this theory of Herbert Spencer is the Religion of Humanity. This phrase was originated by Thomas Paine, and afterward adopted by Auguste Comte. Herbert Spencer recognizes no religion of humanity, but pure, unmitigated natural selection, and pure, brutal, unmitigated Darwinism. But I am glad the speaker has forsaken him, and that there is one church where

" While the lamp holds out to burn
The *wisest* sinner may return." ·

We can not have a religion of humanity taking the place of the God of Battles until we have a federation of trades in the nations, and we can not have that until we have socialism. The ideal which the speaker has so eloquently portrayed is impossible of realization through the individualism of Herbert Spencer.

GENERAL GEORGE W. WINGATE:

It is practically impossible to review such a thoughtful and carefully prepared paper in an off-hand manner in ten minutes. A great deal in the paper meets my cordial approval; a great deal more my experience and common sense lead me to regard as an iridescent dream. It is idle in the light of history to talk about our being civilized. We have a veneer of civilization, but scratch it anywhere and we find barbarism. The most profitable public exhibition to-day in Brooklyn is a brutal boxing match. Christianity as preached and practiced has made no essential change in the condition of things since the time of the Romans. We read of the Basutos in Central Africa, peaceful, and getting along pretty well until they were discovered by Stanley. Then roads were built, and two sets of missionaries—Protestant and Catholic—visited the country. Each set denounced the other, and their converts have killed each other pretty nearly all off. It is the people and not the rulers that make war. Napoleon went to war because the people compelled him to. Until you can get down to the people and change their modes of thinking you will have war. No one can doubt that war is a most terrible and brutal thing; yet there are good things that come out of it. It is well to be inspired occasionally with the idea that there is something more important than money-making, or even studying ethical questions; that there are times when we must sacrifice money and life and social theories to our country. Our civil war gave us self-respect, we don't care now what the London Times or any other European paper says of us. The war made us more energetic and determined. The discharged soldier found the old life too slow, broke away, and built up the great West. Of course war produces an indifference to life; but so do railroading, blasting, and other dangerous occupations.

There is one point in the lecture to which I heartily assent; that is in the matter of pensions. This pension business is absolutely wrong. As it is now conducted, the pension agents are stirring up all who have a shadow of a claim, and it has gone so far that it is said that a man has received a pension who lost his voice in urging his brother-in-law to go to the war. The practical effect is that we have a great army of mercenaries—paid afterward, if not before. A man who lost an arm or a leg can not be paid too much; but it is a shame to pay those who returned sound and became disabled fifteen years after. War is not an unmixed evil. The doctrine of the survival of the fittest applies here. As we need the police to protect us from domestic thieves, so we need the army to prevent our neighboring nations from breaking in.

DR. JANES, in reply:

I wish first to express my indebtedness to both of my critics. They were invited because they were known to hold views somewhat different from my own, and they have not disappointed us in their criticisms. I think General Wingate, in particular, has said about all that can be said in favor of war in our day and generation. My learned friend, Mr. Wakeman, quite outdid himself on this occasion. He first congratulated me on coming around completely to his side, and then proceeded to demolish my positions, thereby, I suppose, demolishing himself. He has at least demonstrated, I think, what I had long suspected—that he was better acquainted with the works of Paine and Goethe and Comte and De Quincy, the writers of fifty or a hundred years ago, than he is with Herbert Spencer and the more modern school of philosophical thought. I do not think that my leading positions are in conflict with Mr. Spencer's. We both recognize the fact that the law of natural selection is a law of Nature—not a figment of the imagination—and being so, it never ceases to operate. It is a mistake on the part of my learned friend to suppose that socialism, or "artificial selection," or anything else can make it inoperative. Mr. Spencer recognizes fully the factor of human volition; but he sees profoundly the necessity of directing the human will so it will work intelligently through and in harmony with the laws of Nature, not blindly in opposition to them. What human volition does is to create conditions of variability in society and institutions on which the law of natural selection can operate. We may do this wisely or unwisely. If unwisely, then the law of natural selection cuts short the life of the nation; but if, on the other hand, we clearly comprehend the laws and, by obedience to them, produce conditions favorable to social advancement, human volition may greatly hasten civilization. Herbert Spencer indeed opposes the notion that any scheme for social amelioration through state agencies, evolved out of one man's inner consciousness, or even promulgated by a majority vote, can succeed. Civilization can only be advanced by natural growth and development; there must be intelligent effort and purpose on the part of man to work in harmony with Nature. Mr. Spencer differs from all who claim that state socialism is the way out of our difficulties—and so do I. So long as our office-holders are as imperfect as they are at present, it seems idle to look to Mr. Wakeman's panacea for a cure. He would remedy trusts by creating one enormous trust; cure the ills of governmental interference with the individual by placing all our interests under the control of Government.

When General Wingate referred to the wars of Napoleon, if he meant Napoleon III I can not agree with him. His wars were " political necessities "—not of the people, but of his own decaying administration. There was the *plebiscitum*, indeed, but we all know that was a delusion and a snare. The people voted under the compulsion of the standing army. Napoleon instigated foreign wars to save himself from a domestic revolution ; and he finally precipitated both.

We need not fear a decay of our combative faculties, even if we have no wars. The competition and struggle involved in earning an honest livelihood offer sufficient opposition to keep the majority of us in fighting trim. If one will simply make it his life work to attack the evils of his own nature, he will find an abundant exercise for his combative faculties, and if he succeeds he will have won the greatest of victories. " He that ruleth his own spirit is better than he that taketh a city." After looking over all the ground, I am convinced that it is quite possible for international arbitration to become a reality much sooner than many of us now dream. With a Court of Arbitration, and all governments pledged to sustain its decrees, no single nation would dare violate them. To this end the entire progress of our industrial civilization seems rapidly tending.

INTERSTATE COMMERCE

BY
ROBERT W. TAYLER

COLLATERAL READINGS SUGGESTED:

The Federalist; Spencer's *Railway Morals and Railway Policy*, in Essays, Scientific, Political, and Speculative; Fiske's The Critical Period in American History; Cooley's Popular and Legal View of Traffic Pooling; Dabney s Public Regulation of Railways; Hudson's The Railway and the Republic; Fink's The Railway Problem and its Solution, Regulation of Interstate Commerce, etc.; Hadley's Railway Transportation; Harper's The Law of Interstate Commerce; Seligman's Railway Tariffs and the Interstate Commerce Law; Reports of the Interstate Commerce Commission.

INTERSTATE COMMERCE.

By ROBERT W. TAYLER.

FORESEEN AND UNFORESEEN CONSEQUENCES OF HUMAN EFFORT.

I TOUCH that class of factors in American civilization wherein the *hand of man*, successfully working with intelligent purpose to predetermined results, has been most conspicuous. Not that what that hand has done is any less the legitimate fruit of man's development, but that it has acted in a more definite manner, with more concrete results. In the development of agencies for our internal commerce, man has wrought with mighty effect upon externals, and, by changing their complexion, has wrought upon himself. It was not always so. The externals upon which the hand of man had not been consciously laid, with any vivid purpose or vital consequence, have always been the potent factors in his development. In the history of the world, from the beginning of time down to the present century, what man has sought to do he has generally failed to do. What he has never dreamed of accomplishing has generally been done. He has been the mere puppet of his environment. He has started out with determined purpose to accomplish certain results, has laid his plans with prudence and with care, has brought to bear all the influences which his foresight had shown him were necessary; he has accomplished something, but that accomplishment has been ingulfed in a vast ocean of other accomplishments of vastly greater consequence and of infinitely more importance. True, man has always been an active agent, endeavoring to do. In earlier times his activities were most positively expressed in his wars of conquest. These were active agencies, undertaken to accomplish positive results. But when the naked and predetermined consequence had been wrought, behold, a thousand other results have sprung into life, and they, and not the intended fact, have wrought upon him and upon his history and career.

The invasion of Italy from Germany succeeded in breaking down the Roman civilization, but it did not succeed in accomplishing what the invaders intended. They, no less than the Romans, were swallowed up in the magnitude of their own victories. They were vanquished, no less than those whom they had conquered. And so, if we go down through the centuries that have followed and trace the purpose, we find it, if accomplished at all, of trifling moment as compared with the stupendous results undreamed of that flowed by logical necessity from the facts of history.

Even the American rebellion, initiated upon certain narrow lines, developed unconsciously and without predetermination upon lines infinitely broader and more potent than existed at the beginning, and produced results the character and magnitude of which were superlatively greater than were intended by the actors in that great drama.

And so I say it has been throughout the history of the human race: that the intended consequences, foreseen by man in his advancing progress, bear but slightly upon the fortunes and destinies of the human race as compared with those consequences which came in spite of the conscious efforts of their inspired sources.

Intelligent Foresight in the Development of our Internal Commerce.

Very different has been the philosophy and the history of the development of our internal commerce. As I said a few moments ago, the hand of man has been here laid with more intelligent purpose, with clearer insight of consequence, than in any other field of action in which the human intellect has ever been engaged. Here, indeed, has the hand of man been laid on the face of Nature with a reasonably clear apprehension of the consequences which would flow from it. If it were intended to throw a line of railway into a country as yet unshod by the iron straps, the consequences—social, political, and commercial—which are likely to flow from that adventure can be predicted with more certainty than from any other human effort of like magnitude.

Looking, therefore, at the history and development of the means of internal commerce in the United States, we discover the play of forces whose scope and influence could not, perhaps, be accurately predicted at the very beginning of railroad development, but which a few years later could be predicted with reasonable certainty. Their influence upon the social, political, moral, and material affairs of this people are perhaps the most stupendous that any people have experienced since the world began.

THE ECONOMIC NATURE OF TRANSPORTATION.

Let us start with a proper fundamental conception of transportation. In its essence transportation is waste. It should never be resorted to except in case of necessity. This necessity, to a greater or less extent, always exists, because all the articles which people need are not produced at the spot where needed. To move a thing from one spot to another costs effort. Effort has potential value. If exerted to unnecessarily transport, it is necessarily waste. To move a thing from one spot to another, where there is already a sufficient supply, or where the article can be produced as cheaply as at the place from whence it is moved, is wasteful. In its new situs it is the same article exactly, and has no more value than at its old situs, unless it could not be produced as economically at the new as at the old situs. Therefore the labor of transportation may or may not add to the value of the thing transported, according as it can or can not be produced more cheaply at the place from which it is moved. Therefore the effort in the first instance should be not to multiply the means and possibilities of transportation, but to multiply the means and possibilities of production as near as possible to the seat of consumption.

To haul three thousand miles a thing that can be produced at the place to which it is hauled, with the same effort that is necessary to produce it at the other end of the haul, is waste.

This has a bearing upon the value and necessity of transportation and of commerce in its widest as well as in its narrowest sense.

It has to do especially with the value and necessity of our foreign commerce; and no foreign commerce, taking this view of the case, can by any possibility be advantageous to us or to any other people if it involves an exchange of the product of one day's labor for the product of one day's labor plus the labor of carriage. We ought always to be making war upon the waste of unnecessary transportation; and that involves, as I have before indicated, the development of the production of those things which can be economically produced—labor cost considered—nearest the seat of consumption; and without going into details, and without wishing to wave a red rag before this audience, this means enlightened selfishness and philosophic protection.

ECONOMIC SUPERIORITY OF HOME CONSUMPTION.

Nor is this all; no foreign commerce can, in the long run, be advantageous if the tendency of that commerce is to dissolve the mutuality of interest between the home producer and his home consumer. The value of the trade of the home consumer depends upon the purchasing power of his labor. If the home producer has such a mutuality of interest with the home consumer as that he shall always be interested to see that the purchasing power of the labor of the home consumer is as large as possible, we then have the condition most likely to result in the greatest prosperity to the producer. But no producer can see the rewards of his own employees fall without finding in it causes affecting alike all other employees, and hence all other consumers at home. And yet, if that producer depends more upon a foreign than upon a home market for his consumption, he must of necessity be constantly employed in the effort to reduce the rewards of his own employees, in order that he may be the more able to compete in the broader markets of the world. And thus, by reducing the power of the home consumer to purchase, he has restricted his own market. I think it will be found to be true that wherever the producer, who is at the same time an employer, looks to the world at large for his market and depends chiefly on that, the mutuality of interest between him and his employees, and thus between him and all other home employees, will be so destroyed as in the long run to very largely diminish the volume of his trade and of his profits.

The iniquity of what is known as discrimination between the long and short haul, other things being equal, is in this connection apparent. Discrimination in favor of one class of our people as against another is bad enough; but a discrimination against our own people in favor of other countries is infinitely worse. When a low and unjustly discriminating rate is made to the seaboard on goods designed for export, the foreign consumer obtains the benefit of the discrimination, and the home consumer must make up in his cost the loss to the railroad in transporting to the seaboard. We thus pay tribute to another people and to another civilization. Unless the trade was essential to us and could not be obtained on any other terms, we have simply permitted the caprice or the cupidity of the railroads to rob us for the benefit of an alien people.

THE NATURAL DIRECTION OF COMMERCIAL INTERCOURSE.

It is a corollary to all this that the natural lines of transportation are between north and south—that is, between different zones; for on the same zone there is a more noticeable similarity in the natural possibilities of production. In all those respects wherein climatic influences operate, it is apparent that one zone may be able to produce more economically than another certain articles needed in other zones. It is, for instance, absolutely in accordance with the fitness of things that cotton should be transported from the South to the North; and that wheat and corn should be transported in the opposite direction. The same does not everywhere obtain as to mineral products, and therefore as to these, Nature has not determined similar lines of transportation.

PRIMITIVE METHODS OF TRANSPORTATION.

I think it may safely be said that all modes of transportation prior to the introduction of steam were primitive. The primitive mind was equal to the conception of oars or paddles, of sails, and even of canals. The most savage tribes must at a very early period have grown to the use of boats substantially on the same lines—though not of the same size—as characterize those in use to-day. A slow development in size took place, and a slight improvement in oars and in sails is noticeable. Perhaps I should modify the expression " primitive " by a passing reference to the fact that the science of navigation, when it came, enlarged the field of commerce, and thereby made demands upon the ingenuity of mankind for vehicles of transportation suited to longer journeys and more uncertain seas.

Primitive transportation was, as now, by land or by water.

By water it was in boats propelled by sail or oars, or by current, or by animal towage.

By land it was carried on either by man, or on the backs of beasts of burden, or in vehicles with wheels or runners drawn by man or beast.

Stated with what I think is substantial accuracy, the effective transporting capacity of a man was one ton-mile per day; of a beast of burden, about four ton-miles per day; and of a wheeled vehicle, about fifteen ton-miles per day. These two latter must be reduced, if we would learn their true value, by allowing for the labor of man in directing the beasts which bear the burden or haul the vehicle.

Looked at in the light of its development, we note that, for some centuries before the steam engine had come, the effort of man was chiefly directed not to the improvement of the moving force, but to the improvement of the vehicle and the surface over which the vehicle must travel; the lessening of incidental friction and of the force of gravity, not an increase of initial force, was the only problem they thought was to be solved; and nothing but a revolution in the mode of investigation could bring about any vital change.

When Copernicus, in the exaltation of his mighty conception, cried, "O God, I think thy thoughts after thee," he was but expressing the thought which came to him when, by a mighty effort, he cast aside the things that were, and, thinking the thoughts of God after him, discerned that perhaps, after all, this planet of ours was not the sole center of omnipotent effort, and that if he gave it a minor place in the universe, the dark places might be made light and the illumination of a divine intelligence might penetrate the human mind. Thence came the science of astronomy; all before was vague, but not futile effort, for it produced Copernicus.

The development of transportation needed a radical treatment. Growth—slow, steady, and effective—might follow the improvement in vehicles and in the surface over which the vehicles must travel; but, in the light of modern conditions, this growth could be but meager. A Copernican conception was needed, and we find that in the discovery of the power of steam and its availability as a motive power.

History of the Development of Internal Commerce in the United States.

The lines along which our internal commerce has developed may thus be analyzed:

I. Natural highways: 1. Coastwise. 2. Navigable rivers. 3. Packing over country.

II. Artificial highways: 1. The ordinary road. 2. Turnpikes. 3. Canals. 4. Railroads.

I. *Natural Highways.*

Until the development of the turnpike system it was impossible that any system of internal commerce could be carried on save along the coast and on navigable streams. It is a fact worth noticing here that south of the St. Lawrence there is no navigable river extending inland for any considerable distance from the Atlantic seaboard; a great water-shed is almost in sight of the ocean. The result was that while people might live at a distance from the Atlantic they could have no commercial relations with those who lived upon its borders. When the charge for hauling a barrel of flour one hundred and fifty miles was five dollars; when it cost a cent to transport a pound of salt fifty miles; when it required a week to go from Boston to New York by stage, and almost three weeks to reach Charleston; and the cost of transporting a bushel of wheat over the Alleghanies to eastern Pennsylvania was absolutely prohibitory—we discover that the conditions that had prevailed for centuries had improved but little and no great development was possible without changed means of carriage.

The means of conveying information were quite as crude and unsatisfactory and even more expensive.

If we could conceive such a thing possible, imagine a New York merchant ordering one thousand bushels of grain from Pittsburg in 1785; it would have taken nearly three weeks for the order to reach Pittsburg and nearly four weeks more for the grain to reach New York, and the freight charges would have been about six dollars a bushel. The same order could to-day be sent to a point five hundred miles back from Sydney, Australia, and the grain be delivered in New York in less time for less money. And yet this last operation would involve sending a telegraphic message ten thousand miles and the carriage of the grain about six thousand miles by water and nearly four thousand by land.

It is sufficient to say here that land commerce over any considerable distance was practically prohibited except in those articles whose value was high and whose weight was relatively low. The embargo on civilization was as great. Only the very rich could enjoy anything beyond the comforts of the vicinage, and only the rich could travel.

II. *Artificial Highways.*

1. The ordinary dirt road was of little consequence in the development of commerce; this the world had had for centuries.

2. *Turnpikes*—i. e., improved roadways. It is now one hundred and two years since the first turnpike was built in this country; but within the forty years following many millions of dollars were spent in their construction. They ameliorated the conditions noticeably, but, after all, when we consider that the reduction in the cost of hauling was only one half, we can, while appreciating the great advance, realize how slight must have been the actual benefit as compared with present conditions. Under this system there was a marked development in the volume of internal commerce, but still communities were necessarily complete in themselves and dependent almost wholly upon themselves. Through Pennsylvania and Ohio, for instance, were scattered small furnaces, with meager output and even more meager trade, for their market was of necessity restricted to the immediate vicinity. A single modern blast furnace, employing one hundred men, with an output of two hundred tons of pig iron per day, involves a freight movement of about one thousand tons daily. Conceive, if you can, the number of people whose employment under the old system would be necessary to manage such a plant and move its material and product.

Canals.—The next great impetus to commerce was given by the building of canals. They still further reduced the cost of carriage; like the turnpike, they developed commerce and civilization. They played their part; but perhaps the most striking result which they produced was this: they, with the lines of natural waterways, in large degree determined the direction of the country's development. There is no large city in this country not built upon the edge of a navigable waterway; every city with two hundred thousand inhabitants is on an ocean, lake, or navigable river. The commerce of the ocean and the lakes has steadily grown; the commerce of canals and rivers has proportionately steadily decreased; wherever the newer and greater, the modern transporter, the iron horse, has opportunity to compete, the extended commerce of canal and river is doomed.

Railroads.—We come now to the greatest achievement of the ages; the great leveler of distance; the great equalizer of localities. The day has passed when regions away from river, lake, or ocean must remain in shadowed splendor unable to use their varied resources. No region has been found inaccessible to the railroad; it has crossed the Alleghanies, it crossed the Mississippi; it crossed the prairies, the alkali plain, the Rocky Mountains; it has climbed to the very summit of Pike's Peak. Wherever man has wanted to lay the rail and run the engine, there it has gone; and what a magnificent empire it has discovered and fructified —nay, what a magnificent world it has created! What we have suffered from it, or what we may suffer at its hands, is but the faintest shadow of a wrong compared with the good it has wrought.

ENORMOUS VOLUME OF OUR RECENT INTERNAL COMMERCE.

The internal commerce of the United States during the last ten years has exceeded in volume all the commerce of all the world from the beginning of the historical period down to the present century. To those to whom figures may convey any intelligent conception, it will not be uninteresting to say that the tonnage of the internal commerce of the United States during the current year amounts to nearly one hundred thousand million ton-miles—that is to say, is equivalent to the hauling of one hundred thousand million tons of freight one mile. The tonnage which annually passes through the Detroit River far exceeds the entire foreign and coastwise tonnage of Great Britain. And the entire foreign commerce of Great Britain is but a small fraction of the commerce by rail, lake, and river among the people of the United States. The internal commerce of the United States measured in dollars is nearly twenty times our foreign commerce; in tonnage it is more than one hundred times as great.

A day's work to-day on overland transportation is two hundred times as effective as a day's work one thousand years ago directed to the same effort.

To move the internal commerce of the United States for the year 1892 would have required five times the total working force of the entire world one thousand years ago.

Its Beneficent Effects on our Civilization.

A brief reference to some of the results of this development is here necessary.

First, it has multiplied the purchasing power of every man's effort by permitting the production of needed articles at the point where they can be produced with the least cost of human effort, and their carriage with economy to the point of consumption.

Second, it has tended to the aggregation of people into communities to an extent permitting the largest possible efficiency in human effort, in consequence of the proximity of its different units; and this in turn has resulted in the broadening and polishing and civilizing of those thus brought together, because of the breadth and polish which follow from the personal contact of people.

Third, it has brought to all these people the fullest and promptest information of the facts of life which are essential to an intelligent living, and thus multiplied the intellectual efficiency of every man capable of receiving information.

Fourth, it has induced and multiplied the means of traveling, and has thus developed the mind and awakened new sympathies and tendencies, and thus multiplied its efficiency.

Fifth, it has indeed made the desert to blossom as the rose, and has uncovered and laid at the feet of man, for his comfort, the untold wealth of useful minerals planted in the earth at points remote from any natural highway. To illustrate by a single example: The pig-iron production of the country for the year 1890 was ten million tons, and involved the use of forty million tons of raw material gathered from a wide area of country; the cost of assembling these materials and distributing the product would have cost, sixty years ago, ten times what the product was actually sold for in 1890.

Sixth, it has furnished, by this development of previously inaccessible territory, a million opportunities for effort and enterprise which, without it, the world could never have had.

Seventh, it has united by such powerful physical, commercial, and social bonds the different units of this mighty empire as to make them one in spirit and in fact.

Power of Congress to Regulate Interstate Commerce.

It is a popular fallacy that we imagine we know more than we actually do know. The fact is that we know much more than we know that we know. It is true that of the thing concerning which we think we know the most, we often know the least. But we are apt to forget the magnitude and importance of the knowledge we have assimilated from our environments, from the constant touch and attrition of affairs which have unconsciously saturated us, so that we seem to know instinctively a thousand things which we hardly realize we know at all. The most intelligent publicists of England and the continent have difficulty in comprehending the relations that exist among the several States and between the States and the Federal Government. Very many wise men of other countries have failed to comprehend them at all. To us they are a part of our absorbed and assimilated knowledge about which we think and speak with a confidence that is so assured as to involve no conscious process of reasoning to reach results.

Interesting, therefore, as a dissertation on the relations among the several States and between them and the National Government might be, and logically necessary as it is in a paper of this kind, time forbids a discussion of it, and such is your familiarity with the framework of our political organization as to render a discussion of it unnecessary. It is sufficient to say here that the most important legislation respecting internal commerce, in the broad sense in which this topic intends to treat it, must be enacted by the General Government. First, because the greater portion of the internal commerce is interstate, and, second, because a relegation of such legislation to the several States would involve us in endless and perplexing confusion.

The Federal Constitution provides that Congress shall have power to regulate commerce among the States, and this has been construed to include the means by which commerce is carried on. In no important sense was this constitutional provision ever appealed to until the passage of the Interstate Commerce Act of 1887. Various statutory regulations existed in the different States; but these, while they cover the whole field of the railroad power and duties, have rather more to do with their physical condition and manipulation. As the power lodged in Congress to regulate interstate commerce arises from a distinct and positive authority in the Constitution, no serious question has arisen as to the power of the National Government in this respect; and it is not thought likely that within the scope of present legislation any serious conflict will arise between those who take the broadest view of the powers of the several States and those holding broader views of the power of the General Government.

How the Railway has modified the Problem.

It is a curious, not to say a momentous, fact that, except as to those parts which relate to the mere machinery of government, our constitutions, national and State, have to confront so many changed and undreamed-of conditions that in their interpretation we are constantly compelled to guess at what is their spirit. A hundred years ago railroad locomotion, with all its attendant political and social accomplishments, was hidden in the germ of an undisclosed future. By no possibility could the framers of the Constitution conceive the conditions under which the construction of railroads could be carried on. As soon as the public character which this mode of locomotion would take on was seen, State legislation began to shape itself to the supposed requirements of the situation. It was not supposed, even at the time when the first development that might take place could be foreseen, that railroads would take the shape and form in which they now appear. The railroads of sixty years ago were not supposed to be common carriers in the sense in which they are to-day. The railroad was merely to be a public highway, as canals were and are public highways. It was supposed that a private corporation, having constructed its way, would devise reasonable rules and regulations in conformity with which individuals who might desire to convey properly constructed vehicles over the road might be permitted to do so. The railroad company might own nothing but its road-bed; a carrier might own nothing but cars and engines. And so far has this conception adhered that to this day, when plans and specifications for the construction of a railroad are, as required by law, presented to the British Parliament with the request for authority to construct it, every detail down to the minutest circumstance is set out, save alone the character and location of stations.

For at the beginning it was not supposed that stations would be needed, since every man with properly equipped appliances was to be permitted to go upon the road and haul his cars. He might stop where he pleased, unload where he pleased, and would have no need for station houses. A side track at most would meet every requirement of the theory upon which it was supposed railroads would be constructed and operated. The changed use of railways has not been accompanied with a corresponding change in the powers built upon it. The railway which is, in the sense that a canal is, a public highway upon which, under certain reasonable rules and regulations, any person may take his properly constructed vehicle, and thus using the highway become a common carrier, does not exist. The railway company is now a public carrier, but the railway is not a public highway. The Pennsylvania Railroad Company has no more authority to run its cars and engines over the lines of the Reading Railroad than to draw them through the streets of New York. Nevertheless, there is practically no limitation whatever upon the power of the railway to take and use private property. It is under no more restraint than if it were in the fullest sense the user of a public highway and itself a common carrier. The original delegation by the State to the railroad company of the power of eminent domain—that is to say, the sovereign power to take and possess any private property, no matter what its character, which the officers of the railroad might deem necessary to the proper construction and operation of the road—was based upon the fundamental theory that the railroad, when constructed, would be in the most literal sense a public highway, and those who put their vehicles upon the road, themselves common carriers. If that conception of the use of private property had been carried out, there would have been the presence of a public use and the absence of a private monopoly.

PUBLIC USE AND PRIVATE MONOPOLY.

It may, perhaps, be fairly said that we now have a common carrier and, to all practical intents and purposes, a public use; but it is a private monopoly which controls it. If it had been possible to thus effectuate the primitive idea of a public highway used by common carriers, our modern railway problems would never have risen to vex us. It is only because in the evolution of railway construction, of railway management resulting in the combination of capital, that the public highway feature of the railway system disappeared, leaving only, as I have suggested, a common carrier having a private monopoly.

It is this that brought us to the state where the victims of innumerable wrongs, subjected to the stupendous power of such stupendous monopolies, were compelled to seek redress in the courts for the violation of their common law rights, and, the machinery of the courts proving unavailing and ineffective, a new and fresh and vigorous demand arose for legislative action which would bring about a prompt and thorough remedy. It is an incident of the public character of a railway company in its capacity as a common carrier (that capacity of common carrier arising out of the fact that to the railway has been delegated the power of eminent domain) that all those who are compelled to make use of this public mode of carriage should be treated alike; and not only that, but that they should be treated fairly as between themselves and the carrier company. This much is their right upon the broad principles of the common law. All legislation, therefore, has been, as I have already indicated, a mere codification and simple declaration of the rights of those who use this public mode of conveyance, and a new and fresh statement of the manner in which those rights may be enforced. Therefore—as a culmination of the long and persistent struggle of shippers and communities, on the one hand, to have their rights more easily and speedily recognized, and of the railroad companies, on the other, to prevent any statutory crystallization of their duties and limitations—we reach the Interstate Commerce Act of 1887, which is an act intended to define the powers, duties, and limitations of owners and users of the common carrier companies transacting business among the people of the different States.

The Interstate Commerce Act.

The public mind has never thoroughly comprehended the scope, or rather the narrowness, of that act. It is what I have just indicated it to be—a slightly detailed statement of pre-existing rights creating a machinery, quite simple and easily operated, whereby those interested, as well as the public at large, may be advised not only as to what their rights are and what their remedy is, but as to what the railroad companies themselves are doing, and wherein, if at all, rights, either public or private, have been infringed upon. The Interstate Commerce Commission is really a commission with visitorial powers. It can hardly be said to be more than this. It sustains in principle the same relation to the railroads and other common carriers of the country at large which some of the railroad commissioners of the various States sustain to the common carriers within their States. Its jurisdiction is ample from an inquisitorial standpoint, but it is a mockery to describe its determinations as judgments.

Stated in a technical form, the interstate act covers this ground: It provides that all charges in connection with the transportation of passengers and freight shall be reasonable, and declares unlawful and prohibits discrimination of all kinds and undue or unreasonable preference or advantage, and makes pooling arrangements unlawful. It creates a commission with semi-judicial and inquisitorial powers, and provides for the hearing before it of violations of the provisions of the act. Very many cases have been brought before the commission, and in some instances actual relief has been afforded to complaining parties. The commission, in the effort to maintain its own power and dignity, has with great ability declared the law, construed the act, and added very materially to the literature of jurisprudence in relation to common carriers. Beyond this the act has been a disappointment.

POWERS OF THE INTERSTATE COMMERCE COMMISSION.

The Interstate Commerce Commission is a body for whom Nature and education have done much, and for whom legislation has done little; it is a body of surpassing intellect and of infinitesimal legal authority; a body whose opinions are of the greatest weight abstractly and of exceedingly little importance concretely. As educators of the people they are worth their cost; as moral forces they are potential; as a legal power they can not even enforce their own order for costs. They have had a very considerable influence upon railroads, not because their determinations had any judicial effectiveness, but because they called the attention of the railroads and of the people to certain wrongs in a semi-judicial way, and thus, by a process of public enlightenment, by a process of moral education, have raised up a higher standard of conduct. They have reared also a set of men who have trained their intellects to avoid the requirements of the act. Just as the development of projectiles has kept pace with the development of fortifications and armor plate, just as the development of burglars' appliances has kept pace with burglar-proof safes, so has the development of the capacity of the railroad officer to avoid the difficulties of legislation kept pace with the legislation itself.

Considered in the light of its legislative intent, I think the Interstate Commerce Act may fairly be said to be a stupendous failure. Considered as a step in the education of the people, as an illustration of what is meant by evolution, it falls little short of being a pronounced success. As a demonstration of how not to do a thing it is complete. No man can truthfully declare that such a step is not necessary to a determination of how a thing ought to be done.

And such powers as the commission has are being so strictly construed by the courts as to still further abridge its authority. Judge Gresham has just held to be unconstitutional that portion of the act which makes the United States courts an adjunct to the commission for the purpose of compelling answers from contumacious witnesses. The commission is now knocking at the door of Congress, begging to be invested with judicial powers. If this request should be granted, a most serious question as to the constitutionality of the act would arise.

The Interstate Commerce Act might be described as an act to fortify the strong roads and to embarrass the weak ones; to benefit the roads whose lines are best equipped, and to injure those whose lines are imperfectly equipped; to advantage the roads which have the shortest lines between competitive points, and to ruin longer lines between the same points; to emphasize and accentuate the natural advantages which one road may have, and to emphasize and accentuate the natural disadvantages of others. This is not quite the purpose for which government was ordained.

LATER ASPECTS OF THE RAILROAD PROBLEM.

I noticed in an earlier part of this address how vividly appeared the hand of man consciously at work, and how conspicuously his efforts had ripened into the predetermined fruit, and yet, while this is true, the unexpected happened. The mighty forces of evolution, almost fatalistic in their overwhelming energy, are, of course, responsible in a large degree for the railroad problem as it exists to-day. The expected development of the natural resources of our country has been brought to pass; the distribution and the concentration of population have come, but the play of unknown and incalculable forces has tossed us about like corks upon the mighty ocean. Let me illustrate, at the same time following the thread of my discussion.

When the railways of the United States were composed of a large number of independent units, as was the case thirty years ago, before what is known as the American railway system had evolved from the incoherent units which preceded it; when every railroad stood upon its own bottom and was a law unto itself; when people paid three to five times as much for railway freight charges as now—they complained less and they were better satisfied. I am not leading up to the consolidation by legal measures of connecting lines, nor to the placing under one head of dozens of roads previously independent. This is really not the root of the situation. I am coming now to the actual, not the merely formal, consolidation of the means of transportation.

The first step was taken when the railroads began to sell tickets good beyond the line of the selling company; then followed the necessity for facilities of transfer from the train of one line to that of another; then followed the transfer of an entire car from one line to another, and its transportation over the line of another road. Incidental to this came the proper division of the purchase price of the ticket; and so this evolutionary process went on, inevitable and unforeseen.

The same process and progress followed respecting the transportation of baggage of passengers. More noticeable still was the development of the freight business. At first there was an arbitrary rate between the point of shipment and the point where the freight was to leave the first road; here there was a physical transfer, with accompanying charges, to the cars of the second road, and a second arbitrary charge for the carriage on that road and its transfer to the next; and so on to the final destination. Following this came the through rate, with the necessity for a division of the freight charge; then came the transfer arrangement, and finally the transfer of the car itself. This involved a uniformity of gauge, until finally there came a time when there was a practically unrestricted use of the cars of one road on the tracks of another; from this necessarily came an historical account of the movement of cars, with a charge for the use of the same. The result is, that one may often see trains of cars representing as many railroads as there are cars in the train, and gathered from every corner of this vast country. It is not necessary to further particularize. The important thing is this: That from all these changes and developments came a system of railways entirely independent of any physical or nominal consolidation. The railroads became welded into a coherent mass, every part of which felt the touch of every other part.

EFFECTS OF COMBINATION.

Now, this magnificent development of a large number of incomplete and unsatisfactory lines of railroads into a magnificent *railroad system* was the result of combination—of combination, however, directed in proper channels, and of inestimable benefit to the people. Combination is not an unmixed evil; but the development of all these benefits preceded the development of other results of combination which have not been so satisfactory. One other result of combination, or one other effort which the railroads have constantly made for the past twenty years by combination, has brought down upon it the malediction of the people, and the people's sense of opposition to it has been crystallized into statute in that section of the Interstate Commerce Act which declares pooling unlawful. Perhaps pooling was not unlawful under the common law. In my judgment, it is not certain that it ought to be declared unlawful by any law. The same rules that apply to other branches of business are not necessarily applicable to railroads. I do not see how it is possible, under the existing system of railroads, to avoid the necessity of pooling business in some form. No two roads between the same points are alike in their physical, financial, and geographical conditions. No road can change the form of its investment. No road can move itself to some more favored quarter. No road can overcome, in a word, the forces of its physical environment. The result is, that at the same rate some roads will get all competitive business except the overflow which they can not carry. Some roads can carry freight and passengers at a rate which affords a margin of profit, while the competing road, affording the same service at the same rate, will have no profit. From this situation have arisen all the trouble of rebates, secret rates, and the other forces that have done so much to demoralize railroads and railroad officials. The only danger which the most sensitive soul can fear from pooling is, that too high rates may be charged. But another and more serious danger is absolutely averted—namely, the hardship of inequitable rates as between different localities. The very essence of a pool is that rates should be scaled according to the distance, all other things being equal. Thus, a rate having been fixed to Chicago by the managing officers, the rate to Cleveland can be determined by clerks at, say, sixty-seven per cent of the Chicago rate. If it is arranged that the Erie road shall carry twenty per cent of the business originating at New York and destined to the principal cities of the West, it is entitled to the profit derivable from hauling so much freight, whether it hauls more or less than its allotment. This, as I said, raises the danger of exorbitant rates, but that is all, and that is a question which Congress can attend to in the event of the railroad failing to interpret correctly the public sense.

Under a system of pooling we can have uniformity and stability of rates. It is doubtful if any other possible advantages are equal to these.

Viewed in its most material aspects, I make free to offer these criticisms and suggestions as to our railroad system.

I. *Criticisms.*

1. There are in most sections of the country too many miles of railroad for the business offered them. Kansas has more miles than New York; and when we have ten lines of railway when five are sufficient for all the business, including its natural development, you will find that each one of the ten roads will conceive itself entitled to one fifth of the business at least, and act accordingly.

2. The railroads have cost too much money. Waste, extravagance, and enormous profits to middlemen, to construction companies, to contractors, and to bankers by way of commissions, have characterized their early stages.

3. In addition to their actual cost, as just indicated, their stock and bonds have been watered to an extent which imposes upon managing officers an apparent necessity to base earnings upon the volume of nominal capitalization; and the people are therefore compelled to pay more to meet the fixed charges.

II. *Dangers to be Feared.*

1. That from these apparent necessities there will continue to be, what we have had, a constant effort to obtain business at any cost. But this effort to get business at any cost does not reach to unfavored points, but to competitive business; and by so much as such business is handled below the necessities imposed by fixed charges and operating expenses, by so much must the charge be increased for handling non-competitive business. Here we come to the most serious danger which menaces us—the danger of discrimination. Nothing can be worse than this. An arbitrary, even an exorbitant, charge is not necessarily oppressive if it bears upon all alike. An inequality of charge results in the destruction of the prosperity of individuals and of communities.

2. Another danger arising from the apparent necessities is that a demand at once exists and persists to control legislation and official action.

The Proposed Remedies.

Three remedies are proposed to cure these great evils.

First. By putting our railroad system under Government control. The United States and Great Britain are the only countries in the world, with an extensive mileage, whose railroad systems are not under Government control, and they are the two countries where the railroad service is most satisfactory and most economical.

When we consider that the railroads of the United States represent ten per cent of the entire wealth of the country, when we consider that to turn the railroads over to Government control and direction means to add to the number of Government employees nearly ten per cent of the entire available working force of the country, we are appalled at the stupendous revolution necessarily involved in so vital a change in social relations.

It is enough to say that the prospect is sufficiently apalling, under the present system of civil service, to effectually prohibit our assent to the proposition.

Second. To relegate the railroads to their primitive use and make them public highways, free to everybody who desires to enter upon them with properly equipped appliances, under certain reasonable rules looking to the safe and expe-

Interstate Commerce. 139

ditious transportation of trains. This might and might not be economical. To effectuate this plan is not as difficult as at first sight it might seem to be. And yet, with our present conditions facing us, it would seem revolutionary in a backward rather than in a forward direction. It would undoubtedly raise a host of new conditions and new problems undreamed of, and, in my judgment, would plunge us into a sea of doubt and disturbance from which we could not easily extricate ourselves. I present it only because it affects to afford a novel and interesting solution of the present difficulties, and because, theoretically, it takes us back to first principles.

THE METHOD OF EVOLUTION.

Third. The third remedy proposed has not the merit of distinctness which marks the first and second, and leaves still a most wide field for the play of individual opinion and consequent uncertainty.

It is the application of evolution and natural causes to the conditions as we find them. It is to go on in the lines now laid down and depend upon an awakened and enlightened public heart and intelligence for remedial legislation and remedial conduct on the part of railway officials that shall harmonize to a greater extent the conditions and the requirements. This is not very definite, but to the Brooklyn Ethical Association it is not without meaning.

The history of railroad development affords us, in the highest degree, encouragement that the growth will continue to be in the right direction. The inestimable benefits from combinations for certain purposes which I have already defined are a striking proof that our hope is justified. As to the cost of transportation, we have so developed along proper lines as to reduce the cost of carriage to less than one half of the cost in any other country; and this in spite of the fact that the wages paid for our labor are fifty per cent higher.

Note this remarkable fact, which demonstrates that something good has come from our railway management. If the freight rates which prevailed in 1870 had prevailed in 1890, the people of this country would have paid one thousand million dollars more for the carriage of their products than they actually did pay. We have suffered not so much from exorbitant as from inequitable rates.

Judging the future by the past, I have no sort of doubt

that the managers of our railway system are as thoroughly convinced as any of us that the only way in which they can bring prosperity to the properties they manage is to duly regard the general prosperity of the country; and that they recognize, no less than we, the operation of an inexorable law of development, before whose might and majesty they will be crushed to destruction if they block its path.

Give us, then, a system which guarantees equality of rates as between shippers and stability in the same, and I think the rest may be safely left to the illumined intelligence and awakened conscience of the American people.

ABSTRACT OF THE DISCUSSION.

MR. JOHN C. WELCH:

The lecturer has presented on very broad grounds a thoughtful discussion of a subject which is the marvel of the nineteenth century. But he has not fully considered some of its perplexities. I agree that if we get stability of rates and undiscriminating rates the problem is solved. The accumulation of large fortunes by individuals through railroad management is not so great an evil as unstable and discriminating rates. Many large fortunes are doubtless ill-gotten; but we can leave this to the enlightened and awakened conscience of the people. One source of our trouble in dealing with this subject is the duality of our Government, State and Federal. State lines are now purely arbitrary, convenient only for the regulation of local government. In transportation there is no natural distinction between State and State. Making such a distinction in our laws introduces a bad element. The tendency everywhere is toward concentration and consolidation. In this way our great railroad systems are built up. Each one is a unity and must have a single head; but its management is hampered by the Federal and State Governments, and by the powers of the corporation in its collective capacity. How to harmonize these is a serious problem. The manager's interest is not always that of the stockholders, as we sometimes see the wrecking of a road for the individual benefit of the manager. Next to slavery, the railroad question is the most perplexing thing our Government has had to deal with. The roads between New York and Buffalo were consolidated by Commodore Vanderbilt, uniting five different lines. Next, the parallel lines were consolidated by Albert Fink. But the public became alarmed by the formation of the pool. Under Fink the pool worked satisfactorily; but it could not always remain in such good hands. There was no assurance that it would be worked in the interest of the people. The objection to consolidation first became prominent in the Western States, in the Granger movement. State laws were enacted which showed a violent feeling against the railroads. Then the matter went to Washington. The legislators were not familiar with the subject and did not know what to do. Reagan, of Texas, had *a priori* ideas adverse to a commission and to pooling. Cullum in the Senate understood the matter better. There was a compromise, and a law was passed instituting a commission and forbidding pooling. It is unnatural to regulate long and short haul rates by law; injustices thus arising are best corrected by public opinion through publicity. To offset the dangers to our civilization arising from the concentration of absolute power and great fortunes in a few hands, it may be necessary to institute governmental ownership or control over railroads. It was great fortunes that destroyed Roman civilization. I am not sufficiently optimistic to assume that success is foreordained for this country. Unless we exercise wise statesmanship in defense of the people's interests it is possible for us to lose our place, and for other nations to take the lead.

MR. J. WHIDDEN GRAHAM:

I regret that the lecturer, in summing up, did not include a fourth solution. I think the real solution is not in Government control or ownership of road-beds, nor in the evolution of public sentiment, but in the abolition of all governmental restrictions whatsoever—*laissez faire* and free competition. Herbert Spencer believes that nearly all the evils of the day spring from governmental interference. In the early days there were certain special privileges granted to railroad corporations, and here is the source of our evils. The opinion that "something must be done" has no further basis than the opinion that we must make laws against corporations. I believe that trusts, monopolies, and pools are good, because they can not exist unless they are giving better service to the people. All legislative interference only aggravates the trouble. The pooling clause in the interstate commerce bill is unsound. We might as well say that the grocer must not sell twenty pounds of sugar at a less rate than he gets for one pound. If the principle of free competition were recognized, and railroads had no governmental favors, there would be no ground for political complications. The Reading combine of last year has caused a great outcry, and a congressional committee has been appointed to try to break the combination. I believe the combination ought to be a good thing. The railroad monopoly depends on a previous monopoly of coal lands. The railroad has its power to extort, not as a railroad, but as the owner of coal lands; this is the true point of attack. Experience has shown that Government management of railroads is a failure. In Canada the Government road is operated at a steady loss and has never paid a dividend, while the Canadian Pacific has given as good service and has been profitable. Henry George confesses that the railroad system of Australia, owned and controlled by the Government, is inferior to ours in the Western States, though I think he still favors Government control. The real solution is to allow free competition, and allow as many companies to build as may choose to organize. I believe railroads have a perfect right to discriminate. It is very curious that in attacking great fortunes people always refer to the railroad, when the most of our great fortunes are built up in the dry-goods trade and other industries.

COLONEL J. HOWARD COWPERTHWAIT:

To write an essay on the play of Hamlet and leave out all reference to Hamlet requires great ability. I concede that kind of ability to the lecturer. He has given us a long and able account of the growth of the country and development of the railroad industry and made no mention of the principal factor in that growth—namely, free trade throughout the whole extent of the country. The Government has never interfered with the growth of trade between the States. One of the best features of the Constitution of the United States is that it prohibits this interference. To-day our rate of wages is far higher than in continental Europe, where there is " protection " between the States; yet freedom in this country has not prevented great differences in wages in the different States. The lecturer says the natural lines of trade are north and south, bearing in mind climatic differences. I should say the natural lines are the lines of least resistance —those over which there is most traffic—and these, as we all know, are east and west. The climatic difference is only a small factor. The great factor is the aggregation of people in the cities of the East, and the breadth of acres in the West for the farmer. The first builders of railroads in our country seldom make money. The roads are sold out at foreclosure once or twice, and the final purchasers, at a low cost, begin to make money on their investment. The individual never counts. He is sacrificed half the time in the great march of progress. The public gets its benefit and the individual loses his money. I do not think it is better to consume goods where they are produced. It is better to consume goods that come from where they can be produced cheapest. This is determined by natural laws and not by governmental interference. The speaker tells us that the cost of transportation is less and wages higher in this country than in Europe, and says that when there is a decline in prices on account of transportation wages are cut down; but in the past twenty years there has been a steady decline in the price of commodities, and also an advance in wages. The facts do not agree with his theory.

DR. LEWIS G. JANES:

I would call attention to the fact that before our Constitution was adopted the States did actually interfere with commerce by tariffs against the neighbor States. Virginia had a tariff on nearly all the products of Maryland, New Jersey on those of New York, etc. It was to break down these barriers, and to "form a more perfect union," that these artificial restrictions were prohibited, as I believe, wisely. In the same line of thought and policy was the constitutional provision authorizing Congress to build post-roads, and thus facilitate intercourse between the States. Congress actually did build such roads in the earlier history of our country.

MR. TAYLER, in reply:

One of my critics complains that I did not discuss free trade between the States. I made no reference to the final cause of America's prosperity for the same reason that I did not refer to the effects of the sun's rays upon our soil, or the geological structure of our country, or war and peace. It wasn't my business. I am quite ready to admit that if commerce had been prohibited among the States there would have been no interstate commerce; but I am not here to catalogue negations. My subject was interstate commerce, viewed in its physical aspects, and the effect of the means used to carry it on. I would have liked very much to speak upon the subject of free trade between the States; that involves the very essence of the protective theory. Mr. Graham's additional remedy was included in my third. It is another mode of carrying out the evolution idea. But I take issue with him as to the wisdom of taking away legislative control. The doctrine of *laissez faire* can not logically be extended to what has arisen by governmental acts. As for things which are not natural monopolies—dry goods, manufactures, etc.—perhaps legislative control would not help us, and trusts may be a proper development. But when a corporation is endowed with the sovereignty of the State, and allowed to take what it wants by eminent domain, and when its possession of the land thus taken may physically prohibit competition, we have peculiar conditions. Its greatness is built up by the power of the Government, the law creates a monopoly, and the people must see that it uses its power properly. As to pooling, we must bear in mind that every danger menacing us to-day, save possibly that from combinations, can be overcome under the general principles of common law. All corporations are bound to deal with all alike. Relief from discrimination was granted before the Interstate Commerce Act was passed. Inequality and instability are, however, the only things we have to fear. I do not think these things can be remedied altogether by Government control. With absolutely no Government control to speak of, we have better service and cheaper rates than the English. In most things we can afford to say: Let the railroads do what they please. That should be what an enlightened public conscience would say they ought to do.

FOREIGN COMMERCE

BY
Hon. WILLIAM J. COOMBS

COLLATERAL READINGS SUGGESTED:

Maine's International Law; Twiss's Law of Nations; Chisholm's Handbook of Commercial Geography; Curtis's Trade and Transportation between the United States and Latin America; Dilke's Problems of the Greater Britain; Gronlund's Our Destiny; Villebard's History of the International; Our Continent: or America for the Americans; Coutillon's Essai sur le Commerce.

FOREIGN COMMERCE.

By Hon. WILLIAM J. COOMBS.

"They that go down to the sea in ships, that do business in great waters; these see the works of the Lord, and his wonders in the deep."

IN this passage the Psalmist breathes the sentiment of the early ages in relation to the voyaging into foreign parts. The geography of the world was little known, natural laws were imperfectly understood, and the imagination had full play.

Under these conditions foreign commerce had its birth. The merchant became the explorer. In seeking new fields for his enterprise, he traversed strange seas, visited unknown lands, and added to the store of knowledge.

The fitting out of a ship for a voyage of trade and discovery was a notable event. Hardy adventurers flocked to enlist in the enterprise. And as the vessel sailed away and was lost to sight beyond the horizon, she was followed by the prayers and anxieties of the community. When, after years of adventurous wandering, touching strange shores, she returned home loaded with the riches of foreign countries, and when the story of the voyage was told, it lost nothing from lack of imagination or embellishment, helped by superstition and ignorance.

THE BEGINNINGS OF FOREIGN COMMERCE.

The earliest traders with foreign parts within the range of history were the Phœnicians, who occupied a small strip of the sea coast between the hills of northern Palestine and the Lebanon mountains on the east and the Mediterranean on the west. Their position was, with reference to the condition of the world at that time, most commanding in its facilities for commerce. Their caravans penetrated eastward into Asia, also into Egypt, Arabia, and Palestine, while their vessels coasted along the northern borders of the great sea, past Gibraltar and up the coast of northern Europe—then in a state of barbarism.

They also traded along the African coast on the south shore of the Mediterranean; and there are indications that their caravans penetrated to the interior of that country.

Crossing the Isthmus, they built vessels in the Red Sea, and traded on the west coast of Africa, even to the gold fields of Ophir.

Their own country was small and insignificant in its productions, but the merchants of Tyre and Sidon were men of enterprise, and became the traders of the world, exchanging the tin and other products of the North for the spices, silks, and gums of the East, thereby acquiring great wealth.

Their successors were the Carthaginians, whom we find about the eighth century before Christ in command of the trade of the then known world.

Tyre, Sidon, and Carthage in time disappeared from the world's activities. The fisherman now dries his nets on the ruins of Tyre. A few crumbling pillars remain to mark the site of imperial Carthage.

THE EVOLUTION OF COMMERCE.

It would be interesting and instructive to follow the history of commerce from the destruction of Carthage up through the centuries. We would find it controlled now by one nation, now by another. As soon as one nation became weak, on account of the accumulation of wealth in a few hands, the supremacy passed to a new people with more enterprise—each, however, adding to the store of knowledge. During our investigation we would witness the development of trade forms and customs which are preserved in many of the usages of commerce to-day. We would trace the transition from the primitive forms of barter to the use of the precious metals, first in the shape of bullion, then as coined money of universally recognized value; and, finally, the development of the banking system, the growth of confidence and credit, and the system of foreign exchange—all indispensable to commerce as it now exists.

That, however, would consume more time than is at my command without neglecting the field indicated by your committee.

The various nations of the world are separate families,

each having its own peculiarities of habits and tastes, as well as its own special products.

The exchange of these products is commerce, and when they are exchanged between different nations it is called foreign commerce. That of the present day differs from the commerce of ancient times in the magnitude of its operations and in the resources of science and the mechanical arts which it has called to its aid.

Then, too, it differs from the commerce of half a century ago in that its tendency and profit incline to a direct exchange between the nations having surpluses.

ENGLAND'S COMMERCIAL INFLUENCE.

Of this change England affords the best illustration. That country for generations occupied the position of trader among the nations. While her home products were large, they bore no proportion to the volume of her commercial transactions. She carried to the East not only the products of her own factories and fields, but also those of other Western nations; and brought back the products of the East in sufficient quantities to supply the other Western nations. She made money not only from the sale of her own surplus, but also from the purchase and sale of foreign products. In that way she accumulated the vast stores of wealth which have enabled her, even under the changed conditions of direct communication, to continue to a certain extent the levy of tribute upon international commerce—by acting as the banker of the world.

MODERN METHODS; IMPORTANCE OF A STABLE CURRENCY.

In other respects England is upon a par with other trading nations. The American merchant now buys the products of the East in the Eastern markets; the merchants of India, China, Africa, and Japan buy American products direct from our country.

The use of the cable has annihilated *time*, the steamship has shortened *distance*, and the establishment of exchanges has eliminated *secrecy* from the problem. With the disappearance of time, distance, and secrecy have naturally come larger transactions at a minimum rate of profit. The merchant who will not be left behind in the race must be awakened to the situation; he must utilize every modern improvement, avoid all intermediaries, and study every economy. In order to form an intelligent judgment of the probable course of exchange, he must keep himself posted in relation to the movements of foreign money markets and the conditions of production in the world. It can easily be seen that the present time requires a greater degree of intelligence and ability in its merchants than did the past, when all parts of the world were not in such close contact. Such being the case, that government is very unwise which adds to the intricacy of the problem by adopting a financial policy tending to throw its circulating medium out of accord with that of other commercial nations, or which substitutes one of changeable value for that which is universally recognized as the standard of values.

DANGERS OF GOVERNMENTAL INTERFERENCE.

It may with equal truth be observed that the legislative machinery of Government is too slow and too uncertain in its action to warrant its use in the regulation of commerce.

Its only useful field of action would seem to be the facilitating of communication, the removal of restrictions where they exist, and the maintenance of the integrity of its currency. All else can safely be left to the ordinary movements of commerce, to the laws of supply and demand, and those unwritten laws of trade that are older than any existing government.

Laws can be of no permanent help where the natural conditions are against us; they may perplex and hinder by attempts to establish unnatural conditions.

Since every nation produces more than it consumes, and since all depend upon foreign markets for a portion of their prosperity, intercourse should be as natural and as untrammeled as possible.

If the statement of economists is true, that the price of the great products of our country is fixed by the price at which we are able to sell our surplus abroad, it becomes manifest that any encouragement or assistance in the direction of facilitating the establishment of a foreign demand for our surplus is not solely in the interest of the merchant, but primarily in the interest of the producer, for whom in the present organization of business the merchant is only a broker or agent. I make this statement for the reason that I found in many of the debates in Congress that representatives from the agricultural sections of the country were apparently jealous of any concessions which were suggested for the encouragement of commerce.

ARE GOVERNMENT SUBSIDIES DESIRABLE?

I do not wish to be understood from anything that I have said that I favor Government subsidies to ocean carriers. The best subsidy it can give us is to open to us the possibility of securing return cargoes. Without return cargoes for our vessels while competitors in the carrying trade have them we can never succeed even with the largest possible subsidies. Our laws have heretofore stood in the way of this indispensable factor in the matter of the building up of our mercantile marine. The people, by their recent decision to remove the duty on wool, have cleared the way toward more favorable conditions.

The agriculturist has, by sacrificing a fancied advantage in the duty on wool, gained a real advantage in making a better and more accessible market for his other productions.

After cheap production the most important factor is cheap transportation, both inland and by sea; each is dependent upon the other. With cheap transportation, both inland and by sea, the producer here is in better condition to compete in the foreign market. With abundant freight to transport the carrier should be able to reduce his rates to a minimum ratio of profit. Profits should be gauged by the capital actually employed and not upon fictitious capital.

If Government touches this question at all, it should be in this direction. There have been many abuses of the public interest in this matter for which it is hoped there may be some remedy.

THE TRADE OF OUR COUNTRY.

My views in relation to the ability of this country to compete with any other manufacturing nation in the world are well known, and it is not necessary for me to repeat them. The great skill of our mechanics and the ability of our manufacturers will soon, if they do not already, lead the world in the quality and cheapness of our productions.

Entertaining these views, I have no sympathy with a policy founded in a distrust of our ability to meet other nations upon equal terms—a policy which would hedge us in from too intimate relations with the outside world, for fear that we may be forced to give more than we receive.

Aside from its antagonism to the advancing liberal sentiments of the age, such a doctrine is lowering in its tendency, and breeds distrust where there should be the greatest confidence.

Had our manufacturers the proper degree of confidence, if they would but use a tithe of that enterprise and ability which they display at home, they could create a foreign demand and reap enormous harvests. Let them drop the crutches, and they would never consent to use them again.

To do this, we must be liberal in our policy. We must interpret in a broad way the well-known maxims of political economy. We must realize the fact that no well-established trade can exist and be permanent in its character when there is a constant depletion by one country of the circulating medium of another. There must be a real, reciprocal transfer of commodities. Exchanges and banking arrangements may in a measure modify, but can not detract from the truth of this statement. When exchange through a third nation is used to correct such inequalities, both trading nations become tributary to her. Witness England to-day. The more direct the transaction, the more reciprocal the benefit; the fewer the intermediaries, the more solid is the condition.

Mexican and South American Trade.

We have an inviting field for commercial intercourse in the republics of this and the South American continent. Especially is this the case with Mexico since she has been connected with us by railroads. Easier communication and cordial relations have had the effect of at least quadrupling the amount of our transactions with her.

It is to be regretted that up to this time no system has been in force to ascertain the amount of our exports to that country. I discovered, upon an examination of the matter, that the reports published by our Government took no account of what crossed the frontier by railroads—and that is by far the largest share (possibly two thirds) of our shipments. A new law has been enacted, through my efforts, to remedy this defect.

While Mexico is a good customer of ours, we are also her best customers, for statistics show that of the sixty-three millions of dollars' worth of goods that she exported last year, we purchased forty-five millions, or over seventy per cent.

The same healthful conditions will exist with all of the other American republics when communication is made easy. We have a large financial interest in their stability and prosperity, and we can afford to meet them more than half way. Above all things, let us avoid the appearance of hard bargaining with them. They are for the most part poor in revenue, and can not afford to sacrifice any of it in order to meet our demands. Having assumed, by the Monroe doctrine, to cut them off from reliance upon European nations, we should feel in honor bound not to make our friendship too expensive for them.

Are Reciprocity Treaties Desirable?

While the reciprocity treaties with the Spanish West Indies and Brazil have had a temporary effect in increasing our transactions with those countries, no one who is acquainted with existing conditions believes that they will be permanently beneficial. Those with other countries, so far, are illusory and unsatisfactory. It is not possible in these days to make so narrow and selfish a theory the corner stone of the commercial policy of a great nation.

Aside from the above objection, reciprocity, as embodied in these treaties, is founded upon a variety of errors, some of which I will specify:

1st. That we can not afford to compete with foreign nations upon equal terms.

2d. That they can afford to reduce their revenues.

3d. That it is a matter of indifference to us whether we have their products or not.

4th. That other commercial nations will quietly submit to discrimination against their trade.

Doubtless that astute statesman, the author of reciprocity, considered it a temporary expedient to palliate an otherwise unpopular measure.

The foreign trade of the United States is not in its infancy. Already the products of our factories have penetrated to all quarters of the globe, and are there waging successful battle against their European competitors. Europe, Asia, Africa, the islands of the Pacific, all draw from our supplies, not in limited but in enormous quantities. Every year we make new inroads on our foreign competitors. At some early day our people will realize the fact that we can meet unassisted the competition of all.

Our Trade in Industrial Productions.

It would be interesting to give a history of the rise of our trade in industrial productions. It has all occurred within a generation. In that time we have not only availed ourselves of the current methods for cheapening the cost of production, but have also invented new methods. We have assimilated all new discoveries in science, and have worked them into practical results more rapidly than any other nation. While we have learned from other nations, they, too, have been instructed by us.

The inventive skill and the enterprise of our mechanics and manufacturers have greatly cheapened the necessaries of life, while at the same time there has been a steady advance in the reward of skilled labor. So great has been the decline of prices within the last quarter of a century that we may look forward to the time when men can live well without exhausting labor. This will certainly happen unless these advantages are diverted from the many into the hands of the few. If *all* the people could receive the *full* benefit of *all* improvements and scientific discoveries, we might reasonably expect a millennium of prosperity. The people could dress better, eat better food, and have more time for improvement.

I can not enter into a consideration of the monopolistic movements which are now seeking to control these advantages and divert them from the people. I have enough faith in the strength of the current of human progress and in the capacity of a free people to take care of themselves to believe that when this tendency is understood by them, and when they begin to be seriously hurt by it, the monopolists will be swept away like straws before a hurricane. Woe to the party or administration that opposes the popular will! We have lately seen such an awakening of the people.

Foreign Commerce. 155

INFLUENCE OF COMMERCE ON CIVILIZATION.

The mingling of different nations and peoples through commerce has had a beneficial effect in advancing the civilization of the world. It has given an opportunity to discard the faulty conditions of social existence and to select the best. Provincialisms are rapidly disappearing under this influence, narrow prejudices are dissipated, and a broader humanity is encouraged.

The life-blood of commerce is confidence, and the tendency of modern trade is strongly in the direction of building up confidence and character.

No man who has been engaged in business with foreign countries during the past twenty years can have failed to notice the gradual disappearance of peculiarities and differences between the nations, and a marked approximation to the same ideas and customs.

We well remember the time when the office of an English merchant or banker was inaccessible to Yankee ideas; to-day they have adopted many of our business customs, while we have wisely adopted many of theirs. Such is also the case with the Germans and French.

Modern commerce moves too rapidly to permit the indulgence of whims and peculiarities; those who persist in them will be left behind in the race.

ETHICAL VALUE OF COMMERCIAL INTERCOURSE.

If a merchant dealing with foreign countries is not naturally honest, he must act honestly if he would succeed and continue to do business. The commercial world soon discards a man or a firm that is not square in business transactions. The amounts involved are too large and the margin of profits too small to permit dealings with those who are not above reproach.

That there has been an immense advance in this ethical direction is proved by the steady decline in losses occasioned by dishonesty. Men who are in the habit of acting upon this high plane in business matters are not apt to be dishonest in their other relations to society or in their public duties.

Is it therefore claiming too much to say that the merchant in his inconspicuous sphere is quietly assisting to build up a better civilization and better standards of character throughout the world? His occupation also serves in a marked degree to preserve peace between the nations and to make war more difficult. Each nation finds in every other a customer for its surplus, or a source of supply for what it needs. The nations every day more strongly realize the fact that they can not live alone, and that war means hardship for all. The nation that goes to war must be able to give a good reason to the others, and to its own people, who are made to suffer on account of it.

The necessities of commercial intercourse will always demand a quick adjustment of differences. The acquaintance with each other's character acquired through commerce is a powerful factor in the settlement of vexed questions.

I trust I have not claimed too great a share for the merchant in the civilization of the world. Full credit must be given to all the other great agencies working together for the improvement of mankind. It is, however, pleasant to the merchant to feel that the world is not the worse for his efforts to gain a subsistence; that while he has sought his own gain in the different markets of the world, he has set in motion instrumentalities that have brought the nations closer together and made not only his own people, but other nations richer and better. He learns many lessons—not the least valuable being that each nation shares in the prosperity or adversity of all others; that it is not always wise to take full advantage of the necessities of others; that in the long run men and nations will get what they are entitled to; that artificial conditions must be only temporary, and that all gained in that way must be in time repaid in some other way.

ABSTRACT OF THE DISCUSSION.

Mr. WALTER S. LOGAN:

The lecturer and myself are like a pair of economic Siamese twins—agreed in all particulars. I wrote to the lecturer some days ago asking him to state some illogical position and give me an opportunity to refute it; but he has not done it. I take it for granted that foreign commerce is beneficial, or it would cease to exist. Exchanges are carried on between individuals when we trade with foreign countries just as they are in our domestic trade. If one is profitable and right, the other must be; there is no difference in principle. Every exchange is justifiable and beneficial which enables the parties thereto to get the greatest amount of goods at the least expenditure of labor. A great deal is said nowadays by philosophers and pseudo-legislators about the seller making all the profit; it is rather the buyer, in my opinion, who is most benefited. You pay five cents for a cup of tea that gives you an inestimable amount of comfort, or ride for five cents from the Battery to the Harlem River. You would not walk it for five dollars. For a few cents you buy matches with which you can light a fire in a minute, when it would take you hours otherwise. In all these cases the buyer is more benefited in the trade than the seller. Trade is the source of all our wealth, and wealth is the mother of civilization. Until you can set gold eagles and hatch gold eaglets you had better keep your money in circulation. There is a current fallacy also in what is called the balance-of-trade theory. It is assumed that it is better for a nation to sell more than it buys. If foreign goods were always purchased for cash, and there were no return trade, and the process went on indefinitely, we should finally get all the goods and the foreigner all the money. We should certainly be better off than he would be. But in reality the matter readjusts itself long before this extreme is reached. As goods or money become scarcer they rise in value, and the exchange goes the other way. There is no more danger of a permanent or serious disturbance of the balance of trade than there is of the ocean piling up on European shores and leaving our own high and dry. In the original savage state of society each tribe was autonomous, and there was no outside commerce. This was the jellyfish stage of society; there was no differentiation of structure. Later on, industries became specialized, and the interchange of commodities followed as a natural result. In this process of social evolution the shop was the precursor of the school; the merchant the missionary of moral and intellectual ideas. To the Phœnicians, the first trading nation, we owe our alphabet; to Greece, mistress of the seas, the early development of art. A Genoese, seeking gold and new fields for commercial enterprise, discovered this continent of ours, and revolutionized the geography of the world. The great Chinese wall is a good illustration of the "protective" spirit. China sought to seclude herself from the rest of the world, and shut out knowledge and progress. We have "statesmen" in our country to-day who would build a Chinese wall around it. There is a dreamer in a Pennsylvania university who says that if he had his way he would make the sea a wall of fire to separate America from the Old World. There is a senator, high in the councils of his party, who would absolutely prohibit, if he could, all foreign commerce. Shall not this Ethical Association, which stands for the moral advancement of the race, stand also for free trade and a world-wide commerce—the best friend of man's moral progress that the world has ever seen? Let the Statue of Liberty in our harbor be a beacon to welcome the seamen, the treasure, and the unrestricted trade of the whole world.

DR. ROBERT G. ECCLES:

To-night's paper is able, interesting, and valuable. It reflects the business interests of the gentleman who presented it. No one could expect him to take any other position. To his view, of course, reciprocity is "an expedient to palliate an unwise measure," and protection causes property to be "diverted from the many into the hands of the few." Many of us claim to be evolutionists, and as such it would be well to see what bearing the synthetic philosophy has upon the subject. I propose to treat the subject from this standpoint—to apply to it the common law which always governs change in evolution, which makes it a transition from indefiniteness to definiteness, from uniformity to multiformity. Is or is not all growth from indefiniteness to definiteness? As evolutionists you must answer, "It is." In the evolution of laws governing commerce we should therefore consider the direction of progress to be toward the definiteness of restriction, and from the indefiniteness of non-restriction. Trade always begins in savagery with perfect freedom, and ends with protection, or restriction, if you please. Commencing with lawless, unrestricted commerce, when every ship could carry what it chose, where it chose, and as it chose, development should go on to that restriction which a proper tariff would place upon it. In the evolution of the nation side by side with the growth of commerce toward restriction we should look for a change from uniformity of business to multiformity of the same. The nation—beginning in the indefiniteness where every man was farmer, hatter, shoemaker, tailor, carpenter, and everything else for himself—went on to the present time when each man seeks to have a business of his own. A barbarous nation is one in which there is perfect freedom of business indulged in by everybody, where the whole nation has but one industry, and that an indefinite industry, mainly but not wholly agricultural. A civilized nation has many distinct forms of industry, and the height of its civilization is measured by their number. For a barbarous nation free trade is the ideal of commerce, since, like itself, it is free from trammels or restrictions. Progress always means definite restrictions, and never freedom. The method of induction is utterly ignored by free-traders. If they wanted to be scientific they would follow the Baconian method of proving their points by experiment and not hurling us into a revolution on *a priori* reasoning. Let them ask that one thing at a time be tested for a term of years, first under protection and then under free trade, and then fairly decide on the results for that one thing, and no scientific mind could reject the proposal. But no. They are sure without trial that free trade in everything will prove a blessing. As the height of our civilization is in direct proportion to the number of useful industries, and as we want to increase civilization, let us see which system applied for a term of years to one article at a time, which we do not now produce, will give us its production the quickest. How does any one know that free trade would be the best policy for us to pursue? Men that have not intelligence or knowledge enough to foresee the consequences of changing the tariff on one thing only, madly believe they can foresee the consequences of changing all. They are utterly and absolutely unscientific. The conditions in our country are wholly unlike those of any European nation. Our country is so vast that our possibilities of internal development are immeasurable. England is a commercial nation. She lives and thrives on commerce. Ours is a developing nation that needs but little foreign commerce. Our territory exceeds that of Europe, and our possibilities are therefore greater than all European nations combined. Our policy of protection has developed our internal resources to a degree that is marvelous. England's policy of apparent free trade was a necessity of her existence, since her territory is scattered through the world in her colonies. She has her ships; we have our railroads and telegraphs. We have to-day more railroads and telegraphs than all the rest of the world combined, and we owe this fact to protection. Free trade between the States is to us an advantage and a necessity; it is a condition of our national unity; but to secure it we must have protection against other nations. Every scientific reasoner knows that all motion is in the direction of least resistance or greatest traction. Why does Texas trade with New York instead of London? Why does California trade with New York instead of Melbourne, Yokohama, or Calcutta? Because it is in the line of least resistance. Does or does not a protective tariff increase the resistance along the coast, making it harder to trade abroad? If it does, then business finds it lines of least resistance at home and of greatest resistance abroad. Are not our railroads and telegraphs the proof of this? Is not the immense volume of home business the evidence? Wherein does the United States differ from civilized Europe commercially except in its perfect freedom between State and State with resistance at its borders? What other explanation is possible of our enormous railroad and telegraph interests as compared with their meager ones? They certainly have more people, more cities, and therefore more commercial needs, yet they have not been able to do as we have done. Free commerce between us and the outside world would mean reduced commerce between State and State to the same degree. If we got everything abroad we would need no internal commerce. If we got everything at home we would need no foreign commerce. The less we get abroad, the more we get at home, and the more the business is kept at home. Patriotism demands that we encourage business between State and State. Where our commercial interests are, there is our heart also. If trading with England will lessen our chances of warring with England, as the speaker tells us, then trading with Florida, California, or Oregon will do the same. Trade between State and State lessens sectional feeling and brings all the States into a common interest. Trade with foreign nations, by lessening to that amount trade between State and State, weakens the ties that bind us. Open our ports to cheap foreign productions, and trade goes to foreign ports. It is useless to say that an equivalent of trade in our products will go abroad. That makes matters worse. The great channels of commerce would be cut along the water routes, where carrying is cheap. Interstate commerce would become next to impossible. Oil and water are no more irreconcilable than is free-trade and interstate progress. Our nation can not live long as a free trade nation. The mutual interests of its various sections, in the very nature of things, would become less and less. Secession would soon be a popular doctrine, and the United States would go to pieces by its own weight. Free trade is the doctrine of secession. Unless commodities are of more value where they are sent than where they are made, there could be no more commerce. Commerce therefore gives us more than it takes; but remote consequences are of as great or greater importance to us than immediate ones. Perfect adjustment is perfect life. Intelligence demands adjustment for the future as well as the present.

If our nation would live, its present conduct must not be suicidal. We are very far from having reached our maximum of multiformity in business. England has long since reached hers. We can not reach ours if we go to pieces as a nation; neither can we if we trade abroad for everything that can not be produced at a profit at home. It is safe for England to open her ports because she has ceased to develop new industries already established in competition elsewhere. It is not safe for us to open ours because we have not reached the limit of our possibilities. The monopoly we cry out against tempts capital from abroad to invest itself here, and so causes our country to grow in wealth. Capital always flows to where it can grow the fastest. Where capital goes, there goes the demand for labor. Where there is a demand for labor, there labor flows. Thus does our country grow in commerce, in wealth, and in population. Who can deny that protection has increased the population of this country? [Several voices: "We deny it." MR. WOLF: "Will the speaker please prove his assertion?"] DR. ECCLES, resuming: If people are not brought here under contract by protected manufacturers, why have we passed exclusion acts? If fortunes were not made here, capital would not flow here. If capital did not flow here, labor would not flow here. If neither came, we would have no need for contract labor exclusion acts. Extreme protection is fogyism and extreme free trade commercial anarchy. Evolutionists should adjust themselves between the two. Use the experimental method of science in letting down the bars. Free one thing at a time, as soon as a test experiment proves that it can be freed. The wholesale freedom clamor is wild nonsense, and makes scientific adjustments of the tariff impossible. Such clamorers are the nation's greatest foes and the assassins of the workingman's best interests.

MR. JAMES A. SKILTON:

In this essay we have an object lesson of peculiar value and significance—the presentation of the combined view of the merchant and the legislator, the two dominant classes and factors in foreign commerce. The view of the evolutionist and of evolutionary sociology is, however, conspicuously wanting.

Undoubtedly, in the early time they that did "business in great waters" did "see the works of the Lord, and his wonders in the deep," and also gave the Lord a more or less loyal credit therefor. But the modern merchant, legislator, and average man fail to make this recognition in its full significance.

The historical data of the essay are complete but melancholy. Are fishermen, then, hereafter to dry their nets among the ruins of New

York, Brooklyn, London, and Liverpool? And if not, why not? is the one pertinent question the evolutionist asks. What he seeks to know here, as elsewhere, is the true law of survival and progress. Recognizing the danger of it, he still refuses to be discouraged by the sad fate of the many Tyres, Sidons, and Carthages of the past. To the evolutionist the origin and order of succession is, in fact, necessarily and according to a higher law, quite otherwise than that indicated by the lecturer. The merchant does not and never did become the explorer; but the freebooter and the pillager, following well-marked and necessary lines of evolution through the stages of animalism and war, became the explorer, and eventually the explorer or his successor became the merchant; and the merchant has yet to become the complete peripatetic philosopher, moralist, and benefactor of the race he now imagines himself to be. When, therefore, the evolutionist brings foreign commerce into the field of inspection, he will expect to find in it the more or less imperfect acceptance and application of scientific moral principles with the active survival of these only partially aborted characteristics. Not only is it true that such is and must be the order of development, but even in the last year and this very day of grace we have all the grades of the past actually at work, the Arab slave drivers and pillagers, followed by the European missionaries of trade and civilization, destroying whole tribes and villages "in the interest of trade."

The essayist himself, by what the lawyer calls "apt words," incidentally and naïvely used, fitly describes the character even of modern foreign commerce when he refers to England as continuing "the levy of tribute upon international commerce by acting as the banker of the world," our factories as "waging successful battle against their European competitors;" and when he uses other militant figures of speech to set forth the operations and effects of foreign commerce. Why use soldiers, guns, and warships, or continue to imitate the enterprising merchants of the Barbary Coast, when the "tribute" can be so easily levied through banks and bankers? Apparently unconsciously, the distinguished essayist treats foreign commerce as still militant in character and methods, if not military in the sense of using arms to accomplish its ends. And he truly says the curriculum of foreign-trade nations has from the beginning been first bold and enterprising, then wealthy, then weak, and then a fit subject for pillage and destruction by some stronger nation, that stronger nation eventually in turn following the same road to ruin. The evolutionist, however, and the scientific moralist, want to know when and how this eternal round of ruin throughout the ages, inevitably following a preliminary term of apparent prosperity, is to be brought to an end, and continuous human progress and development established and made certain. The essayist says, substantially, that the way of safety and progress is through freedom—freedom without definite limit. In this he agrees exactly with the freebooter and his congeners. But freedom—unchecked freedom—enthrones superior strength and tramples on the weak. Whether the instruments are guns or finance, militancy rules most arbitrarily and most ruinously where freedom is most free. And we are reminded by Mr. Spencer himself that we now have more freedom in America than we know what to do with, if not more than is safe for us.

If, then, freedom is to give full license after legislation has facilitated communication, removed restrictions, and maintained the integrity of the currency, what hope of rescue have we left ? We rebelled against a tax on tea and stamp duties, and have imagined for something over a hundred years that we had established an independent nation and taken control of our own affairs; but it seems to be all a mistake, since " the merchant," "primarily in the interest of the producer," kindly arranges matters so that "the *price* of the great products of our country is fixed " for us by the merchants and bankers of other nations—even of the very nation from whose governmental tyranny we have thought we had been free for a century. Furthermore, this even is not enough, according to the doctrines of modern foreign commerce. We must in addition, and on altruistic grounds, continue to bribe these philanthropic strangers to perform this high duty of deciding what pay we are to get for our products and labor by that " best subsidy," " return cargoes."

If, truly, things have come to this complexion at last, what a pity we ever became " independent," or imagined we became so! If matters could be so arranged that everything we have to sell and to buy must pass through the hands of foreign merchants, then we should have a new order of tyrants more terrible than that from which political freedom has relieved us. If we did not know to the contrary, it would seem that all men must recognize at a glance that a freedom tending to such a condition must be a " freedom " that enslaves. The objection is made that "our laws have heretofore stood in the way." It is not the human, but the divine law that stands in the way. It is the constitution and the laws of the world and the universe, and not those of the Union or the State, that we are called upon to consider and respect.

Cheap transportation, both inland and by sea, is offered as a means of salvation. Mr. Tayler has shown in this season's course that transportation adds no value to products, but rather consumes it through cost of carriage. When transportation consumes all the value, there cometh still cheaper transportation seeking products of regions and peoples beyond, and ever still beyond, for its hungry and capacious maw.

In discussion of the Land and the Race Problems * last year I presented an evolutionary and historical view of the barbarizing effects of untrammeled foreign trade and cheap transportation on America, and I can not here repeat the presentation. Subsequently Dr. Janes † brought to our notice the discovery of Prof. Atwater that soil exhaustion due to removal of products had already caused great degeneration in the food value of all American products of the land. Is foreign commerce, then, to take from us, in the sacred name of freedom, even our brain- and muscle-making power, with the certainty of producing further and continuous deterioration of our individual and national life, and that of the entire civilization of America, the present hope of the world?

But one of the surprising results of the system approved is that gentlemen who grow frantic in their fears of Gresham's law and its effect on our money, entirely ignore the effects of that law as already applied and realized in the marked deterioration of our population and our citizenship, and the turning over of political control in all our cities to a class of voters who are already demonstrating to us the failure of the republican principle by their complete surrender to the political boss with all that is thereby implied in State and national affairs. The currency of the country must not be debased, say these frantic gentlemen, but the population and the suffrage may be; and on the whole, it is said it is rather better that they should be, since otherwise cheap production, cheap transportation, and access to new lands may be prevented. This degeneration began with the work on the Erie Canal and cheap foreign labor, and has continued *pari passu* with the building of railroads throughout the country, and with their effects in building up great exporting centers of populations in response to the demands of foreign commerce.

Cheap transportation is the instrument by which England especially uses the existing system of foreign commerce, in skinning the globe and preparing it for return to wilderness and desert. Particularly the railroad, the chief instrument of cheap transportation, began as a beggar and a beneficiary, but has now reached the horseback or imperial stage. In early and in later years it has been the child of bonded cities, towns, and counties, and of land grants, and the pet of legislation which has relieved it from its proper share of the burdens of taxation, generally made it the product of special legislation and protection, and eventually, through ingenious systems of railroad wreck-

---

* See Man and the State, pp. 131-143 ; 383-402.
† See Id., p. 179.

ing, enabled a few men to own and control property that had been paid for by the many out of hard earnings, which property has come into control of all other values and interests. In the new hands these railroads have frequently if not universally become the masters, and those who originally paid for them their bond servants, been compelled to deliver to their masters a share of the earnings of each and every day of the year.

The question is not whether we shall go back to the go-cart and the dug-out of the past for transportation requirements; it is whether the splendid facilities the people have built and paid for shall be made the instruments of the waste, devastation, and destruction of their remaining property under the pretense of valuable service.

The lecturer finds evidence of the beneficial effects of foreign commerce in "the gradual disappearance of peculiarities and differences between nations, and a marked approximation to the same ideas and customs." Evolution, on the contrary, finds beneficence and progress only a differentiation and departure from the homogeneous, and either decay or stagnation in the wake of the opposite movement. The lecturer finds hope of relief from monopolistic movements and control of advantages not in obedience to any law of Nature and things, but "in the capacity of a free people" and in freedom of trade. But every tyro in business knows that practically all the great trust and so-called monopolistic movements of the day are directly caused by a freedom so great as to develop a competition that brings men and their business to the verge of destruction, and makes combination a matter of life or death. In reality the struggle is for survival rather than monopoly. It is this principle, acting with the constancy and certainty of the law of gravity, that has caused the coal railroad combinations which our friend is just now engaged in investigating, as chairman of a congressional committee. It is indeed a freedom greater than we know how to use wisely, giving imperialism to superior power, that is exalting the few at the expense of the many, as it is cheap transportation and railroad control that are producing our large crop of railroad and merchant millionaires on the one hand, and infesting public office everywhere, from high to low, with mediocrity and venality on the other. Instead, therefore, of favoring ethical advance, we may look to foreign commerce, *as now conducted*, as the one great and guilty cause of eventual moral and national decline throughout the world. My objection is not to foreign commerce *per se*, but to that conducted in the now and still dominant destructive spirit.

Undoubtedly the system, even though it works ruin to the world, requires, as he says, "honesty" among its workers. It is, however, a part of the work of evolutionary sociology to ascertain, by the establishment of better standards, what are truly right ways and ends, what are the duties of righteousness, and what is the more comprehensive definition of the word honest, by extending the domain of scientific morality to the utmost limits of human activity.

Mr. Spencer having shown that the perfect moral status is that in which the egoistic and altruistic forces are in equilibrium, it is not to be wondered at that the world of business has not yet accepted the principle for its guidance, seeing that the same principle has been before the world at least eighteen hundred years in the form of the golden rule equally with only very partial acceptance. The evolutionist agrees, once for all, that the practical acceptance of the principle as a rule of affairs is a work of time, governed by evolutionary law like all the rest of life. What he insists upon is a progress not too hasty toward it and what he protests against is retreat from it and whatever forces that retreat upon men. The true, descriptive word I would suggest for the banner of evolutionary sociology and true progress is the word ABOLESCENCE, meaning slow growth from bad toward better and higher things.*

Instead of freedom, the missing factor of promise and hope is a combination of sturdy faith with intelligent obedience to universal law. In the absence of such a combination, the high possibilities of human progress must remain in abeyance for many generations yet to come.

The system I condemn has its philosophical foundation in a theory of rent, so called, which suggests the names of Ricardo and Malthus. The system I commend suggests the names of Carey and Spencer and a different theory of rent. These theories attempt to explain how a new society is started or planted, and how it continues or grows. According to the former, the first comers naturally and selfishly take and hold possession of the best and richest lands, and those who come later unwillingly take poorer lands in succession. This method establishes selfishness, jealousy, and class differences as the initial controlling forces of the new society, with the inevitable result, flowing from the selfish principle, of eventual disorganization, decay, and poverty after a term of apparent prosperity and increase in wealth. According to the other view, first comers necessarily take and occupy the poorest lands and the later comers the richer lands; but the richer lands can only be subdued and compelled to give up their riches by the continued altruistic and mutually helpful co-operation of all comers. This method produces a society that grows strong and rich by consideration of the family first, and nearest neighbors and their children

See Man and the State, p. 388.

next, substantially in the order of proximity, thus preventing waste and leaving foreigners, strangers, and commerce with them to follow the same order. The first naturally develops a foreign commerce based on the immediate and supposed interests of select individuals only, the second a foreign commerce based on the first, the ultimate and the highest interest of both the community and its component individuals, and later on of those of foreigners and strangers. Necessarily each has its own co-ordinate system of morals, and eventually of politics and life, and therefore gives form, method of action, and survival or destruction to the society. I stand by the last mentioned. So long as the foreign merchant approaches consciously or unconsciously in a way to weaken such a community, by removing its capital or exhausting its soil, my contention is that he is not completely differentiated from the pirate or the pillager, and I find the foreign commerce of this age is still practically of this kind and order. And I also contend that a foreign commerce of the other and more altruistic order will be the richer, larger, and better commerce for all trading peoples, while that with which I contrast it is the guilty cause of moral decline, because at one stroke it injures the wealth and the weal of the victim community and of its individuals, as well as those of the victimizer. Admitting that the pirate and the warrior have each had shares in the progress of civilization, I complain that they still "lag superfluous," although partially aborted, in modern foreign commerce. Freedom of intercourse here gives them opportunity of survival. Protection laws tend to their extinction. These laws must be wisely framed and administered with the clear, strong, and resolute purpose of self-preservation. Attack upon the interests of other communities and nations is allowable in any form only when it becomes the true and only policy of self-preservation. It is because under the other system, revolution, war, and the decay of governmental or national forms become the inevitable, necessary, and only possible means of shackle-breaking, emancipation, and reform for individuals and races that I object to it as not the way of true prosperity, peace, progress, and sound scientific foreign commerce.

I congratulate Mr. Coombs on having been instrumental in making a law for the preservation of a record of exports. It is a step in the right direction. But the practical and logical necessity beyond and behind such a law is an amendment of the Constitution permitting the collection of duties on exports. Protection, like charity, begins at home. Until the nation can control native products, it can not properly control foreign products. Until the United States has had experience with protective export duties and protective import duties working co-operatively to common ends, the American people can not be said to have begun the study of the true principles of either protection or free trade.

I therefore venture to suggest that Mr. Coombs may add to our obligation to him by agitation for such an amendment of the Constitution, and the preservation of all export records equally with import records.

DR. LEWIS G. JANES:

While I agree with Mr. Skilton in his dissent from the theories of Ricardo and Malthus, and in his deprecation of land exhaustion, I can not adopt his view of the dominant tendencies of foreign commerce in this or any era of the world's history. He may be right in tracing the evolution of the merchant and explorer back to the pirate or freebooter; but, in my judgment, there was long ago a far more complete differentiation of the two classes than he has recognized, so that, in fact, throughout the historical period the pirate has been, next to the extreme "protectionist," the chief enemy of the merchant. Upon what historical grounds it can be asserted that foreign commerce, as now or as at any time conducted, is "the one great and guilty cause of moral decline throughout the world," I can not imagine. Certainly I have not so read history. The consolidation of the Roman Empire, which first paved the way for general commercial intercourse between nations, was the precursor of that period when, as Gibbon declares, the masses of the people were more prosperous and contented than at any time before or since. The merchant paved the way for the Christian missionary; a merchant vessel carried Paul to preach the new gospel in Gentile lands, and then, as later, the pirate was the enemy of both merchant and missionary. In fact, the function of the freebooter, since his class became distinctly differentiated, has always been essentially identical with that of the prohibitory tariff in rendering foreign commerce difficult. In the far-away and forgotten period, when the pirate monopolized the commercial function, even he was a benefit to civilization, as the warrior also was in earlier times. This Mr. Skilton substantially admits, while he claims that they now "lag superfluous" in foreign commerce. That our country, the *pro rata* wealth of which is greater than that of any other country in the world, has been since we emerged from England's "paternal" protection in the colonial period, or is now in any sense a "victim" of foreign commerce, seems to me a proposition at once absurd, unpatriotic, and self-destructive. The influence of international commerce in promoting the world's civilization has, in my judgment, not been second to any other factor—not even the spread of Christianity. As a rule, isolated communities are certainly sessile and unprogressive. Only where there is free communication with external influences has progress been considerable. I can accept the doctrine of protection as advocated by Prof. Gunton, involving the imposition of a tariff no greater than is necessary to equalize the wage-level between competing countries and thus encourage fair competition; but not when it becomes prohibitory and interferes with free intercourse between nations. Nor do I find the true remedy for land exhaustion in such interferences, as I have elsewhere explained.* The whole question is simply one of historical fact, and the facts, as evolutionary factors, seem to be on the side of the merchant, and not of his traducers.

MR. COOMBS, in reply:

My paper, as most of you will agree, does not advocate free trade, but merely the removal of restrictions upon trade as far and as fast as practicable under existing conditions. I have tried to confine myself to the state of things as it actually exists. We must have a revenue to meet the expenses of the Government, and this implies a certain degree of interference with commercial freedom.

I have the greatest respect for the argument of Dr. Eccles, though I am free to confess that his positions are new to me, and I do not understand them. I think I detect one error in his assumption that the Government is competent to frame and administer laws with the accuracy needed for a fine scientific experiment such as he has suggested. My experience has been that our legislative methods are too cumbersome and complicated for judicious legislation; it is as likely to mar as to make, to retard as to forward. My faith is not so much in legislation as in the character and intelligence of the individual man. I believe that what we can make to advantage in this country we will make, and what we can not without the artificial stimulation of protective tariffs we had better leave alone. I do not believe that a hothouse forcing process will result in the healthful development of our industries. I view this subject wholly from the common-sense standpoint of a practical business man. The theoretical discussion of underlying principles may be a delightful mental exercise to you philosophers, but for myself I must beg to refrain from entering the lists in such a contest.

* See Man and the State, pp. 179, 180.

THE SOCIAL AND POLITICAL STATUS OF WOMEN

BY
JOHN W. CHADWICK
AUTHOR OF THE BIBLE OF TO-DAY, CHARLES DARWIN,
EDUCATION AND CITIZENSHIP, ETC.

COLLATERAL READINGS SUGGESTED:

Mary Wollstonecraft's A Vindication of the Rights of Woman; Mill's The Subjection of Woman; Spencer's *The Rights of Woman* and *The Constitution of the State*, in Justice (compare chapter on *The Rights of Woman* in Social Statics); Mrs. Stanton and Miss Anthony's History of Woman's Suffrage; Mrs. Fawcett's *Why Women require the Franchise*, in Essays and Lectures by M. and G. Fawcett; Chapters on *Woman's Suffrage* and *The Position of Woman*, in Bryce's American Commonwealth; Clarke's Sex in Education; Miss Brackett's Education of American Girls; Bushnell's Woman's Suffrage a Reform against Nature.

THE SOCIAL AND POLITICAL STATUS OF WOMEN.

BY REV. JOHN W. CHADWICK.

THE PRESENT STATUS OF THE WOMAN QUESTION.

THE woman question, considered in its entirety, might be likened unto an army in order of battle. It has its center and its wings. The center is political enfranchisement; the wings are industrial and educational opportunities co-equal with those which men enjoy. Now it will not, I think, be denied that our army has advanced with unequal steps; the right wing and the left have left the center a good way behind; the industrial and educational advancement of woman has been much greater than her political advancement. Nevertheless, from first to last, the army has been one, and the victories of the parts have been the victories of the whole. The center has not been weakened by the advance of the right wing or the left. It has been greatly strengthened by the advance of both. And there are few, if any, lovers of the general cause of woman's larger life who do not feel that the disproportionate advance of women's suffrage, as compared with their industrial and educational advance, has been a fortunate order of precedence. If disproportion there must be, it had better be of this sort than of another. It is better for suffrage to lag behind industry and education than for either industry or education to lag behind suffrage, although unquestionably the exercise of the right of suffrage by women would have a tendency to remove many of the hindrances that still bar the way to an industrial and educational opportunity for women equal with the opportunity for men. We can at least concede so much to those who think that women should not be allowed to vote until they are "perfect, even as their Father in heaven is perfect," that the larger their industrial freedom and capacity, and the fuller their educational opportunities and their use of them, the better qualified will they be for the exercise of their right of suffrage in a just and noble way. In the mean time that principle of which Darwin made so much in animal structures, "the correlation of growth," and which Paul anticipated long ago, when he said, "If one member suffers, all the members suffer with it; and if one member rejoices, all the members rejoice with it," is nowhere more conspicuously operative than in the development of womanhood. Industry, education, suffrage, like Barbara Locks and Mrs. Aleshine and their male companion in Mr. Stockton's funniest story, are all in one boat. Improvement in one direction helps improvement in every other. Every year that suffrage is delayed women are becoming better fitted for its exercise by the enlargement of their industrial and educational spheres. Suffrage pays for this favor in advance. The agitation for it has been more influential than any other intellectual and moral force in bettering the industrial and educational condition of women. It would be impossible to find an advocate of woman's suffrage who is not equally an advocate of the fullest possible extension of the industrial and educational sphere of womanhood. And the plea for such extension has come very largely, and always most effectively, from the women suffragists. The advocacy of others has been sicklied over with the pale cast of a most natural fear that one thing would lead to another, the inch of industry or education to the ell—I have not dropped an "h"—of complete political enfranchisement.

RECENT CHANGES IN WOMAN'S INDUSTRIAL OPPORTUNITIES.

It would be impossible to overstate the change that has been brought about in the industrial and educational status of women within the last twenty-five or thirty years. Scores of employments that were monopolized by men in 1863, with no deliberate intent, are now open as freely to women as to men, and tens of thousands of women are engaged in them with honorable advantage and a new happiness and self-respect. The fear that every woman in a new employment would drive out a man has not been justified by the result. If men have been driven by hundreds out of certain classes of employment, it has been to be driven into others much better suited to their physical ability—from the desk and counter to the machine shop and the ranch. But for all that has been done, much still remains to do. The range of woman's work is still capable of indefinite enlargement, and, within the scope of those employments to which women are freely admitted, the inequality of wages for the same amount and quality of work furnishes both the political economist and the philanthropist with a problem which is very difficult to solve. Here is undoubtedly, to some extent, the defect of a quality—the quality of impermanence —which belongs to women's labor in the mass, because the factor of marriage enters so deeply into it. The readiness with which women frequently abandon a first-rate employment for a tenth-rate husband would be comical if it were not tragical, but we are dealing now with general laws and not with special instances, and, in general, this factor—the probability of marriage—has certainly an injurious effect upon the average character of women's work beyond the precincts of the home, there also where her position is one of household service, and the average character of the work of any class is extremely influential in determining the average pay. Nevertheless, the inequality of pay for equal work is often monstrously unjust. Everything will help to remedy that which helps to make the general equality of men and women more assured. (Nothing will help so much to make the general equality of men and women more assured than an equality of their political status.) Let there be so much as general school suffrage and the shameful inequality in the wages of men and women doing equal work as teachers in the public schools will show an immediate tendency to disappear. Nor can one wrong of this sort be righted and that be the end. By a process of capillary attraction the next wrong will be righted; then the next and next. It is all one chain, and whether you strike the tenth link or ten-thousandth you strike the whole.

How Industrial Advancement Aids Political Enfranchisement.

The industrial development of women aids their political enfranchisement in many ways. Every enlargement of the sphere of womanhood makes the ultimate political enlargement a less radical change. We have the ultimate enlargement broadening slowly down from precedent to precedent. Moreover, many of the arguments against woman's suffrage were equally arguments against woman's industrial expansion thirty years ago. As the event has proved their fallacy in the case of industry, the presumption is that it will prove their fallacy in the case of suffrage. Take but a single instance: Surely the argument from woman's natural physical disabilities was much stronger against a free industrial life for her than against suffrage. Now the event has proved its absolute futility in the case of industry. Men lose more time than women in the employments in which they are engaged together. As the first steamship crossing the Atlantic brought to America the first copies of Dr. Lardner's book proving that an ocean steamship was an impossibility, so our good ship of state goes plowing on her way to equal industry and education and political rights for men and women, her hold well stuffed with literature proving beyond peradventure that such a voyage is an absolute impossibility. What funny reading Dr. Lardner's book after the lapse of fifty years, when twice a week a fleet of ocean steamers leaves New York for various European ports, and five or six days are sufficient for the trip across! There are scores of books prophetic of the impossibility of equal rights for men and women in education, industry, and politics that will be even funnier after an equal lapse of time.

Woman's Progress in the Higher Education.

Woman's advance along the educational line of her ideal development has been hardly less than her advance along the industrial line. No barren virgin that "Female Seminary" which Emma Willard and Catherine Beecher and Mary Lyon nourished with such affectionate and tender care. Its children and grandchildren are high schools and academies and normal schools innumerable, in which separately, or in healthier co-operation, girls are enjoying equal advantages with boys—yea, verily *enjoying them*, and proving their ability to do as much with them as Tom and Harry. At the same time colleges for women have multiplied, and the most venerable universities have afforded women opportunity to show that even without the advantages of their direct instruction they can attain the highest honors which their graduates are able to command, and these object lessons in some cases have availed to break every barrier down and make women of the gate and court free of the temple to its inmost shrine. Not a collegiate year goes by that does not chronicle some new advance. Now it is a woman's professional chair at Brown, and yesterday it was an alumni petition at Harvard for the admission of women to the theological school, while Harvard tutors and professors in the "Harvard Annex," so called, whose nickname gives the ancient mother credit for a virtue she does not possess, while they are teaching the young women, are learning how absurd the barriers are that keep them from the full enjoyment of the best on every line old Harvard has to give. These are but straws that indicate which way the wind is blowing. Urged by its gathering stress, the bark which bears the hope of woman's final conquest for herself of "all that harms not distinctive womanhood" is drawing steadily near and more near to its desired haven. How many prophecies of what woman could and could not do have been shamed by the event! You know the story of the man who criticised the owl. "A bad piece of taxidermy! A live owl never looked like that; never carried himself after that fashion." All at once the owl changed his position! He wasn't a stuffed owl at all! He was a live owl and could do what he had done, and a good deal besides. And the live woman of our time has already done a good many things which the sagest critics have declared to be impossible for her. (She is not an ornamental fixture, but a living organism.) The trouble with the whole business of this criticism on the higher claims of woman is that it is rooted in the old idea of a world finished in six days, not in the new idea of a world which is still in process of creation; *going to be created* like Adam in the mediæval play.

"Where is one that born of woman altogether can escape
From the lower world within him, moods of tiger or of ape?
Man as yet is being made, and, ere the crowning age of ages,
Shall not æon after æon pass and touch him into shape?"

Man and woman are both on the way to their creation. Neither is half finished yet. Certainly what women are industrially, educationally, politically, is no measure of their possible attainment. What they are is the resultant of countless disabilities acting upon them through successive centuries. Loose them and let them go, and you will find they were not dead, but sleeping—not too sound to hear the voice that summons them to the full use of every faculty which they possess.

WOMAN'S PLACE IN THE PROFESSIONS.

There is one feature of the situation that is more impressive than the expansion of woman's intellectual opportunity. It is the "fruits meet for repentance" on their part who have denied to woman her fitness for the highest intellectual things. There are to-day hundreds of women practicing medicine with unquestionable success. They will do better now that Miss Garrett has completed the five hundred thousand dollars necessary to secure for them at Johns Hopkins University the full advantages of the medical curriculum of that noble institution. "The attractions are proportioned to the destinies," if Fourier was right; hence it would seem that it is not woman's destiny to be a lawyer in the coming civilization, seeing that her attraction for the profession of law has so far been very weak; though if they could dress and look as Ellen Terry does as Portia it might be a different matter. Architecture is much more attractive; and what more natural than that she who mainly builds the home should also build the house? She will not be likely to make the mistake of Balzac, whose completed house had two mutually independent stories with no stairway of any sort connecting them; nor to have the kitchen shunted off upon a siding, while the smoking-room and billiard-room have the main track to themselves. A few years ago the wonder was that the ministry attracted women hardly more than law. But there has been a change in this particular, especially in our Unitarian ministry, and with such success that more are sure to come. To Dr. Johnson's bearishness the wonder was not that women could preach well, but that they could do it at all. It was as wonderful to him as a dog's standing on his hind legs. In our time he would not even wonder that she can do it well; she has done it well so often that her success is no longer a matter of surprise. The pulpit, however, has witnessed only the least of her successes. The best of them have been in committee rooms and club rooms and upon platforms where important charitable and social and educational religious matters have been discussed, and where men of high repute as public speakers have often wished that they could speak as clearly and as forcibly, as eloquently and persuasively as their sisters in the craft. The improvement in the public speech of women during the last thirty years has certainly been very great. It has left far behind that smartishness which formerly infected it, and it has stopped girding at the men as if our inferiority or absurdity were their only stock in trade. Nowhere, I imagine, has this progress been more strongly marked than in the New York League of Unitarian Women. And so far there has been no perceptible falling off of womanly grace and sweetness in the women whom this enterprise attracts; at least within the limits of my own personal observation. The early agitators of the question of "women's rights" were made nervous and self-conscious by the novelty of their position, and therefore did themselves less credit than they might otherwise have done, and were less helpful to their cause than they might otherwise have been. Then, too, you will remember that "when the sons of God came together Satan came also among them"; to the antislavery meettings, Abigail Folsom, "that flea of conventions," as Emerson called her, and others who were "very trying" in their day. The daughters have not been more fortunate. Fools have rushed in where angels feared to tread, and the management of the enterprise has not infrequently fallen into the hands of women with so little culture or intelligence, so little judgment or common sense, that one has had frequently to brace himself with Beecher's following-up of the woman who had spoken long and not well at the prayer-meeting, " I believe in women's doing these things, nevertheless."

➤ WOMAN'S WORK IN RECENT LITERATURE.

But it is as a writer even more than as a speaker that woman has of late brought forth intellectual fruit so fair and large that the talk about the intellectual inferiority of women, which "motley" was almost the only wear twenty-five or thirty years ago, now seems as antiquated as a rope harness or a Navarino bonnet. I have not now in mind the creative genius of George Sand or George Eliot or Mrs. Stowe, to name no lesser lights. The disabilities of women have never been able to repress their creative genius. The social circle in which Jane Austen lived was as narrow and conventional as possible, but she is to us the only novelist of her generation whom we care to read, except as Sir Walter was writing his first novels as she was writing her last, and named her for all time " the dear, delightful Jane." I have not even in mind the host of women of the same general standing as the " mob of gentlemen who write with ease," in a purely literary way. I have in mind the literary work which is not literature for its own sake, but a vehicle for the discussion of the greatest intellectual and social and political and religious questions of our time. Nothing has been more characteristic of the last quarter of a century than this sort of work as done by women. There are many noble books to witness it, but its best witness is the pages of our great reviews and magazines. In this respect the English periodicals are more distinguished than our own, in which the emotional is apt to overtop the intellectual part, though in the way of pure literature our American women are not at all behind, if they are not in the lead. How often in the *Nineteenth Century* or *Contemporary Review*, side by side with the essays of Frances Power Cobbe and Julia Wedgwood and Millicent Garrett Fawcett, do we find those of noble lords and bishops, the lawmakers of England, which, but for the artificial dignity of their authors, could not gain admittance to those magazines which rely for their support on the subscriptions of those contributors who " work for nothing and find their own thread," as we used to say in my shoemaking days—write for nothing and subscribe in order to enjoy the satisfaction of reading their own contributions!

Now, these phenomena have an important bearing not only on the educational and practical life of women, but also on their political enfranchisement. For one of the most popular arguments against this has been that woman is a being " inferior to man but near to angels." Not only is this nonsense put to shame by woman's later intellectual development, suggesting the absurdity of measuring her possible force by any past achievement—though that from Sappho to De Stael and Helen Hunt has been no poor affair—but her later intellectual work has dealt so largely with questions approximately or absolutely political, and with so much calmness and clearness, that it furnishes a special argument of no little weight for her political enfranchisement. It is a significant fact that in the United States, where the appointing power of the President is the most important of all political questions, the solid monograph on this subject by Miss Lucy Salmon, a Vassar graduate and teacher if I am not mistaken, is by far the ablest and most exhaustive contribution to it that has yet been made. There the Spoils System draws its vile length along, a wounded snake, "scotched but not killed"; but that it must be killed, if we are not prepared to see it crush the nation in its slimy coil, it would seem only necessary to see it as it is in this dispassionate presentation to believe.

WOMEN IN THE CIVIL SERVICE.

There is a feature of the employment side of womanhood that is even more suggestive of her political possibility than her educational and intellectual triumphs. It is the steadily increasing hold of women on the civil service of the Government and upon allied positions of responsibility and trust. In Grant's second term there were already five thousand women acting as postmasters, and since then the number has been much increased. In the Treasury and other national departments the number of women doing their work with undeniable efficiency is large, and, like the family of Dr. Isaac Casaubon, "augments itself annually." Consider, also, in how many States women—to whom every electoral privilege and position is denied, except possibly voting on school matters and being voted for on school committee—have been appointed upon boards of charity and correction, and with what good average results. For the discharge of official business women have shown a striking aptitude, and they have brought to it a sense of responsibility and a conscientiousness which the male animals might emulate, if they would, to their advantage, and not theirs alone. It is the height of the ridiculous that, in a State where Hill and Murphy have attained the highest offices the people have to give, the right to vote against these crafty politicians is beyond the reach of women who in every intellectual and moral attribute are as superior to them as gold to silver; as real gold to counterfeit silver.

A little deeper and we shall come upon the right and duty of enfranchisement. It is only a step from the position of women in the civil service and upon boards of charity and correction to their position as voters for school committees and school appropriations, and to their service upon school committees as managers of such appropriations. Another step as long would take us to municipal suffrage, possibly to something broader than that of England and Scotland, where only the unmarried women vote who have a certain amount of property, without that abolition of the poll-tax, which is a step in the wrong direction—which, wherever it has been taken, ought to be retraced. Those who can not individually contribute so much as two dollars a year to the support of the Government had better stay outside the poll until they can. Let no bugbear of a property qualification frighten us from this position. The man or woman who can not save half a cent a day for public education, roads, lighted streets, and other Government expenses, has not the stuff in him or her out of which to make a decent citizen. From municipal suffrage not merely as an experiment, but as a proved success, to State and national, the way would not be long, or not too long for the security of our public life.

OBJECTIONS TO THE SUFFRAGE MUTUALLY DESTRUCTIVE.

But there are those, it seems, who heartily rejoice in both the industrial and educational expansion of woman's sphere, and even in so much of political expansion of this sphere as is necessary for the inclusion of voting for school committees and appropriations, and being voted for upon these lines, who are either indifferent to the general political enfranchisement or earnestly opposed to it; and sometimes with passionate heat. There are even those who have done much for the expansion of woman's work and education and her social usefulness, who have exposed themselves in furtherance of their ends to "the oppressor's scorn, the proud man's contumely," and to the disapprobation and dislike of other women, who are hardly less strenuous against the general political enfranchisement of woman than they have been for the widening of her industrial and educational and social life. Sometimes we find an ardor in the negative position which the positive could not excite. Here are the bayonet points that thrust the advocates of women's suffrage back on their reserves of courage and conviction. What reasons can they give for the faith that is in them that are equal to this novel state of things?

None, let us say frankly, that have not been given over and over again in general advocacy of the cause, or to meet the objections which its more or less trivial or intelligent opponents have brought against it all along. Perhaps it would be safe enough to leave these objections to their own mutual destruction. The first English sparrows sent to this country were sent all in one cage. The consequence was even more fatal than when the parrot and the monkey were allowed to entertain each other while the lady of the house was out to do her morning's shopping. They used each other up. There were no sparrows to speak of on the arrival of the cage here in America; only a lot of feathers and a few osseous remains. If the objections to woman's suffrage could be shut up by themselves, we might expect a similar result. Thus, for example, the objection that women are dominated by priests and clergymen would neutralize the objection that the voting of women would break up the institution of marriage and the home, seeing that the influence of priests and clergymen is generally conservative of marriage and the home. The objection that women could not be made to vote is neutralized by the objection that there are too many voters already; and the objection that the new system will breed difference and dissension in the home is negatived by the objection that women would vote just as their husbands told them. There has been, I think, a good deal of domestic difference as to the right and wrong way of voting in the United States during the last few years, and I doubt if it has been sweetened by the exclusive privileges of the men folk. The women who have said so warmly, "I wish *I* could vote," would have felt better if they could have done so; the repression of their ardor has sometimes been injurious to the domestic peace. As for the objection based on woman's sexual disabilities, it is much stronger against industrial than against political equality, and there the event has proved its general futility. Then, too, we hear, "Women have all the rights they want"; but, if this is so, how are we to account for the agitation for the suffrage which has been going on for forty years? "But only a few want it, and the majority ought not to be obliged to vote against their will." But if the considerable minority of men who do not care to vote should be increased to a majority, would that be a sufficient reason for general male disfranchisement? I think not. But it might be better to let the majority decide than for parties in the Legislature to outbid each other for the women's votes. If there is no natural right of suffrage as of individual liberty, as Mr. Spencer, I believe, contends, this objection applies to men and women equally and does not affect the question of women's voting in the least degree. "But women are already overburdened; why add to their responsibilities? It is the last straw that breaks the camel's back." Well, if they gave as little time to qualify themselves for voting as men give generally, they would not know the difference.

But this is a contemptible reply. There is a better: that women might give up some of their present burdens and responsibilities and nobody be the worse for it. Not many years ago the sentimental objection *par excellence* was, " But think of women going to the polls!" This objection never had much weight. In twenty-five years before the introduction of the Australian system I never saw a sign of rowdyism at our Brooklyn polls and no more tobacco juice than frequently in a horse-car or railway carriage

"Bids the rash gazer wipe his eye."

"Who will take charge of *you*," said some one to Lucretia Mott when one of the many anti-abolitionist mobs was in progress in New York. "This gentleman," she said, and slipped her hand into Isaiah Rynders's arm—and he the leader of the mob. It was a happy ruse and one of which any lady might avail herself in such distress. A few years ago Colonel Higginson's vision of "beauty for ashes" at the polls seemed a deceptive one; but already the sign "No smoking here" has been put up in many a polling-booth in deference to the women, as if "the smoke of their torment" were not "ascending forever and ever" in their own dining-rooms and sitting-rooms at home. The Australian system has, however, made all the sentimental and æsthetic objections to women's voting null and void. "There is retirement in the crown of a hat," said the devout sailor upon Nelson's deck. There is the same felicity in the sentinel's box where you are left alone for five minutes with your country, your conscience, and your God. But none of these objections could ever have had any weight for women who do their own marketing, feel the attractions of a "bargain counter," or go on friendly visits to the slums. The imagination of the objectors has been extremely fertile in devising possible contingencies of the most dreadful character. There was the saintly Bushnell telling us how much more easily women can disguise themselves than men. They could vote early and often—five or six times a day! One is reminded of Frank Stockton's complete letter-writer, in which he provides for various remote contingencies that are not provided for in the letter-writers generally. For example, " No. 6. From the author of a treatise on molecular subdivision, who has been rejected by a cascarilla-bark refiner, whose uncle has recently paid $63 for repairing a culvert in Indianapolis, to the tailor of a converted

Jew on the Eastern Shore of Maryland, who has requested the loan of a hypodermic syringe." "Never cross a river till you come to it," was Mr. Lincoln's sage advice and sound philosophy, which would have saved the obstructionists of every great reform from a world of vain imagination. But behind every ballot we are told there is a bullet; that the right to vote implies military duty; and Mr. Spencer, whose lightest word receives attention here, gives to this objection the most serious attention and evidently attaches to it great importance. But every child *in arms* is there by jeopardy of a mother's life, and in bearing the men who bear arms for their country it has been suggested that women do their part; getting no pensions, whatever loss of health the hard experience entails. But they do vastly more than this, as a bright array of Florence Nightingales and Clara Bartons testify by their unspeakable devotion to the sick, the wounded, and the dying; surely as indispensable to war, if war there needs must be, as any facing of the enemy's fire or storming of some bristling parapet. If war there needs must be; but it is Mr. Spencer's hope and faith that war will be eliminated from the better social state to which we are moving on. Then, if not before, his principal objection to woman's suffrage will entirely disappear. And, perhaps, in this connection Jael, the Kenite's wife, and Joan of Arc, and the Maid of Saragossa, and some other fighting women, ought not to be forgotten.

WHY WOMEN SHOULD DESIRE THE SUFFRAGE.

But what shall we say to the objection that, if it is woman's right to vote, it is her privilege to abstain from voting? But every person's right is every other person's duty, and it is no one's privilege to abstain from any duty, be it ne'er so disagreeable or hard. But "politics are so vile." "Women are viler," Ouida says; so keep the women out if you would not have the political elements more basely mixed than they are now. This is a very different way of putting it from that of the old sentimentalists, who imagined that the enfranchisement of women meant for every woman voter a new moral influence, simple, undefiled, into which no defiled thing could fall. Now, I have myself no sentimental persuasion of the absolute indefectibility of feminine morality, though I have imagined that when the psalmist said that men are a *little* lower than the angels he came pretty near the mark. It means something, I suppose, that in the reformatories of Massachusetts there are five times as many boys as girls; in the prisons twice as many men as women; in receipt of charity the same proportion. In vices of the tongue Smith and Wellesley and Vassar, I warrant you, differ from Harvard, Columbia, and Yale, as light from darkness and as heaven from hell. But no matter for all this. It is not pertinent. Personal character does not fix the character of the individual's vote as good or bad. However it may have been in the past, made wiser by experience, those who look to woman's voting for the immediate and complete regeneration of politics are few and far between. I am sure that I have never thought of arguing the enfranchisement of women on this ground. But take the other horn of the dilemma: It is the privilege of women to abstain from "dirty politics." Not if they can help to make them cleaner than they are. To those who tell me that the best women do not want to vote I answer: "By that sign they whom you call so are not the best women." The best women must want to vote, because they must want to help their husbands and their brothers, their fathers and their sons, in the good work of building up here in America a righteous nation whose God is the Eternal Righteousness and Truth and Love. Grand words are those of my friend Gannett: "Not suffrage for women so much as women for suffrage is the hope beyond the hope. The whole 'sex' argument against woman suffrage in low-level politics reads as argument for woman suffrage in high-level politics." That is to say, assume that politics are irretrievably corrupt, and women may well hesitate to enter into them. But such an assumption is unworthy of any noble person, man or woman. The corruption is not irretrievable, and every noble woman, equally with every noble man, will desire to do her part in bettering the bad and bringing in the best; if not by voting, then in some other way.

"Inexpedient!" says a remonstrant, who has as good a right to her remonstrance as any other who has lifted up her voice, "Yes, forever inexpedient until the highest type of morality and the clearest sense of justice . . . are reached by all women." But what if men had been obliged to wait for this degree of excellence? Republican government would not have yet begun to be. In the exercise of their political functions men have heightened the type of their morality and clarified their sense of justice. This placard, "None but angels need apply," is like telling a boy "You shall not swim till you can swim perfectly," or "You shall not play till you can play like Rubinstein." But Rubinstein, when asked how he could play the Erl-King so wonderfully, as if a god were thundering at the keys, said: "Simply by practice." By practice women must come into the fullness of political knowledge. They must learn by failure and mistake. There is no other way.

> "Cast the bantling on the rocks,
>   Suckle him with the she-wolf's teat;
> Wintered with the hawk and fox,
>   Power and speed be hands and feet."

SOCIAL LEVERAGE OF THE BALLOT.

You will think, perhaps, that I am keeping this thing too much in the air; treating it too theoretically; not with sufficient reference to the actual status of women in society and to the actual working of the experiment of women's suffrage where it has been tried. But you can not think so more confidently than I do myself. And I shall not deny that the actual status of women in society is such to-day that one of the very strongest arguments for women's suffrage thirty and forty years ago has been shorn of so much of its strength that it is very different from what it was. For that argument was that not till women had the suffrage would they have those rights of property and that control over their minor children which are enjoyed by men. In short, the argument for self-protection was the strongest argument that women had to offer for their suffrage, though others, much more sentimental, were perhaps urged more frequently. But in the years that have elapsed since the beginning of the agitation there has been a progressive amelioration of the status of women in these particulars. It has been to a considerable degree a consequence of the agitation, but in part a resultant of the general tendency to social betterment and a more equitable adjustment of all personal relations. The amelioration has been welcomed cordially by the women suffragists with but the faintest apprehension that some of their best thunder was being carried off by the manly Greeks who were bringing such fine gifts to their sex. It has gone so far in several of the States that a counter-agitation has been seriously demanded to redress the balance which has been depressed too much upon the women's side. And still the fact remains, however equitable the laws, their operation as controlled by special legislation and even by the courts is not by any means so favorable to women as it would be if they were on the ground to look after their own affairs. When I was in London I went to Christ's Hospital, where Charles Lamb and Coleridge went to school, and tried to imagine them still sitting there among the hundreds of blue-coated boys. Hundreds of blue-coated boys, but not a single girl there or anywhere else on the foundation! But there was nothing in the terms of the foundation to give boys its exclusive privileges. Here is one instance of a thousand where moneys and privileges have been diverted from their intended course, because women have had no part in their appropriation and control. The chivalry of American gentlemen is proverbial, but our legislators are not always gentlemen. The average man upon the street car or the ferryboat has been known to shield himself consciously with his newspaper from the pleading eyes of the tired lady standing up before him. The doors of senate chambers and assembly rooms are a much better protection than the newspapers from the pleading eyes. But few of the legislators that sit behind these doors have Governor Flower's indifference to the votes. Their sensitiveness to them is remarkable, and that of the whole body of elected and appointed public servants. A prospective vote is that wonderful oiled feather of the story which makes keys, otherwise abominably refractory, turn as if to music and admit the bearer to innumerable advantages from which, without it, he would be debarred.

RECENT EXPERIMENTS IN WOMAN SUFFRAGE.

Consider next what is the bias on the argument for women's suffrage of the actual working of the experiment so far as it has been tried, and this means widely in the direction of municipal and school suffrage both in this country and Great Britain, but very narrowly in the direction of the general suffrage of women on the same terms with men and to the same extent. The latter we once had in Utah, but it was a brief experiment. In Washington Territory the experiment was a much longer one, but did not finally commend itself to a majority when the time came for making a State constitution. In Wyoming the present

Governor assures me that it is a complete success, but his *ipse dixit* is accompanied by no facts by which I can judge for myself or help you to an intelligent judgment. There are those who are not unfriendly to woman's suffrage who have followed the course of it in Wyoming with a troubled mind. It certainly has not had that elevating influence on the politics of the State which its more sanguine friends had confidently hoped to see. It has gone far to justify the fears of those who prophesied that the emotionalism of women and their amenableness to personal considerations would be a tremendous and injurious bias on their votes. In Kansas the municipal voting has done much to controvert the doctrine that women do not want to vote, while it would appear that even more violently than the men of that unhappy State they have been carried away by the vagaries of the People's party. In England and Scotland municipal suffrage has drawn out a heavy vote, courted alike by the Liberals, who are persuaded that women are liberally inclined, and by the Conservatives, who look to them to prevent the disestablishment of the National Church. That its general influence has been favorable to good government I am assured by those who are upon the scene and whose judgment I can trust. In Massachusetts, which must be regarded as the banner State of the reform, the history of the experiment of school suffrage is better calculated to make the judicious grieve than to encourage the reformers' hearts. But then it has been biased since 1888 by a most unfortunate controversy growing out of Roman Catholic opposition to a statement in Swinton's *Outlines of General History*, which a teacher had perverted to the effect that "an indulgence is a permission to commit sin." The statement in the book was quite within the bounds of truth; the perversion of the teacher hardly an exaggeration of the practical working of the system of indulgences under conditions favorable to its abuse. The history was dropped in deference to the Roman Catholic demand, as it should not have been, and thereupon ensued a violent Protestant crusade against Roman Catholic influence, demanding the ostracism of all Roman Catholics from the school board and the expulsion of those Protestants who had favored the concession to the Roman Catholics implied in the dropping of Swinton's History. Seldom in this country have fiercer religious passions been engendered than by this controversy. The anti-Romanists went far to justify the application to themselves of the name Know-Nothings, formerly applied to the Native American party. Twenty-two thousand women registered, Protestants and Catholics in about equal parts, and the anti-Catholics elected their whole school ticket. The next year the registration fell off to ten thousand, probably a sign that the Roman Catholic clerical leaders had resolved to let the Protestants do their worst, and make that the basis of their demand for a part of the school fund for their parochial education. Since then the controversy has had a various ebb and flow. In this last election the anti-Catholic women dictated the school ticket to the Republicans, and it was carried by the fusion of these bodies, leaving the situation as precarious and miserable as it has ever been. My impression is that this course of events has been viewed with much satisfaction by a large majority of the woman suffragists of Massachusetts. To have the women vote and show their power and exercise a controlling influence has been a result so dazzling that it has blinded them to the substantial merits of the case. But there has been a goodly company of women, the Massachusetts School Suffrage Association, that has made a splendid fight against the narrowness and intolerance of the anti-Catholic movement.

There is little in this series of events to encourage any one to hope from woman's suffrage as such an improved condition of our political and social life. The bias of that suffrage has been distinctly on the wrong side of the controversy, and has done serious injury to the Commonwealth. But there has been nothing here that should surprise, however it may pain, the woman-suffragist who knows the history of woman and her emotional temperament and her subjection to traditional influences in religious matters. In 1854–'55 there was an outbreak of this silliness among the men of the United States, and great good came of it in that it broke up the old party lines and made new combinations possible. When people begin to think on any subject they generally think unwisely, especially if they think with their hearts, not with their heads. They do better as they go on. The last Boston election especially demonstrated the capacity of women for careful and efficient political organization. Throughout the State evidence would seem to be upon their side who say that women do not care to vote. In my native town hardly a baker's dozen out of a thousand or twelve hundred women gave an affirmative answer to the assessors who put the question on their annual round, and their negative was sometimes expressed with vehement contempt. But towns and villages do not frequently divide upon school questions. Not infrequently both parties support one and the same ticket. And still the friendliest to woman's suffrage must confess that even where the agitation has been kept up longest and most powerfully, only a small minority of the women apprehend the suffrage as a crying need, or the duty to exercise it, where it has been accorded, as one from which they may not be excused.

(EQUAL SUFFRAGE A LOGICAL NECESSITY UNDER A)
(REPUBLICAN GOVERNMENT.)

Reverting from the practical experiment and the objections that are made to the enfranchisement of women, we come upon the central fact that the phrases which are more dear to us than any others in the political sphere, which express our loftiest political ideals, are phrases that carry along with them the necessity for women's suffrage if they are not going to be shorn of half their meaning. "Governments owe their just powers to the consent of the governed." Of course any one who cares to do so can say with Rufus Choate that the phrases of the Declaration of Independence are "glittering generalities." But Wendell Phillips's reply that they are "blazing ubiquities" is also worth remembering; and if Government does derive its just powers from the consent of the governed, seeing that women are governed equally with men, how but by voting can their consent be given? The family is the unit, we are told. But how about the innumerable women who have "no visible means of support" except their own brave hands? Then there is the great phrase of Lincoln and Parker, "Government of the people, for the people, by the people." It will hardly be denied that women are the people equally with men; and if they are, we have not government by the people till they obtain the franchise. "No taxation without representation." Here is another golden phrase—the watchword of the Revolutionary War, the principle on which it was fought to a successful issue. But women have "virtual representation," we are told. And James Otis answers for us : "No such phrase as virtual representation was ever known in law or constitution. It is altogether a sublety and an illusion, wholly unfounded and absurd." This "virtual representation" is but the "family unit" by another name which does not make it smell a bit more sweet. No class can safely be permitted to make laws for any other. Women may be no wiser than men. In political matters, without immediate experience, how can they be as wise? But equally with men they have the inherited experience of the race, for they inherit from both sides of the house equally with the men. They may not at first be wiser for themselves than men can be for them. But after some blundering and indirection they will be so. The instinct of self-protection, like the instinct of self-preservation, is exceeding strong. There are doubtless women like the Irishman who preferred his grievance to its abolition. But the woods are not full of them, and they are not likely to increase their numbers with the lapse of time.

EDUCATIONAL VALUE OF THE SUFFRAGE.

But I believe there is a higher ground than this for the enfranchisement of women. It is that the exercise of political privileges is itself an education. When women vote they will begin to cultivate that much-neglected branch of study—American history; and perhaps they will discover that it is the grandest history ever written. Suffrage will enforce the duty of the educated women to educate the ignorant of their sex. Those who are now remonstrants will be found obedient to this heavenly vision. Once when my little boy was in a pet I said to him, calling from my study, "Come up here." He remonstrated, saying, "I don't want to." "Well, then," said I, "stay where you are." "No," said he, "I'll come up if I don't want to." And so, I doubt not, the remonstrants against woman's suffrage will come up *if they don't want to;* come up to the exercise of their right when it is once accorded them; come up to their duty of advancing the general and political education of the women of whose political influence or subservience they are afraid.

That the right use of suffrage requires the highest possible intelligence and the noblest character—this is the highest ground of all on which the enfranchisement of women can be urged. Every woman that hath *this* hope purifieth herself. How can she make herself more wise, more just, more earnest, more sincere, if haply she may help to bring a nobler wisdom and a higher justice, a grander earnestness and a more absolute sincerity, into all civic, state, and national affairs? "For their sakes I consecrate myself," every true woman that cherishes this hope will say of those whose social circumstances have been less favorable than her own. But the elevation of her sex will not be the highest aim of her ambition. This shall be to make the nation that surpassing good which it can be only through the harmonious co-operation of both men and women for all highest ends. Whom God hath joined together let no man put asunder.

ABSTRACT OF THE DISCUSSION.

Dr. Louise Fiske Bryson:

I have been thinking it was very unkind to ask me to follow Mr. Chadwick, for he is exceedingly clever, and full of wit and learning too. I am inclined to wish I were not here, for I do not agree with anybody, and I never did. I liked to hear what Mr. Chadwick had to say about the great women who lived so long ago and so far away as Sappho or George Sand or Joan of Arc, and who had so much courage and ability. But how does it apply to us here? I venture to say that not one of us here has the courage to do what George Eliot did. We like to have compliments paid us; but how would the men like to be told that they were delightful creatures because Shakespeare wrote so wonderfully; or how would the sailor like to be praised because Columbus discovered America? What are women doing now?—that is the question. The men or women who are not doing this or that great thing may nevertheless be doing their simple duty. It is no compliment to a woman to say she is just like some man. Tell her, if you wish to praise her, that she is like herself, and is doing a work that no man can do. Some women complain that they are no longer treated with consideration by men in public places. In the street car and ferryboat I feel that I have a right to stand up when I am going out for pleasure and when men are out for work, or returning home weary at night. If women want seats, why not be as prompt as the men who get them? Women who are trained to business have to learn to be prompt.

It is hardly fair to speak in terms of generalization, but I should say that men are beasts of burden that clear the way and overcome obstacles, while women are the artificers of life. It is a matter of nervous structure and physical and mental adaptation. The chief mental sexual difference is a greater distribution of the lower or vital nerve centers in woman than in man. Women are capable of enduring much more than men. Humanity is divided into two parts, working in different directions but meeting again in the home to enjoy the fruits of their labor. The more social an art is, the more woman excels in it. She is pre-eminently social. In that line she does her only distinctly original work. Women have a talent for affairs. They are good diplomats. As the world becomes less militant, the woman question assumes a different aspect. No woman has a good time when wars are going on.

The Social and Political Status of Women. 195

How little we know of this subject as it presents itself in other countries! I didn't know that there was anybody living who hadn't the right to do the things we have been doing in America since the colonial days. But I have just been reading a German book, by Miss Heléne Lange, asking that women might become teachers! There are no women teachers in that country, it seems. The condition of women in Germany is traceable to the fact that Germany is a militant country, where woman has other things to do than take part in social organization. In an ideal community all men and all women would work; but there are three conditions necessary: no one should work too hard or too long; there should be variety in the work; and the work must be productive. I can not speak about the suffrage. I don't know anything about it. I only know of woman's adaptation to this work of social organization, and that her functions and qualifications for work, in general, are entirely different from man's.

MRS. EMMA BECKWITH:

It is idle to talk about what woman would or would not do under certain assumed conditions, for the simple reason that we have no data on which to base an opinion. We can only judge from what we have actually seen, or what we hope might be true. What the inhabitants of one State, either men or women, have done, might be offset in another by actions entirely diffferent. Because women citizens in Wyoming behave in a becoming manner on election day, it is not therefore to be counted as certain that women would do likewise in New York. Celia B. Whitehead once said : " It is this eternal lumping of women that I object to." And I agree with her. In the plan of creation as generally accepted, though it is rather shaky when the search-light of investigation is thrown upon it, woman was the last thing created. Hence she should be the best. But, according to history, she has become side-tracked in some unexplained manner, and was reduced to the level of the animals. She was not allowed a soul worth saving. Afterward, in the general evolution of all things, she somehow became possessed of that commodity. She acquired sufficient intelligence to be taught how to read—the Bible only, however, at first. The enemies of her advancement here builded better than they knew. She has been limited in her advancement by her exclusive devotion to that book. With her reasoning powers lulled to sleep, how can she have intelligent opinions regarding worldly matters? Little girls come into the world destined, yet a while, to be reared just as their mothers have been. Fashion has made a few changes in their dress, but from birth their training is different from man's. If of Chinese birth, their feet are not allowed to grow. I have heard that a society has lately been formed in China for "the advancement and growth of natural feet." The whole end and aim of woman's existence, the world over, is to become a wife. She must look pretty, not redden her eyes by crying, not cause wrinkles by scowling, not romp or play with the boys. Girls are made to feel their sex all through life. This is all wrong. Take away this ever-present feeling of sex. Make all children feel they are human beings, with like desires for advancement. Daughters are made to feel their dependence on their fathers in a most uncomfortable manner. Marriage is thus made to seem preferable to living a life so odious as that of an "old maid." So the young girl makes vows she does not intend to fulfill, and then comes trouble. If women had always been counted as human beings, allowed to work and live as men do, we might then begin to talk of the "political status" of women. Now they have none. Men say women must demand the ballot before it will be granted; but not an Indian or negro in the South demanded it; yet it was granted to the ignorant as well as the competent. The only reason I could ever find in favor of free trade is the havoc so much "protection" has wrought among women. But the demand for equal rights is bound to grow. Woman's voice was never heard to such an extent as in this last presidential campaign. Two women sat as delegates from Wyoming in the National Republican Convention. The Democratic Convention, not to be outdone in gallantry, allowed the women's protest to be read. I sometimes think the "boss" idea in politics was evolved out of the habit men have acquired of "bossing" their wives at home, and that it has gotten so strong that they do the bidding of the political boss, recognizing his authority as rightful from sheer force of habit.

MR. CHADWICK, in reply: The New Testament says that the priest in the temple profanes the law of the temple and is blameless. It is already past ten, and though I am a priest in the temple I will not profane it or violate the rules of this Association by prolonging the discussion. I will only say that in so short a time I have seldom heard so much matter with which I so strongly agreed—and disagreed. I most heartily agreed with Dr. Bryson's strong insistence upon the fundamental difference in sex. Because I so strongly believe in this fundamental difference, I believe it is safe for woman to do anything she can do, and the difference in sex characteristics will not be disturbed. I remember when I was a boy, in Marblehead, they were afraid the old almshouse would tumble down, so they put a charge of gunpowder under it to get it out of the way; but they could not blow it up, it stood so firm. So this difference between men and women will persist through all time, in spite of all the justice we can do to woman.

THE ECONOMIC POSITION OF WOMAN

BY
CAROLINE B. LE ROW
AUTHOR OF THE YOUNG IDEA, EDUCATION AS A FACTOR IN CIVILIZATION, ETC.

COLLATERAL READINGS SUGGESTED:

Spencer's Principles of Ethics, Principles of Sociology, and Social Statics; Mill's Subjection of Women; Gunton's Principles of Social Economics; Adams's Woman's Work and Worth; Carroll D. Wright's articles on *The Working Girls of Boston, The Economic Position of Women*, etc., in the Arena and Forum; Helen Campbell's Prisoners of Poverty, and other writings; Miss Martin and Miss Henrotin's The Social Status of European and American Women; Le Roy Beaulieu's Le Travail des Femmes aux XIX Siècle; Helène Lange's Higher Education of Woman in Europe and Woman's Work in America; Anna Nathan Meyer's Woman's Work in America; Virginia Penny's Think and Act, Employments for Women, and Work and Wages; Caroline H. Dall's College, Market, and Court; Thorold Rogers's Work and Wages; August Bebel's Woman; Dr. Kay's Moral and Physical Condition of the Working Classes; Gail Hamilton's Woman's Worth and Worthlessness; Dinah Mulock Craik's A Woman's Thoughts about Woman.

THE ECONOMIC POSITION OF WOMAN.

By Caroline B. Le Row.

The Fundamental Facts of Evolution.

There are certain fundamental facts of the physical and social universe with which the student of evolution is as familiar as with the syllables of his own name. These are the persistence of force; the tendency of all living forms to adjust themselves to their environment, resulting in the struggle for existence and the survival of the fittest; the law of natural selection, of segregation and differentiation, and that all advancement is from the simple to the complex, from the uniform to the multiform, from the indefinite to the definite, from the homogeneous to the heterogeneous.

In support of these propositions is offered a mass of testimony gathered from the most intelligent study of physical science, of biology, and of the life of man through his entire development and in all his relations—physical, mental, social, and moral. So far nothing in the profoundest study of these subjects has been found to weaken or refute a single one of these premises. On the contrary, the more extended the study in regard to the field covered and the time devoted to the investigation, the greater becomes the amount, the more satisfactory the nature, of the proof afforded; and the heart of the evolutionist is repeatedly gladdened by the beautiful consistency which characterizes all phases of the discoveries made by his hand and his head, each fact being related, and often in numerous ways, to all other facts in the universe, these fitting with and into each other as perfectly as the tiny wheels in the lady's thumbnail watch, or as the spiral gears which drive the mightiest engines in the world.

The Woman Movement no Exception to Evolution's Law.

Such being the consistency everywhere observable of what we call "law," the believer in evolution accepts the additional fact that this law is the governing power and decides certain matters in certain ways, regardless of personal prejudice or preference. He early learns submission to this law, whether the result of its working please or offend him, or even if it prove to be at variance with all his preconceived notions of things.

The evolutionist can make no exception, for in this philosophy it is not the exception which proves the rule; one real exception would prove the whole rule to be worthless. If he concedes the truth of the laws underlying the evolution of vegetal and animal life, just as submissively must he concede the truth of those governing man's social and industrial existence, no matter how repugnant to his feelings may be the conclusions forced upon him.

Additional emphasis is laid upon this point because of the almost universal opposition which exists to what is popularly known as "the woman movement." Disregarding the action of a universal law in all nature, the modern attitude of woman has been looked upon, even by many otherwise clear-sighted and logical observers, as an abnormal condition, the only comfort to be derived from a contemplation of it consisting in the belief that it would be as self-destructive and as transient in duration as it was monstrous in development.

It is not difficult to find the explanation of this feeling. This new element in sociology is utterly opposed to all the doctrine, belief, and practice of all the ages. It has revealed itself with comparative suddenness, and in every phase which it presents, it shows itself to be at variance not only with long-existing tradition and custom, but with the selfishness from which the race is but gradually emerging.

THE PRIMITIVE INDUSTRIAL STATUS OF MEN AND WOMEN.

Starting in our consideration of this subject from the same point where we would begin in the investigation of any sociological movement, we first give our attention to the primitive condition of society, the economic relations therein of men and women to each other and to the world.

In the first or savage state of man we find him merely a huntsman and a warrior, always on the alert to secure food for himself and family, to defend himself and them from the attacks of wild beasts and the assaults of his enemies.

What more natural or logical than that his mate should remain indoors to prepare the food and clothing and care for the children of the family?

In the primitive social condition which in due time followed, men and women labored alike in their efforts to supply the simplest wants of life; the former engaged in agriculture and commerce, the latter making clothing and attending to the household. In this stage of social development nearly every family owned a loom and a spinning-wheel.

Compare for one moment this simple condition of family and social life with the conditions which exist to-day throughout the homes of the civilized world and the society of civilized man. Can any sane person, especially can any philosopher or evolutionist, wonder that the difference in the needs, ideals, and aspirations of the race is as marked and as significant as that between its past and its present form of life?

From the earliest ages and through the entire world woman has been literally a beast of burden, doing in field, mill, and mine such work as is done by ass, ox, or horse, and in many cases being the silent sharer in their labors. To this day in some parts of the Old World she is driven in the same harness with these other domestic animals.

The transition from field to house labor, or rather the division of one from the other—for at no time, no matter how hard woman has worked outside, has she been exempt from the work of the family inside—was a little advancement for the sex; but D. D. ("Domestic Drudge") have, until the last half century, been the only initials indicative of her employment which woman has been privileged to attach to her name.

THE HIGHER EDUCATION OF WOMAN AS AFFECTING HER ECONOMIC POSITION.

The writer Diesterweg says, "Education is liberation," and most emphatically true have his words been proved in the matter of woman's employment. Opportunities for her employment have increased in direct ratio to the skill and ability developed by education. Nothing is more gratifying than the ready appreciation she has shown of every educational advantage offered her, and the practical use she has endeavored to make of it. Half a century ago not a college for women was in existence; the world evidently was a convert to the doctrine of Fénelon: " Keep young girls within bounds, and teach them that there should be for their sex a modesty with respect to knowledge as delicate as that inspired by the horror of vice." To-day there are twenty-five thousand students in women's colleges, and sixteen thousand women in co-educational institutions. Switzerland, Sweden, Norway, Denmark, Italy, Belgium, even Russia, have opened to women the doors of their universities. German Austria and Hungary are making a beginning in the same direction. In most of these institutions women enjoy the same rights and privileges that the men have in regard to higher education, and acquire the same degrees in the arts and the professions. In Holland women have never been debarred from the universities, and are enrolled in four of the leading colleges. Spain and Portugal are gradually following these good examples, leaving practically the women of Germany as the only ones in the Old World debarred from university study. Who can doubt that such a tremendous educational evolution as this indicates corresponding advancement along all lines of the world's thought and work?

WOMAN'S INDUSTRIAL PROGRESS IN AMERICA.

Fifty-eight years ago Harriet Martineau found American women engaged in only seven industries besides that of domestic service. To-day the occupation of professional diver is mentioned as the only one upon which women have not entered, and the avenues to trade, art, and the professions which, according to evolutionary law, are constantly becoming more numerous and varied, are daily spreading out in new directions for her eager and ambitious feet. Nothing is more difficult than the securing of reliable figures which shall represent the amount of time consumed and the rate of progress made by woman in her efforts to become a wage-earner, and thereby a self-supporting member of the community. At no time could we say " Lo, here!" or " Lo, there!" and state precisely either what woman was doing or how much ground she was gaining in industrial fields. Her taking possession has been like the flowing in of the tide upon the shore—scarcely perceptible from one hour to another, yet surprising us at last with the advance which has been quietly and almost imperceptibly made.

So while from year to year woman has been steadily advancing in the ranks of the world's workers, it is only recently, and in the perplexing complications growing out of our rapidly-changing social conditions, that we have begun to realize all that is implied by her radically-changed attitude toward the work of the world; to realize also the necessity for greater care and skill in the collection of figures bearing upon this great industrial revolution, the future results of which no man can foresee, to the end that the significance of this vast sociological movement may be fully understood and wisely dealt with.

WOMAN IN THE COLUMBIAN EXPOSITION.

One of the most important features of the Columbian Exposition of 1893 is the gathering of statistics respecting the industrial condition of women. These statistics have been tabulated in every township by reliable individuals, and their data compiled in a monograph which will form the basis of a valuable history of the social and industrial status of women in this age, for future reference by students of sociology. The Woman's Building was designed by a woman, erected for women, and is to be controlled by women. In its exhibits will be told the chronological history of the origin, development, and progress of the industries of women from the earliest time to the present. The building is intended to symbolize the discovery and recognition of woman's talent, the association of women in the stupendous work of its design and erection, and in the discussions of the great congresses to be held during the Exposition, representing the spiritual and mental growth and status of civilization as the different exhibits illustrate its material resources; and, above all, in the organization of women themselves with its delegates from every country in the world save one—Turkey—and representing every industry, art, science, and interest of the age.

EARLY STATISTICS OF WOMAN'S WORK IN AMERICA.

An attempt was made in 1830, and still another ten years later, to procure statistics relating to woman's work. But correct figures were difficult to obtain, and the results proved to be so valueless that they were not even preserved. This apparent waste of effort proved to be, however, a valuable lesson in experience by which our legislators profited. It showed the necessity of a change in methods, and the need of more time in carrying them out. Even then the methods were for a number of years largely experimental, and are still far from perfect. But woman had not been idle even in the literary and professional field, although little statistical recognition was made of her labor.

Out of seventy-eight newspapers published in the colonies, sixteen were edited by women, all but two championing the cause of liberty and justice. The first paper to publish the Declaration of Independence was edited and printed by a woman.

The trade of shoemaking employed at first only a few dozen women. The census return of 1880 gave the total number of women in that field of labor as twenty-one thousand.

When in 1789 Miss Betsy Metcalf, of Dedham, Massachusetts, discovered a method of bleaching and weaving straw for hats and bonnets, she opened a new avenue for woman's work, and ten years ago twenty thousand women were engaged in the straw-braiding industry.

Until 1826 the manufacture of stockings was woman's exclusive province. At that time knitting machines were set up, but the work has always remained largely as the occupation of women and children.

James I of England, wanting to utilize the mulberry trees indigenous to the soil of America, forwarded silk cocoons to this country, offering bounties in tobacco and money to those who made the greatest success in this line of manufacture. These prizes were invariably taken by women, three of whom—Mrs. Pinckney, Miss Grace Fisher, and Miss Susan Wright—became famous before the Revolution as silk growers and weavers.

Influence of the Factory System on Woman's Economic Position.

Carroll D. Wright tells us that "the entrance of woman into the industrial field was assured when the factory system of labor displaced hand labor. The age of invention must be held accountable for the entrance of woman into a field entirely strange and unknown to her prior to that age. The attraction to woman to earn more than she could earn as a domestic servant, or in some fields of agricultural labor, or to earn something where before she had earned nothing, became the economic force which induced her to assume the position and submit to all the conditions of a new economic factor."

The invention of the cotton gin is credited to Eli Whitney, but it is said on good authority that it was really invented by Mrs. Nathanael Greene, widow of the Revolutionary hero of that name, and that she permitted Mr. Whitney to claim the patent through fear of the ridicule and loss of social position which recognition of her work might entail.

The cotton gin, brought into being in 1794, has been truly called "the foster mother of slavery in America." The invention made slave labor valuable in the South, and caused in the North the erection of many factories into which women flocked by hundreds, altering thereby the whole status of the labor market in America.

Twenty years afterward came the power loom and the introduction of what is known as the modern factory system. In 1816 sixty-six thousand women were employed in the work of spinning. At that time all the weaving was done by hand looms. The census of 1860 shows that of all the mill workers in New England, sixty-five per cent were women.

THE SEWING MACHINE AS AFFECTING WOMAN'S WORK.

The sewing machine inaugurated another industrial period for woman. This invention appeared in 1846, though it was not in general use until nearly ten years later.

The civil war was a very natural cause for thousands of women to seek means for self-support. In 1868 there were in Boston twenty thousand women working at starvation rates, most of them at the needle, and fully one half of the number earning only twenty and twenty-five cents a day. In the same year in New York there were thirty thousand women engaged in shirt-making, the wretched conditions of whose existence, according to the New York Herald, "beggared all power of description." Women who could get machines worked for two dollars and fifty cents a week; those who could not, for even less than that sum; and a similar condition of things existed at the same time in many of our other large cities—the direct result of a war which deprived thousands of women of home and support.

RECENT INDUSTRIAL STATISTICS REGARDING WOMEN.

The United States Census of 1860 was the first one which gave any definite statement as to the work of women and children, the figures even then being difficult to obtain and known to be in some measure inaccurate.

The New York Bureau of Statistics, in 1885, under the direction of Mr. Charles M. Peck, reported the number of working women in New York—not in domestic labor, but in actual handicrafts—as two hundred thousand, nearly one third of this number living by the needle.

In all such estimates it must be borne in mind that large numbers of women are deterred by pride from reporting themselves as members of the working class.

The gain of women in trades over the census of 1870 was sixty-four per cent, the entire percentage of women workers for the whole country being forty-nine. It is reasonably expected that the returns for 1890 will indicate a further increase of ten per cent.

Miss Clare de Graffenreid, special agent for the United States Department of Labor, divides woman and child labor into five classes, New England being pre-eminently the textile district. In Boston alone, out of 17,427 workers, one tenth earn only from $100 to $150 yearly.

The second group she locates in New York, where the employments are much more various, and the foreign element largely predominates.

The third group goes west, the city of Philadelphia leading in population and in women workers.

The Southern group Miss Graffenreid considers unique, and says concerning those who form it: "Nowhere else in the world do so many well-bred women, bankrupt and bereft of male providers, labor at manual callings as at the South, pursuing, without loss of caste, vocations which elsewhere involve social ostracism."

The last group is found farther west. Here it becomes hard for the native workers to hold their own against the enormous foreign population.

At the close of the war about one hundred new avenues of industry had been opened to women. In the ten years following the number more than doubled, while to-day there are over four hundred occupations which women are following with more or less social and financial success. In the great manufactories of America there were, in 1885, 281,822 men and 112,762 women. Woman has now entered every field, and is distinguishing herself in art, music, the drama, in medicine, journalism, literature, education, theology, and science.

MRS. MERIWETHER'S STATISTICS.

Mrs. Lide Meriwether, of Memphis, Tennessee, reported the following figures in 1888. They were gathered from the editors of various magazines—literary, medical, agricultural, etc.—and their accuracy is vouched for: There are in the United States of America, among women, 110 lawyers; 165 ministers; 320 authors; 588 journalists; 2,061 artists; 2,136 architects, chemists, pharmacists; 2,016 stock-raisers and ranchers; 5,134 Government clerks; 2,438 physicians and surgeons; 56,800 farmers and planters; 13,182 professional musicians; 21,071 clerks and bookkeepers; 144,650 heads of commercial houses; 155,000 public-school teachers.

In Massachusetts there are 300,000 bread-winning women, of which Boston has 20,000. In New York there are 200,000 working women and girls. The American Cultivator gives the following figures based upon the census of 1890: In Germany there are 5,500,000 working women; in France, 3,750,000; in England, 4,000,000; in Austria-Hungary, 3,500,000; in America, 2,700,000, making a total in five countries of 19,450,000 self-supporting women.

WOMAN'S INDUSTRIAL DISADVANTAGES.

In the industrial field woman labors under great disadvantages. She has no capital to begin with, and to earn her own capital under the present rate of wages is plainly impossible. Even man can not do it as he once did. Small beginnings can not survive competition with trust companies, corporations, and long-established wealthy business firms.

Society has not been educated to regard woman as an employer, except in household service, and a realization of her ability in this position is yet to be brought about.

Public opinion is still largely opposed to the idea of women being independent socially, and financially self-supporting. The seclusion of the home is still considered to be for them the only safe and honorable environment. Time must be allowed for the gradual dying out of this long-cherished belief, but when it dies—as die it surely must, and its dissolution is already begun—with it will also perish a host of pernicious notions which will leave the world better for their departure.

DEPRESSING INFLUENCE OF WAGE DISCRIMINATION.

In many cases want of skill, due to the lack of proper training, is accountable for the low rate of wages which women are forced to accept. The law of supply and demand rules in the field of woman's work as in every other direction, and in precisely the same way. Again, much of woman's labor is intermittent from its very nature, causing many and long periods of forced idleness. The universal belief, inculcated in the minds of girls from the time that their minds are capable of receiving an idea, that marriage is the only desirable destiny of a woman, has much to do with this indecision, lack of preparation, and, in some degree, irregularity, in the beginning and the carrying on of any kind of work.

There can be no profitable discussion of the question whether women should receive equal pay with men for the same work unless the work done by the woman is in every way as good as that done by the man. Not the sex of the worker, but the amount and quality of the work is to be considered, and when in these respects the work of a woman is fully equal to that of a man, it is not easy to see upon what ground any inequality of wages can be defended.

Everywhere women are discriminated against as to wages. In the Government departments at Washington women doing exactly the same work as men get only two thirds as much pay. And this is simply because they belong to a disfranchised sex. A certain senator, on being appealed to on this subject a short time ago, replied: "Madam, if we should give as good pay to women as to men, all of the women would soon be driven out of the departments. The voters of the country are males, and the demand for the places by men is so great that we are able to retain women only on the plea of economy because we can get them cheaper."

WOMEN'S LACK OF INDUSTRIAL ORGANIZATION.

The lack of organization among women is another powerful hindrance to their industrial advancement. Organiza-

The Economic Position of Woman. 209

tion has lifted many trades to the dignity of skilled labor; has raised wages for thousands of laborers; has shortened the hours of labor for thousands more; has forced reforms in factory laws and living; has encouraged many feeble workers, supported many a weak but righteous cause, and has changed the entire structure of the working world. That there are thirty-seven thousand telegraph operators alone, and enormous numbers of bookkeepers, typewriters, and stenographers, gives one some idea of the power which organization among women would effect for their interest. "In this way, too," says the Social Economist, "would be overcome the opposition of men to women as competitors, and would give the latter the advantage of an increased rate in wages."

WOMEN'S IGNORANCE OF BUSINESS METHODS—THE PROTECTIVE UNION.

What women suffer from their ignorance of business methods no mere words can portray. Thousands of them answer advertisements for "girls to learn a trade" only to find that after the trade is learned there is no more employment for them, thousands more standing ready to take the same places on the same terms—that is, on no terms at all— kept only so long as they are content to work without pay, in the hope of becoming able to earn something in the future.

To remedy this state of things the Working Woman's Protective Union was formed in New York in 1868. On an annual outlay of $5,000 it has fought and won battles for twelve thousand women who would otherwise have been defrauded of their wages, the suits representing sums of from a few dollars to several hundreds. During the years of its existence it has gratuitously furnished more than three hundred thousand women with advice, relief, and employment. Similar societies, born of the dire necessities of the working woman, have been founded in most of our large cities by influential and wealthy men and women disposed to assist the working class in some practical fashion.

THE DISFRANCHISEMENT OF WOMAN AS AFFECTING HER ECONOMIC STATUS.

The principal obstacle at present to woman's business success is the fact that she has no elective franchise. History shows that a disfranchised class is always at a disadvantage in labor contracts. Political inferiority always begets industrial servitude, and this result is in a straight line from cause to effect. Says a clear thinker on this subject: "Business prosperity implies the ability to contract with others on terms of equality and a reasonable confidence in results. Some sudden turn of the political machinery over which they have no control may hurl the disfranchised from their places or upset their most carefully-laid plans. It is also difficult for them to keep in touch with commercial tendencies, so intimately are these blended with political issues in a country governed by popular vote."

To the truth of all this society must assent, and it would be well also at the same time to bear in mind Captain Cuttle's assertion that "the bearing of the observation lies in the application of it." So long as woman suffers will society suffer, and the day will surely dawn when even its blindest members will see that political equality for woman is one of the first principles of a sane political economy.

It is true that much temporary mischief has been wrought by woman in the industrial world. She has cheapened labor, and driven out of the field a large number of male laborers because she could manage to live on less than would support them; and because unskilled, disfranchised, and consequently helpless, she must generally choose between starvation and poor pay. The present condition of affairs is proof of the truth embodied in a wise man's word that "maladjustment of a new good may be worse than the old evil." Yet good is always to be preferred to evil, and maladjustment is a trouble which time is very sure to cure.

How Woman's Industrial Progress Illustrates Evolution's Law.

In even the most superficial study of woman as an economic factor there can be found confirmation of the laws underlying every form of evolution. She has nobly illustrated the persistence of force, and in her struggle for industrial existence has adjusted herself to her environment in a way which seems little less than miraculous, considering the nature and the number of the obstacles continually piled up in her pathway. The New York Tribune lately said: "A woman may be defined to be a creature that receives half price for all she does and pays full price for all she needs. She earns like a man; she pays like man; she is paid like a child. Her brain is clogged; her hands and feet are tied."

Dr. Emily Blackwell wrote of a period hardly more than a century ago: "Women were hindered at every turn by endless restraint in endless minor details of habit, custom, and tradition. Most women who have been engaged in any new department would testify that the difficulty of the undertaking lay far more in these artificial hindrances and burdens than in their own health, or in the nature of the work itself."

Woman's Special Work in the Economic Field.

It is no longer a question of a woman doing a man's work in a man's way, or a man's work in a woman's way. Woman has her own work in the world, and asks only a fair field and no favor that she may do it in her own way, and that it may be recognized, if it is good work, regardless of the sex of the worker. Faithful in few things she has become ruler over many things, and the day can not be far distant when her rule shall be acknowledged, her labor adequately rewarded.

The late George William Curtis once said: "I know of no subject upon which so much intolerable nonsense has been talked and written and sung and, above all, preached, as the question of the true sphere of woman, and of what is feminine and what is not, as if men necessarily knew all about it. The pursuits of men in the world to which they are directed by the natural aptitude of sex, and to which they must devote their lives, are as foreign from political functions as those of women. There is nothing more incompatible with political duties in cooking and taking care of children than there is in digging ditches or making shoes, or in any other necessary employment, while in every superior interest of society growing out of the family the stake of women is not less than men's."

Woman's Right to Work.

First among "woman's rights," then, is her right to work. Labor has been denominated prayer; it is no less happiness. It was a woman who wrote—

> "Get leave to work
> In this world—'tis the best you get at all,
> For God in cursing gives us better gifts
> Than men in benediction."

Man is tenacious of his right to life, liberty, and the pursuit of happiness. Every step which he has taken through the ages has carried him forward to a better life, greater liberty, and surer enjoyment of all life's benefits. In this progress woman has been his helper, and it is not strange that at last she has come to the conclusion that she is entitled to become partaker and sharer as well. Having helped him, she is asking now for the privilege of helping herself, and not only asking for it, but taking it; showing, too, how abundantly able and inclined she is to make good use of it.

HERBERT SPENCER ON WOMAN'S EQUALITY WITH MAN.

"Equity," says Herbert Spencer, " knows no sex. In its vocabulary the word *man* must be understood in a generic, not a specific sense. The law of equal freedom manifestly applies to the whole race—female as well as male. Many admit the axiom that human happiness is the divine will; from this axiom what we call rights are primarily derived. Why the differences of bodily organization and those trifling mental variations which distinguish female from male should exclude one half of the race from the benefits of this ordination remains to be shown."

THE MORAL INFLUENCE OF WOMEN WORKERS.

The moral influence of woman's employment, considered in relation to herself, the family, and society at large, has been one of the most potent factors for good in the progress of our civilization. A woman who can take care of herself is no longer that general nuisance and special drag, "an unprotected female." She is no longer obliged to marry for support—and the significance of that statement is too far-reaching to be grasped by even the most profound student of sociology. She is no longer, to the same extent as formerly, the despairing victim of a condition known as " the social evil "—one so fraught with risk of destruction to the race that even among many evils it is distinguished by the definite article. The "mischief" which Satan so easily "finds for idle hands to do" is not limited to the masculine members of society; and when to idleness is added want, it is not strange that so much mischief is perpetrated.

WOMAN'S WORK AS AFFECTING THE FAMILY AND SOCIETY.

Whatever affects the individual woman affects family life. The woman who can take care of herself can always take care of others, even of husband and children, when misfortune, failure, or illness, makes such care incumbent upon her. And in how many cases this is done, and done successfully, there is no need of words to demonstrate to those who live with their eyes open.

Whatever affects family life affects society. Our society —not using the word in its superficial sense—is what woman makes it. The education of woman, which has made her a better—because wiser, and therefore more efficient—sister, daughter, wife, mother, housekeeper, has improved family, and consequently social, life beyond all power of estimation. The man who stands in the way of woman's advancement is standing quite as surely in his own way, and hinders himself exactly in proportion as he strives to hinder her. He is opposing the progress of civilization and putting stumbling blocks in the pathway of his children and his children's children.

There is nothing in all human development which so directly antagonizes the natural, selfish instinct of man as the self-assertion of woman in social and political affairs, and especially in the industrial world, where the effects of this assertion are felt in the most direct and material ways. Just in proportion as the egoistic yields to the altruistic sentiment will the way be made easy for woman to take without opposition and hold without contest the place to which she aspires, the occupation for which she is best fitted, and the freedom which is as dear to her as to man.

BENEFICENT INFLUENCE OF WOMAN'S ADVANCEMENT.

"In all respects," says Carroll D. Wright, "I bespeak for the great influence which shall come from the industrial emancipation of woman a happier and rer social condition! And this I say not as an advocate of woman suffrage, not as woman's champion, but simply from a recognition of justice and from the inevitable trend of social forces which is hastened by industrial processes."

The age of the simpleton and the sentimentalist is fast dying out. The age of the scientist and evolutionist is even now with us, and in the latter as well as in the former day a tree is known by its fruit.

The industrial emancipation of woman, already largely accomplished, to be followed in fullness of time by her political freedom and equality, is a thing which "means intensely and means good" to herself and the civilization of which she is so large and so important a part. She has come to her own not to destroy but to fulfill the laws of social obligation, and her coming—as strictly in accordance with the laws of evolution as is the growth of life upon the planet—shall help to prove not only the certainty and consistency, but also the beneficence of those laws which man can neither make nor mar, but with which, if he be wise, he endeavors to place himself in harmony.

ABSTRACT OF THE DISCUSSION.

PROF. ALMON G. MERWIN, PD. D.:

In listening to these discussions, I am reminded of one of my experiences when I was a boy in the country. In driving hoops on casks, I used to pound away on one side and get it all right, and then find the other side was up, out of place; pound that side down, and then the first would go up. So each of us believes in some reform which is to regenerate the world, but we forget that while we are fastening down one side of the hoop which binds society together, the other is coming up. Is it not possible that the advocates of equal wages and equal political privileges for woman are driving the hoop too far down on that side? I have heard it asserted recently that among savages the woman was the equal of man in strength. If I was to reason about it *a priori*, I should ask, How came it, if she was originally equal to man, that she quietly submitted to his rule? She was oppressed, it appears to me, because man had superior strength. In the animal world we find it generally true that the male is the stronger. It is the stallion that leads the herd of wild horses. The bull is stronger than the cow. There are exceptional cases, it is true, as when the mother is goaded to desperation in defense of her young; but it is the exception which reveals the rule. There is one truth which appears everywhere : When there is one all-absorbing thought or passion in man or woman, equal strength can not be given to anything else. In woman, the all-absorbing thought is the love and care of children. That being the case, she can not use her full strength in other directions. This is an insuperable barrier to woman's equality with man in the industrial world. If we take from the earth the work of man, what would be left ? To him we owe our great cities, our ships, and all the thousands of inventions of the age. To him we owe the best there is in literature. Where, for example, shall we find a female Shakespeare or a female Plato ? The simple fact is that the care of the family has rendered it impossible for woman to give to other pursuits the steady and persistent thought and application necessary to the accomplishment of great things. As to wages, assuming that women should receive equal wages with men, this rule should apply everywhere. Not only can the woman typewriter do her work as well as a man, but the nurse girl can take care of the baby better than its father; hence, I suppose, she should receive his wages. So with the cook and the seamstress. I regard it to be all-important to preserve and perfect the family, which is the unit of our social commonwealth. I admit that woman should be free to marry or not, as she pleases. But why should she acquire property if not to support a family? If the ablest women go into business or professional life—and it is this class only which can win success there—it follows that the best women will not become the mothers of families; the maternal function will be left to a lower order of women. The best women will thus be prevented from transmitting their superior qualities to their offspring, and the race will deteriorate. Why is it that the wages of women are lower than those of men? The wage-level must always be sufficient to support life. Wages also depend on what is required of those who receive them. If women receive men's wages they must have equal responsibility. But if they marry and have the care of a family this is impossible. It is not the single woman that suffers from woman's introduction into business and the professions; it is the married woman. If as a teacher she earned as much as her husband prior to marriage, now the two have to live on half their former income. Woman can not go out and earn money if she has the care of a family.

PROF. GEORGE GUNTON:

Let us look at the actual facts as we see them around us. Woman is not lower in the social scale, but higher than she has ever been before. Let us see what has taken place in her condition as a matter of fact and history, and, if possible, by the application of evolutionary tests, discover what conditions have brought about what we see—what has been the real cause of this progress.

Mr. Chadwick asserted in his recent lecture on the Social and Political Status of Woman that woman's wages are discounted because she is likely to marry. I hadn't heard this argument before. I do not think this is the true reason why her wages are less than those of men. The true reason is her greater cheapness; her wants are fewer than those of men. For the same reason children and Chinamen are employed at low wages. Factory girls' wages in America are higher than men's in Russia. There are more than twice as many women workers in Austria-Hungary as here in proportion to the population. Is that country therefore ahead of us in its civilization? The first speaker struck the key to the situation. The family is the great factor in the evolution of society. Woman has become free and independent as she has become expensive and masterful. Neither man nor woman can get more from Nature or society than the power he or she can exercise is competent to exact. The Chinaman can exact only ten cents a day because he has only a rice-eating power. As woman has advanced in her social demands—in consumption—she has advanced in social importance. In the last century it was the men who wore ruffles and laces. When the frills left the man and went to the woman, the hobnails left the woman and went to the donkey.

The tendency of evolution is to specialize. It is not to make woman like man, so that either can get along without the other at a pinch, for the development of unlikeness creates importance in the thing developed. Woman is going to fill a special function in society, and not run looms like a man. Her specialty is in the social line—refining, broadening, and elevating—a sphere man becomes less capable of filling as he advances industrially. Her special sphere is an enlarged social life. That is a higher function than dickering about wages. The more she stays at home, the more man gets; the more she goes into the factory, the lower are his wages. When she is his counterpart there is no trouble about her freedom. Freedom doesn't come through the ballot, but the ballot through freedom.

Dr. Lewis G. Janes:

My own position on this subject is a very simple one. I disclaim for myself, I deny to any man or any number of men, the right to dictate to woman as to what functions in society she shall perform. Woman has the right to decide these questions for herself. I agree with Prof. Gunton and Prof. Merwin that the family is the fundamental factor in social evolution; but I believe that the more interests woman has in common with man the more harmonious and perfect will be the life of the family. It is not, as a rule, those families wherein the wife and mother is an advocate of the equality of woman in which serious domestic misunderstandings arise; nor do women trained to self-support often make unhappy marriages. The practical knowledge of human nature developed by business or professional life serves them well in the choice of husbands, while their pecuniary independence saves them from grievous temptation to *mariages de convenance*, which, without genuine love and mutual respect, are simply legalized immoralities.

Prof. Gunton apparently sees the law of evolution fulfilled in the differentiation of sex attributes and the relegation of the two sexes to different walks of life. But the true test of evolutionary progress, as he himself has shown in another department of investigation, is the creation of conditions favorable to a more complete integration of society by the voluntary action of its individual members. This, too, is Herbert Spencer's idea. A higher form of differentiation, it seems to me, supplementary and complementary to sex distinction, is that which gives variety to individual choice in the pursuits of life, which enlarges the mental horizon of women, makes them self-supporting, and gives them common interests with men in the affairs of the day. This furnishes the conditions of a higher sympathy and more complete accord, which lead to more perfect integration and unity of aim and sentiment, both in the family and in society at large. Under freedom I doubt not that woman will find her true place in the world's work, which can never be completely accessible to her under a system of arbitrary compulsion. We need have no fear that woman will be unsexed by a larger freedom. That would defeat the very end for which this larger opportunity affords the means. It is the ever-womanly, the peculiarly feminine attributes which are needed to supplement the masculine in every department of social and industrial life.

MISS ELLEN E. KENYON, PD. D.:

I have nothing to say in criticism of the just and able lecture of Miss Le Row. I rejoice to have this important subject handled as the aims of our Association demand it should be. It is said by opponents of woman's equality with man that the dignity and independence of woman are to be attained by feminine differentiation, not by equal wages and equal rights. Women are to become more and more the elevators of society, and consequently more and more unlike men, more and more separated from men in their pursuits, more and more specialized in their social and domestic functions, and thereby more and more necessary to men and able to name the terms per inch, yard, or mile for which they will do this work. Methinks we must look backward rather than forward for a differentiation wider than that of the present. In the days of chivalry the knight sang his serenade at the foot of his lady's castle wall. She opened the lattice and bade him within; elevated by several stories, he entered her presence, and she made him forget the battlefield and took him into a land of poesy. Becoming his wife, she dispensed the hospitality of his house and took exactly such charge as Prof. Gunton relegates to the future woman. Not that this is wrong or is past, but that something was lacking, who but a poet will deny? Let but Amy Robsart's dying shriek pierce our poet's ear and surely he will come out of his rhapsody and cease preaching the helplessness of woman as her crowning glory and *Magna Charta*. Since the days of Amy Robsart the reverse of this process has steadily taken place. Fathers have become more motherly, mothers have become more fatherly; men have become social elevators beside their wives; men have spoken in public potent words put into their mouths at home by thinking women; women have sunned themselves under better laws more strictly enforced, have lost their timidity, come out from their castle walls, engaged in competitive labor of every kind suited to their physical strength, fought their way into the colleges, and organized—yes, *organized*—for humanitarian work of every kind. They have thrown a fresh and revivifying force into moral progress that—well, who knows but one of its results is this very Ethical Association? Only Mrs. Janes can tell! The public and industrial activity of woman will go on increasingly, but will it unsex her? Is she less a woman than in the days of chivalry? Are mothers less tender, wives less faithful? O ye of little faith! O evolutionists who rhapsodize till you lose the points of the compass and watch the western sky for the rising of the sun! Give woman equal justice in every form and trust the rest to the future.

Yes, even when she declines the maternal function grant her the free choice that is her right. True that all our benefits from the past imply debts to the future; but here the double question arises, Is it necessarily a benefit to be born, and must all debts be paid in their own coin? Our poet, coming down to practical ethics, which at least brings him within reach of reason, says to the able woman, "You can do more *good* by bequeathing your splendid qualities to another generation than by directly applying them on behalf of children already born." Then he proudly asserts that there is "no female Shakespeare," and hence woman is not adapted to a literary career. Had Shakespeare been the mother of a family of children, the plays of Shakespeare would have borne a markedly Froebelian character, at least outwardly. And, seriously, does any business veteran advise a neophyte to stake his entire capital on one venture? This has been the shipwreck of women always. No! The sex is grateful to the few women of genius who have maintained sufficient freedom to save us by their works from a sweeping charge of mediocrity.

"But," says our friend the enemy, "if women receive equal wages and political justice they will not be obliged to marry." Ergo, marriage is a hateful condition into which women must be forced at the bayonet point of starvation. Ergo, the race can not continue on earth without the immolation of an entire sex. Question: This being granted, how long is it desirable that the race should continue? Evidently, poets should beware of entering the field of logic. It will be noticed that all poets of the Grant Allen class make the impossible classification, "women and workmen." Upon this, all their fallacies rest.

We *do* like to have sonnets sung to us, and better still do we appreciate the practical poetry of the street-car, where, all having equal access, the stronger tenders to the weaker a seat that is rightfully his own. This beautiful moral deference is heroic and poetic in the highest degree.

But it would not be desirable to continue this terrestrial race life of ours were its prime prerequisite the degrading flat that women must be starved into marrying. Nor is this assumption held by any but men who feel that *they* wouldn't marry if they were women unless forced to. Nor has it any truth whatever. Though I have raised the question, Is it a benefit to be born? I am too much of an optimist to believe that life is really a burden. Women will go on marrying as long as there are men worthy of the great reliance a wife must place in her husband. When women are free and equal they will be more likely to marry only worthy men; and will *this* work deterioration for the race? And when women marry from higher, purer motives than the desire to be financially taken care of, wifehood and motherhood will stand some chance of becoming what they should be.

We are asked, "Who built the cities and railroads?" Very true, this is the house that Jack built; but who built the men who built the cities? It is taking a very unfair advantage, because men's stronger muscles have laid the stones in the bridge piers that remain to visibility, to claim that they are the builders of civilization. The best part of civilization is invisible. What about the plum pudding over which these workmen smacked their lips? It requires no more brains to lay a brick than to put salt in the oatmeal. And why are not housework and the care and education of children as good a preparation for the suffrage as building railroads and selling tape over a counter?

But now these friends are aching to ask the question, Who *planned* the cities and railroads? Well, who went to college and studied civil engineering? When as many women shall have passed through the vigorous mental training that the effective men of the ages have had—I care not whether it be in the German universities or as Spencer was educated—when women shall have numerically caught up with men in their enjoyment of these advantages and in their pursuit of occupations whose results last to the eye, then, and then only, can a fair comparison be made on the line suggested by our unreflecting brethren. This, of course, can never be, for those pursuits that can be followed in the shade of domesticity will ever be the chosen ones of woman, and will ever demand her gentler touch. But out of the comparatively few women whose destinies have placed them in the walks of men, let us see what the showing of inventive genius begins to be, even without waiting for the very general help of the college course.

The list of women to whom patents were granted from 1790 to 1888 comprises twenty-five thousand names in all parts of this country and a few in foreign countries. Up to 1830 they numbered only ten, increased by forty-five during the next thirty years. After 1860 they came forward thick and fast, in some years averaging nearly one a day. The most striking feature is the *variety* of articles invented by women. Many have special relation to women, children, and domestic affairs—baby jumpers, tidy fasteners, dolls' cradles, rocking chairs, cooking utensils, bird cages, etc.—such are numerous; but also articles belonging to masculine industries—a machine for sawing wheel-fellies, folder cutter, mowing machine, currycomb, even a smelting furnace and a new war vessel, a process for mounting fluid lenses, a submarine telescope and lamp, fire alarm thermometer, non-heating axles, safety car heaters, locomotive smoke consumers, screw propellers, spark arresters, sleeping-car berths, rails for street railways, hoes, shovels and barrows, chicken-coops, wagons, bale ties, and roller-skates.

A Brooklyn woman in the human hair business invented a machine that would take the single hair from the tangled combing and turn it the right way, so that the root of the hair, not the wrong end, was woven into the strand. A Brooklyn girl of eighteen invented a machine to bottle up the momentum of a horse-car when it stops and release the force at starting, to ease the strain upon the horses. This was never patented, though competent judges pronounced it workable. The inventor was engaged in feminine work and far from accessibility to the world of business, of machinery, and of capital. I mention this to suggest what probably becomes of ninety per cent of women's inventions.

The supernal conceit of the husband who has climbed back fences, played ball, and otherwise exercised, untrammeled, every energy of his nature while still a youngster, in active and aggressive contact with things and society, who has grumbled his way out of school and into an office at fourteen, there learning a business and business economics, who has gone back to school and through college with a lot of real knowledge to underly all his study, who has freely roamed the woods and fields at all seasons and at all hours, who graduates with the lore of ancient nations and what ought to be a good share of the wisdom of the moderns in his head—the supernal conceit of this man as he complacently puffs at his club-room cigar and thinks of what he chooses to characterize as his wife's " limited mind "—will some one please tell me what thing earthly is equal to it?

Thanks to the mothers of men, some of them have grown up with more just perceptions. Too many to name, were my whole time devoted to the roll-call, are and have been the men who appreciate, allow for, and seek to remove, when unnecessary, the trammels of woman. If they see "the cheapness of woman," they also see *why* she has been cheap, and grieve to think that their sex still has a powerful hand in the cheapening. They see that woman is to man almost as the canary is to the wild bird—a poor, caged, half-atrophied creature. And *yet*, what noble work she has done! Work immeasurable, and consequently not down in the books of the accountant. Woman's work is too great to be definite. That she has done it so well, in the mental darkness that has been thought good for her, is magnificent testimony to the fineness and power of her mind. That she has often failed is due to the *blinders* that form so prominent a feature of her harness. "Don't tell mother that!" exclaims the schoolboy in relation to something that he would be shocked to have her know about; and he grows up feeling that there is a side of life about which the mother and sister and the lady friend should not know. Why should men worship ignorance for innocence?

Only when woman *knows* all that awaits her son in the battle of life, only when she knows about the horrible doctrine that is calmly taught by so-called respectable men, only when she knows the horrible laws that are made by man-elected legislators, only when she knows *about* the world of vice in which Mr. Gunton gives her credit for an equal and equally intelligent place with men—only then can she *prove* her womanhood by organized and peremptory opposition to this man-ruled cheapening of her sex and poisoning of the race's life-blood! Not that man alone is to blame. Not that any one is to blame. We are all what evolution has made us. Only, the day of eye-opening has come on the tide of evolution to some women and to some men, and they would fain pick open the eyes of the rest. The woman question is the race question. Upon the economic position of woman depends her social position. Only financial independence can enable woman to maintain in all respects her own dignity. Only when she has dignity unmenaced can she dignify motherhood. And only when motherhood is in every instance free and willing can we hope to see that ideal race of men grow up who shall build a bridge of broader span than any we yet know—a bridge into Utopia.

These consistent friends of ours exalt the process of intuition as the highest known to mentality. They accredit this power of automatic reasoning to woman, and on the same page they classify woman as a non-reasoning animal. They exalt the mother instinct as the most beautiful sentiment known to poetry. They accredit it to woman as her chief distinguishing characteristic, and while it serves the purposes of their argument, they rhapsodize over it until woman thinks she is enshrined. But a few minutes later they find this wonderful trait common to all mothers, and guardedly or recklessly point out that while it may distinguish woman from man, it does not at all distinguish her from the brutes below man.

These sophists—some of them are worthy a better name, but their leaders are not—they have mothers, sisters, wives—opportunities of looking into women's lives and seeing by sympathy what arithmetic fails to teach them—these sophists or unthinking disciples of sophists make much of the physical claims of woman, ever exalting the lower that the higher may be obscured. There is nothing noble about the physical relation of motherhood. It is *mentally* that the mother rises above the father. The work of supplying the family with daily bread is one of self-sacrifice and heroism, but the work of rearing the children at home is one requiring the highest and the steadiest inspiration. If woman is to go out into the world as a bread-winner, let her have man's training; but if she is to perform her own natural function in the social economy, let her have a better. If she is to enter on a profession, put her through college; but if she is to *mind the baby*, by all means put her through college and give her a kindergarten besides.

EVOLUTION OF PENAL METHODS AND INSTITUTIONS

BY
JAMES McKEEN

COLLATERAL READINGS SUGGESTED:

Spencer's *Prison Ethics*, in Essays, Moral, Political, and Æsthetic; Wines's State of Prisons and Child-saving Institutions; Wilson's Science and Crime; Macdonald's Criminology; Boies's Prisoners and Paupers; Marquis Beccaria's Essay on Penal Methods; Lombroso's L'Uomo Delinquenti; Palm's The Death Penalty; Reeve's The Prison Question; Altgeld's Live Questions, including our Penal Machinery and its Victims; Morrison's Crime and its Causes; Du Cane's The Punishment and Prevention of Crime; Tallack's Penological and Preventive Principles; Ryland's Crime, its Causes and Remedy; Green's Crime, its Nature, Causes, Treatment, and Prevention; Ellis's The Criminal; Pike's History of Crime in England; Dugdale's The Jukes; Prof. E. S. Morse's *Natural Selection and Crime*, in Popular Science Monthly, August, 1892; Dr. Robert Fletcher's Retiring Address as President of the Anthropological Society of Washington, D. C.; Seventeenth Year Book of the New York State Reformatory; Papers in Penology, issued by the New York State Reformatory.

EVOLUTION OF PENAL METHODS AND INSTITUTIONS.

By James McKeen.

SOCIETY AND CRIME: PRIMITIVE PENAL METHODS.

It is observed by John Locke in one of his political essays that an ideal government is incompatible with an ideal society, because an ideal society will require no government. This reflection and some of its corollaries are pertinent in the consideration of the morbid excrescences which afflict society. The very existence of penal institutions is a constant reminder of social imperfection. The highest aim of such institutions must be to accomplish their own extinction. Thus the jailer says in Cymbeline: "I would we were all of one mind, and one mind good! O, there were desolation of gaolers and gallowses! I speak against my present profit, but my wish hath a preferment in it." The criminal class seems to attend civilization as its shadow, growing and diminishing as civilization approaches or recedes from the high noon of meridian splendor; though, indeed, that shadow sometimes seems to increase in intensity with the increasing brightness of noonday, suggesting the philosophy of Leibnitz, that evil is the inseparable accompaniment and condition of the highest good. It is not certain whether or not primitive men were solitary or gregarious animals. It is certain that long before the dawn of history they had become gregarious. For the rude beginnings of penal methods we need not depend upon imagination. We may see to-day suggestions, if not instances, of them in the herds of lower animals and in savage tribes. Some individual liberties begin to be surrendered for the common advantage. Certain courses of conduct are enforced by the many against the few. A herd of buffaloes, it is said, will turn and gore to death one of its number which by mere misfortune has become disabled. A rude consciousness has been bred by the slow processes of natural selection that the movements of the herd must be free and unhampered. The penalties of savage tribes make few moral distinctions. The recalcitrant is exterminated. The physically and the morally deformed are in much the same category. A seeming vigor in the surviving individuals of such tribes is gained at the cost of moral attributes. The failure to perceive this was the fallacy of the Rousseau school of sentimental politics, which went back to the simplicities of barbarism for its social ideal. And a kindred fallacy is discoverable in the logic of many of the anarchists of our own time. As humanity emerges from savagery, as the interdependency of men supplants their isolation, discipline of the recalcitrants takes the place of extermination. The consciousness of the value of independence breeds tolerance toward occasional excesses of it in individuals. The spirit of philanthropy increases the burden which society carries, but that same spirit of philanthropy, in an enlarging ratio, increases the power to carry the burden.

An occasional recurrence to primitive methods of dealing with crime has been disastrous to the general good. Thus, when England sought to rid itself of its criminal class by an extension of capital punishment to the lighter felonies, the air at every cross-roads vibrated with the hideous music of the creaking of gibbet chains, with the result of deadening the general moral sense, and hardening those social sympathies which constitute the best safeguard against crime.

THE EVOLUTION OF PENAL METHODS.

It would be an interesting thing to endeavor to trace along purely scientific lines, by the application of *quasi* Darwinian methods, the changes from age to age in dealing with criminals; to note how it is that many of the convicts of one epoch have been regarded as martyrs in another epoch; how certain perverted theories of government have resulted in enacting "injustice into law"; how priestcraft has for certain ages dominated communities, branding as felons the real leaders of human thought; how the right and duty of private vengeance have been surrendered by individuals to the community; how special outbreaks of crime attend special social conditions; how, in certain stages of progress, temptations increase more rapidly than the power to resist them. Thus, it seems an undeniable fact that of late years a marked proportionate increase of crime among women has attended the widening of their spheres of political and industrial activity. One observer of such a phenomenon says: " Alas, it is still true that the daughters of Eve can not be

Evolution of Penal Methods and Institutions. 229

let loose even in the Garden of Eden!" Another discovers only one more argument in favor of the wider liberty and the freer indulgence in the apples from the tree of knowledge, though it be knowledge of good and evil.* Such a line of discussion is perhaps the one primarily suggested by the topic of the evening. It has, however, occurred to me as equally in accordance with that topic, and certainly more compatible with the limitations of my own powers, rather to suggest something of the growth and present aspects of what has come to be known as Prison Science.

Time compels that the glance at the history of the subject must be very cursory. The difficulties confronting modern society are formidable. In the effort to surmount physical obstacles in the path, we sometimes go back to gain impetus. I may safely promise in an historical review to skip down the centuries with a rapidity which will afford the momentum, if not the agility, wherewith to overleap some of the hurdles which are in the track of this generation of reformers.

The Growth of Prison Science.

It is not without significance that we find in one of the earliest surviving historical records, the history of Rameses II, carved upon the walls of the temple of Karnak, an extradition treaty whereby escaped criminals were to be mutually surrendered between Egypt and the King of the Khetas. In Egypt itself the prison had already, centuries before Rameses the Great, become a recognized penal institution. It is necessarily an institution of a stable society. Migratory tribes, however well advanced in moral development, necessarily use flagellation, mutilation, or some form of slavery for the discipline of delinquents. Even in Greece and Rome the prison seems to have been merely subordinate and ancillary. The noble precepts of Plato on the subject found no realization in actual administration. Great as is the contribution of Rome to the development of criminal as well as of civil law, Roman history adds little to the solu-

---

* The proportionate increase of crime in women is positively asserted by students of English statistics. In the United States there is a difference of opinion. The matter may be determined upon the completion of the census of 1890, which can be compared with that of 1880, when the numbers of male and female convicts throughout the country were first separately stated. But, as is observed by Mr. Frederick H. Wines, much uncertainty attends such comparisons. He says, too, that wicked women usually persuade men to commit crime for them! attributing to men a gallantry certainly not inherited by them from Adam.

tion of modern prison questions. Although Cicero says, in one of his orations against Catiline, that their ancestors had wished the prison to be made the punishing instrument for offenders against the law, nothing approaching the modern reformatory prison seems to have existed in ancient Rome. Naturally the dark ages are a chaos. We penetrate the feudal donjons and torture chambers with a sense of horror, finding there oftener evidence of the gratification of the impulses of despotic political vengeance than of any truly governmental reformatory, or even punitive efforts. The earliest emergence from this feudal chaos was in Italy and in the Netherlands. Notably, Popes Innocent X, in 1655, and Clement XI, in 1704, had devised and built essentially reformatory prisons, and already when Howard made his famous tour of the Continent, he found at Ghent and other cities of the Low Countries institutions which may be compared to those of our own time. In Europe generally a great progressive step in the treatment of crime had been made when the feudal chiefs had handed over criminal administration to professional magistrates, who gradually evolved something like a system of law founded upon precedents. But down into the eighteenth century it is surprising to find, even in the most enlightened countries of Christendom, to what an extent even the definition and gradation of crimes, and the nature and extent of punishments, were left to the discretion of the magistrates. Whimsical survivals of priestly inquisitions pervaded the courts. Criminals were tortured, with the idea of thus purging them of the infamy of an offense, which often they had never committed but had first been tortured into confessing. The devil of depravity was exorcised like the possessing demon of insanity. It was in this state of criminal law, or lawlessness, that the essay of the Marquis Beccaria appeared, first published in Milan, about 1764. Pre-eminently this essay is the foundation of modern penal literature. Its value is perhaps not less because Beccaria's reasoning is largely *a priori*, although he was amply fortified with the credentials of practical knowledge of his theme. In our own devotion to the inductive methods of modern science I sometimes think we do scant justice to the great social idealists of the eighteenth century. It is true that Beccaria's influence was rather upon penal legislation than upon penal institutions; yet the influence rapidly ripened into the intelligent consideration of the management of convicts. And this practical side of the subject had its chief impulse in the work of his great English contemporary, John Howard. Howard's name has come to be so constantly associated with every sort of philanthropy that he is often thought of as a sort of amiable and kindly old gentleman, who went about with gingerbread in his pockets, which was dealt out with discriminating partiality in favor of naughty children. He is often and erroneously believed to have been the apostle of that pernicious rose-water prison system which Mr. Carlyle so vehemently, and I think righteously, denounces in his famous pamphlet on model prisons. A very different man was the real Howard. He was not a genius. He might easily,

"Along the cool, sequestered vale of life,
Have kept the noiseless tenor of his way,"

and become the tenant of a forgotten grave in a country churchyard. A mere accident in his political career as an English country gentleman made him, when already past the prime of life, the high sheriff of his county, and thus brought home to him knowledge of the fearful state of things in the county jails. Fortunately, he did not acquire with the position that official shrug which shakes off the blame of patent evils upon other men's shoulders. He set himself resolutely at the task, in Parliament and out, of devising and carrying into effect remedies. He journeyed again and again through Europe, at a time when that journey involved great personal discomfort, knocking at the doors of the fortresses of official prejudice with the vehemence of a Macduff. Pre-eminently by Howard's efforts and example has come about the conviction which inspires the best efforts of our own time, that the State shall endeavor to treat its criminals as they deserve, but also after its own honor and dignity. England tried extermination in vain. It tried transportation, with results disastrous to its colonies, and a disastrous reaction to itself. Now, under the firm, centralized administration of its Home Office, it has adopted, with the many modifications incident to actual experience, the reformatory system of Sir Walter Crofton, which, coupled no doubt with the vastly increased efficacy of preventive measures, has reduced the average convictions in England during the prevalence of the system more than fifty per cent.* Sir Walter Crofton's earlier reforms were

* Taking the figures of Sir Edmund F. Ducane (appended to the Report on English Prisons, made in 1884 to the New York Prison Association by Mr. C. T.

in Ireland, and the Crofton System is often known as the Irish System. Some of its methods have been abandoned. The great Queenstown institution, intended for use in connection with the management of parole convicts, is in ruins. Like all progressive systems, it has moved on, leaving behind some of its rollers. Its fundamental idea is the reformatory idea. The sense that his imprisonment is a punishment for heinous misconduct is often impressed upon the delinquent by a term at the outset of absolutely solitary confinement at hard and isolated labor. Later he is permitted to labor with others, and there is a method of promotion for good conduct from one class to another. It has been found in England, as with us, that short terms of imprisonment have little reformatory value; and it is a part of the system to substitute for minor offenses some other form of punishment.

IMPROVEMENT OF PRISON SYSTEMS IN AMERICA.

America during this century has been conspicuous in the improvement of prison systems. The so-called Pennsylvania plan, still enforced at its Eastern Penitentiary near Philadelphia and in many of the smaller prisons, is that of continuous solitary confinement, each prisoner working in his own cell. This method is the prevalent one in Belgium. It may be mentioned that all devices seem to have failed to prevent more or less intercommunication between the prison inmates. By actual experiment a few years ago at the Eastern Penitentiary an item of exciting news made known to the occupant of a solitary cell at one end of a corridor was found to have been communicated to the other extremity of the prison a few minutes later. The pipes of modern plumbing have aided in this intercommunication; but where

---

Lewis), it appears that the ratio of persons in England and Wales sentenced for indictable offenses was as follows for the years given:

In 1850, 1,085 to the million of population.
" 1860, 508 " " "
" 1870, 495 " " "
" 1880, 415 " " "

1860 appears to have been an exceptional year. But comparing decade with decade, there is still shown a steady diminution in the proportion of sentences.

According to the United States Census, the proportions here were for the same years:

In 1850, 290 to the million of population.
" 1860, 607 " " "
" 1870, 853 " " "
" 1880, 1,169 " " "

The United States Census returns are untrustworthy for such comparisons, however, because of carelessness in not separating misdemeanants from felons.

there are no pipes, wall taps and other telegraphic devices are speedily learned. The weight of authority is against the solitary system, unless its application be discriminating. It is found to be mentally and morally disastrous in very many cases, destructive of the social sense, which is perhaps the most notably deficient sense in very many classes of criminals, and requires strengthening, not weakening. The New York or Auburn system associates the prisoners in labor during working hours; and this is the method generally prevalent in our State prisons and penitentiaries. But New York, in its Reformatory at Elmira, has an institution combining all the best methods of penal discipline, and confessedly in the front rank of the institutions of the world. It is there sought to combine with the rigorous discipline proper to punishment an education in lines which may curb the criminal propensities.* The State of New York also now has a general system of prison law which is admirable. As to certain classes of offenders, the sentence, within limits may be indeterminate, so that the confinement may be shortened by good behavior, and there may be in certain cases releases on parole (this being not now limited to the Reformatory). The labor of the prisons is no longer sold to contractors, but is controlled by the State in a business conducted entirely on public account or in filling contracts at piece price, where the dealer with the State furnishes the machinery and the raw material. Provision is made for allowing to the prisoner a proportion of his earnings, which may be applied to the use of those whom his crimes have deprived of the support which was their due, or which may be available to the prisoner upon his discharge. Owing to sluggishness on the part of the State Superintendent, the permissive features of the New York law have not yet been fully availed of, nor have its provisions for the gradations of criminals been adequately enforced; and the judges have not yet duly availed themselves of their power to impose indeterminate sentences. The prison labor question has been satisfactorily dealt with in the New York statute. The general scheme contemplates the employment of the less hopeless class of offenders in industries such that the primary purpose of the

* The annual reports of the Elmira Reformatory command an authoritative place in prison literature. The seventeenth and latest, just submitted to the Legislature (wholly the mechanical product of the Reformatory), as a specimen of book-making merits a place on the shelves of the Grolier Club. The book is a compendium of practical wisdom evolved by experience in conducting a great compulsory industrial school.

labor shall be educational, and that it shall fit them to earn an honest livelihood. All the labor in our prisons is essentially productive, though the State's profit is subordinated to efficacy in discipline. Experience has amply demonstrated that unproductive exertion, like that of the old treadmill, or of pumping water from one tub to another, is cruel and demoralizing. Provision is now made by law limiting prison products of any one kind to a small percentage of the total product in the State, and primarily devoting the products to the supply of the prisons themselves and of other public institutions, so that the State shall not materially affect prices by unfair competition with its own citizens. It is a whimsical illustration of the inconsistencies which attend many popular agitations that the very classes in the community who vehemently oppose the utilization of prison labor by the State for the common good call with like vehemence upon the State to take control of almost everything else.

THE FLAGRANT ABUSES IN OUR COUNTY JAILS.

But while our State prisons and most of the penitentiaries are now upon a sound legislative basis, and promise to become efficient agencies of penal discipline, the county jails in this State are most deplorably inefficient. Their management remains largely local in the sheriff and supervisors. These jails should be used simply for the detention of persons arrested on civil process, or for persons awaiting trial; never for the incarceration of persons convicted even of petty offenses. In the present condition of things they are schools of crime, largely attended, especially in the winter, by tramps and vagrants, many of whom look upon their commitment in the light of a favor by a friendly magistrate. In only five of the sixty jails in the State of New York is there any attempt at systematic labor. The sheriff's income is increased by an increase in the number of his jail boarders, and he comes to view the criminal classes as specially ordained by a beneficent Providence for increasing the private emoluments of his public trust. The flagrant abuses of the county jails have been again and again called to the attention of the Legislature, but the system is so intrenched in local prejudice that it will yield only to the assault of some American Howard. Notable among American penal institutions are several distinctively for female convicts, the government of which with marked success has been devolved upon women. America, too, has made most valuable contributions to the general literature of the subject. Few writers have brought to bear upon it a philosophical acumen more penetrating than that of Edward Livingston; and no one has recorded so lucidly and accurately the history of prisons and child-saving institutions as has Dr. E. C. Wines in his monumental work. The annual conferences of the National Prison Association have brought about intelligent comparisons of the different phases of State legislation, and the introduction of interstate regulations. Not the least among the practical difficulties of the classification and control of convicts in the United States has been the facility with which they shift about from State to State; and wherever newly arrested, they always claim the privileges and immunities of first offenders. A knowledge of a given criminal's antecedents is of the utmost importance, not only for the judge in determining the sentence, but for the prison officers in assigning the disciplinary labor. To overcome this particular cause of perplexity, the French Bertillon system is now being here introduced, largely by voluntary interstate courtesy. It is a matter of constant surprise that, notwithstanding the seeming resemblance of men's hats, thousands of which are turned out by factories upon a common pattern, still every man, unless far gone in inebriety, knows his own hat, and certainly knows the moment he puts on another man's. I refer to this as giving briefly some idea of the Bertillon system. Bertillon found that there are certain dimensions of the human skull which are marvelously persistent, in spite of other changes in the physical organism. These skull measurements in the system are supplemented by a great number of others, of limbs and features. The result makes what has been found to be an almost infallible test of identity. The records are indexed for ready reference. The shrewdest of old offenders have vainly endeavored to break through the meshes of this web. In France, where English and American presumptions of innocence do not prevail, accused persons are, when arrested, subjected to the Bertillon measurements—a humiliation from which the notable victims of the Panama scandal have not been spared.

RECENT INCREASE OF CRIME IN AMERICA.

But, in spite of all these American agencies and institutions, we are confronted with the appalling fact that crime for several years past has seemed to be steadily increasing. Statistics warranting such an assertion must, of course, be skeptically scrutinized. A mere increase in the number of convictions may prove, not increase in crime, but an increase in police efficiency. I am, however, reluctantly compelled to the belief, by the assertion of students of the subject who fully understand the necessity of double verification of criminal statistics, that depravity has made large gains here, while decreasing in England. This is measurably accounted for by the process of selection, which has facilitated the transfer to our shores of the worst elements of foreign populations. In the days of the early settlement of America there was some systematic transportation of criminals. Some were leased as servants—a form of slavery; but, as a rule, the condition of things, political and religious, selected for America the ablest, best, and bravest sons and daughters of the Old World. Down almost to our own time it was the ambitious, the courageous, the enterprising, who in the natural course of things came hither. Now the asylum of the oppressed is becoming the dumping ground for the oppressors.* But I have mentioned this great and dominant immigration question only in its bearings on the subject of the evening. The lamentable increase of crime is not entirely accounted for by immigration. The vicious lawlessness among the young has led so scholarly and conservative a man as Dr. Francis Wayland, of New Haven, to say at the recent meeting in Baltimore of the National Prison Association:

"Take them [the children] in hand before they have any other taint than the inevitable taint of heredity. It is, of course, an outrage that the State stands idly by and permits

---

* It appears by table in the seventeenth year book of the Elmira Reformatory that of the total inmates (5,899) since its establishment in 1876, 1,163 were foreign-born, and of the 4,521 born in the United States, only 2,274 were the sons of natives. Thus, counting as of foreign extraction sons of foreign-born parents, about 55 per cent of all the inmates come into that category. These figures, however, do not warrant a statement as to percentage of foreign convicts in the country at large, because a large majority of Elmira inmates are from the cities of New York and Brooklyn.

It is due to our foreign population to state that the conclusion is reached by the statistician of the Wardens' Association (on the basis of figures compiled in 1890) that in high crimes the proportion of convictions of foreign-born citizens is not noticeably greater than of native.

Evolution of Penal Methods and Institutions. 237

the intermarriage of paupers, vagabonds, prostitutes, and felons, thus becoming a party to the wholesale manufacture of probable criminals."

And then he adds : " It seems hardly rational to contend in this stage of nineteenth-century civilization that the State has no right or power to prevent the probable from becoming the positive criminal ; that it is compelled to wait with folded and helpless hands until the child whom it might have saved is brought within the reach of existing laws by some overt act of wickedness. Such a theory of the limitations of the State is monstrous. If the bugbear of a paternal government terrifies us into such a lame conclusion as this, our condition is indeed hopeless."

THE PATERNAL SYSTEM: SUPERIOR EXCELLENCE OF
VOLUNTARY PREVENTIVE MEASURES.

Now, I will not venture here, perhaps on reflection will not venture anywhere, to enter upon the contravention of the position of so thorough a student of this subject as is Dr. Wayland; but I may say that if he did not reside so far away as New Haven is from New York, he might think that the paternal theory, at least, of city government more resembles a bear than a bugbear, and he might venture to hesitate to commit to its embraces even our incipient criminals. In the slums of the metropolis are many children who may wisely be transferred from the care, or rather carelessness, of faithless parents to child-saving institutions. But what sort of salvation is likely to come from fostering influences of a State represented by a mayor who goes into the criminal haunts to select members of his municipal cabinet and committing magistrates ? I am quite prepared to admit that the pendulum has swung back a good way from the extreme *laissez faire* of the Manchester economists. The State in many of its functions may be wisely redirected into channels of more fructifying influence. The compulsory features of public-school education may be strengthened. Already the courts upon proper process may, upon due inquiry, take children from unworthy parents and commit them to other guardianship. But when the citizen, young or old, may be deprived of liberty for anything short of due conviction for actual infraction of law, a road is entered upon which leads backward and downward to the administrative processes of

Russia and the *lettre de cachet* of the Bastile. We must keep in mind Locke's suggestion, which I quoted at the outset, that the ideal society will require no government. We may be compelled to extend the power of the State, but if so, it must be in the confession that we are in a stage of retrogression, not progress. The one constant aim of penal measures must be the enlargement, not the diminution, of individual liberty. The point is not to undervalue the paramount importance of preventive measures, but to suggest that they be brought more and more within the province of voluntary organizations and agencies.

RECENT ADVANCES IN CRIMINAL ANTHROPOLOGY.

While in England and America the progress in penal administration has been along the lines of experimental reform, an intellectual movement of immense importance has more distinctively engaged attention upon the continent of Europe, especially in France and in Italy. Since the time of Beccaria, and as a natural result of his great essay, Italy has been at the head of the world's scholarship on the subject. In comprehensiveness and in philosophical arrangement the penal code of Italy is unapproached in the whole domain of modern jurisprudence. But I referred rather to the scientific study known as criminal anthropology. The zeal of many students has culminated or had its apex in the great work of Professor Lombroso, of Turin. It may perhaps be said that the conspicuous theory of the anthropologists is that the criminal is a racial type of man, recognizable by physical diagnosis. These views, and many of the observed facts upon which they are founded, were forcibly presented at the International Prison Congress held in Rome in 1885, where Lombroso and his friends carried everything before them; a prestige continued, but with diminished ardor, at Paris a few years later. It was thought that at last the criminal question had been solved or was on the eve of solution. Boards of experts (after the manner suggested in Plato's Republic) were to tell by examination in advance what children are predisposed to crime, so that they can be set aside and their race checked and exterminated. From these sanguine, if not sanguinary views, there has been in Europe a very pronounced reaction. At just about the time last summer when Dr. Fletcher was urging Lombroso's views before the Washington anthropological meeting, and Professor Morse was promulgating them in The Popular Science Monthly, the Continental *savants* assembled in Brussels were admitting that study and reflection since the meetings in Rome and in Paris had compelled a revision of many of their utterances. While I am persuaded that many of Lombroso's generalizations are erroneous, and some of them unsound and possibly mischievous, I would not for a moment be misinterpreted as not commending his investigations. There has been merely the proper reaction from extravagant praise. Some of his followers heralded his book L'Uomo Delinquenti as, next to Darwin's Origin of Species, the book of the century! Its merits and demerits may more pertinently remind one of Mr. Buckle's History of Civilization. Mr. Buckle promulgated, as the inductions of a new philosophy, many social facts which had been commonplaces for a hundred generations, and it seems to me that many of the criminal peculiarities set forth by the anthropologists as the results of the study of cranial measurements and cerebral convolutions are peculiarities which have been patent to every policeman; and many propositions of the new science were long ago demonstrated in the pages of the Newgate Calendar. It is apparent that if a distinctive criminal man has been developed, a vast and confusing number of different types of criminal men have come into being contemporaneously. Of course, the relations of heredity to crime, and of race to crime, are subjects of the utmost importance, and the scientific arrangement of statistics bearing upon these points is fruitful in practical suggestions to the administration of penal institutions. As to heredity, it is from present data unsafe to generalize. When we read of the corrupting environment in which the members of the Jukes family grew up, it tends against the heredity theory that any of the children escaped being criminals; and the annals of Newgate confirm, what is indeed the common knowledge of all of us, that criminal propensities break out in the best of families, inexplicable by any rational theory of "atavism." Those who delve in the earth for its precious minerals incidentally bring to the surface a vast quantity of rubbish, and a like result is attending the work of those delving into the obscurer depths of human nature; but the sifting process will in time yield nuggets of importance.

SCIENTIFIC STUDY OF FACTS: PHYSIOLOGICAL PECULIARITIES OF CRIMINALS.

Of course, no one who has studied Darwin can say that science can afford to discard any facts, however seemingly trivial and minute. It is accordingly well that one of the Italian enthusiasts has devoted a considerable portion of his energies to the study of the criminal nose. Of course, the skull and brain have been the chief subjects of physiological investigation, but the ears, mouth, cheek bones, viscera, limbs, lungs, and livers have been duly classified and compared with normal types. Observation has shown, what might have been safely alleged *a priori*, that the eyesight of the average criminal is exceptionally good. A less obvious but important physiological fact is that the average criminal is lacking in sensitiveness to pain. This is a concomitant, or probably the cause of, that indifference to suffering in others, and thus of a want of sympathy, explanatory of the commission of a large class of crimes. But, as before stated, a minute knowledge of individual peculiarities in criminals is of immense importance in determining to what disciplinary treatment the individual may best be subjected, and also in determining what exemplary influences may be most efficacious in preventing crime. A few years ago the duty was devolved upon me of examining Sing Sing Prison, especially its night schools. It happened at the time that there were among the fifteen hundred felons in confinement about seventy Jews, and about the same number of Italians. Every one of the Jews had been convicted for crime against property, and every one of the Italians for crime against the person. Indeed, one explanation of the increase of crime in America is that a system of penal law, which was directed distinctly against the criminal propensities of the Anglo-Saxon race, has not been readjusted to the propensities peculiar to other races; and it is obvious that such differences in race call for radically different correctional methods. But now, once within the ordinary prison, the State subjects most of the inmates to substantially the same treatment. Inevitably, without a much greater differentiation and classification than has yet been attempted except in a few of the foremost institutions, the prison treatment which checks some evil propensities increases other evil propensities. Indeed, it is a discouraging fact that very many well-appointed institutions, except in their exemplary

Evolution of Penal Methods and Institutions. 241

influence, seem to increase crime. By the criminal class, as commonly known to the police, is generally meant the class who have graduated from the prisons. Very many of the peculiarities which enable a police detective to discover criminals when intermingled in crowds with ordinary citizens are peculiarities which the prison itself has engendered. The quick glance, the abnormal walk, might be forced upon an innocent man subjected for a considerable term to the ordinary prison discipline. Then the fellowships formed in prison are oftentimes disastrous; for crime, like disease, is contagious. For great numbers of offenders the Pennsylvania or Belgian system of isolation is unquestionably the best, but for other men of unsocial instincts the character may be strengthened by even convict friendships. "Honor among thieves" is largely a mythical affair, but not entirely so, and even that kind of honor is better than none at all. Experience and enlightened reason concur in impelling the conclusion that the reformatory idea is the sound basis of all penal systems. It is rarely indeed that any one who is an instinctive criminal can by any influences be converted into a lovable character; but it has been found in a sufficient number of cases to warrant persistent effort that even hardened offenders may be occasionally turned into law-abiding citizens. In the interests of reform itself certain convicts must be sifted off into prisons for incorrigibles, separated from the hopeful classes, relegated to a position where they can not prey upon society. It will follow upon adequate classification of convicted offenders that the courts need not be so much perplexed as now about the relations of insanity to crime. Violation of law, whether the result of sane or of insane impulse, is equally a thing which society must stop. The insane perpetrator must be confined to be cured, and the method of confinement and treatment may be best determined in the actual administration of the institutions.

IMPORTANCE OF JUST PENALTIES: CAPITAL PUNISHMENT.

But while prison treatment must be so ordered as to fit the criminal rather than the crime, and opportunity be given by an indeterminate sentence for the convict to win his release by good conduct, the penalty attached by law to offenses must be commensurate with the offense. The exemplary effect of punishment is of paramount importance, and a swift execution of the law is not only deterrent upon the criminal class, but is also more widely effectual in stamping crime as iniquitous. For this reason, it seems to me, capital punishment is still warranted, although the fact that Italy has abandoned it is a strong argument against its continuance. Still, it seems to me that in the present stage of social development nothing has been devised to take its place as an approximately adequate penalty for the very gravest offenses. It is said society can not impress upon the individual consciousness the sacredness of human life by itself deliberately taking human life. But the fallacy of this reasoning is in that while society acts with deliberation, it does not act with malice. It may take the life of a guilty murderer for the general good, as it may impel the innocent soldier to death for the general good. I can not concur in the teaching, though it is ably put forth by many authoritative writers that the retributory idea should be eliminated from our penal system. Looking from the side of jurisprudence, retribution is essential in a scheme of government by law, as distinguished from despotism. And in the education of public conscience the distinctive and proportionate penalty of the law must be associated with the prohibition of the law. Righteousness must sometimes be wrathful.

IMPROVEMENTS IN PRISON ARCHITECTURE.

As the prisons have come gradually to supplant other forms of penal institution, architecture has become a most important factor. Indeed, the development of the science of dealing with delinquents may be traced in the change from such dungeons as the Mamertine at Rome to the imposing structures of our own time. In this particular America was so far in advance that in 1834 England sent a special commissioner to examine our prisons, and his report contributed suggestions for the erection of Pentonville, the pattern upon which most English prisons have since been built. Sir Joshua Jebb has been called the English originator of modern prison architecture, because he superintended the erection of the Pentonville prison. So eminent an authority on this subject as Mr. John R. Thomas seems to concede to Jebb this distinction. Unless, however, I am much mistaken, many of the essentially novel features of Pentonville were borrowed from the plans devised by Jeremy Bentham, whose "pan-opticon" was one of his most deeply cherished schemes for practical reform in governmental administration. The "pan-opticon" was essentially a prison with radiating corridors supplemented by reflecting mirrors, so contrived that the entire prison could be visually commanded from the supervising center. Whatever may be the ethical defects of Bentham's philosophy, it has been the lot of few single individuals to inspire so many reforms in legislation and governmental administration.

ETHICAL ASPECTS OF THE CRIMINAL PROBLEM.

But the limit of time assigned to the opening essay of the evening has been reached, and I will in a few moments gladly yield the floor to the gentlemen present who bring to the consideration of the subject the results of observation and experience much wider than my own. The attempt at compression has resulted in many distortions. Many phases of the topic have not been mentioned—phases which might profitably engage exclusive attention for an entire evening. The problem of crime is the paramount perplexity of ethics. In approaching the consideration of it one may well recall Milton's sublime invocation to the Heavenly Muse. Few may venture to climb the height of his great argument, much less to "assert eternal Providence and justify the ways of God to man."

To many of us the theological labyrinths and metaphysical fog banks are impenetrable. But whether the moral sense be the result of experience and of the association of ideas accumulated along those courses of conduct which promote the greatest happiness, or a more immediate inspiration from that "Power in the universe which makes for righteousness," it is the most priceless of human faculties. In many delinquents it is so far wanting or defective that they may properly be classed as moral imbeciles. In many others it is so far perverted that they regard themselves the victims of social tyranny. But a vast number have a clear apprehension of their wrongdoing. They know, when violating the law, that they are seeking the gratification of their own passions at the cost of suffering to others. They know that their punishment is just. But each, with Milton, may urge of the spirit of enlightened philanthropy—

"What in me is dark,
"Illumine; what is low, raise and support."

Even over the entrances of its prisons for incorrigibles the State should never affix the mournful legend which Dante found at the gate of Hades. And the most miserable delinquent may find courage in the thought that escape was found by Bunyan's pilgrims even from the dungeons of Despair, and that a few steps from those dungeons brought them to the Delectable Mountains, from which were gained visions of the Eternal City itself.

ABSTRACT OF THE DISCUSSION.

Mr. NELSON J. GATES:

I see but little in the lecture to invite unfavorable criticism. It seems to me that modern science in the departments of psychology and sociology has convinced thoughtful men that the moral and mental natures of men are controlled by inexorable law, and in considering the question of punishment and its effects upon the community we must take into consideration the causes that produce crime. If we are to be sympathetic our sympathy must be based upon these principles. Emerson says: "While the code of natural law is so brief and simple that it could be written upon the thumb-nail or upon a lady's signet-ring, every bubble upon a dashing stream is a key to some mystery of the universe." The cause of vicious volition: that is the mystery. What has produced it? How far is it due to heredity? How far to environment? The lecturer has not put much stress upon heredity; but the subject is a subtle one, in regard to which we have no better teacher than analogy. Look at an orchard of a thousand trees of a natural stock. They may have the same amount of rain, sunshine, and cultivation, but they will grow differently, and the differences all come from heredity—the nature of the organisms. But by culture and environment—budding, grafting, etc.—we can produce grand and nearly uniform results. So with the child; but we can not eradicate entirely his fundamental nature. Experience shows that it is not safe to depend entirely on reformatory institutions to make good citizens. It is impossible to reform all.

The volition of men is not wholly controlled by judgment. It may be my judgment that I should have an appetite, but that doesn't insure my eating. It is my judgment that I ought to avoid certain things, but that doesn't affect my strong desire for those things. The actions of the will are the exact product of antecedent causes. Good or vicious thoughts can not arise without causes which lie beyond the power and scope of the senses; and therefore we are not to be too hard in fixing the penalty for criminal acts in a spirit of revenge. I believe the will is fully conditioned. If this is so, nothing could have been any different. Why, then, should men be punished? One may say in five minutes after an act is performed, "I wish I hadn't done this," but a new factor has come in to change his determination. If the cold law of necessity prevails in mind, what right have we to punish? The penalty may be imposed as a deterrent to others. The knowledge of it becomes a part of their environment and education. Society is thus organized on the basis of the recognition of the fact that the will is conditioned. We punish for self-protection. Why kill a rattlesnake? Not to punish the snake, for he simply asserts his nature. So the criminal asserts his nature, and is not to be punished unless he intrudes on our interests. Laws do not make men moral in essence. If the only things that prevent me from robbing are police and jails, then I am a robber. Society is protected by the police and jails, but it is no help to my moral nature. A man who is restrained from violence by a sense of right is a good citizen, and he who is not so restrained must be restrained by fear. I do not think the criminal is to be considered. Whether he is in a solitary cell or working is of no moment. We must not be cruel, of course; but we must use whatever means are necessary to protect society.

It is a matter of record that three quarters of the crime and extreme poverty are the result of intemperance. What is intemperance? It is a purely physical condition—the effect of certain gases or drugs upon the brain; but the law imposes the full penalty whether the crime is committed in soberness or in drunkenness—and it does this very properly. Crime as well as intemperance is really a disease. In the light of our present knowledge it is an insult to science to say that moral depravity is not purely the result of physical derangement.

MR. Z. R. BROCKWAY, Superintendent of the Elmira Reformatory:

No better statement of the change of theory in the treatment of criminals from the old to the new penology can be found than that in the January number of an English quarterly, The Journal of Mental Science. It is as follows: "(1) The old principle of punishment must give place to the idea of social protection; (2) the criminal must be studied instead of studying the criminal act; (3) there are two factors in crime—psycho-physical organization and external circumstances."

From this premise it would seem to follow that the true function of the criminal trial is simply to determine the question of the guilt of the criminal, and whether the safety—perhaps the welfare—of society requires his restraint. When the Court has committed the criminal to custody, then its whole duty is discharged. Another tribunal of administering experts should prescribe what shall be the treatment of the prisoner and what the period of his detention, and the extent of his supervision afterward.

Not any salutary treatment can be prescribed, nor can restraints be

Evolution of Penal Methods and Institutions. 247

wisely relaxed without a very full inquiry into the corporeal, the psychical, and the emotional or spiritual idiosyncrasies of the man; and it is equally important to know what obstacles to recovery lie in the inherited impulses, and what has been wrought into the being by environment as well.

I know not whether there is an anatomically-determined criminal type, but the daily close observation of fresh criminals reveals asymmetries and peculiarities that suggest congenital physical degeneration, giving a defective human machine incapable, under the strain of social contact, of good or orderly performance. The criminal is one who is, for one reason or another, out of adjustment with his social relations, and the treatment should be to adjust or readjust him to his environment. It is found that some young criminals are not subjectively criminous, but are out of place in society, and it comes to pass that for such to find the true niche and place them in it recovers them from the predatory to the productive class. The great mass of imprisoned criminals, however, require for safe rehabilitation much more than that; they need, throughout their complex natures, to be made over, reformed, and, if it were possible, they should, some of them, be literally born again. This regeneration can not be accomplished by imprisonment under the usual punitive sentence system and under the ordinary circumstances of confinement in the average State prison, for such imprisonment affords neither adequate motive nor needed facilities for improvement. Within a few years past it has come to be generally accepted by those best informed upon the subject that for the protection of society by the treatment of criminals in prison there are at least three essentials—namely: (*a*) The indeterminate sentence in place of time sentences; (*b*) some measure of classification and graduation of prisons and prisoners, which again necessitates a thoroughly worked marking system, covering and accomplishing physical, technological, disciplinary, and scholastical training; (*c*) the conditional release or parole of prisoners with subsequent legalized supervision and control.

At the Elmira Reformatory, by the legislative act, and in actual administration, these conditions are supplied, and my observation of their application in very nearly six thousand cases during the past seventeen years shows that prisoners, when first received at the prison under the improved system, are by it brought into a favorable frame of mind. The inevitable, if unconscious, antagonism between the prisoner who wishes to go and the warden determined to keep him is dissipated, and in place of it there exists complete unity of purpose, the warden and the prisoner consulting and working together for the prisoner's early release. There is afterward, when the prisoner desires ease and the warden demands exertion, frequently a difference between them, but never a difference of aim, only of method, which is more readily reconciled.

The prisoner becomes at once interested and usually anxious to progress in the way pointed out to him as the condition of liberty, and, however feeble his ambition or deep his discouragement, hope is never entirely quenched; there always remains a point of growth, the possibility of new endeavor with improved behavior. The concord of the management and the man, together with the vitalizing element of hope, constitute a favorable subjective condition for elevating educational processes which, stimulated and assisted by superimposed training, is irresistible, and is quite sure to accomplish desirable improvement when there is a sufficient physical basis—soundness of tissue—to sustain a degree of intellectual life and moral self-control necessary for properly regulated conduct when again the prisoner is in the associations and competitions of free life.

The cure or reformation of the criminal consists not alone in better intentions, for intentions change as the weather-cock changes, with altered outward circumstances; but there must be created new habitudes—the old when repressed gradually lose strength, and new activities bring in new tastes and impulses dominating the old. When by any means, persuasive or compulsive, the life of the prisoner is so directed and practiced that the vital currents course in new molecular channels, giving satisfactory or safe instinctive conduct under conditions similar to those he must meet on his discharge, then the prisoner should be released, for the State seeks not evangelism but citicism (good citizenship) only.

The new prison science has for its sole object the reformation of the prisoner for the protection of society, and it is confidently declared that there is no other sure protection. Of course, the prisoner, while immured, can not continue his depredations, but he is an object of the public care which is maintained at considerable expense; and since he must sooner or later be released, he is likely to be then tenfold more dangerous, unless changed, reformed, during his confinement. Indeed, every conceivable purpose of imprisonment for crimes, whether it be protection, punishment, vindication of the majesty of the law, or the satisfying of clamorings for vengeance, is best accomplished by aiming solely at reformation.

The true reformatory is not the product of sentimentalism, yet the sentiment of humanity underlies and pervades it. Little or no importance is attached to the pleasure or momentary happiness of inmates, but rather regard is had for their welfare, which is more than present enjoyment. They are compelled to observe the *condi-*

Evolution of Penal Methods and Institutions. 249

tions of happiness, instead of childishly chasing a phantasm of happiness.

The institutionary government of the modern reformatory is, and must be, an autocracy under which voluntariness has full scope when it is manifested in the right direction; but, as has already been intimated, the principle of compulsion is necessary and must be freely and vigorously applied whenever there is need of it. As the system of sentence, under the new law, is without regulation of punishments, so the administration of the prison discipline leaves retribution out altogether, and discourages, too, all waste of time and effort for retrievement. The low landing place of the prisoners who fall is made at once a new point of departure for another ascent; each achievement is the foothold for another effort.

The administrative methods are, when summarized, substantially as follows: In place of the stereotyped superficial inquiries of the old system, the prisoner on admission is now most carefully examined for a very complete biographical record, the inquiry covering the ancestral history for one or two generations; evidences of degeneration and disease; mental endowment and conditions; degree of moral sense and general sensitiveness. During such an examination, which is always made by the superintendent in person, impressions are received and information obtained which naturally readily suggest the best course of treatment, a record of which is made at the time. After full explanations, instructions, and such inspirations as the officer may be able to impart, the prisoner goes into harness in physical training, the military organization, technological instruction, the school of letters, and to any special prudential conditions or treatment to which, after medical and expert educational examination, the superintendent may assign him.

Now the marking system, losses and gains under which are expressed in monetary terms, meets him on every side; there is before him a long (it should be actually indeterminate) period of possible imprisonment or the desirable alternative of an early release, if only he can earn it. A straight and narrow path of honest conduct, with manly self-control, is before him as the condition of enlargement; every attempt to find a short cut or by-path casts him backward; he can not escape it and he soon finds that he can not be comfortable and refuse or neglect to walk in it. As men more mature, burdened in free life with reponsibilities and cares which for some legitimate ambition they bear and guard, regulate their life and conduct so as to promote their object, so these ignorant or thoughtless and selfish young men take up duties to be performed, incur risks that jeopard their progress, and find it necessary to restrain as well as exert themselves, first, for the love of liberty, then afterward, with very many of them, for the love of the pursuits and prospects themselves, whose ennobling influence supplies new and better satisfactions.

At Elmira there are fifteen hundred young felons of average age, say, of twenty-one years. The powerful incentives of their situation, the choice opportunities supplied them, the stimulating control that is over them, serve to supply an animated mass of mind and men whose direction and guidance calls for vigilant skill and constitutes a most fascinating occupation. The current experience of the director is full of interesting and instructive incidents illustrating and proving the soundness of the principles of reformative instead of punitive treatment for prisoners; but I must not communicate them here.

I will conclude by saying that we may congratulate ourselves and our fellow-citizens that we live to see spread upon the statute books of so great a State as New York the somewhat modified, but nevertheless the advanced, principle of the indeterminate sentence, whereby it is decreed that they who offend against us shall be forgiven, not when they have suffered an estimated equivalent of pain as penalty, but when they can show reasonable evidence that they are so changed as to be safe, self-supporting members of the community. Not only this, but that out of the resources of the people whose laws are violated is generously supplied institutions and apparatus and instruction to recover our enemy, the criminal, to a respectable place in society again, and that the enlightened public sentiment throughout the Commonwealth enables discharged prisoners from the reformatories to find entrance into business and friendships in good society.

And, finally, let us be glad that, having emerged from the hard doctrines of former times into more scientific and humane sentiments about sin and crime, we have at the same time learned to rely for reformation of character less than formerly on the preaching to prisoners of purely religious dogma, and more upon education. Not mere common school cramming, but a broadened educational *régime*, whose fullness embraces physical renovation, technological training, increase of mental powers, and such presentations and study of Nature and of society, that there appears in consciousness the dawning idea of a Creator who is the common Father of us all, and with this the sense of universal kinship.

DR. LEWIS G. JANES:

Mr. Emerson has somewhere said: "An acceptance of the sentiment of love throughout Christendom for a season would bring the felon and outcast to our side in tears, with the devotion of his faculties to our service." We are beginning to see, however, that the mere

Evolution of Penal Methods and Institutions. 251

sentiment of love is not enough. There are those who, in their sentimental attitude toward the criminal classes, love "not wisely, but too well"; or, if not too well, at least far from wisely. Here love must be tempered by justice and wisdom; it must call to its aid the counsels of science and the teachings of evolution. I have just been reading anew the noble essay of Herbert Spencer on Prison Ethics, printed in the British Quarterly Review a third of a century ago, and have been forcibly struck with its exceedingly modern tone. Indeed, it may be truthfully said that all our advance in the treatment of criminals in recent years has been along the lines laid down in that essay. Comparing it with the able lecture of this evening, and the admirable paper of Mr. Brockway, one could not help noting the identity of purpose, and usually of method, therein indicated. Mr. Spencer herein advocated the indeterminate sentence, wise methods of prison labor with compensation, the mark system, and the physical, intellectual, and moral culture of the criminal, now so admirably enforced by Superintendent Brockway at that model institution the Elmira Reformatory. Mr. Spencer lays down the principle that "institutions are ultimately determined by the nature of the citizens living under them," and therefore recognizes the relativity of the law as to the application of penal methods, whereby harsher methods are required under an arbitrary government and in an immature stage of social development; but he strongly emphasizes the fact that harsh measures are always liable to survive when society has advanced to a higher status, which renders their administration barbarous, unscientific, and positively injurious, and that justice is best satisfied when it is wisely tempered with humanity. I agree with Mr. Spencer and Mr. Brockway that retributive punishments are wholly out of place in our modern civilized communities, and must here dissent from the position taken by the lecturer. I also strongly dissent from even his qualified advocacy of capital punishment. It seems to me that the demand for a swift and certain execution of the law with which he introduced his remarks on this subject is, in fact, a powerful argument against capital punishment; for all our experience proves that public sentiment in this country will not permit the swift enforcement of this supreme penalty, or its general enforcement at any period, even for homicidal crimes. Within the past year (1892) there have been six thousand seven hundred and ninety-one cases of homicide in this country, and only one hundred and seven legal executions. To these may be added two hundred and thirty-six lynchings. The fact that Italy and other European countries have outstripped us in abolishing this relic of barbarism, and that no evil effects have followed its abolition, even in a country which we habitually associate with the ready appeal to the stiletto, should lead us to wiser conclusions. The certainty of imprisonment for life at hard labor, or even for a limited period of sufficient duration, with wise restriction of the pardoning power, would be far more effective as a deterrent than capital punishment as now administered in this country. I agree with the lecturer that Dante's mournful legend should never bar out all hope, even from the breasts of the most hardened criminals; and when life is taken, hope is extinguished forever.

On one other point it seems to me that an unjust conclusion may be drawn from the statistics presented by the lecturer. It is said that fifty-five per cent of the inmates of the Elmira Reformatory are of foreign birth or parentage. But Mr. Brockway informs me that two thirds of the inmates of that institution came from New York city and Brooklyn, and in these cities, I believe, a much larger proportion of the population than that is of foreign birth and parentage.* It would therefore appear that here, as elsewhere in this country, the alarming increase in crime in recent years has been proportionately greater among our native than among our foreign population. However painful may be the confession, we are bound to look at the facts as they are, and to do no injustice to our foreign population. The question of preventive measures is of prime importance; but lack of time forbids its discussion. Above all things, the management of our penal institutions should be kept out of politics and placed only in the hands of enlightened and competent officials. It is our duty as citizens to use every influence in our power to this end. In our State Reformatory we have a noble object lesson, showing how such institutions should be conducted. Fortunate indeed shall we be when all our prisons, jails, and reformatories have wardens and superintendents as just, firm, wise, and enlightened as Superintendent Brockway.

I do not agree with Mr. Gates that the criminal is not to be considered. We are bound to deal justly by him as by any other citizen. A criminal forfeits his rights only in proportion as he violates the rights of other individuals or endangers the peace of society. Experience at Elmira and elsewhere proves that a certain proportion, not small, of persons with criminal tendencies may, under proper discipline and training, be made good citizens. It is our duty to bring all possible means to bear toward this end.

MR. McKEEN briefly thanked the audience for its cordial reception of his paper, but declined to reply at length to criticisms.

* The census of 1890 shows that in the entire State of New York only forty-two per cent of the inhabitants are of unmixed native parentage. In the cities the proportion is still lower.

EVOLUTION OF CHARITIES AND CHARITABLE INSTITUTIONS

BY

AMOS G. WARNER, PH. D.

PROFESSOR OF ECONOMICS IN LELAND STANFORD JUNIOR UNIVERSITY
LATE SUPERINTENDENT OF CHARITIES, WASHINGTON, D. C., ETC.

COLLATERAL READINGS SUGGESTED:

Spencer's Principles of Sociology and Principles of Ethics; Fawcett's Pauperism, its Causes and Remedies; Eden's State of the Poor; Mrs. Lowell's Public Relief and Private Charity; Wayland's Outdoor Relief and Tramps; Riis's How the Other Half Lives; McCulloch's The Tribe of Ishmael, a Story of Social Degradation (address before the National Conference of Charities and Correction, 1888); Elizabeth Bisland's *London Charities,* Cosmopolitan, July, 1891; Dr. Seaman's *Social Waste of a Great City,* Science, vol. viii, p. 283.

EVOLUTION OF CHARITIES AND CHARITABLE INSTITUTIONS.

BY AMOS G. WARNER, PH. D.

HOW NATURAL SELECTION OPERATES IN RACE IMPROVEMENT.

NEXT to its efficiency as a means of race improvement, the most striking characteristic of natural selection is its enormous wastefulness. Heedless of the lapse of time, prodigal of life and indifferent to suffering, the forces of Nature-apart-from-man work out surely, but at fearful cost, the differentiation and improvement of species. A hundred different characteristics may be essential to the survival of a given organism under given conditions, and to fail in one essential is as surely fatal as to fail in all. For a defect in any one of many essentials the punishment of Nature is death. If a given person, fitted in all other ways to promote the advancement of a race, can not resist an attack of small-pox, that person, setting aside conscious effort to prevent the disease, must die, and so must perish all who are similarly weak until the race shall be made up of persons impervious to this disease. If a young man who is fitted in all other ways for high success under the conditions of modern life has neglected to learn to swim, and then permits himself to fall into deep water, Nature calmly eliminates him as one of the unfit. If the population of a thriving town is indiscreet enough to live beneath a reservoir not adequately strong, Nature hurls over them the waters of a Conemaugh flood, and all that quantity of prosperous and useful life is obliterated, merely to give to other communities a hint that they must employ engineers more competent or more honest.

From the extermination of young codfish to the decay and disappearance of the races of men, nonsentient Nature operates in the same successful but remorseless way. The wolf that can not bear starvation, or the Englishman that can not bear the tropic heat of India, must pay the penalty of death for their respective weaknesses. But early in the development of living beings instincts appear which tend to economize time and life in the process of evolution. One of the earliest instincts of this sort is that which prompts animals to care for their young. Some shield is interposed between the helpless infants of the lower orders and the remorseless operations of nonsentient Nature. In the higher orders of life the sentiment extends beyond the family, and an instinctive desire to preserve the life of others defeats the uneconomical ruthlessness of Nature. Thus comes in what may be called instinctive selection as opposed to natural selection in a narrow sense. The charitable impulse, the desire to help the destitute to prolong life and make it happier and fuller, has, until recently, been an instinct only.

THE CHARACTERISTICS OF HUMAN SELECTION.

Finally there has been introduced an element which may be termed rational selection. It comes to be perceived that those who, for some reason, are not capable of coping with the local and temporary conditions which surround them, may yet be of great use to the race, if preserved from Nature or from instinct by the conscious and purposeful intervention of man. It thus happens that we practice vaccination that the scourge of small-pox may not run its former course and harden the race only after it has destroyed the larger part of it. We see, or think we see, that the time of the race can be better employed than in becoming inured to small-pox, and we modify the process of natural selection in order that the process of evolution may take a short cut toward its final goal. For similar reasons, if it be possible, we throw a life-preserver to a drowning man that all the energy and time that had been spent in rearing him may not be wasted merely because he did not know how to swim. We send relief to Johnstown in order that cold and famine may not supplement the devastation of the flood. We hold it to be our business so to modify conditions as to make certain the survival of those who are fit from the standpoint of race improvement. As Professor Ward puts it, "the environment transforms the animal, while man transforms the environment."

" So we, considering everywhere
  Great Nature's purpose in her deeds,
  And finding that of fifty seeds
  She often brings but one to bear "—

Evolution of Charities. 257

considering these things, I say, we study agriculture, and try to plant the seeds so that more of them will germinate than under the natural *régime*.

For the purposes of this evening, then, we consider human selection—that is, selection as it affects human beings—to be made up of three elements. First, natural selection in a very narrow sense, meaning by this the selection that results from the operations of the blind forces of Nature—from winds and floods and droughts, from cold and heat and earthquakes, and from all pestilences having their origin in causes beyond human control. Secondly, there is what may be called instinctive selection, by which I mean that selection which results incidentally from the instincts of man or from his purposeful acts which are not designed to influence selection. As examples of this we may take the extermination of a tribe in which the combative instincts of the individuals are so strong that they can not co-operate for mutual defense, or the death without surviving issue of the debauchee and the prostitute, or the extinction by pestilence of the instinctively dirty and unclean, or the tendency to survive and multiply of sober and thrifty people like the Friends. Thirdly, there is an element in human selection which we may call rational selection. We have an example of this when the State enacts laws against murder and suppresses private war; when it drains a malarial swamp or provides for sanitary inspection in order to lower the death rate; when it forbids child labor and endeavors to prevent the unhealthful employment of women; when the community guarantees the destitute from starvation or death from exposure; whenever, in short, any action is taken for the set purpose of affecting the death rate or the birth rate, or for promoting the public health.

COMPARISON OF NATURAL, INSTINCTIVE, AND RATIONAL SELECTION.

Natural selection, using the term in the narrow sense above indicated, is perfectly ruthless and fearfully wasteful. Instinctive selection is a step toward something better, something more economical of time and energy and life; but the advance is still made blindly with many halts and retrogressions and excursions into no thoroughfares. The excessive development of the sexual instinct which at one time is necessary to the survival and development of the race, may at another destroy the welfare of the race which it once promoted. The instinct of the fighter, at one time necessary to preserve its owner in the rude struggles of the time, may at another get its owner hung for murder. The instinctive impulse to aid the destitute and to keep the poor from starving, which results in more economical evolution at one time, may at another be the agent which wastefully prolongs the existence of those who are unfit from the standpoint of race improvement.

Rational selection at the first, and at its poorest, is only a shade better than instinctive selection. Indeed, in cases of definite blundering it may have worse results than instinctive selection. Indeed, it is hard to tell in any given case how far we should allow our reason to dominate our impulses. But it is manifest that rational selection, at its best, and in its possibilities, is the superior of the other two forms, and those races will eventually survive which practice it most constantly and most wisely.

In so far as the impulse to aid one's fellow-men has heretofore affected human selection, it has formed a part of instinctive rather than of rational selection. Pity for the helpless, the diseased, and the destitute did not originate in the reasoning faculties any more than did maternal love. Indeed, it might have seemed that a people that charged itself with the task of supporting the weaklings would have been fatally handicapped; that it was irrational to assist incapables to survive; and we frequently hear it urged to-day that the giving of relief promotes the survival of the unfit. But experience has indicated that those communities and peoples that have developed largely the charitable instinct, properly so called, have been the ones that survived. In the many instances that might be cited where the dependent classes have become so numerous as to drag down the community, a closer examination will show that the altruistic impulse had degenerated or been counterfeited, and we do not recall any race that is even reported to have become extinct through the excess of genuine brotherly love.

Utility of the Charitable Impulse.

The survival of those peoples that have the altruistic sentiment strongly developed is perhaps a sufficient answer, from the evolutionary standpoint, to those who object to all philanthropic undertakings as mischievous meddling with the benign course of Nature; and yet, perhaps, it is worth while to introduce a parenthesis, in answer to the questions, Why not be brutal? Why not chloroform diseased babies and aged paupers? Why not shoot down the Indians and drown the inmates of our insane asylums? Perhaps for the purposes of this parenthesis these questions sufficiently answer themselves if we add to them the question, What would be the effect of such a course upon the state of feeling existing between employer and employed, between debtor and creditor, and between all the myriad atoms that make up modern society? Do we not know instinctively that a return to barbarism in this way would return us to barbarism in other ways? The question, Why not be brutal? has further been answered by anticipation: Because it is not economical. And, finally, if we are asked why the vicious and the profligate, the dirty and the diseased, can not be allowed to exterminate themselves, run their course and perish, we can answer that gangrene will not do the work of caustic. Social cancers infect a larger portion of the body politic than they eat away.

INFLUENCE OF RELIGIOUS SANCTIONS ON THE CHARITABLE IMPULSE.

Whatever begot the charitable impulse in the first place, it survived because it was useful; and any impulse or habit that is for the good of the race is likely, in the course of time, to be fixed and its practice insured by religious sanction. Almost all customs, including the organization of the Government and of the family, and even habits of cleanliness and diet, have been thus confirmed. For present purposes we need not bother ourselves with teleological considerations, nor inquire whether the religious sanctions begot the useful habits *de novo*, or whether the useful habits originated through spontaneous variation, and were then seized upon and perpetuated by the religious instinct.

To whatever source we may trace the sentiment of pity and the desire to relieve the destitute, this, at least, is sure that it had not been in existence long before it was re-enforced by religious sanctions. In the language of the Vendidad, as quoted by Mr. Crooker: "The riches of the infinite God will be bestowed upon him who relieves the poor." Or, according to a Hindu epic, "He who giveth without stint food to a fatigued wayfarer, never seen before, obtaineth merit that is great." In China, long before the Christian era, and in some sort with religious encouragement and guidance, there were refuges for aged and sick poor, free schools for poor children, free eating-houses for wearied laborers, associations for the distribution of second-hand clothing, and societies for paying the expenses of marriage and burial among the poor.*

But religious sanctions sometimes deteriorate the very impulse that they are supposed to strengthen. When the religious re-enforcement of a charitable impulse has been the desire to do the will of the Heavenly Father, wishing only good to his children, it has not only strengthened the altruistic impulse, but has uplifted and ennobled it. When, on the other hand, it has been a mere desire to escape hell and enter heaven, or to propitiate a more or less unreasonable deity, we have had the acts of charity without the motive, the letter that killeth without the spirit that giveth life. The grim threat of the Talmud—"The house that does not open to the poor shall open to the physician"—is typical of many passages that might be quoted from the older religious writings. Under the influence of such threats or of more direct ones, many a man has felt constrained to aid the poor for purely selfish reasons; to do some overt act that he thought prescribed, in order that it might be accounted to him for righteousness. We all know how the teachings of the New Testament were so distorted by the mediæval Church that princely gifts to the poor were made for the selfish purpose of benefiting the giver's soul, and with entire disregard of the results upon the recipients of relief. Indeed, so purely selfish, and even commercial, were the reasons which led the people of the middle ages to give to the poor, that one person, whom Prof. Huxley has quoted, spoke of such gifts as "merely a species of fire insurance."

ALMSGIVING NO CHARITY; FAILURE OF THE CHURCH AS AN ALMONER.

We shall find, as we review the various forms of the charitable impulse, that the objective effects almost invariably deteriorate in consequence of a deterioration of the subjective motive. When almsdeed takes the place of charity, the

* See Crooker, Problems in American Society, p. 51. I am indebted to Mr. Crooker for any symptoms of erudition that may appear in this part of the lecture.

poor are not helped, but merely fed and clothed, and too frequently degraded. Further than this, however valuable religion may be as a motive power urging people to charitable deeds, the ecclesiastical organization, the Church, as an administrator of relief funds on a large scale, has seldom been a success. The work of the Church and of religious people has been most successful as an initiator of charitable undertakings. New classes of sufferers have been sought out and helped; new methods of helping them have been invented and applied; but when the community had been educated up to the point where it saw that a large charitable work needed doing, and when the methods of doing this work had been quite thoroughly elaborated and reduced to a routine, the usefulness of the Church organization as the community's almoner has been pretty well at an end. Specialists in spiritual matters do not appear to be the best administrators of material relief. This comes only in part from the deterioration of the charitable impulse already referred to, and only in part from the worldliness which creeps into a wealthy church organization. It comes very largely from the tendency of ecclesiastical almoners to forget the material effects of their work, through concentration of their thoughts upon things spiritual. In our modern churches there is very little of the selfish element which induces the church members to give for the sake of their own souls, but there is too much of the giving which serves only as a bait to bring the unrepentant within the spiritual reach of a particular denomination. The "fire-insurance" element has disappeared, but the element of interdenominational competition takes its place. Material relief is scattered about as a farmer scatters corn about his feet when he wishes to bring the chickens about him in order to catch some of them. So blind are many of the workers to the effect upon the poor of this sort of relief-giving, that a charity organizationist in a large American city once told me that the relief-giving female missionary was the bane of his life.

THE STATE AS ALMONER.

So common has been the failure of the Church to be a good almoner when administering large funds, that in most countries the heaviest part of the burden of relieving the poor has been transferred to the state. In England the Church was deprived of her almonership at the time of the

Reformation; in France, only at the close of the last century; and in Italy the great charitable endowments administered by the Church have been secularized only within the last few years. But so complete has this change actually been that a recent volume by Hubert-Valleroux, urging that the public authorities in France should loosen their hold upon the relief funds now administered in that country by the Bureaux de Bienfaisance, and that the Church should again become the community's largest almoner, is a reactionary plea to which no one seems likely to give heed. And yet this author is right when he claims that the charities of France were largely begotten and developed by the Church. It is mainly through church influence that the community has been educated up to a point where it insists that this large mass of relief work shall be done. None the less, it is proper that after individuals and the Church have experimented and found out what needs doing, the doing of it should often be intrusted to the state.

This tendency from ecclesiastical to state administration of relief-giving was confirmed at the close of the last century, when the religious dogma of the brotherhood of man was paralleled by the political dogma of the equality of men. Among the rights which the revolutionary governments of France held to be inherent in the individual was the right to labor and the right to be saved from starvation. The "passion for humanity" not only led to the extravagant guarantees given by the revolutionary governments of France, but indirectly it encouraged the lavish giving of outdoor relief, which proved such a curse in England. This lavish giving of public outdoor relief, which has been repeatedly cited as an example of the limitless power for harm inherent in the state, resulted, as Chalmers pointed out, in taking money from the thrifty by taxation and giving it to the thriftless in the name of charity. It was altered greatly for the better by the Poor Law reform of 1834. In the modifications of political philosophy that have come about since 1848, the justification of public poor-relief has been much changed. It is now oftenest justified on the grounds of expediency, and, curiously enough, those countries which theoretically give relief as a right which the individual may demand do not differ greatly in the practical administration of the poor law from those which give relief as a favor and as a matter of expediency.

INFLUENCE OF THE LAISSEZ-FAIRE DOCTRINE.

But "equality" was not the first word in the political creed of the revolutionary epoch from 1776 to 1848. The first word was "liberty," and while the passion for humanity, acting on political theories, tended greatly to extend public relief, at the same time the passion for liberty, operating through economic theory, begot the doctrine of *laissez faire*, and tended to limit public relief work or to abolish it altogether. Really, though not avowedly, the economists put the emphasis on "liberty," and the politicians the emphasis on "equality," and in both cases the emphasis was rather too strong. The economists rendered invaluable aid in the reform of the poor laws, but the fact that they several times said "Don't" to good purpose emboldened them to say it sometimes when they had much better have said "Do." Napoleon's maxim, "Open the way for talent," is an excellent maxim for those who have talent, but how about those who have it not? While the former press on to the opening made for them, it is likely that the latter will be crushed. "Whoso in the press," said Carlyle, "is trodden down, has only to lie there and be trampled broad," and this was his way of formulating the conclusion which he thought he found in some poor-law commission reports that had been written by economists. The school of political economy of Cobden and John Bright—the Manchester School, as the Germans call it—implied in their teaching that philanthropy was only a mischievous tinkering with matters much better left to themselves.

But utilitarianism was triumphant on the side of both political and economic theory, and practice was brought to conform with the new philosophy. People were no longer lavishly given relief simply because abstract reasoning indicated that they had a "right" to it, and, on the other hand, the community never consented to let the destitute suffer and die, simply because the "dismal science" indicated that that was the proper thing to do. The relief work of the Church, the state, and the individual has been brought to the base of expediency, and neither theological nor philosophical considerations are sufficient to compel the continued doing of that which experience indicates to be unwise.

It has already been indicated, in a general way, that between the time of the Reformation and the present a very large amount of relief work has been undertaken by the state. In New York State alone—the Empire State of a country that was once thought to be quarantined against pauperism by the Declaration of Independence—considerably more than one million dollars per month is paid out from the public treasury for charitable institutions. But are public charities charities at all? Mrs. Lowell, you know, has called her work Public Relief and Private Charity, indicating a distinction. When a special committee of the Legislature of Pennsylvania was investigating the expenditures for charities in that State, the committee took the ground that an institution supported from the proceeds of taxation was not a charity at all. The Indiana State Board of Charities, on the other hand, say that it is proper to call a public institution for the relief of the poor a charitable institution, since it is sympathy for the poor that induces the legislators to vote the money; and it is sympathy for the poor that induces their constituents to uphold them in so doing. It would surely be unwise to quarrel with a popular nomenclature for the sake of a fine distinction which after all may not be justifiable.

DIFFERENTIATION OF EDUCATIONAL FROM CHARITABLE INSTITUTIONS.

Historically we find, as already indicated, that what the state is now doing was formerly done by the Church, or by private associations, or by individuals. When the work became large, and it was certain the community demanded the doing of it, and the methods of doing it had been well developed, then it was unloaded upon the state, and the state still bears the load. But there has been a tendency for some of the enterprises which started as charities to cease to be classed as such after the state has had control of them for a considerable time. I refer especially to educational institutions. These were formerly considered charities, and in law an incorporated school or university is still classed as an eleemosynary corporation. The charities commission which investigated the endowed charities of England found some of its hardest work not in reforming and revising the institutions for the giving of material relief, but in the grammar schools and other educational enterprises supported by endowments. The free schools of England were long spoken of as "charity schools," but in this country we would no longer think of so classifying them.

Lying between what we now call educational institutions and what we now call charitable institutions are the establishments for the education of the defective classes, as the blind, the deaf and dumb, and the feeble-minded. It is within the memory of men still living that such institutions as these were supported almost entirely by private contributions and classed by their promoters as charities. Yet now they resent such a classification and wish to be considered purely educational. While this development has been going on, the character of their support has also changed and they are now, for the most part, maintained at public expense. As regards the feeble-minded, the development is behind that of the other two classes of defectives mentioned, and in the work of caring for inebriates public enterprise has as yet done almost nothing. Whether or not other groups of institutions, now classed as charitable, shall eventually come to be classed otherwise can not be definitely foreseen; but my own impression is that there is an important practical and theoretical distinction between the giving of material relief—such as food, shelter, and clothing—and the giving merely of instruction and opportunities for self-development. There is in the former class of undertakings a possibility of degrading the recipient, which is almost entirely absent in the second class; and it seems likely that the "taint of charity," whatever that may be, will always cling to the giving of material relief.

EVILS AND ADVANTAGES OF STATE ADMINISTRATION; THE SUBSIDY QUESTION.

The state has been an unsatisfactory almoner in some ways. The element of brotherly love is at a minimum in relief work when it is done by public officials. Sometimes the blight of partisan politics falls upon the charities of the city, or the county, or the State, as it did in the old days of outdoor relief in Brooklyn; as it has in Marion County, Indiana, where the volume of outdoor relief varies with the intensity of election excitement; as it has in Nebraska and many other States, where positions in the insane asylums and other institutions are part of the political spoils. But in the main, where the work to be done is large, the state is the most reliable almoner that we have; at the same time it should be said that the large measure of administrative awkwardness which has fallen to the lot of American local government makes it undesirable that the state should undertake work which can not be done in a routine manner and according to pretty thoroughly generalized rules. For this reason outdoor relief in American cities and counties has usually been a source of degradation to the poor and of corruption to local politics.

The advantages of public relief work are that an income adequate to all that needs doing can be depended upon, and that under a just system of taxation all are compelled to contribute according to their ability. The advantages of private charitable organization are great economy of administration, more personal and sympathetic interest in the beneficiaries, and a greater measure of inventiveness and adaptability of means to ends. It has therefore been frequently attempted to unite the advantages of public and private charities by the giving of subsidies from the public funds to the private charitable institutions. Few, perhaps, know how far this tendency has gone. In New York city alone nearly two million dollars per year is paid into the treasuries of private charitable institutions. In New York State a single private institution receives over two hundred thousand dollars per annum in the form of such subsidies. The objections to this hybrid form of organization are, that by disguising pauperism it promotes it, as in the case of the fourteen thousand dependent children in New York city; second, that it leads to the needless duplicating of institutions, as where in Maryland there are two sets of juvenile reformatories—one administered by the Catholics and the other by the Protestants; third, that it does not take the charities out of politics, but merely transfers their representatives from the executive offices to the legislative lobby; and fourth, that it tends to dry up the sources of private benevolence. As illustrating this last point, it may be noticed that as public contributions to institutions for the education of the deaf, dumb, and blind have increased, private contributions have fallen off. Private donors do not like to have their mites hidden by the large contributions from the public treasury, and turn their attention to charities that do not receive state support. In the District of Columbia I have studied this matter with care, and it is almost uniformly true that as public support has increased private contributions have fallen off, and in many cases they have finally ceased altogether. The subsidy system, as a transition from private support to public support, may sometimes be advisable, but, wherever practiced, the state should have some effective means of supervising the institutions it subsidizes, and should have absolute control over the admission and the discharge of the inmates whom it supports.

PUBLIC AND PRIVATE RELIEF WORK IN THE UNITED STATES.

At the present time the state is responsible for the great mass of relief work in the United States. In its almshouse it provides for all classes not otherwise provided for, and especially for the aged and infirm poor. In relief of the sick it usually provides free hospitals in the large cities, but where endowments have accumulated, as in Philadelphia, the larger part of this work is done by private institutions. Either directly or through subsidized institutions, it provides for the care and training of dependent children; it provides for the education, with free board and lodging, of the defective classes; in its asylums or hospitals it provides for the ever-increasing number of the insane; to a happily increasing extent it provides education and custodial care for the feeble-minded; and, finally, in some cities, as Boston, and recently in Washington, there is public provision for the homeless poor. The state having undertaken all these forms of charitable work, what now remains for private benevolence to do? The same work that has always fallen to the lot of private benevolence—that, namely, of invention, experimentation, progress. Private benevolence showed what was possible in the way of friendly inns and wood-yards, and now that branch of work is about ripe for transfer to the public authorities. It has shown and is showing what can be done in the way of free kindergartens for the children of the poor, and that work is being transferred to the educational department of the local governments; it is showing in New York, Baltimore, and elsewhere what can be done in the promotion of thrift through dime saving institutions, and that work we hope will eventually be transferred to a postal saving department of the Federal Government. Private benevolence has shown and is showing, in the great children's aid societies of the country, the advantages to be derived from boarding children in private homes instead of herding them in great institutions; and this lesson has also been learned by progressive public authorities in Michigan, Minnesota, the District of Columbia, and elsewhere. There also remains for private benevolence a very considerable amount of work which the public authorities can not properly undertake. At present private benevolence should do all that is done in the way of outdoor relief. It is conceivable that if we improve in the administrative branches of our Government, a time may come when the work of relieving the poor in their homes can be undertaken by public officials; but such a time is yet far distant. However this may be, there will always remain for private undertakings the relief work which must necessarily be re-enforced by religious exhortation and spiritual uplift. The Salvation Army can do much that no public authority can ever undertake, and there will always be relief work which can best be done by the minister and the missionary. Finally, there remains for private benevolence the work of seeing that public authorities do their duty; and, most important of all, the work of organizing and co-ordinating all the charitable agencies of our cities, counties, and States. The former is especially the duty of the State Charities Aid Association, and the latter of the Charity Organization Society.

ETHICAL ASPECTS OF THE QUESTION.

In the outline of this lecture, which was prepared before the man who was to give the lecture had been chosen, the heading is inserted "The Effect of Indiscriminate Charity on Character." I ask to be excused from treating that subject. It is easy to talk upon the subject of philanthropy as a failure, and I have myself discussed that subject many times and at length; but, as a student of political economy, I hold it to be my duty to say very little about it. Economists have harped enough on that string already. From Walter Bagehot, who said that it was doubtful whether or not the efforts of philanthropists to relieve their fellow-men had not resulted in more harm than good, to the last college sophomore, who has written an essay on Pauperism, they all know how to insist upon the dangers of relief work. At present and to this audience it seems a more helpful thing to shadow forth, however dimly, the place of charitable work in evolutionary economy, and to show that we are not obliged to look upon all the works of philanthropy as a gratuitous blunder.

The charitable impulse persists because in the long run it

is useful to the race that possesses it. It has a distinct value in so modifying environment as to save from needless extermination all who are in any wise fit from the standpoint of race improvement. It is useful in that it minimizes suffering, lengthens life, and economizes energy. In the complex conditions of modern life self-sacrifice must manifest itself and do its work through modern machinery. It must take into its service all the implements of scientific research and school itself to be wise as well as sympathetic. With the same care and for the same reasons that it would give shelter to neglected and abandoned children, it must see to it that it does not encourage parents to neglect and abandon their children; with the same care and for the same reasons that it would feed a hungry man, it must see to it that that man works for what he gets; with the same care and for the same reasons that it assists and helps a woman who has been abused and abandoned by her husband, it must, if possible, punish the man who has abused and abandoned her; with the same care and for the same reasons that it would insure a feeble-minded woman against starvation, it must insure that same woman against the possibility of having offspring. Charity, as has been well said, must no longer be a means of securing merit, but a method of helpfulness.

At one time it was supposed that self-seeking was invariably and inevitably bad, but the early economists " changed all that " and taught that enlightened self-interest was the salvation of industrial society. Bastiat, the rhetorician of economists, almost takes our breath away as he describes the "economic harmonies" latent in enlightened selfishness. That which produced so many evils, the economists declared, was only a very short-sighted species of selfishness. Now, if enlightened self-interest is a good thing, which it is, enlightened self-sacrifice is a better thing. One instinct, as well as the other, may be blind and so harmful, but one instinct, as well as the other, is capable of enlightenment; one, as well as the other, may be rationalized.

Your lectures this winter have dealt with "The Factors in American Civilization." Among such factors, enlightened self-sacrifice must find a place if America is to be loyal to the "high calling wherewith she is called"; if, as thousands have fondly hoped, she is to prove herself to be that nation which at last shall "serve as model for the mighty world, and be the fair beginning of a time."

ABSTRACT OF THE DISCUSSION.

Miss M. E. RICHMOND, Secretary of the Charity Organization Society, Baltimore, Md.:

Some time ago I had occasion to attend a meeting called for the purpose of organizing reformatory work among homeless young women. Two protests were made, I remember, against the plan of work as there explained. One good lady complained that it was narrow to limit the organization to one purpose; that so much good work could be done for worthy old couples too. Another objected that the children were neglected—nothing appealed to her heart so much as the cry of little children. Inspired by these examples, a third person present moved that we bind ourselves to nothing definite; that we remain (though she did not so word it) in a state "of relatively indefinite, incoherent homogeneity." When I wrote to an officer of your association, Mr. Skilton, soon after about the evolution of charitable methods, and he replied with great frankness that the *non*-evolution of charities had attracted his attention for a long time, I thought that possibly he too had attended recently a meeting for the organization of reformatory work.

Perhaps, to one who is in the field, the minor obstacles and discouragements assume undue importance, and such a one should express her gratitude first of all to Prof. Warner for the larger view which gives charity its rightful place in the evolution of life on our planet. It is my purpose, however, to dwell on some of the discouragements, hoping we may find an indication here of the path which progress must follow.

Taking the more objective of these first, the daily press of our large cities, with some notable exceptions, is the enemy of charitable progress. It parades the needs of our poorer neighbors in grossly exaggerated descriptions, it advertises the poverty of particular families, with name, street, and number, in local items, where the policeman and the newspaper reporter figure as guardian angels; and, worse still, it fosters that vanity which delights in the cheap, local notoriety of a charitable leader.

Another and most discouraging element in modern charity is the gross materialism of the charitable—a materialism which pins its faith to charitable cash and charitable bricks and mortar, a materialism which thrives too often in our churches, and finds its expression, on cold days, in loaves of bread sent for distribution to police headquarters, or in free soup for the idle. Still another discouragement, and the natural corollary of this materialism, is the wasteful expenditure for charity in our large cities. In Baltimore, which is not the most wealthy city of its size in the East, we spend a million and a third of dollars yearly in running the public and private charities of the city, and this takes no account of individual benefactions, which certainly amount to a third of a million more. Those who know the work of these charities most intimately feel that only a very small part of this money is spent in making our people permanently better, and therefore happier.

The tendency of charities to revert to a lower type should be noted. The wave of reform which reached our country from Elberfeld during the forties and resulted here in associations for the improvement of the condition of the poor, purposing to teach habits of thrift and self-help and to discourage beggary, subsided again to leave us with a number of relief agencies, many of them still engaged in no better work than the distribution of coal and groceries. The history of these associations reminds me of the career of that "missing link," the ascidian, who gave promise at one time of a backbone, but reverted later into a mere stomach.

It has been said that the most liberal of us are superstitious in spots. A physician would discover your medical superstitions, and it is but natural that I should find myself wondering how many charitable superstitions are still yours. The power over us of outworn charitable traditions is so great that nothing but a perpetual readjustment to the best knowledge and experience of our time can save us from fatal fallacies. Take an illustration from Boston, of whose philanthropic progress we are accustomed to speak with awe. The mayor of that city appointed a special committee of men and women to examine and report upon the condition of its public charitable institutions. Last year, in their final report, the committee summed up many pages of admirable and most practical suggestions with the statement that prevention and cure appear to form no part of the policy of the administration; that there seems to be "no policy except that of feeding and housing cheaply, and, on the whole, humanely, all who come." A critic, commenting upon this report, remarks: "Remedial charity is in everybody's theory but in no one's practice." I am not prepared to agree with him, but it is quite certain that we are all of us supplied with a larger body of doctrine on this subject than we have ever used.

Is the situation quite hopeless, then? By no manner of means. I take the report of this Boston committee as a most hopeful sign of the times. When men and women are willing to spend months in the careful examination and tabulation of facts for no possible personal gain and with the certainty of giving much necessary offense, when they consent to become intimately acquainted with the most disgusting conditions and their loathsome causes, and when this knowledge is informed by a spirit of enlightened helpfulness, the battle is not lost. A new spirit is abroad—the spirit which Dr. Warner calls enlightened self-sacrifice. It demands a thorough acquaintance with the facts in their totality, and an appreciation of what others have done and are doing in any given charity work. In sharp contrast to the old school, it insists upon the same standard of manly and womanly independence for every human soul, and seeks to develop habits of self-help by wise giving and by wise withholding.

This new spirit came to us with a second wave of charitable reform, which was first felt in 1878 from the work of Edward Denison and Octavia Hill in England. This wave has not subsided and left us in the state of the ascidian—its force is developing, through what is known as the charity organization movement, a well-defined vertebral column.

Over eighty cities and towns in the United States have organized charity organization societies; but it would be unfair to leave the impression that the spirit of the new charity has been confined within these bodies. On the contrary, it has leavened the whole charitable lump. Orphan asylums are being replaced by technical schools; unwieldy institutions by cottages, and, in the case of children, by carefully selected homes in the country; Dorcas societies, where the ladies of the parish met to do some sewing for a remote and shadowy class known as "the deserving poor," have given place to sewing schools and industrial workrooms; and educational philanthropy is everywhere on the increase.

In searching about for some logical progression in the history of charities, it has occurred to me that a hint of the possibilities as yet undeveloped in the race's charitable instinct may be found in the growth of that more highly developed but, as I believe, parallel instinct— maternal love. Most permanent now of all human ties, it is hard to realize that, in the early communities, mother and child held this relation to each other during the period of infancy only; that motherhood ceased when physical helplessness was at an end. Mr. Fiske has shown, in his able chapter on moral genesis, how the maternal instinct grew with the growing faculties of man and with the increasing need of ante-natal education; the more complex the needs of the child, the deeper the mother's love.

Trace the history of mother love through the ages, and you can not fail to find many interesting analogies to the history of charitable development. If, in the lack of permanence in our charitable relations, we are forced to compare ourselves to the gregarious communities of barbarism, the comparison may give us an enlightening glimpse of our unrealized possibilities. If, in artificial states of society, we find the mother relegating her mother's privileges and duties to hirelings, it will not be impossible to discover those in our own day who are willing to pay others to discharge their charitable duties. If the mother instinct, unenlightened and uncontrolled, has hindered race development at times, so too have we petted and coddled into helplessness those we would have helped.

But for mother love as we know it at its best—that primal passion so elevated and transformed by self-sacrifice, so keenly alive to the threefold responsibility of motherhood, so conscious that from the plastic lump of flesh is demanded a symmetrical development of body, mind, and soul—for such love we have no parallel in charity. Such love must be our teacher. When we have failed in efforts to help our fellow-man, is it not because we were blind to the claims of his threefold nature? Is it not because the woe of impecuniousness or of physical suffering appealed more to our sluggish imaginations than the mental and moral lacks behind them? When we know about and care intensely for the whole man, when no sort of giving will content us which fails to carry with it our time, our thought, ourselves— then, indeed, may we feel that the charitable instinct has become a powerful factor in civilization.

PROF. ROBERT FOSTER:

Those who have watched carefully the evolution of charities, as I have done for the past forty years, must have noted certain features as awakening interest, inspiring hope, and accomplishing the best results. Among the features referred to are these:

1. The decrease of indiscriminate almsgiving.
2. The use of scientific methods, with love as the impelling motive.
3. The substitution of remunerative employment for the dole of alms.
4. The divorce of institutional charity from politics.
5. Improved dwellings for the poor, in which real and pure home life is possible.
6. The establishment of benevolent agencies which are or are likely to become self-supporting.

All these principles have been adopted to a considerable extent, and all are essential to large progress in right directions. There are, it is true, many persons who dissent from this; some who are reformers on one line, who insist that all effort and energy should be concentrated on the work of shutting up the dram shops, for example, or on the care of neglected childhood. These, surely, are important; are, like the others, indeed, essential; but no one is sufficient in itself, no one is the single panacea for the ills of poverty; no one can do more than a part of the work of redeeming Brooklyn or New York city from the want and woe and wickedness which, alas! so largely abound there.

In the time allotted I can only dwell on one or two of those features indicated as prominent in the evolution of charities. The decrease of the pernicious custom of indiscriminate almsgiving is more and more manifest, and we rejoice in it chiefly because the deserving poor are greatly the gainers thereby. The greatest curse possible in any community is the bestowal of alms without previous inquiry. The consciousness of this has led gradually but surely to the adoption of scientific methods in charity. Especially during the past decade there has been a persistent endeavor to bring the teachings of science to bear practically on this great subject, and, without suppressing the sentiment of charity in the individual soul, to accomplish the greatest good to the greatest number through organization—through wisely directed institutional activities; to do this in obedience to the dictates of common sense and yet without sacrificing that spirit of human sympathy which Paul exalts above faith and hope, and which Henry Drummond rightly styles "the greatest thing in the world." That noble society, the Bureau of Charities, in this city, is the finest illustration known to me of the wisdom of focusing the earnest sentiment and sympathy of the community, and without check directing their flood into common-sense channels. I am deeply impressed with the value of the work done by this bureau, and I am amazed to learn from time to time that they lack the funds needed to carry out the plans they so wisely project. Would that more of the surplus wealth of this rich city might find its way into their treasury. There is one other local institution with the operations of which I am thoroughly conversant, and I think no one will gainsay the affirmation that it is doing its share, and a very large share, toward solving the problem of the poor. During the past week there were taken from the free library of the Union for Christian Work an average of more than six hundred books to be read in the homes of the people. During almost every week employment, in many cases permanent, is provided for at least seventy persons. The Union is unique in its policy, which is strictly adhered to: No money is paid out to its beneficiaries, and no money is received from them. This Free Labor Bureau of the Union, probably the largest of its kind in the world, has for its motto and motive this proposition: *To promote self-help is to help the most effectually.*

Mr. Bolton Hall:

I think it may be shown that in many cases, instead of saving reckless waste, charity has increased it. Charity is a palliative designed to sustain the *status quo* in our social institutions. On account of charity men are induced to endure the conditions in which they find themselves. The time is past when charity was a kind of fire insurance against the contingencies of the future life, because we have ceased to believe in the fire. But it is now an insurance of another kind—an insurance against social tornadoes. But for charity, men would long ago have swept away the whole order of things as it now exists. What would be the effect upon the people of Brooklyn if, on some such morning as we have had of late, fifty people should be found frozen to death? The public mind would be immeasurably shocked; yet many of the poor of this great city go where they had better be frozen to death. Our police lodging-houses save the body but destroy the soul. Here is an entire field that charity now occupies which ought to be left vacant. It attracts to the cities a large number who, if left in the country, would support themselves well. They come to the city assured that if they find nothing to do there are at least plenty of places to "turn in." The best way to relieve this kind of distress is to do nothing. We have made no progress in the relief of poverty for eighteen hundred years. We have not fewer poor people; we have not less distress. The charity organizations have done one good thing: they have collected statistics and discredited the old claim that the cause of poverty is drunkenness. It is the other way: the cause of drunkenness is poverty. They have also shown conclusively that the cause of poverty is not laziness. Forty per cent of those who apply for assistance need no help but the opportunity to work. When the Pilgrim fathers came to this country they had nothing and found nothing—but land. As long as men can get the land there is no lack of work. But we allow individuals to monopolize the land: this is the cause of poverty—and charity. What are we going to do about it? Divide the land anew? That would do no good. The sensible and natural course is where anybody has a monopoly of any kind let him pay to the rest of the community a reasonable value; as in law, when property is divided among heirs, if one takes all the land he pays the others who have none. What we need is access to the land. Make it unprofitable to hold natural opportunities without using them. Tax natural monopolies up to their full rental value. It should be as absurd for a man to be "out of work" as out of air, and if we remove the artificial barriers to opportunity it will become so.

DR. WARNER, in reply:

With the last speaker I realize the lack of time to treat the subject adequately. Voltaire said: "The way to be stupid is to say everything." I have at least, I hope, avoided that accusation. I am aware of the truth of Spencer's dictum: "The final result of saving people from their folly is to fill the world with fools." As to the idea that charity will not be necessary if we have a proper social organization—that giving free access to land will abolish poverty and do away with the problem of charity: If any one thinks he can cure the complex disease of poverty with a single panacea he is assuming as much as that all bodily diseases can be cured by one drug. I am reminded of a man on the street corner giving a lecture on physiology. He conveys a good deal of tolerably accurate information, but finally traces all diseases to one organ, holds up his twenty-five-cent bottle of stuff to regulate that organ—and there you are! About a quarter of all the poverty in our society originates in bodily disease, and it is as impossible to obviate that poverty as the bodily disease from whence it comes. There is one distinction which Mr. George makes in his books which he could never have made if he had ever acted as a "friendly visitor." It is as absurd to speak of "voluntary poverty" as of voluntary stomach-ache. We may choose to do things that give us the pain, but we never choose the pain. Poverty arises not from one thing, but from many things. One who has lived in the West, where access to land is free, must know that a great deal of poverty comes from disease, is caused by bad habits, etc. Access to land is not a cure for these evils. I believe private property in land is based on expediency, and has been, on the whole, a great social advantage. If by having private property in air we could increase the amount and improve the quality of air for the people, I should favor that also.

THE DRINK PROBLEM

BY
T. D. CROTHERS, M. D.
EDITOR OF THE QUARTERLY JOURNAL OF INEBRIETY

COLLATERAL READINGS SUGGESTED:

Spencer's Principles of Sociology and Principles of Ethics; Mill on Liberty; Dr. Bowditch's Intemperance in the Light of Cosmic Laws; Kerr's Inebriety: Its Etiology, Pathology, Treatment, and Jurisprudence; Inebriety and Crime; Ribot's Diseases of the Will; Parish's Alcoholic Inebriety; Galton's Natural Inheritance; Oswald's The Poison Problem; Iles's The Liquor Question in Politics; Pitman's Alcohol and the State; Gustafson's The Foundation of Death; Wheeler's Prohibition; Fernald's Economics of Prohibition; Sermons and Addresses on Temperance by Rev. Dr. Howard Crosby and Rev. Dr. W. S. Rainsford.

THE DRINK PROBLEM.

By T. D. Crothers, M. D.

Alarming Prevalence of the Drink Habit.

Some general conception of this problem may be obtained from the single statistical fact that in 1891 over half a million persons were arrested in this country charged with intoxication and petty crimes associated or following from inebriety. It is a reasonable assumption that at least half as many more persons used spirits to excess that did not come under legal notice. If to this be added the opium, chloral, and other drug takers, the numbers will reach enormous proportions. Admitting the possible errors that may exist in such statistics, there are many facts and reasons for believing that the extent and fatality of the drink evil are more serious and of greater magnitude than have ever been represented. Personal observation in almost every town and community confirms this; and each year the nature and extent of this evil become more and more prominent.

There is apparent in the public mind a growing sense of danger which is manifest in temperance agitations and various efforts to neutralize and break up this evil. This feeling of alarm has concentrated into various great crusade movements and organized societies, with a vast machinery of county, State, and national divisions. A political party fully organized is in the field, with the central object of obtaining power to control and break up this drink disease. Great church societies are urging moral means and remedies for the same purpose. Revival orators are holding meetings and creating a public sentiment of alarm in all parts of the country. In this country and Canada there are eighty newspapers and magazines published, weekly and monthly, exclusively devoted to this cause. Books, pamphlets, sermons, and tracts, almost without number, are coming from the press constantly. A literature that is sensational and aggressive is scattered in all directions.

With this increasing agitation, apparently, the sale of spirits is increasing; and many persons are confident that inebriety is also increasing. Statistics undoubtedly show that the fatality, injury, and losses following the use of alcohol have increased far beyond the growth of population.

There is a deep psychological meaning in this which indicates the movement of unknown laws and forces above the confusion and roar of agitation. If we take a higher point of view, this problem appears to be one of the great natural eliminative processes in the evolutionary march of the race. Here the armies of inebriates, the weak and defective, and those who resort to alcohol, and are unable to adapt themselves to the changes of life and environment, are driven out as unfit—separated and crowded out by the larger, stronger types of the race. This view is sustained by the history and appearance of the drink victims in every community. From both inheritance and neglect, they bear physiological and psychological marks of degeneration. Even those who deal in spirits show the same signs and indications.

ORIGIN AND GROWTH OF THE DRINK HABIT.

It is an interesting inquiry where this army of inebriates began; at what point in the march have they reached at present, in what direction is their movement, and what laws and forces are controlling and shaping their course?

The use of spirits can be traced back to the infancy of the race and has ever been associated with its ignorance, weakness, and disease. While it has followed the march of humanity from the lower to the higher, from its infancy up through all stages of growth and development, it has manifested a peculiar movement of its own. Thus, in some ages, it has been very prominent, creating alarm and attracting the attention of historians; then it has declined and been unnoticed. Then it has come again into prominence and disappeared as before. This very significant tide-like movement has extended over the drink history of centuries, and has followed in some unknown way the great convulsions and revolutions of nations and races. In modern times it is traceable in the statistics of courts where inebriety is punished, and points to the operation of laws at present unknown. This oscillatory movement of inebriety is receding and appears to be governed by the growth and mental vigor of the race.

Up to the last century the use of spirits was almost universal. Total abstainers were very rare and excessive use was common and unnoticed. Nearly all authorities agree that the inebriety of the past was not marked by the delirium and frenzy of modern times. The less sensitive brains of our ancestors became early palsied from spirits, and they suffered from dementia and death. At banquets the standard of strength was ability to keep awake while drinking spirits. Men used spirits and became stupid, and continued to drink for a lifetime, or until death from some acute or epidemic disease. Little or no reference is found in medical histories to alcohol as the cause of insanity, epilepsy, or idiocy, or, in fact, as the cause of any disease. Any excessive or fatal use of spirits was explained as the result of vice, free will, or demoniacal influences. The common people drank the coarser and heavier spirits, and the wealthy drank wine and light alcohols.

CHANGE IN TYPE OF THE HABIT WITH INCREASING BRAIN DEVELOPMENT.

Evidently the excessive use of spirits in all classes has slowly declined with the increase of knowledge and progressive development of the race. The drink evil has followed the race march as a shadow in outline, generally growing less and less distinct up to the last century. From that time it has appeared in a new form. The old-time stupor from the effects of spirits has changed to delirium, delusions, and crime symptoms. Mental exhaustion, insanity, and acute brain and nerve degeneration have become prominent in most cases. Moderate drinking is becoming more and more impossible. The moderate drinker of to-day becomes the inebriate of to-morrow, and dies the next day of acute disease, or is laid away in some asylum.

The type and forms of inebriety have changed. The developed brain of the modern man is more acutely sensitive to alcohol, and is more likely to find in spirits a relief from the mental strains he is subjected to. The drink evil has become a mental disease, an insanity whose origin, progress, development, and decline can be traced and studied.

ORGANIZED EFFORTS TO COMBAT THE EVIL.

This fact was unconsciously recognized at the beginning of the century in the organization of societies and efforts to break up and combat its influence. The drunkenness of the past appeared in a new light, and with it came the growing faith that it could be removed and prevented. From the first temperance society in 1816, with eight members, down to the present, there has been a steady increase of efforts and means to check and prevent inebriety. The armies of total abstainers and temperance reformers have rapidly increased; and literally no topic of civilization is more widely discussed to-day in all circles of society.

Although statistics may show an increase in the sale of spirits proportionally greater than the increase of the population, and the number of persons drinking may appear to be larger for a time in certain sections, yet a wider study, extending over a series of years, will show that this drink army is disbanding and disappearing. The tide-like oscillation of inebriety to which we have referred is often traceable in temperance revival movements which spring up suddenly and disappear mysteriously; or, in other words, inebriety increases up to a certain point and then recedes. The retrograde movement begins when the highest level is reached in sudden temperance reformatory efforts which go on with intensity for a time, then die away abruptly.

Through all this, the same eternal laws of evolution are moving the race upward and outward, and crushing out the defectives and all who are or may become incompetent and unfit to bear the burdens of humanity.

FAILURE OF REFORMERS TO RECOGNIZE THE CHANGED CHARACTER OF THE HABIT.

It is startling to find that through all this movement and agitation there has been no change in the theory of the nature and character of inebriety. This drink problem has changed in form and prominence, and is the central topic of thousands of moralists, reformers, and philanthropists, and yet the same theories of a moral origin, the same explanations of a heart deceitful and desperately wicked, the same story of vice and moral depravity, are repeated and accepted as the true explanation of its character and causes. All the literature and the remedial efforts to check and prevent inebriety are based on such theories. All physical agencies in the causation are unrecognized, and nothing but the moral weakness and the wicked impulses of the victim are supposed to be active causes. Such are some of the facts which appear from a general study of the drink problem of to-day.

The Drink Problem. 283

THE APPLICATION OF SCIENTIFIC METHODS TO THIS STUDY; HEREDITARY INFLUENCES.

If we ascend above the conflict and agitation of the present and lose sight of all such theories, a different view appears. The drink army stretches away before us like a river, with a resistless onward sweep beyond the uncertainties of human will and the feebleness of human effort. To understand this, we must go back to the sources, to the springs and streams and causative influences which have accumulated and united in forming this drink current. This is done by a careful study and grouping of the histories of a large number of cases. The conclusions from such a study by many observers agree that *heredity* is the most prominent cause and is present in over eighty per cent of all inebriates.

This heredity includes the degenerations which are transmitted from consumptive, insane, idiotic, epileptic, hysterical, and other nervous diseases, together with alcoholic and moderate-drinking ancestors. Inebriety may be the direct legacy of any of these diseases, and especially from alcoholic and drug-taking parents. If drunken children should not follow from inebriate parents, some other of these allied forms of disease is sure to appear, either in the first or second generation. The drink craze is a symptom of physical degeneration and tendency to early exhaustion, and a hint of the incapacity of the brain to regulate and continue the vital processes along the lines designed by Nature.

Parents who use alcohol are literally crippling their children, lessening their vigor and the possibility of living natural lives. Thus parents are literally trustees to receive and transmit to the future the germ form and force. If they fail by neglect or ignorance, they come into conflict with inexorable laws which punish by pain, suffering, and extinction. This army of inebriates are, to a large extent, the product and result of the diseases of their ancestors—a reflection of the physical and mental degeneration of the race that has passed away.

The use of wine at meals, defective nutrition, ungoverned appetites and impulses, neglect of healthy body and brain exercise, break out in the children in inebriety or some allied disease with almost absolute certainty. It is our physical sins and diseases of to-day that are preparing the ground for all sorts of nerve diseases and inebriety in the next generation. It is our failures, neglect, and weakness that are transmitted in low vitality, defective power of resistance, and tendency to disease, making every condition favorable for a short, degenerate life and early death.

INEBRIETY AN INHERITED DISEASE, AFFECTING THE WILL.

The free will we urge these poor inebriates to exercise only existed in their ancestors. They alone could have diverted and changed the currents of health and made *free will* possible in the children. The hereditary inebriate is born into the world with a low power of vitality and states of central brain exhaustion which are ever seeking relief; and alcohol, by its narcotic action, supplies this demand. This impulse to degeneration may pass down one or two generations before appearing as inebriety again.

No other disease is more positively transmitted than inebriety, either directly or indirectly, in some associated disease. A study of heredity reveals a most startling view of the forces at our command to change and prevent the inebriety of the future. In the good time coming, not far away, this field will be occupied by practical scientists, and we shall be able to break up this great polluted spring and stop the tide of disease which follows.

INFLUENCE OF INDISCRIMINATE MARRIAGES IN PERPETUATING THE HABIT.

Another active factor more apparent and controllable in the problem of inebriety is that of *marriage*. At present indiscriminate marriages are largely influential in intensifying and continuing this alcoholic stream. The assertion that inebriety is bred and cultivated by indiscriminate marriages can be proved in the experience of every community. Stockmen, who have only the most selfish interests, act on an analogous fact, and avoid raising defective stock by the selection of the strongest and best types for the continuation of the race. Our neglect to recognize this great principle of Nature is seen in the common marriages of many persons who are literally human wreckage and remnants of a race stock approaching extinction. Criminals, paupers, inebriates, and others notoriously far down on the road to dissolution, are permitted to marry and raise children freighted with a truly frightful legacy of degeneration. The dangerous classes of every community, the inmates of hospitals and asylums, are the living witnesses of this blunder.

Higher up in the social scale unions are constantly taking place the progeny of which must be defective and incapable of living normal lives. Were it not for the higher laws of Nature, which continuously throw out and exterminate these unfit, the race would soon be doomed to helpless degeneracy. The children from these dangerous marriages are so far crippled as to be unable to live normally and in accord with laws of health, and hence become diseased and subject to the laws of dissolution.

One of the saddest facts in the history of these degenerates is the very common sacrifice of noble women, who marry them under the delusion that they are suffering from a moral disorder which can be reached and cured by love and sympathy. The marriage of chronic inebriates on this principle is a crime and offense against the highest laws of humanity that should be punished by the severest penalties. In the near future the State will recognize this fact in its laws. It is this defective heredity, increased and intensified by marriages with equally bad stock, that is the great fountain-spring from which inebriety comes.

DEFECTIVE NUTRITION AND OTHER CAUSES OF THE DRINK DISEASE.

There are other active sources from which inebriety springs that may be seen in every community. Thus starvation in childhood by overfeeding and underfeeding is followed by defective nutrition and growth, and finally by inebriety. Degenerations and defective growths from diseases of childhood slumber along to the period of maturity, then break out into inebriety from the slightest exciting causes.

Injury of the brain and nervous system in early and mature life, such as sunstroke, shocks, blows, and diseases which are attended with delirium and unconsciousness, often develop into inebriety. Want of rest, strains, and profound drains of the body bring on exhaustion and changes in the nerve centers that are often manifest in inebriety. The moment alcohol is taken in large quantity a tremendous activity and concentration of degenerative forces begin.

INFLUENCE OF ALCOHOL ON THE BODILY TISSUES.

Alcohol, of all drugs, seems most to intensify and provoke disease, and to afford the most favorable conditions for the destruction of cell and nerve tissue. The incline to acute disease and final death which follows the use of spirits is sharp, and the rush downward is rapid and deceptive. The history of a large number of these cases points to the same symptoms, the same progress, direction, and termination.

Like a river springing from certain sources and moving on down, diverted here and there by rocks, mountains, banks, and islands, so this drink stream changes and winds about, but always passes the same sections with the same course, and always reaches the same ocean. It is a startling fact that inebriates are literally a new army of the insane, which have sprung up and camped all along the frontiers of modern civilization.

DELETERIOUS INFLUENCE OF THE SALOON.

One of the most unaccountable facts of this drink army and problem, notwithstanding all the agitation of means and methods for relief, is the *saloon, its support and defense by the public.*

Everywhere, for the mere formality of a license, saloons are permitted and encouraged for the sale of spirits, under the most attractive conditions and surroundings. Art, luxury, comfort, and elegance combine to make these places attractive resorts; mirrors, flashing glass ornaments, colored liquids, pungent odors, are arranged to create thirst and stimulate the sense of taste.

Thus the senses are appealed to in the most powerful way to use alcohol in all forms. As a result, the saloon has become a terrible power over the minds and conduct of a vast number of weak, defective persons, whose mental and physical health it breaks up and destroys. Nothing can be more certain than this fact. In every community, under all possible circumstances, the saloon is destructive, antagonizing every effort to struggle from the lower to the higher, and every law of growth and development. Why should the saloon be tolerated a moment in any intelligent community? Whenever the dangers from the use of alcohol are even partially realized, why should not the saloon be the first object of attack? What right has the saloon to exist? What right has it to peril every interest of law and order?

The answer is to be found in the same old realm of superstitious theories that cling with deathless grasp to the public mind; theories of the food value of alcohol, and its moderate use as favoring longevity and happiness—these are the real supports of the saloon.

The saloon is the real schoolhouse for the cultivation and development of inebriety, and is the most dangerous disease center that can exist in any community. The only word that can be said in its favor is that its real power is eliminative—it hurries on the process of dissolution in the individual. It makes all its patrons unfit, and then speedily drives them down to death and extinction. It destroys the individual by switching him from the main line on to the side track, ending in destruction. It will be the wonderment of the future that the saloon should exist so long, with nothing but the densest and most criminal ignorance to support it. Alcohol must be recognized in its true character as a medicine, and used in the same way as arsenic or strychnine.

These are some of the facts that are not understood practically, that are not studied in the temperance literature and lectures, and are literally unknown even to the poor drink victims.

PSYCHOLOGICAL FACTORS: ABNORMAL MENTALITY A PREDISPOSING CONDITION OF INEBRIETY.

There is a psychological factor in this problem that is still more obscure and startling, and yet it enters very minutely into the practical solution of the question. It is the unequal growth and decay of the several brain faculties in each individual which come into prominence from the use of alcohol.

From heredity, disease, starvation, injury, and other complex causes, certain parts of the brain undergo degeneration or are undeveloped. Some parts become atrophied or shrunken; others are enlarged into abnormal proportions. As a result, some faculties seem highly developed, others are exhausted early, and an abnormal mentality follows in both cases. Inebriety is a symptom of this abnormity. It indicates that the brain faculties are disorganized and out of harmony. The natural adjustment is broken up either temporarily or permanently. The two most commonly observed faculties which diverge most widely are the moral and intellectual senses. Often these are at different levels in the same individual. In the alcoholic victim the moral sense suffers first and is always the most diseased. The inebriate may have a complete palsy of this sense and yet have all the other faculties fairly acute or so slightly deranged as to be unnoticed. This moral or ethical sense is the highest perfection of character, and always degenerates rapidly in all persons who use spirits to excess. The capacity to think right and act right is blunted, palsied, and destroyed, while the intellectual sensibility may be apparently unimpaired. This inability to adjust conduct ethically is the direct result in many cases of the paralyzing action of alcohol. No doubt in some instances this faculty was very feebly developed before spirits were used, or it may have been wanting altogether. In that case the degeneration from alcohol makes all efforts to build this up impossible.

WHY MORAL APPEALS ARE USUALLY INEFFICIENT.

The practical bearing of these facts is illustrated in many ways, particularly in the failure to restore inebriates by appeals to their moral sense alone. The influence of the pledge and prayer on persons who have no sense of duty or moral obligation is almost useless. Often such persons have an intellectual sense keen enough to take advantage of the circumstances and exhibit a cunning characteristic of criminals, passing as reformers and martyrs, and arousing interest and enthusiasm only to profit by it in some unusual manner.

In this way temperance revivalists, by passionate appeals to the moral and emotional senses of inebriates, may secure thousands of pledges and conversions to a life of total abstinence, followed by relapses startling and unexplainable. The moral or ethical sense of this new army of inebriates is paralyzed or destroyed, and efforts directed to this side alone are worse than failures.

The only road possible to reach this class of cases is by the physical, by the use of means and measures that appeal to the entire organism. The degeneration of brain cells, nerve tissue, and organic forces, combined with defective and diseased moral and ethical senses, presents a condition of individual disease that seems difficult to cure. This fact opens up a new field of effort and suggests a different class of means and remedies. The question arises, Can we halt this army and turn it into other paths? Can we stay this tide of destruction and the terrible losses which follow from it? Can we solve this problem and stop its evils?'

Appeals to the moral nature of the inebriate are useless, because that part of his brain is palsied. Intimidation by punishment and suffering fails for the same reason. The pledge is powerless because the will is unstable and incapable of consistent action. The prayer fails because the emotional nature is incapable of permanent impressions. Thus education, morals, law, and religion are powerless to remove or check this disorder.

RESTRAINT AND QUARANTINE OF INEBRIATES A NECESSITY.

The inebriate is literally a madman, who persists in destroying himself at all hazards and irrespective of all interests of his relatives, friends, and the community. Such conduct forfeits all right to personal liberty and makes him an outlaw and an antagonist to all the highest interests of society. Any one who persists in drinking to intoxication is dangerous and may at any moment peril the interests of individuals or the community he lives in and commit acts of very serious consequences. He should be restrained and be confined in a hospital, where his conduct can be regulated by others.

Rev. Dr. Bellows said long ago in an address on this subject: "No man has the right to peril the interests of others. Society learns nothing by tolerating the presence of any one whose liberty is dangerous. Society gains nothing by holding for an hour any one who is fit to be at large. Liberty and human rights gain nothing by allowing any man to be at large for a moment who is destroying himself, his family, and neighbors. All we need is what we are fast gaining a possession of—the tests and gauges of this fitness or unfitness."

The true remedy is a united public sentiment that this army of inebriates are diseased and dangerous, and the highest interests of society require that they should be quarantined and their personal liberty restricted, not as criminals for short sentences in jails, not as willful sinners, to be helped or cured by fear, suffering, and the law of vengeance, but as diseased and helpless people needing guardianship, medical care, and the direction of others. Like cases of mania, smallpox, typhus fever, and contagious diseases, they need isolation and treatment in special surroundings. We want a clear public recognition of these facts; then means will be adopted to prevent the victim from going on to chronic stages before any efforts are made to help him.

INEFFICACY OF LEGAL EFFORTS TO SUPPRESS INEBRIETY.

The legal efforts to cure this evil are more fatal and dangerous than the saloon, by increasing the very evil they seek to remove. Thus saloons are licensed and protected, and, both directly and indirectly, the use of spirits is encouraged and made attractive. The victim is excused and tolerated until he reaches a chronic stage and violates some law; then he is fined and imprisoned under conditions that intensify and increase his disease. Statistics show that ninety-nine per cent of all victims who are punished by the courts the first time by fines and imprisonment relapse and appear again and again for the same offense as long as they live. They receive the name of *rounders*, and are not infrequently sentenced hundreds of times in the course of years. The station house, jail, and machinery of the law, from the absence of physical and mental aids, are fatal in their influence.

Yet public sentiment hugs this terrible delusion of vice and sustains the police courts in efforts that make it more and more impossible for the victims to recover. Thus the law destroys the inebriate by punishment as a criminal, and the Church disowns and drives him away as a sinner; society looks down upon him as having a vice that can be controlled at will. It is the same old superstitious theory of a theological or moral origin of evil, which from time to time has been used to explain every phenomenon of Nature, that sustains and keeps up this delusion.

HOSPITALS, ASYLUMS, AND REFORMATORIES AS REMEDIAL AGENCIES.

Science has opened up a new field of remedial forces, and points out a solution of this drink problem, in special hospitals organized as industrial military schools. Here the inebriates may be housed and kept for a lifetime if they are incurable. These hospitals are to be organized with every means to build up both body and mind, to protect the victim from himself, and to provide every hygienic and physiological agency requisite for a normal life.

Laws should be passed authorizing the arrest of any one known to be drinking spirits continuously or at intervals. There should be no waiting until the victim is intoxicated or commits some overt offense. He should come under legal control as soon as evidence of his habitual use of spirits can be obtained. Thus all classes, from the poor pauper to the rich man or his son, who are in the early stages of inebriety, should be forced into conditions of sober, rational living, and continued under legal restraint, either in an asylum or out on parole, until their mental and physical health is restored and evidence of temperate living can be established.

If such asylums were in operation and such laws in force, supported by public sentiment, this army of inebriates would disappear from our streets, and with it the crime, losses, and suffering so apparent. The saloons and distilleries would pass away in obedience to a higher law than legal prohibition.

This is the voice of science: to quarantine the inebriate in a hospital, as if suffering from a contagion; to stop the disease at the fountain, to remove the victim from all causes and conditions favoring inebriety. If the inebriate is curable, he can be restored to health and society again; if not, he should remain a ward of the State, and be kept under conditions most favorable for health and the public good.

Industrial hospitals for this army of inebriates can be built and supported by a tax on liquor dealers, and thus relieve the producer and taxpayer. To a large extent, after they are established they can be made self-supporting. The general principles and many of the details of these industrial hospitals are already practically worked out in most of the asylums, prisons, and reformatories of the country. The Elmira Reformatory and many of the present inebriate asylums are literal demonstrations of this fact.

A Scientific Study of Causes Absolutely Essential.

In a wider sense, this solution of the drink problem promises not only to house and check the present evils, but to place these victims in the best possible conditions for scientific study. Here the great underlying causes—physiological, psychological, and sociological—which have developed and set apart this vast army of what has been aptly termed "border-line maniacs" can be discovered and understood. There is no way to comprehend inebriety except from exact studies of inebriates in the most favorable surroundings.

It is something more than the impulse to use spirits to excess, more than a weak will and moral carelessness, which is the cause of inebriety. This disease is beyond cure by punishment or appeals to the emotions, beyond educational and religious influences, beyond remedy by license and prohibition. Back into those silent realms, where the great natural laws of evolution and dissolution move in a majestic sweep, there we shall find its causes and the means of relief.

Declaring the inebriate diseased and restraining him in special asylums for cure is not a new theory of modern times, but has been urged and discussed for over two thousand years. But, like all other great truths in the world's history, it has waited for an audience and a favorable time for acceptance. That time is rapidly approaching, and the principle is already recognized by an increasing number of scientific men in all parts of the country. The State of Connecticut has passed laws for the organization of such a hospital. Bills have been introduced in many of the State Legislatures for this same purpose, but the opposition of moralists who still cling to the vice theory has so far prevented any practical work.

Empirics and charlatans, ever eager to profit by the half-defined truths just dawning on the mental horizon, rush in with claims of secret specifics for the cure of inebriety, arousing enthusiasm among the poor victims and creating expectations that will only end in disappointment. This in itself is an unmistakable sign of the rapid growth and evolution of the real truth, which is now passing through the empiric stages.

We must have hospitals in every city and town for inebriates: First, for the paupers and criminals, the saloon loungers, and those who are constantly before the police courts for offenses of all kinds associated with excessive use of spirits. This class must be committed for five or ten years, or on indeterminate sentences depending upon their improvement and restoration, under certain conditions being permitted to go out on parole. Hospitals for their retention must be organized in the country, on large farms, where all the inmates should be required to work every day at some profitable employment, according to their capacity and strength. All the conditions of life and surroundings should be regulated with military exactness. All sources of debility and degeneration should be removed.

Nutrition baths, healthful surroundings, exercise, mental and physical remedies to build up and restore all the energies of the body, should be enforced. Rest, in the highest sense of change and growth, should be favored by every means known to science, and all acts and conduct should be under the control and guidance of others. Each man should be organized into the working force of the hospital, made a producer in some way, and kept in training not only for the purpose of self-development, but also of increasing the value and usefulness of the institution. If he shows capacity, or can do more than become self-supporting, the surplus thus earned should be credited to him or his relatives.

The possibilities are almost unlimited along this line. Vast numbers of inebriates, if they could be restrained from the use of spirits in such institutions and given medical care and work in the best conditions of health, would become active producers and support their families besides. After a long period of medical and institutional care and training such cases would be restored, and in many cases become useful citizens. If after repeated trials on parole they should continue to relapse, their commitment should be permanent. The incurables would thus be placed in the least harmful and most humane and economical conditions of life. The present losses and contagions which follow this class would be prevented. The crime, insanity, pauperism, and disease centers which are always found associated with them would disappear.

CLASSIFICATION OF PATIENTS DEMANDED.

Hospitals must be provided for a second class of persons who are not so far down the road to final dissolution. Inebriates who are constant drinkers or who have periodic excesses, and who keep up the delusion that they can stop any time and are not so bad as their friends represent—such persons are literally an army of exhausted, brain-toppling drinkers, who are on the verge of insanity, crime, suicide, and sudden death. These should be committed to hospital care, the same as others. The same military control of exact obedience and exact living—exact use of all means and appliances; every hygienic, physical, and mental remedy known—should be applied to build up and restore them to temperate living. The terms of confinement should be shorter, and the remedies suited to recent cases. Employment should be required of each one, and, if able, they should pay for their care in labor or otherwise.

A third class of hospitals would be required for the wealthy and recent cases. The general plan would be as before: military care and training, with nerve and brain rest. The same special object would exist to ascertain the conditions and causes which provoked the inebriety, and remove them; also to build up the entire man to resist and overcome these disease impulses in the future. To this can be added all the moral forces of prayer, faith, and conversion, together with every possible stimulation of the higher brain centers. The application of such remedies where the physical health and surroundings are the most favorable would be followed by the best results.

The study of inebriety in these hospitals would reveal many of the great underlying causes and laws which are active in producing this drink evil. The power and influence of the saloon and unregulated marriages would be seen and realized.

PHYSICAL ASPECTS OF THE DRINK PROBLEM.

We have arrived at a period where all phenomena of loss, suffering, and evil must be regarded from a physical point of view. They are the results of tangible causes that may be known and understood. The drink phenomena and problem must be solved along this line.

If we consider the great evolutionary principles which underlie and control all these movements of individuals and races, this subject appears in a new light. All students of science understand that disease and degeneration, either inherited or acquired, come under the operation of great natural laws which may be studied and understood.

Social Evils Preventable under Scientific Treatment.

Degeneration, disease, and premature death are conditions that are preventable beyond the wildest dream of the enthusiast, but along lines that are yet to be discovered. Already the possibility of averting insanity, idiocy, criminality, pauperism, and other afflictions, looms up like the mountain ranges of a new continent that is yet to be explored and mapped out. The armies of inebriates are the same degenerate, diseased victims, who become unfit, disabled, and sorely wounded, and are left on the field to die. In our ignorance we fail to realize this, and join in the delusion that they are able yet to do battle for civilization.

The laws of elimination go on crowding them out everywhere, and the losses and injuries they inflict on both the present and future generations are great obstacles to the survival of the fittest. Here Nature is teaching the true remedy in the elimination and separation of those unfit, and hurrying them on to death by insanity, criminality, and various allied degenerations: the grinding, crushing battle of civilization; the struggle of man upward and outward, with its exposure, its strains, and drains; its shot and shell, wounding, crippling, and disabling; and its force of hereditary injuries, coming from the past and reaching out into the future. This is the struggle along the front line, in which over a million of poor victims are engaged.

Nature separates, eliminates, and destroys. Science teaches that separation and isolation may be followed by restoration. The same laws and forces which accelerate dissolution may be turned into currents of evolution. This army of inebriates can be halted and forced back to the rear, and diverted into conditions of growth and development. Already the polluted springs of heredity and the recruiting stations of the saloons and unregulated marriages are apparent. Already there are in sight vast ranges of causes and conditions that can be utilized and sent into practical operation for the prevention as well as the cure of inebriety.

Away on the outlying posts a few scientists, like picket guards, look over into the coming century, confident that "where the vanguard rests to-day, the hosts shall camp to-morrow."

ABSTRACT OF THE DISCUSSION.

MR. JOHN A. TAYLOR:

The advocates of so-called temperance reform rarely listen, in the great number of meetings held by them all over the country, to any one who represents the other side of the question, and therefore fail to give due consideration to certain cardinal facts of the situation, which, nevertheless, form a very great hindrance to the success of the cause so advocated. Indeed, quite often the opinion seems to prevail that there is no other side. On the other hand, the purveyors of intoxicating liquors and the consumers very rarely allow themselves to consider the very serious objections to their trade and habit, and the very important manner in which the interests of society at large are affected by the unrestrained indulgence in intoxicating liquors. Nor does it avail either side of the question to array statistics of science or of political economy which are susceptible by biased and adroit manipulation of appearing favorably or unfavorably, upon either side of the problem, according to the preconceived opinion of the manipulator.

Several considerations seem to be apparent, I think, to the unprejudiced observer as very important elements of the situation, which nevertheless are habitually ignored or erroneously denied by the advocates of either extreme view:

First. It may be fairly stated, I think, that it is at least an open question whether or not alcohol is a useful, important, and necessary article of food or of therapeutic value.

Second. It is a fact that only a very small part of the community wholly abstain from its use, either as food or as a remedial agent.

Third. It is a fact that thousands of people during long and useful lives do use it, both as a food and a medicine, without apparent harm to themselves or evil to the community about them.

Fourth. It is a fact that society as now constituted has a clear right to protect itself from any trade or personal indulgence which palpably renders the community dangerous or unhealthful or in any way materially interferes with the right of the community at large to life, liberty, and the pursuit of happiness.

Fifth. It is a fact that the community may lawfully avail itself of the police power of the State and of penal legislation to preserve from infringement these conceded rights.

Sixth. It is within the proper purview of the organic law of the

State to levy upon the resources of the community a reasonable tax out of which to maintain asylums for such portions of the community as by incapacity not produced by responsible misdemeanors or crimes may be a menace to the rest of society if not so sustained. It is obvious that these, and many other considerations vitally affecting the entire problem, are habitually ignored by one side or the other of this controversy.

The tactics of moral suasion, while meeting with occasional good results, and while they are by no means to be discouraged, do not, I think, bear any such important results as are made to appear from the marshaling of the thousands of people who are said, and I think truly, to have signed the pledge of total abstinence. On the other hand, the attempts to coerce by legislation the abandonment of either the sale of or the indulgence in intoxicating liquors must be seen to be replete with disappointment, and largely found to result in either the more firmly established existence of the rum traffic, or the greatly enlarged consumption in intemperate ways of intoxicating liquors. The latter result seems to be due to the anomalous situation that by far the most effective allies of the rumsellers and drink-lovers in dealing with the law-making power of the community have been that portion of the temperance army known as Prohibitionists. Periodically this handful of men and women have demanded extreme measures from the Legislature, and have been surprised at the readiness with which their demands have been answered by laws so wide-reaching in their effect and so far beyond the normal demand of the communities for whose benefit they were enacted as to be utterly incapable of execution. Now, from the standpoint of the rumseller and the drink-lover, a law so radical as to be incapable of execution is far less dangerous to their respective interests than a law which, restraining to a moderate degree the traffic and the indulgence, is so sustained by the moral sense of the community as that its enforcement will be insisted upon. This aspect of what may be called the legislative influence in favor of temperance seems latterly to have been recognized by various communities that have virtually surrendered the attempt to inhibit the use of and trade in intoxicating liquors, and have turned to the regulative power of the Commonwealth as a means of restraining the evil of the traffic and the habit.

I am in hearty sympathy with that part of Dr. Crothers's scheme of temperance reform which would subject the victims of inebriation to scientific treatment, and the employment of such energies as they have to the advantage of the community which supports them. I must confess, however, that the statement of Dr. Crothers that "the moderate and periodic . . . drinkers are always sources of danger to themselves and others" resembles very closely a great mass of overstatement which has tended for more than a generation to hinder the acceptance of well-considered schemes of reform at the hands of the calm and unimpassioned citizens of the country. That a moderate drinker *may* become a confirmed drinker is true. This is equally true of every advocate of total abstinence and of each of the rank and file. In the last analysis it is the personal equation which is to determine this result. So long as young men and young women are told that it is impossible to control the indulgence in intoxicating liquors, when they are every day witnessing their fathers and uncles and mothers and aunts indulging moderately in the use of intoxicating liquors without sacrificing in the least degree any element of moral worth, they will be apt to repudiate all suggestions coming from people making such false assertions, and the cause of intelligent reform will lack their affiliation and support.

The two classes who need to become temperate are the hopeless sots and the bigoted advocates of total abstinence, who alike refuse to recognize truths which every one else sees, and who suppress important factors of the temperance problem which do not fail to be witnessed and believed in by the rising generations. If these conclusions are sound, it is time to throw aside the prejudice and indisposition to acknowledge the whole truth of the situation and to deal with the question from the standpoint of what is best not only for the individual but for the community, and to carry restraint only so far in the direction of reform as shall be certain to receive the hearty sanction of a pronounced majority of the given community.

MR. E. J. WHEELER:

It was said of Thomas Carlyle that he spent fifty years shouting at the top of his voice that people were talking too much. So the gentleman who preceded me has, in a series of intemperate statements, denounced the intemperance of temperance advocates. I have never heard temperance orators make the statements the gentleman has attributed to them. I do not think the lecturer meant to say that every moderate drinker becomes a drunkard. What he said was that there is no drunkard who does not start as a moderate drinker, and this, I think, is undeniable. The gentleman says a great many doctors advise the use of liquor. A great many doctors are shrewd men, who understand how to please their patients. He says thousands use liquor without harm, but he doesn't prove it. The contrary statement has behind it some of the best medical authorities—Dr. Richardson, of England, Dr. N. S. Davis, of Chicago, and others equally distinguished in the profession. He says prohibitionists go to Albany and bulldoze the Legislature into extreme legislation. I have been in a position to know how much of that has been done, and for fifteen years past I have not known of a delegate going to Albany. We make our demands at the ballot box. I believe it is a mistake for legislation to go ahead of public sentiment; but there is no reason why we should not try to educate public sentiment up to the point we wish to reach — and that is the object of the Prohibition party.

I believe with the lecturer that inebriety is a disease. That disease has its beginning with the first glass taken as a stimulant or for the gratification of desire. I am willing to leave the question of the therapeutic use of alcohol to the doctors. The medical societies say it is the part of science to prevent as well as to cure disease. Last summer a ship with cholera on board arrived in our harbor. The State went down to it and said to the captain, the crew, and the passengers, "Do not dare go to the city," and soldiers were called out to prevent them from landing. What about the personal liberty of those passengers? The personal liberty of individuals must come to an end when public safety demands it. The quarantine failed to quarantine, and the cholera somehow got into the city. Does any practical gentleman say "Because the quarantine did not keep the cholera out it is a failure, and we must not quarantine"? Does any one propose licensing disease instead of quarantining it? I believe in quarantining disease. The radicalism of prohibitionists in regard to inebriety is the conservatism of commerce and society in regard to other diseases. Prohibition doesn't prohibit; neither does the quarantine; but nobody claims that for that reason we should abandon all efforts. I wish we might have the evolution of the temperance reform discussed. Every specific that has been tried has been a failure or been only partially successful. In 1808 the first temperance society was organized in this country to prevent the excessive use of liquor. In 1813 the movement to secure total abstinence by moral suasion was inaugurated. This held the field for a long time, but the whole moral-suasion movement came to an end. The trouble was, they forgot the ratchet—like the brakeman who winds up the brake and then lets go; if he forgets to put up the ratchet, whiz-z-z! it goes, and the work is all undone. Third, we had the Washingtonian movement to reform the drinkers. Fourth, the local-option movement, which collapsed in two years. Fifth, constitutional prohibition, in eight or ten States, which has proved, to a great extent, a failure, because it does not enforce itself. Sixth, an effort not only for prohibitory enactments in the States, but throughout the nation, and for a political organization to make them effective. All other measures have been tried—Dr. Rainsford's, the

Gothenburg system, and the rest—and all have failed. Let us now enforce the quarantine, and so reduce the disease to a minimum.

MR. GEORGE ILES:

However much our current political philosophy with regard to alcohol may lack correspondence to fact, the case is very different in the sphere of business. There is no stouter help to reform than that which spontaneously arises as an incident to the pursuit of gain, which springs up as industry and commerce make new demands upon their leaders. Here can be no charge of insincerity or fanaticism, no taint of patronizing or intrusiveness. A rule of conduct is laid down and obeyed, because it pays both parties to it in dollars. An American loom to-day is more elaborate and costly, more highly speeded than ever; therefore the operative who tends it must be sober. The press which strikes off one's morning paper is worth a fortune; an unsteady touch from a tipsy printer means the delay of a vast edition. The tonnage of an average railroad train was never so great as now; it runs at higher and higher speeds; life and limb are more than ever in the keeping of the engineer, of the army in charge of track, switch, and semaphore. Hence we find such a corporation as the Long Island Railroad Company insisting that its servants shall be strictly sober men. Because machinery is ever extending its dominion, and in ways which more and more bind up the welfare of the hive with the good of the bee, the war on alcohol is in these latter days receiving powerful re-enforcement from new friends.

And aid from the ranks of business is well worth having, even when indirect. At our doors we see men of enterprise, with no other thought than that of dividends, who are nevertheless doing much to weaken the attractions of the taproom. In replacing the horse by the electric motor and the steam locomotive, they are doubling the areas of our cities at a bound. Soon every thrifty man may buy for himself a house where he can know the cheer of home, where the gilding and the glitter of the saloon will in vain entice him.

We hear much about the intensity of modern competition, of the tremendous strain it puts upon mind and nerve; but is it not a good thing for your merchant or manufacturer that he can no longer afford to have any of his brains a-soak?

In paths untrodden by the man of business much, too, is being done in unpurposed alliance with the cause of temperance. We can not as yet afford to dismiss the public servants who work without fear of reward. A few lovers of art in New York have administered the Metropolitan Museum so well that three quarters of a million visits were paid to it last year, one third of them on Sundays. In connection with

Columbia College, lectures are given this winter gratis at the Art Museum, at Cooper Union, and at the Natural History Hall. The lecturers are men of the stamp of Prof. Chandler, Mr. Russell Sturgis, and Mr. Albert Shaw. On substantially the same lines is Mr. Walter Damrosch's excellent music at prices poor people can pay. All this activity on behalf of popular culture lifts the ideal of life, and creates an atmosphere in which such a vice as drinking is none the less repressed because it is never so much as mentioned.

CHARLES H. SHEPARD, M. D.:

The moralist, who claims that the drink habit is a vice, and seeks by pledges and by surrounding the victim with a cordon of preventives to shield him from temptation, too often realizes that all is of no avail; and those who would by law and force at once obliterate the whole evil, find that the time has yet to come when man can be made virtuous in that way.

By the most advanced thinkers it is claimed that the drink habit is a disease, subject to all the laws of disease, and thus it becomes more than probable that from the medical profession the world may yet receive the solution of this problem.

The great majority will agree that the saloon is a public nuisance that should be abolished. It is a source of danger as much as the pest house; but if there were no demand for the saloon it would soon pass out of existence. Let us get at its cause by approaching the subject from the sanitary and scientific side. No essential progress toward the solution of the question has been made or is assured along the moral side. It is *not* a political question to be settled by the politician, nor can the pledge, or even prayer, avail much, because these means do not recognize the causes or the laws which govern them.

It is said in England, and the same will apply with more or less force in this country, that alcohol has become so much the reliance of the overworked classes that there is great danger of its stamping children with a new and peculiar heredity. The inheritance of the child is at the best tainted with the animal and the savage, and when we add that of an exhausted, overworked, drunken parentage, the result is sure to be disastrous.

The eminent French scientist and pathologist, Lancereaux, concludes his observations on the effect of alcohol and the progeny of the drunkard by saying that alcoholic liquors, such as are now consumed, prevent the action of the most important and noble faculties of the man who abuses them; they disturb his nutrition, they make him old before his time; nay, more, they affect his progeny, whom they change and often kill. Thus a stop is put to the wide degeneration of the race, which might otherwise occur, by the fact that alcoholism tends to lessen reproduction as well as to increase mortality.

The full penalty must be paid for all disobedience to the laws of life. Health is to be found only in obedience to physiological law; there is no law of cure in the universe except the condition of obedience. Disease is not a devil to be cast out; it is the *vis medicatrix*, or the action of vital energy, which defends and restores.

The responsibility of physicians in regard to this question is one of great magnitude. The effect of continually dosing with this drug is too apparent wherever it is used, benumbing the senses and rendering more difficult every natural function. Alcohol never sustains the powers of life. It sometimes changes the symptoms of disease, but always at the expense of the vitality of the body. What is called its supporting action is a fever induced by the poison, which but prostrates the patient the more.

There is one encouraging fact to be noted in this connection, that the use of alcohol in medicine has very much diminished during the past twenty-five years, and the present tendency is constantly in that direction. Right here is the central point which I wish to make. When the physician ceases to prescribe alcohol as a medicine, the drink problem will have reached the final stage of its solution.

We talk about temperance as though abstinence from alcohol were the fulfillment of the law; but there is a greater temperance yet to come, more in accordance with the dictates of an enlightened reason. The sin of overeating produces as much or more trouble to the community as that which comes from the use of alcoholic drinks. The use of tobacco is the occasion of harm second only to that of alcohol. The evil wrought by the excessive use of coffee is by no means one of the minor ones. The baneful effects of the coffee habit in Brazil are equal to those of the beer habit among the Germans. The use of opium and other narcotics is another fruitful source of injury to the community. The evils of overwork and worry do not fall far behind. In fact, we exhaust ourselves every way—in our work and in our play, in eating and drinking, in our sexual relations, and even in those athletic efforts that are supposed to be hygienic and recuperative. Furthermore, these very excesses are the occasion of much of the demand for alcohol to drown the nervous rebellion that would otherwise shield us from the result of our own foolishness.

The drink curse is not an accident or theory, but a condition—the direct result of cause and effect—and can be successfully grappled with only by the application of physiological laws and forces. Of all men, the inebriate is the most incompetent to judge of them or their effects.

Yet, strange to say, much of the literature on this question is built up on his statement of the case.

As evolutionists it is permitted us to look forward to the time when an age of temperance, an age of cleanliness and purity, an age of freedom from tobacco, an age of sanitary reform, an age of plain living and high thinking, an age of health, which is holiness, shall have so regenerated man that he will walk the earth one hundred years and more. Then the time will come when he shall not seek vicarious atonement through the doctor or the priest, but, by obedience to law, both physical and moral, fulfill his true destiny.

DR. LEWIS G. JANES:

I have no infallible panacea to propose for the solution of this problem of intemperance, nor am I as certain of the good results of suggested specifics as some of the other speakers. As a physiologist, I am convinced that the habitual use of alcoholic beverages can only work injury to the human constitution. I will not question the value of alcohol as a medicine in certain abnormal conditions of the system; it may then be of service, like other poisonous drugs, though less frequently, I think, than is popularly imagined. Nor will I enter into a discussion of the abstract question whether alcohol should ever be regarded as a food. To any one familiar with the chemistry of alcohol, however, it is evident that, being pure carbon, it must have its limitations as a food, if so regarded. It could only nourish the adipose tissues at the expense of the muscular, bony, and vital tissues of the body. Already, owing to the deterioration of our food elements and the excessive use of starchy and carbonaceous fat-producing foods, we are suffering serious physical ills, such as heart failure, kidney troubles, and fatty degeneration of the tissues, which are certainly aggravated by the habitual use of alcoholic beverages.

As to the legal regulation of the sale of intoxicants, it behooves us to look for some method on which all good citizens can unite. High license has been suggested; but this is repugnant to the moral sense of many. Personally, I do not believe that high license ever saved an individual from a drunkard's grave. Moreover, the license system, like legal prohibition, throws the question into politics, which is one of the greatest evils we are called upon to combat. Prof. Monks, the Superintendent of Education in the Elmira Reformatory, who has given much thought to the matter, suggested to me a method which appears to offer features worthy of consideration. His plan implies restrictions which are prohibitory in principle; but he does not aim at absolute legal prohibition, deeming it impracticable in the present state of public sentiment. Even so stanch an advocate of prohibition as Mr. Wheeler has admitted here this evening that it is useless to pass such laws in advance of public sentiment. Prof. Monks proposes that any person who is a male citizen of the United States, of legal age, and who has not been convicted of offenses against the law, shall be permitted to sell intoxicants under certain uniform restrictions. These are, in effect, that this business shall not be associated with any other, except the giving of meals or lodging, or the sale of drugs; that no liquor shall be sold to minors, aliens, or women; that none shall be sold to intoxicated persons or those known to be habitual drunkards; that none shall be sold after twelve o'clock at night or on legal holidays. He would also cause an official estimate of all public expense incurred directly or indirectly by the abuse of intoxicants in a given community to be made, and a tax to be assessed upon local venders sufficient to cover such expenses. This would not partake of the nature of a license; the conditions imposed on sellers would be uniform; there would be no personal or political favors to be granted, and therefore the question would be taken out of politics. As promising relief from the crying evil of saloon politics, and some wise restrictions on the traffic tending to the disuse of intoxicants, especially by the young, this method, I think, is worthy of thoughtful consideration.

THE LABOR PROBLEM

BY
NICHOLAS PAINE GILMAN
AUTHOR OF PROFIT-SHARING BETWEEN EMPLOYER AND EMPLOYEE,
SOCIALISM AND THE AMERICAN SPIRIT, ETC.

COLLATERAL READINGS SUGGESTED:

Thorold Rogers's Six Centuries of Work and Wages; Ely's The Labor Movement in America; Barnes's The Labor Problem; Atkinson's Capital and Labor Allies, not Enemies, and Taxation and Work; Gladden's Working People and their Employers, and Tools and the Man; George's Progress and Poverty, and The Condition of Labor; Gunton's Wealth and Progress; Wright's Relation of Political Economy to the Labor Question, The Factory System, Uniform Hours of Labor, and Present Actual Condition of the Working Man; Ruskin's Fors Clavigera; Toynbee's Industrial Revolution in England; Gilman's Profit-Sharing between Employer and Employee, and Socialism and the American Spirit; Sedley Taylor's Profit-Sharing between Capital and Labor; Schloss's Methods of Industrial Remuneration; Bushill's Profit-Sharing and the Labor Question; Mary W. Calkins's Sharing the Profits; Donisthorpe's Individualism; Powderly's Thirty Years of Labor.

THE LABOR PROBLEM.

BY NICHOLAS PAINE GILMAN.

SLAVERY CONTRASTED WITH THE WAGE SYSTEM.

IN the various courses of able lectures which the Brooklyn Ethical Association has conducted, but one address has touched on the subject of this evening. Prof. Gunton delivered in the course of 1889–'90 a lecture on The Evolution of the Wages System. It is a pleasure for one often obliged to disagree with Prof. Gunton to recognize the soundness of his defense of the wages system. It is one of the commonplaces of current socialism that this system is a later form of slavery; but the lecturer well pointed out the essential differences between a system entitled to be called slavery and that under which the laborer lives at the present day. Under real slavery the worker himself is a commodity, owned by his master. He receives payment in kind sufficient for a bare maintenance. The amount of this is determined by the sole will of the master, and the slave can never become a capitalist. He has no choice of masters, and no freedom to forsake one occupation for another. The wage-earner is the political equal, at the polls in this country, of his employer. He is paid in money according to regular rates determined largely by associations of his fellow-workmen. He can leave one employment and take up another; he can move with comparative freedom from one place to another; in fact, were he not informed by over-ingenious people that he is a slave, the fact would probably never have occurred to his mind, in most instances. Thinking people recognize that, in a rhetorical sense, all men are slaves to circumstance; that we are too often the serfs and not the lords of our condition, things being in the saddle and riding mankind. Every man who has to work for his living is, in a degree, the slave of his work; the problem for him is to alleviate the rigor of the conditions under which he works and increase his leisure.

The labor problem is one part, perhaps the most important part, of what is roughly known as "the social problem." The social problem includes a great variety of difficult questions relating to modern man under civilization. To be precise, however, there is in fact no such thing as "*the* social problem." As Gambetta once said, "there are social problems." There are a great many of them, and they are likely to continue long, if not to multiply greatly as the years go by. What we less loosely denote as "the labor problem" is a more restricted and more manageable question. I take it to include, as its main matter, the problem of the best relation of employer and employed in this great, complex, and marvelous world of modern work and modern machinery. Certainly, whatever minor issues may be connected with this chief issue, they would, in all probability, be adjusted with comparative ease could we once have and maintain a friendly union of master and man.

THE PERPETUAL NEED OF LABOR.

That there will always be, at least for many centuries, two such parties to labor contracts as master and man, or employer and employee, is altogether probable. We need observe but a few specimens of our common humanity to learn that this distinction has its roots in great natural facts. Differences of mental ability, differences in strength of character, as well as differences in fortune, are the causes of the persistence of this distinction. The need of labor is perpetual. This world of ours is a world in which he that worketh not shall not eat. To be sure, his work may have been done for him, in a few cases, by his fathers, and he may come into large leisure by inheritance, not having earned it through his own personal exertion. But the rule is that work is the condition of food as well as of leisure; we find no one eating whose food has not been paid for by himself or by others who have given it to him. We find no one enjoying leisure who has not himself earned it by hard work, or to whom the hard work of others has not given it.

The first of labor problems, then, for man, who must work to live, is to find some work to do. Happily, the stimulus to exertion through the complexity of human needs is very great, and the world is crowded with work needing to be done. As fast as one want is satisfied, it creates a dozen others. If one piece of work is well done, it points the way for a hundred times as much to be done in the same line or elsewhere. Nothing is more irrational in the conduct of modern labor unions than their attempts to diminish the hours or the tasks of laboring men, under the impression that there is a fixed quantity of work to be done so that, if ten men can do it all while there are twenty needing food, the only way out of the difficulty is for the first ten to do half as much as they can do, and leave the rest of the work to the other ten. It is a pure assumption that the second ten could or would do this half of the work if it were surrendered to them. Probably it would be found by trial that they were neither competent nor willing to equal the performance of the first ten, selected by a long sifting as the most capable and successful workers. The "lump-of-labor" fallacy, as Mr. Schloss calls it, will not stand examination. As a matter of fact, however, there is plenty of work for the first ten and plenty of work for the second ten also, if they are able and willing to work and will go where the work is to be had. The theoretical competition supposed by the orthodox school of political economists under which the workman is always perfectly free to seek work in any quarter is not indeed an actual condition, and there is much room for exertion in bringing the work and the worker together.

If a man is working for himself, he will turn out the largest product, under existing human nature. There is no means for extracting industry, thrift, skill, and all the virtues of work, from the most unpromising character, to be compared for a moment with the magic of private property, as all the economists have noted. The peasant proprietor in Italy, France, or Germany, for instance, or the independent farmer of New England or Dakota, sets the highest standard of achievement. Self-interest, whatever we may say of its excesses, is the most potent motive to exertion with the ordinary man. Working his own few acres, the small farmer will rise early and go to bed late. He will economize time, tools, and materials. He will perform prodigies of work in the hard contest with the powers of Nature if he is sure from the beginning that the whole result of his labor will be his own. We are not speaking of pure selfishness; "his own" includes that larger self, that most natural and persistent of all associations, the family of which he is the head. Not all men, of course, take the sturdy and heroic view of work on their own property; but when a man has thus before him every reason for exertion, and prefers idleness and dissipation, the labor problem is purely a moral and personal question of the individual.

HOW THE SYSTEM OF WORKING ON SHARES ARISES.

Let us suppose that our small farmer has so far prospered that he has outgrown his few acres and can not even superintend satisfactorily the numerous workers whom he is obliged to hire for his several farms.

He has not had to look far before finding other men who are not independent proprietors, and who, for this reason, are seeking work from such as he, which will give them daily bread. As long as his hired men were few in number and he could work with them, the result was fairly satisfactory. But suppose that he inquires how he shall derive the most income from one of the farms which he is no longer able to superintend in person. He need know but little of human nature to be sure that if he leaves this farm to be worked by hired men without superintendence the product will be small. The complaint of all employers of labor is perpetual, and to a considerable degree well founded, that the laborer is *not* worthy of his hire, if to be worthy of the hire means to display as much zeal and interest as the proprietor himself. This expectation, however, is irrational. The owner of the farm can not in reason expect that his hired workers shall manifest that extreme zeal and that persistent interest in making a large product which he himself displays, if energetic and capable. They are not working for their own interest in any such degree as himself; although if they work side by side with him his example will be to some degree contagious. The hired worker has, of course, the stimulus of need to keep him up to an average standard of work, but this standard is much lower than that of the independent proprietor. One need not dilate before people who have ever had occasion to hire another person to do work which they themselves understand and are capable of doing, upon the shortcomings, the neglects, the waste of time and material of the hired worker, as compared with the employer.

For our farmer there is an alternative. He may agree with one of those workers, whom he has found to be the most industrious and competent, to take a farm on shares and pay, not a fixed money rent, but half of the net product as rent. The system of product-sharing, which has had a wide prevalence in numerous countries, practically assures the owner as large a rent as the renter can earn. Though the worker has not before him the force of the motives to industry and economy which would be his were he the full owner of the place, his half-share of the product will augment with his own zeal and skill. With his eyes fixed, perhaps, on the ownership before long of this very place, he will not be slow to make this half-share as large as possible, and may even rival, under the spur of this ambition, the energy of the actual proprietor.

LIMITATIONS OF PRODUCT-SHARING; THE FACTORY SYSTEM.

The system of product-sharing is naturally restricted to such vocations as agriculture, the fisheries, and mining. It is not easily applied to the great variety of manufactures. But that which can be said of the excellence of the system in the fields where it has been so largely practiced can also be said, in considerable degree, of the system which is logically its successor. I refer to that modification of the wages system known as profit-sharing, in which the employer adds to fixed wages a bonus to labor, varying according to the prosperity of the business. No one will pretend that the employee in a large manufactory, working on the ordinary wages system, has every possible motive to exertion held out to him. As a matter of course, his usual exertion will be far below the standard of the man who carries on a small business at which he works by himself or side by side with his few workmen. As manufactories increase in size they become more and more unwieldy, and there is even more need than in the earlier days of the factory system for improvements in the labor contract practiced in them. There is much more demand in a large concern where no one person can effectively superintend the whole business, than in a small one under the view of a single eye, for enlisting every motive of self-interest on the part of the employee. The same tendencies which have built up the great manufacturing concerns of our day will probably long continue. They illustrate very forcibly the aristocratic principle which calls to the front the natural leaders of industries and commerce, and they forcibly exemplify the well-known Scriptural doctrine that "to him that hath it shall be given." Great changes may take place through the application of electricity to industry, rendering possible some return to small factories, and even to house production. For the present we must make up our minds to the continuance of such methods as we see practiced so extensively. We have bidden a long farewell to the familiar association of the employer with a small body of workmen; we must accept as inevitable the massing of workers in great buildings, often far removed from the commercial department of the industry. The practical problem is, first, how to counteract the natural tendency of the wages system to an inferior grade of accomplishment. The system which gives the largest product to be divided is the best.

TRADE ORGANIZATIONS.

We must accept just as much the natural and inevitable organization of workers among themselves for the purpose of raising wages and otherwise improving their condition. However much we may lament the loss of personal touch, and however much we may deplore the almost warlike array of workmen drawn up on one side against the smaller but more compact body of employers on the other, we must accept the situation as it is, and consider every method of feasible evolution before we, for a moment even, talk of revolution. The violent introduction of socialism as a fully developed scheme of collective capital and state production is quite out of the question; nor is the more peaceful revolution of pure co-operative production near at hand. The tendencies of modern industry are almost as hostile to pure co-operative production as they are to numerous small concerns.

MODIFICATIONS OF THE WAGES SYSTEM; CO-OPERATIVE PRODUCTION.

The deficiencies and disadvantages of the wages system are obvious to clear-sighted observers. One plain reason for this is that it is the system under which the work of civilization is actually being conducted. In this respect the system has, of course, great inferiority to fanciful schemes which have never been tried. Putting aside these imaginary constructions, we may say that the choice in the solution of the specific labor problem lies between the continuance of the unmodified wages system, the system of co-operative production, and such an intermediate measure as profit-sharing, shading off into forms of co-operative production. It is necessary to draw some lines of distinction here which do not everywhere exist in the same clearness, for there are various modifications of the wages system—such as piece-work, premiums, and "progressive wages"—which tend toward profit-sharing and answer some of the objections made to the method of simple day wages. Thus the wages system runs into some method of profit-sharing, and profit-sharing naturally tends to some form of co-operative production. Mr. David F. Schloss, in his recent valuable work on Methods of Industrial Remuneration, has well described the different modifications of pure wages in vogue in England. He has done a special service in this work, as the information which he gives could not be found anywhere else in such convenient form as late as three or four years ago.

The advocates of co-operative production usually contrast with this plan the unmodified wages system, under which no special inducement is held out to the workman to do his best. The prevailing tendencies are to make him satisfied with an average amount of work, corresponding to the ability of the mediocre, unsatisfied, uninterested worker. The objection which the advocate of co-operative production and the socialist also make against the wages system, that it is entirely "unjust," I prefer to pass over, for the present at least, for the reason that the application of abstract ideas of justice to complicated questions like this is generally very unfruitful. The employer has one idea of justice and the workman has another idea. A more fruitful method asks which system, the wages system or co-operative production, succeeds best in actual experience. The success of the co-operative productive enterprise is to be determined by the amount of product and its quality, actually realized, and the resulting income to the workmen, year in and year out.

Every one who desires the progressive elevation of mankind must heartily sympathize with the system of co-operative production as laid down so admirably by such writers as Judge Thomas Hughes and the late Mr. Vansittart Neale. The system is evidently near to the ideal, since it promises to all the workers a just division of the entire profits of the business. But it can not be said that the actual record is very inspiring. There are, to be sure, in England at the present time some eighty productive societies more or less connected with the co-operative movement.

Although some few of these are important and well established, the great majority are small, or yet in the trial stage. In America the imitation of societies like these has been almost as slight and intermittent as the reproduction of the English co-operative stores here, of which we have so few. The difficulties in the way of co-operative production are very great. The financial obstacle increases rather than decreases with time. Manufacturing in these days is carried on in such large establishments, demanding such elaborate machinery, that the capital needed to compete successfully with existing enterprises is almost entirely lacking to ordinary workingmen.

MORAL DIFFICULTIES IN CO-OPERATIVE PRODUCTION.

If the necessary capital for a comparatively modest undertaking in co-operative production is at hand, if a considerable number of workingmen of unusual character and ability put together their hard-earned savings, the moral difficulties are still before them. One of the first of these is an entire willingness on the part of these workmen to submit to the orders of one of their own number, placed at the head of the business of manufacturing and buying and selling, with that readiness which is indispensable for competition with other establishments. A man may very well be a workman in one cotton factory, as in Oldham, England, and a stockholder in another; but when he is at once a worker in a mill and a part owner of it, he will not obey orders from a superintendent whom his own vote has helped to put in office, and whom his vote can also help to depose, as readily as he will conform to the discipline of a mill in which he has no financial stake. The ordinary corporation, which is, in one sense, a plain instance of co-operation, seems to be the nearest approach to co-operative production now feasible under most circumstances. In large corporations the great majority of the stockholders own so few shares that the conduct of the enterprise is practically in the hands of a few persons, whose financial interests teach them to combine, rather than to fight each other. When one considers how difficult it is to get a number of people usually regarded as above the average in intelligence and character to co-operate in schemes demanding but a limited amount of money from each, and but a small part of his time, it will be seen how severe a demand the developed scheme of co-operative production makes upon the workman, for he is expected to put in all his available capital, to give all of his working time to the enterprise, and to surrender the management to one of his associates. This associate must be a man of great ability and high character to carry on the business successfully. He must be willing to receive, for the most part, a much smaller compensation for his uncommon business talent than he would receive under the wages system as foreman or superintendent. The opportunities for suspicion and distrust are very many, and the first financial reverse may be sufficient to bring down a very promising attempt at co-operative production. But however discouraging the record of the system may be thus far, there is an undeniable fascination in the idea itself that the capital requisite for carrying on a business should be furnished by those who are to do the work, and that they should divide equitably among themselves the entire profits of the enterprise. This surely would seem to be the application to industry of obvious notions of justice, right, and equity. But the workmen must furnish from their own body not only the manual labor but the faculty for superintendence and commercial management; besides this, they have to reach a higher level of character, leading to a much greater mutual confidence, than we find in the ordinary world. The place of that constraint and discipline which the present wages system enforces, and which sentimentalists call a system of slavery, must be taken under co-operative production by a high moral development, which shall justify complete confidence by the workmen in each other. This confidence they must have not only in those who work with them at the bench or the loom, but most of all in the men of unusual ability, belonging to their own condition in life, whom they select as responsible managers of the enterprise.

PROFIT-SHARING IN INDUSTRIAL EVOLUTION.

Such considerations as these of the tendencies of the existing wages system on the one hand, and of the immeasurable discontent which workingmen penetrated by the democratic spirit naturally feel; of the actual weakness of the system of co-operative production, owing to the large demands, intellectually and morally, it makes upon working people—lead one to inquire if there may not be meth-

ods which may lead up by easy transition from the pure
wages system to the more ideal system of co-operative production.
The system of industrial partnership, for which
term profit-sharing is an inadequate designation, has at least
this much to recommend it: It has, in several very important
instances, bridged over the gap between the wages system
and a system of co-operative production entitled to
that name by its actual results, although not corresponding
in every respect to the usual ideal of the workingman.
Such houses as the Maison Leclaire and the Bon Marché of
Paris, and the Co-operative Paper Mills of Angoulême,
France, for instance, show how profit-sharing may be induced
upon the wages system and developed into a substantial
system of co-operative production. The process in
these three instances has been long and slow, but such is
the nature of all sound and durable education. The numerous
years occupied by the transition sufficed to educate
the employer and the employed alike; they justified the
employer in gradually divesting himself of his powers and
responsibilities; they taught the workmen very gradually
the virtues and the faculties demanded by the employer's
position, and they rendered easy the gradual supersession of
the original proprietor by men from the ranks of his own
establishment. In these cases regulations have been made
for the continuous application of a system of promotion, so
that a body like the Mutual Benefit Society of the Maison
Leclaire can furnish out of its membership at any time of
need the partner or partners, as they are called, to direct
the working of the entire business. These partners, or
managers, however, when they assume their new position,
find a moral condition about them such as no co-operative
productive enterprise starting out *de novo* could furnish.
The new manager, fresh from the ranks of the workers,
finds the whole body of his former fellows ready and accustomed
to obey orders from the heads of the establishment,
and to give them as full powers as partners enjoy in establishments
conducted on the ordinary wages system. The
new partners have been chosen by a sensible body of workingmen
because of their approved character and their tested
ability. They have been shown by time to belong to the
natural aristocracy of ability and character, and their fellow-workmen
take pleasure in promoting them, and a rational
pride in co-operating with them, not henceforth as
complete equals, but as members, each in his own place, of

an establishment proud of its history and determined to maintain its high standard in the years to come.

Such instances as the Maison Leclaire and others of a similar nature lead me to believe that we shall obtain in time, in a large number of cases at least, the substantial benefits of co-operative production through the process of education by means of profit-sharing. The details of the systems thus worked out may not be in all respects those laid down even by the wisest heads for a scheme of co-operative production ideally just. Deference to the democratic principle may easily lead even such thinkers astray, while the experience of such firms as I have mentioned supplies the needed corrective, in paying the due tribute to the aristocratic principle, just as natural as the democratic.

PROFIT-SHARING AN EVOLUTIONARY METHOD.

I am decidedly of the opinion that the labor problem, considered as substantially the problem of the best kind of contract relations between the employer and the employed, is to be solved in the gradual development of the existing wages system, through profit-sharing, into some system of co-operative production. I am not here to undertake the office of prophet, and I quite decline to predict even how soon there will be so modest a number as one hundred such co-operative establishments as the Maison Leclaire in the whole civilized world. With confidence, however, I declare my conviction that such a development itself does more justice to all the factors in production than any other measure which I know. Profit-sharing is thoroughly entitled to the full credit of being an evolutionary method. The one great and crying defect of the wages system is that under it an immense amount of work is not done which could be done, to the great benefit of mankind, if the whole body of workers were thoroughly interested in producing just as much and just as good work as possible. This being so, we should be quick to make modest attempts toward a system which brings into play a great reserve force. Under the wages system this reserve of unusual power lies largely among the workingmen; but one need only stop and think a moment to realize how the extreme friction of the existing system diminishes the actual working power of the employers. Under a system which secured to them the hearty co-operation of their men, their own force would undoubtedly be largely increased. We want to increase it.

Looking at the system of co-operative production, as usually practiced to-day, in comparison with such an evolutionary system as I speak of, it is a striking fact that its advocates virtually leave out of sight the immense working power of the present captains of industry. It is not to be supposed that we can immediately convert any considerable number of the great manufacturers and masters of transportation, for instance, so that they will be willing to put all their ability at the service of the workmen for modest salaries. Imagine, then, if you can, the effect if to-morrow morning the skill and ability of all business men above the grade of common hand labor were withdrawn. Imagine the city of Brooklyn, for instance, left to-morrow to be run, so far as private business is concerned, by the workingmen alone, with nearly all the brain capital of the present system reduced to temporary idleness. It would require but a few hours of such a *régime* to convince even the most determined advocate of the democratic principle in industry of the fallacy of his theories of manual labor as the source of all value and of the equality of all heads in business. Any system which, like most plans of co-operative production, makes little account of the men who are really leading the business of modern civilization and furnishing employment and bread for the great army of hand workers, neglects one of the vital factors in the situation. In point of fact, we need every particle of ability and of working force in head and hand to do even the larger part of the work that must be done. The captains of industry of whom I speak are not yet sufficiently moralized to be willing to accept the very modest position which the system of co-operative production would assign to them. This is no reproach to them; the level of morality among them is at least as high as that among workingmen or any other large class of people. They need, however, education into some larger ideal and up to some nobler standard, like all the rest of us, and it is to some gradual process of taking their workmen into partnership in the profits of industry, managed on substantially the present lines, that we are to look for the educating agency needed. Both the employer and the employed under present conditions need to evolve new capacities and new virtues to give co-operative production a fair field in which to develop.

The question just how large a share of the profits the employed shall receive is not important at the outset. The fact that a regular dividend paid to labor out of the profits of the year has been shown to be good business policy in a large number of cases, resulting in at least as large net profits to the employer himself as before and in the general improvement of the industrial situation in the establishment—recognition of this fact is the main matter at the beginning. If the workman is guaranteed by his employer a modest dividend of five or ten per cent on his wages, varying according to the returns of the year, he is taken into a kind of partnership such as he did not before know. He will in time, if he belongs to ordinary humanity, begin to have the feelings and the ambitions of the partner. The increase in the amount of product and the improvement in its quality, and other gains from economy of material and care of machinery, and from the absence of labor difficulties, which have usually resulted, are arguments of great weight for such a limited partnership. Into the details of the very considerable body of experience furnished in the last fifty years by the numerous firms which have tried the system, beginning with the Maison Leclaire in 1842 and coming down to the three hundred firms which now practice profit-sharing in Europe and America, I can not here enter. My chief claim for profit-sharing, as compared with the wages system now in force and with that system of co-operative production which is desired by so many, is that it does more complete justice to all the factors in the situation than either of these two systems—that which is now a fact and that which is now largely a hope. The objection commonly made to profit-sharing—that it does not include the sharing of losses by the employed—rests upon a gross misconception of the scheme. It is a limited method to be distinguished carefully from the more developed system of co-operative production under which loss-sharing is plainly inevitable. I have elsewhere so fully shown that under the ordinary systems of profit-sharing the workman does bear fully as much of a share of the losses as is just and fair that I simply refer to the matter now.

The progress which has been made in the last few years by the system of industrial partnership is encouraging to all believers who have never allowed themselves to put it forward as the one solution of the labor problem or as a panacea for social difficulties. If I may speak for the great body of advocates of the system, we see in it one excellent method of improving the relations between the workman and his employer, which it is highly desirable should be applied and tested in a great many directions in order to ascertain the fields in which it will prove itself to be a better system than any yet practiced. If in one direction a system of premiums for economy in the use of material, or in another direction a system of increasing the wages according to the amount of good production, is found to bring a larger return to the workman and a better result for the employer than profit-sharing, we are entirely ready to acknowledge the fact. There are directions in which profit-sharing is likely to justify itself at once, as in trades where a large amount of skilled labor is employed; in others, owing to the great use of machinery, there is less room for wise economy on the part of the employee. A large part of the business of the world, of course, is done on a no-profit basis. There are numerous fields, from such matters as common domestic service to the work of the teacher in the public school and the professor in the college, from which the whole notion of profits is absent, and to which consequently such a system as profit-sharing has no application. In these fields, if service is defective and unsatisfactory, means of improving it must be sought in other ways than by resort to such a system.

PROBABLE TREND OF FUTURE INDUSTRIAL PROGRESS.

If we look forward in a general way to consider the parts which the three systems—of wages, profit-sharing, and co-operative production—are likely to play in the comparatively near future, it is only rational to suppose that they will for a long time continue side by side. As the world grows older, wiser, and more humane, and as the democratic principle asserts itself more and more vigorously, the wages system, which is now virtually monopolizing the field, will gradually suffer modifications. Profit-sharing or industrial partnership, under the various forms which as a guiding principle it readily admits, will steadily make converts, encroaching upon the wages system to an indefinite extent. The wages system, however, will persist in some quarters because no other system is so well adapted to the demands of the situation; and in other quarters it will yield place but very slowly to more democratic methods. The wages system, however, will probably be much more influenced by the advance of profit-sharing for a considerable time to come than profit-sharing will be by the spread of co-operative production growing out of it.

A steady and permanent increase in the number of true co-operative productive establishments, in the light of all the experience which profit-sharing can give, we must all heartily desire. No industrial future, however, is likely to be less complex than that which we behold in wonderful variety round about us to-day, and he would be a rash prophet who should predict the day when any one system of the three under consideration will have driven out the other two. He would be much less wise who should protest that no system which the human mind is capable of imagining will ever supersede co-operative production. In all these matters we do well to keep ourselves free from the conceit of inerrancy and infallibility. We have no call to legislate for an indefinite future or to lay down an industrial or economic creed for all our descendants. It is our one imperative duty to consider the existing situation, not as capitalists, not as employers, not as workingmen, not as members of a particular profession, but scientifically and philosophically. It is our business to see facts as they are and to consider them calmly, with a view to that improvement which a progressive civilization demands. We can not escape the application of the notion of evolution to these matters, and such an application at once forbids our declaiming against the wages system as a system of slavery, or exalting co-operative production as the sacred ideal to which the future must conform, or preaching profit-sharing as the one panacea for all our industrial woes.

THE LABOR PROBLEM AS A FACTOR IN OUR CIVILIZATION.

The labor problem, I began by saying, is a problem of finding work and finding the just reward for it. More specifically, it is the problem of the best relation between the man who has more work than he can do himself and the man who must find work. The interests of these two parties are not directly and obviously identical; but society includes both the employer and the employed, and a good many other persons not to be ranked under either of these heads. The interest of entire society unmistakably is that as much work and as good work as possible shall be done without overworking any human being; that every worker shall receive a fair return for his toil; that the whole product of all the workers shall be so increased by such material agents as improved machinery, and such moral agents as greater interest in the work on the part of all, and a closer union and harmony, that the share of every worker may be augmented.

The labor question grows out of the advance of civilization and the development of humanity. While we isolate it for the purpose of clearness of thought and to facilitate the adoption of practical measures of improvement, we have to remember that it is not the only problem, perhaps not the chief problem, of mankind from age to age. The present absorption of so many earnest and able minds in labor problems and social questions does not mean that these are to be perpetually so absorbing. The present deep interest is a sign of progress; it is a sign of the elevation of mankind; a sign of hope, not of despair; it is a token of the increasing spread of sound morals and rational religion. It is, we may firmly trust, the sure omen of a gradual and incessant improvement in the condition of civilized mankind.

The Labor Problem.   323

ABSTRACT OF THE DISCUSSION.

PROF. GEORGE GUNTON:

The lecture to which we have listened was quite exceptional in its character. Few people who are looking for a departure from the wages system have any idea of sticking to the doctrine of evolution. They generally assume that the system is the invention of an evil genius, and aim at its immediate abolition. If I am anything I am an evolutionist. I believe in growth along the lines of existing tendencies. The lecturer navigated among the rocks toward the goal of co-operation, with a good, long stop at profit-sharing, in a way that takes the edge off of criticism. But I am expected to differ, and fortunately, in this instance, I can. You will remember how 'cutely and successfully Mr. Gilman handled the socialist when he reached co-operation—how clearly he showed why the socialistic scheme wouldn't work. Socialism aims chiefly at co-operative production, and this has everywhere failed under practical tests. In Lancashire co-operative production was tried extensively before co-operative distribution. It failed so completely that the aristocratic element had to be introduced, and they changed the counting of noses to the counting of shares. The lecturer showed that democratic co-operation is impracticable, and then claimed that profit-sharing is a half-way place toward the thing that will not work.

What we have to do in order to help along civilization—and this the lecturer declares to be his aim—is to see that the next step is in the right evolutionary direction, so that the next generation will not have to accuse us of guiding them wrong. We must head toward the future and not toward the past. The guide to be consulted is the past experience of the race. Great stress was laid upon the importance of having us work more than we now do. Somehow, the capitalist's whip isn't keen enough. He wants another motive. I do not think that is quite along the line of evolution. My idea is that we should make Nature do more and more and man less and less. Every real improvement is in the direction of letting us work less; toward getting less out of us and leaving more in. Enjoy and be, rather than drudge and do. The speaker regretted the loss of the system of working on shares. When that system prevailed we didn't go to the theatre, we enjoyed none of the comforts of life; we couldn't afford them; we didn't earn as much money as we have since it was given up. That kind of co-operative industry has changed to another and better. The shoemaker, weaver, and all the other factors of our complex society are serving everybody. This is unconscious co-operation, but that is the best kind. The idea of dividing the profits is a thing of the past. It was the method employed when people were nearly all alike. We can not return to it without returning to the simple methods of life that permitted it. Are we better off under our present system? Yes. Society has evolved into a higher state. This means a higher individual development, a state of industrial specialization, minimizing the precarious and maximizing the sure and definite. Profits are doubtful and contingent. It isn't possible for everybody to have profits, and therefore it isn't possible for everybody to have the benefits of profit-sharing. The tendency is to concentrate the contingent into the hands of economic specialists, and make the laborer more and more sure of what his income is to be. Uncertainty is more harassing than lower incomes. The evolution of this element out of the labor problem is the elimination of a great chunk of social gall, and the liberation of a great amount of social sweetness and light.

MR. ALFRED DOLGE:

It is admitted that the relations of capital and labor need readjustment. While labor seeks to enforce the constantly increasing demands which a continual rise in the social scale of the wage-earner calls for, capital seeks to resist these demands. In this industrial war, all parties, including the community, suffer; labor naturally more than capital, since it has less to lose. The problem therefore is, what readjustment of the relations of labor and capital can be made which will be satisfactory to both parties, and how can such a readjustment best be practically carried out?

It is obvious that a method must be discovered sufficiently elastic to meet all the changing phases of business life, and one that will be satisfactory to the wage-earner, because it is founded on justice. Production and not philanthropy, therefore, must be the basis of any economic distribution of wealth. In other words, the first thing to do is to find out what the man actually earns in the production of wealth, and the next thing is to give it to him. This is why I have called my system "A Just Distribution of Earnings." A wage-earner will be satisfied with, say, fifty dollars a year over and above his stipulated wages if he be convinced that that is all to which he is justly entitled, while he will not be satisfied with five hundred dollars if he believes that he has earned more. To determine the actual earnings of a wage-earner irrespective of the wages he gets is a matter of book-keeping. It will be agreed that justice is a rare quality in human life, and that if the settlement of the labor problem is to depend upon it alone, failure may be expected; but if to justice self-interest is added we have a combination that is irresistible. When it can be demonstrated to capital that by being strictly just to labor and no more it serves its own self-interest most, capital will adopt such a policy purely from self-interest, and then that policy will succeed.

My system of the "Just Distribution of Earnings" involves three main features: First, the system of pensions, by which employees can retire with a pension of from forty to one hundred per cent of their wages according to the length of their service. After twenty-five years' service employees can retire on a pension of their full wages. Second, the system of life insurance, by which each employee receives a policy for one thousand dollars after five years' consecutive service; another thousand after another five years of such service, and a third thousand after the third term of five years of such consecutive service. The firm, of course, pays the premiums on such policies. Third, a system of endowment, by which all employees who, by their skill, improve methods of manufacturing, save material, or benefit the firm in any way outside of their regular work, are credited with such a portion of the firm's earnings due to such efforts as the books show they are entitled to after all proper charges have been deducted. These sums draw six per cent interest per annum, but the capital is only payable when the beneficiary is sixty years of age, or to his family at his death.

This system has been in practice in my business for the past sixteen years, and produced the most beneficial results. Aside from the fact that it made the men employed contented and satisfied, it enabled me in one instance to dispense with the services of a man who had for seventeen years been a most faithful worker, but who had passed the stage of "economic efficiency," without throwing him upon the world at the time when he was incapable of earning a living. He has been on the pension list for three years now, drawing over five hundred dollars per year, and his place has been filled by a young man to the benefit of the business.

The insurance plan suggested itself to my mind because of the general well-known improvidence of wage-earners, and having been a wage-earner myself I know that it is not in the power of the majority of them to even acquire a habit of saving. This plan prevents, to some extent at least, the pauperism of the second generation by the death of the bread-winner, and secures to his family the home which he may have bought, paying for the same in installments according to his wages. My experience has been that the majority of those who have insurance policies have become house-owners because of this insurance. It is self-evident that a widow and children of a wage-earner must sink in the social scale when losing their supporter, and must begin a hand-to-hand struggle with poverty, and that the bright future of the boys will be impaired if not destroyed. Into this situation enters first the money from his life insurance, and then the money from the endowment account, to sustain the home and to assure the future of all.

Whatever efforts may be made in the direction of adjusting the relations of capital and labor, the basic idea should always be a proper recognition of the necessity that the wage-earners must enjoy the most favorable conditions while working, and that they must be placed beyond the fear of want in their old age or for their families in case of death. Every progressive manufacturer is continually aiming to improve his methods. In his calculation he makes proper allowance for the wear and tear of his machinery, so that he may be able to buy better machines. Why should he not do the same for his men? Why not insure them, so that he can replace them with younger men when they get old and have given all their strength to him?

I beg to refer to my essay on this subject in the Social Economist of January, 1892, in which I have explained my ideas more fully than this paper would allow. I believe that ultimately the wage-earners will become virtually partners of their employers. The tendency of the times is toward concentration, and the great combinations which are almost daily formed are all in the direction of securing the greatest economic efficiency at the lowest possible cost. These great corporations will be better able to treat the labor question justly and successfully than any large number of small manufacturers or business men could ever be expected to do. As the factory system elevated the working classes from serfdom to personal independence, self-protection will also impel these industrial institutions of the future to recognize the wage-earner's title to all he earns.

MR. WILLIAM POTTS:

The speaker who followed the lecturer used two or three expressions which are significant. He referred to co-operation as if it were identical with socialism. As I understand it, co-operation and socialism are diametrically opposed. Co-operation is voluntary, socialism is compulsory. He objected to co-operation, and to profit-sharing because it leads to co-operation. He advocated the wages system pure and simple, because it leads to certainty of income. I do not see that it is desirable to know every year just what one has to rely upon. It is the contingent that stimulates and makes character. It is the prize in every package that is good for human beings, the something that makes them think all the time whether they can do a little better. If one knows just what he is to get and is satisfied, he is simply a polyp —a stomach fast to a rock into which the food is washed. "The whip of the boss doesn't do it, so some additional incentive must be devised." I am surprised to hear it intimated that it is not a good thing to have something put before the worker that will lead him to feel that if he does his work better he will get more for it. The interests of employer and employed become identical when the employed is given a fair proportion of what is produced. Each must be compensated for his investment, for work, capital, and time, and the profits and losses should be shared. The rate of wages should be fixed sufficiently low to meet the contingency of losses. It may be a difficult thing to adjust, but we must do it as well as we can. An agreement in the interest of employer and employed will remove the struggle between capital and labor and increase the profit, enabling capital to secure as large a return as before and perhaps larger. The best statement of the principle which I have seen is in the chapter on Labor Capitalization in Wordsworth Donisthorpe's book on Individualism. He speaks of the condition of the capitalist as threefold: (1) As a speculator watching markets; (2) as an organizer and director; (3) as an insurer of incomes, a payer of wages. He can not go into the insurance business with safety unless he gives something less as salary than what he thinks is a just share. Profit-sharing enables him to remove the injustice in the insurance element. Let each man take his chances and not be a part of a machine worked by steam, doing nothing but what the steam compels him to do.

DR. ROSSITER W. RAYMOND:

I also am an evolutionist. I found when I began to teach evolution that my clerical friends were scared; but many of them have passed from that stage to an abnormal appetite for evolution. They swallow it undigested and apply it to questions in a way that would make Darwin turn over in his coffin. "First the laborer was a slave; then the capitalist owned not the worker but the tools; then," they prophesy, "the next step will be for the workman to own the tools," and so on. There never was a time when any one could predict on the lines of evolution what was going to happen next. When it gets hold of the best thing it holds to it; it doesn't evolve into something else. The highest thing found yet is a man with a backbone, and he continues to live. There is devolution, and by it we may get co-operation and socialism, in which man ceases to have a backbone and degenerates into a polyp.

The system which is indispensable is free contract; that and not the wage system is the one now prevalent. The contract may be for wages, for profit, or for anything. Wage-paying is only a part of our system. My contention is that we have no right to cram down the throat of the laborer anything he doesn't want. I have been a workingman, and I don't like profit-sharing. I want my pay, and then I strive for something else. Workingmen don't want to run any risks. They would rather have a definite amount fixed and let the employer take the risk. The disturbance of the conditions of free contract is due to philanthropists and demagogues who by legislation try to remove the responsibility from one party or the other. They have coddled the labor unions—the men who have organized systematic robbery and call on us to stand and deliver. The employer can not make a free contract under this system. There is no labor question until we settle the primary questions of order and justice. There was no labor question at Homestead or at Buffalo. When you give to me and to others the protection of the law, first in making the contract free, and second in making both parties responsible, I will agree to undertake the settlement of the question as far as it can be done without making matters worse than they now are. I have no patience with the critic who says that this can not be endured by the public and we must give up our liberty. Our fathers gave blood and money and life for liberty, and we might at least give a little personal inconvenience.

MR. GILMAN, in reply:

I should like to say in regard to Prof. Gunton's point of not getting more work out of people, that we know that the kind of work which hurts a man is that which he does against his will. He is not hurt by the work he wants to do. Zealous work does not bring wear and tear and injury to the worker.

It is utterly impossible to eliminate from modern industry the contingent element. This element is the most interesting feature—helpful, inspiring, for employers and equally so for the workmen. Under profit-sharing the employer says he will give certain wages, and more if he makes it. All work together. How that is going back to barbarism I don't see.

In conclusion, Mr. Gilman read an extract from a letter from Prof. James Bryce, M. P., author of The American Commonwealth, in which he expressed his approval of profit-sharing as the most practical solution of the labor problem.

POLITICAL ASPECTS OF THE LABOR PROBLEM

BY
J. W. SULLIVAN
AUTHOR OF DIRECT LEGISLATION BY THE CITIZENSHIP THROUGH THE INITIATIVE
AND REFERENDUM, ETC.

COLLATERAL READINGS SUGGESTED:

Powderly's Thirty Years of Labor; Wright's Historical Sketch of the Knights of Labor; Miller's Trade Organizations in Politics; Chamberlin's Sovereigns of Industry; Sullivan's A Concept of Political Justice, and Direct Legislation by the Citizenship through the Initiative and Referendum; George's Social Problems, and The Condition of Labor; Jacobson's An Ounce of Prevention; Lloyd's A Strike of Millionaires against Miners; Hubbard's The Coming Climax in the Destinies of America; Huxley's Social Diseases and Worse Remedies; recent decisions in the United States Courts respecting the rights and obligations of laborers and labor organizations by Justice Brewer, Judges Taft, Ricks, and others.

POLITICAL ASPECTS OF THE LABOR PROBLEM.

BY J. W. SULLIVAN.

IN one short hour, how small a part of my subject can be even touched upon! Labor, ever a world-wide, many-sided, complicated, vexed problem; labor in politics, to-day in all civilized lands becoming a foremost problem. In an hour, surveying labor in politics from a labor standpoint, I may be sketchily descriptive, bluntly dogmatic, perhaps here and there suggestive; little more.

What political strength of its own has labor? What reason exists for setting up labor, that is class, politics? What definite social reforms await labor's vote? These queries map out my evening's task.

First, can labor of itself do for itself? Are "laborers" and "hands" merely "laborers" and "hands," or does potent variety dwell in them, as in other men?

WHERE DOES LABOR'S STRENGTH LIE?

I find that my first set of facts relating to labor's political strength begins with a once common prejudice. I well remember how this prejudice was sown in me. When I was six years of age, a certain Irish ditchman's work was to me a never-fading novelty. I would often stand on the ditch dirt-pile and look down at him joining pipes, and I would wonder and admire. He had a helper, a raw and awkward Irish lad, the butt of the whole force. My ditchman bossed this lad, taunted him, and called him descriptive names. One day, after exhausting on him his usual list of fanciful and opprobrious epithets, my artist, his patience worn out, shouted at the lad: "Don't ye do thawt, ye–ye–ye–ye cigarmaker! Yer fit fer nawthing but fer a cigarmaker!" To me from that moment on for years the least man in labor's hosts was the cigarmaker. This was a prejudice. I never rid myself of this prejudice until I moved among cigarmakers and men of less skilled occupations, and saw how, as I shall explain further on, the former prejudice of trade against trade has largely been dissipated.

Some classes of men may yet entertain the idea that the cigarmaker is below the ordinary. Certainly, the business and professional world bar him out; and the society reporter finds in him no material for write-ups. Those persons present who have noticed the cigarmaker at all have perhaps observed that his is not a distinguished air on the promenade; that his week-day clothes are rumpled and baggy and shiny where they rub; that his collar and cuffs are often the shade of his tobacco-stained fingers; that his abode is in a tenement-house district, and that, if accurate, his parlor-wall legends would usually read: " God bless our fourth flat—rear."

In other words, the typical cigarmaker is the typical man in the long procession which hurries homeward from work of evenings through the short-cut streets running from factorydom to tenementdom. Have you ever stood for half an hour and watched one of these processions? There is nothing like it among the lower animals.

Why does the cigarmaker live in the city? He reads the Monday morning papers containing that weekly politico-economic sermon counseling the wage-workers to stay in the country, where there is no work at their trade, and not to come to the city, where there is sometimes work. But he lives in the city because in a small town there is no room for even one idle cigarmaker; in the city, there is always room for thousands, half-idle.

Why does the cigarmaker not start in business for himself? There are reasons. The cigar factory that to-day competes under advantageous conditions buys its own tobacco direct from the planter, minutely subdivides its labor, establishes its own retail agencies, and obtains the best credits. A hundred thousand dollars is a small capital for such a factory. The journeyman cigarmaker, setting up trade for himself, buying his own stuff, making his cigars in a tenement-house, and peddling them, barely earns current wages.

Why does the cigarmaker not learn another business? There are reasons. Commonly his sure purchase on the necessaries of life permits him to risk neither the time nor the money necessary. So he is shut off from the professions, and such like. And why should he drop one poor trade to take up with another? Why quit cigarmakers' conditions for shoemakers' conditions?

Why does not the cigarmaker save a part of his wages and invest?—But this question is mockery.

No betterment to be looked for through an advance in his own business, little or nothing to be promised in a change of place or occupation, no store of wealth in his possession beyond what at the furthest may insure a few months' existence, his condition simply that of the swarms of city wageworkers among whom he dwells, what can the cigarmaker do to better his lot?

THE CIGARMAKERS' UNION—A TYPE OF TRADE ORGANIZATIONS.

Some thirty years ago, having tried in various ways to answer this irrepressible question individually, a group of New York cigarmakers asked it of one another collectively. Together they found a promising idea. They adopted that idea. It has turned out well. In noting its development, we may ascertain if labor has any strength by which it may lift itself up.

This idea was to ask for more wages in a body, and if refused to stop work in a body. That is, the group formed a trades-union. That is, like the great financiers and producers, the cigarmakers formed a trust; like many retailers, they put a price on what they had to sell (their labor) and refused to break the price; like certain professional classes, they decided that before candidates could be admitted to their ranks they must possess a certain instruction, skill, and character. But the cigarmakers never rose to that respected height of insolence at which they could ask that their union rules should be bolstered up by statute laws— that non-union men should be fined or jailed for practicing the cigarmaker's profession.

I know that the first committee of union cigarmakers that ever waited on an American employer were all discharged on the spot; I know that the first American union cigar shop hands that demanded an increase of wages were promptly met by a lockout; I know that public sentiment (among the wealth-holding classes) was arrayed against the locked-out men—ingrates! to conspire and rebel against a kind employer who had furnished them work! I am morally certain of these facts because they are uniform in all trades-union experience.

But the united cigarmakers justified themselves, first, by a conscientious appeal to their own interests, and, secondly, by getting the best of their employers. The union has gone on victorious until to-day, when it has in the United States and British America 330 local unions, combined in one international union; it has 27,000 members, including the great bulk of all the skilled workers at the trade; it has succeeded, without government aid, in firmly establishing the eight-hour workday; and it holds in its treasury nearly $600,000.

These results are enough to challenge even a strong prejudice. The cigarmaker, after all, may be a creature of fair business intelligence. His methods, too, may be worth looking into.

But first a word further as to results. To all hands out on strike or lockout, the cigarmakers' union pays $5 a week for sixteen weeks; after sixteen weeks, $3; to a member out of employment at any time, $3 a week for six weeks; to a sick member, $5 a week for thirteen weeks; to the next of kin on the death of a member, $50 to $550, according to duration of membership. To a member traveling in search of work, the union lends up to $20 car-fare and up to $12 for other expenses. All union funds are considered part of the international treasury, are equalized proportionately among the local unions, and are deposited and drawn in such manner as to be as safe as money can be made. A handsome official monthly journal, of twenty newspaper pages, certain important articles being printed in German and Bohemian as well as in English, is mailed gratuitously to every member. I am not quoting from a prospectus: the union has done these things for twenty years or more.

As to the mechanism and routine processes of the union: When a cigarmaker joins the organization, he is given a little thin official blank-book, his pass to good cigarmakers' society. Without this book he can not get work in a union shop. In it are printed blank forms for his accounts with the union. These accounts he keeps himself, doing so by means of stamps, different colors for different sums, bought of the secretary. These stamps, pasted in their date-spaces, show union officials if a pass-book bearer has paid his dues, fines, and assessments. Paid up, all union shops are open to him.

Who is more to be pitied than a poor man seeking for work—begging his fellow-men for leave to exercise his own faculties? How haunting his fears! When the last penny is reached, what is to become of him, and, if married, of his dependent family? Human hearts, how far away all then are! The crowded streets how desolate! Perhaps poorly clad, and none too well fed, the anxious man walks about to a score of places, to find posted outside each: "No help wanted!" Other places he enters, to be regarded as a something in the way; so many like him have been coming, it is a nuisance. Humiliated, distracted, nerve all gone, the man may commit the horrid social wrong of taking a stimulating drink; and, it is a fact, news of jobs is to be had in barrooms. But sometimes—what is the weekly average in New York?—the man out of work does better for himself than getting drunk: he falls, of his own act, out of the ranks of the living.

Among union cigarmakers, no friendless man loses heart in fruitless quest of work. Fruitless at times the quest may be, but unemployed cigarmakers need apply for work only at the union headquarters, where the boon of vacant jobs is reported by the shop collectors. Once acquainted about town, union cigarmakers may also find jobs through trade rumors and the fellowship of old shopmates.

Who so tormented as the workman disliked and nagged by an unrestrained foreman? There are thousands of factory hands in this city who quail before the foreman a hundred times when they never think of the Almighty once. They must have bread for their bairns; and that bread they must gain not only by the sweat of their brow but at the cost of their self-respect. Hourly they swallow insult and never dare look the foreman in the eye. Could the statistician probe to the facts, he might find hatred of the tyrannical foreman at the bottom of many a strike ascribed to the desire for higher wages. But that column—like certain others representing sentiment—is rarely printed in the tables.

The union cigarmakers have toned down the foreman's voice and helped him bridle his tongue. The union enforces defensive shop rules. Once in a while union shop committees have a word with the foreman—which enriches his character.

Favorites are seldom conscious of the favoritism to themselves. Good turns to them they see as rewards of their own merits. Shrewd employers, acting on this fact, are prone to pay a few hands better than the average, or to give them advantages at the expense of the rest. The favored are then not apt to be agitators, and in case of strike they may side with the employer.

This situation the union cigarmakers have attacked sanely. Under their shop rules, all hands share burdens and enjoy privileges alike. The work is fairly divided.

How pleasant to the weary worker is sympathy! Pity it is it is so often merely a word.

The union cigarmakers have learned how to turn sympathy into coin. On every box of cigars made by them they paste a blue label. All smokers who truly sympathize with the cigarmakers' union buy only blue label cigars. The cigar manufacturer reflects twice before he breaks with his union hands and loses the blue label.

The most remarkable feature in the union cigarmakers is their spirit of unionism. In the beginning, they were panicky, undisciplined, mutually suspicious; their plans were unproved, their spokesman untried; they stood in some awe of public opinion. To-day, confidence in the union reigns; the officials are experienced; the body moves like a veteran army; for newspaper, pulpit, or employing-class sentiment the members do not care a button. Against them or for them, in no way has so-called public opinion ever been worth to them a button. Two points only demand much thought of a well-organized union: How much is in the treasury? What is the state of the labor market of the trade? These two questions settled in the union's favor, public opinion, employers' arguments, the justice or injustice of the dispute, all matter little. The contest is one of endurance. Against justice, reason, and a general clamor, those great trades-unions of capital, the trusts, win five times in six fights.

DEMOCRATIC CHARACTER OF TRADE ORGANIZATIONS: DIRECT LEGISLATION.

It may be asked, What great mind, what Carlylean hero, appeared among the cigarmakers, built up the organization, and devised and discovered ways and means until the present high plane of efficiency was reached? The reply is, The fertile mind was one that will never die while man lives; the hero is one more stalwart than any that ever animated Carlyle's fancy. The name of the god-endowed genius is pure democracy.

Every cigarmakers' local union is perfectly democratic. No project is ever carried out by such a union until all the members have had opportunity to discuss it and a vote has been taken on it. Since 1877, the international union has made no law without a vote of the entire body. In 1892, the tens of thousands in the union voted on more than eighty propositions. On February 11th, last, the nine international officers were elected by the entire membership, the candidates having previously been nominated by the entire membership. No step involving a new principle or a serious result is taken by the international union until a majority (in cases two thirds) votes aye. Any law or action may be proposed to the international union if voted by twenty local unions. To put the idea into terms of political science: the cigarmakers' unions, local and international, practice, in lawmaking and electing officials, direct legislation through the Initiative and Referendum.

The cigarmaker having led the way in these purely democratic methods, he has been followed by the baker and the printer, the brewer and the carpenter, the tailor and the granite cutter, and so on, until 200,000 American trades unionists to-day perform their principal work by direct legislation. The several hundred thousand Knights of Labor employ in some measure the same method.

Here, then, is one important political aspect of the labor problem—the internal political methods of the great labor unions, with the surprising results. Because of those methods and these results, one may look forward to incorruptible labor politics in the State. That direct legislation will be practiced in American politics, all must be convinced who learn of its success in Switzerland. There (as I have elsewhere quite fully described) direct legislation has within the past thirty years simplified the structure of government, left representatives to be simply committeemen without power, transferred in some cantons taxation from the masses to the classes, placed many monopolies under government control, fostered if not created industries by extending free trade, strengthened home rule, quite abolished the politician and fettered the plutocrat, and it is now effectively clearing the way for a settlement of the economic labor problem.

In labor organizations, one effect of direct legislation has been to still the voice of the strike orator and to bring to the front level-headed men. In State politics, one equivalent effect of direct legislation in this country will be, if Swiss experience is repeated here, to kill off the professional labor politician and to permit the labor advocate of politics without party to speak freely. It takes a bold man to talk party politics on the floor of his trades-union to-day. His fellow-members are inclined to regard him as pushing for a political office, and if he ever gets one he at once becomes a dead quantity in the union. No so-called unionist leader is good for the delivery to a political party of any vote except his own. A standing joke to the unionists are the bogus politicians, with their ghostly unions, who year by year dicker with campaign committees and figure in interviews in the partisan newspapers as uttering "the sentiments of labor." To all behind the scenes, these bogus unionists, and the few real unionists good for one vote who prey on the political machines, are as well known as the quack political economists who sell their mouths and pens to the monopolists. With direct legislation, however, a new era opens to the unionists. To the State is to be transferred the internal political methods of the unions. This fact brings up with renewed force the query, What can law do for labor?

PROFESSOR HUXLEY ON SOCIAL DISEASES AND THEIR REMEDIES.

What attractively scientific reading is Mr. Huxley's "Social Diseases and Worse Remedies" (referred to in the Ethical Association's printed schedule for this evening's address), until we arrive at page 27! On that page, moving swimmingly with the smooth sentences, we come upon this statement: "At the present time the produce of the soil of England, Scotland, and Wales does not suffice to feed half its population." Mr. Huxley, accepting this fact as normal and inevitable, unscientifically leaves it at once and hurries along to dwell on his social remedies: technical schools, improvements in foreign trade, free baths, etc.—all in the strain of conventional charity to the helpless. But on page 53, in mentioning as a cause of the remediable misery in England its "faulty social arrangements," he opens up, but does not follow, other considerations than those of charity and the helplessness of the workers.

Mr. Huxley, however, does not argue that the workingman is growing better off. On the contrary, he describes to us (page 31) that social condition which, he says, the French emphatically call "*la misère*"—"a condition," to quote him, "in which the food, warmth, and clothing which are necessary for the mere maintenance of the functions of the body in their normal state can not be obtained; in

Political Aspects of the Labor Problem. 339

which men, women, and children are forced to crowd into dens wherein decency is abolished and the ordinary conditions of healthful existence are impossible of attainment; in which the pleasures within reach are reduced to bestiality and drunkenness; in which the pains accumulate at compound interest, in the shape of starvation, disease, stunted development, and moral degradation; in which the prospect of even steady and honest industry is a life of unsuccessful battling with hunger, rounded by a pauper's grave." "Any one," continues Mr. Huxley, "who is acquainted with the state of the population of all great industrial centers, whether in this or in other countries, is aware that, amid a large and increasing body of that population, *la misère* reigns supreme." "I take it to be a mere plain truth," he asserts, "that throughout industrial Europe, there is not a single large manufacturing city which is free from a vast mass of people whose condition is exactly that described, and from a still greater mass who, living just on the edge of the social swamp, are liable to be precipitated into it by any lack of demand for their produce. And with every addition to the population the multitude already sunk in the pit and the number of the host sliding toward it continually increase." And further on he speaks of "the constant gravitation of industrial society toward *la misère*." Mr. Huxley declares that in making these statements he in no wise pretends to the character of the philanthropist, he has a special horror of all sentimental rhetoric, but, as a naturalist, he is merely trying to deal with facts, to some extent within his own knowledge, and further evidenced by abundant testimony.

Mr. Huxley is a respectable witness. What a flood of inquiry, then, do these statements of his suggest! Is the present produce of the soil of Great Britain the highest possible? What are the faulty social arrangements at which he hints? Could the horrors of the widespread misery which he depicts have ever been worse in the civilized world? Can not the poor of the European cities find escape in the country?—or in other lands? Or has Mr. Huxley exaggerated? Whatever our impressions, our feelings, on the subject, surely what he here says is enough to call for some further examination into the facts as to poverty in the civilized world.

CONDITION OF THE LABORING CLASSES IN ENGLAND.

What as to poverty in rural England? Let us get a comprehensive statement. In 1878, Mr. Wm. Stubbs put into book form the results of his thorough investigations in that field. Last year, Mr. Frederick Verinder, traveling about in several agricultural counties in a van, followed up many of Mr. Stubbs's observations, and published his own evidence in the London "Church Reformer" (Episcopalian). Space here only to quote from Mr. Verinder's summary: "The English rural laborer," he says, "is obliged to live in houses where the very first principles of morality, cleanliness, decency, or modesty are impossible." The bedrooms are wretchedly small, damp, and draughty, mere lofts, probably less comfortable than the cottage owner's dog kennels. Bedrooms without windows; sometimes without fireplace or windows; with windows that will not open at all, or open on to the cesspool or the pigsty. "What wonder," Mr. Verinder exclaims, "that pleurisy, and bronchitis, and diphtheria, and influenza, and typhoid fever are rife in England's picturesque villages! The overcrowding of the houses is as bad as in the city slums. Two families are often crowded into rooms not sufficient for one. Beside the nameless horrors which result from the crowding of growing up brothers and sisters into single bedrooms, even the returns of illegitimacy hardly seem shocking, and the early and improvident marriages, against which the thriftmonger rails so unceasingly, appear to be meritorious actions." "There are probably hardly a dozen villages in England where the water supply is throughout pure and abundant." Frequently the village water is drawn from roadside ponds fed by surface drainage from the fields, ponds to which resort ducks, geese, cattle, and passing dogs. The settled policy of the rural landlords seems to be to drive away the laborers from the villages and to make their return impossible by tearing down the cottages almost as fast as they fall empty. This is in part done, as it has been in Scotland, for the preservation of what pays better than tenants—game.

An enchanting Britain, city and country, that of Messrs. Huxley and Verinder!

But, Oh! at once comes the reply: Mr. Giffen's statistics? Mr. Robert Giffen says the condition of the poor in England is not half so bad as it was fifty years ago.

In preparing this address, I wrote here an analysis of Mr.

Giffen's "Progress of the Working Classes"—but it took up so much space that I have omitted it, and will publish it elsewhere. I will, however, outline the main points of that analysis. Mr. Giffen begins by throwing grave discredit on his historical sources of information; from these sources, however, he then draws a few skeleton facts relating to wages fifty years ago in fifteen occupations; next, he compares what on these data he calls the wages then with wages in the same occupations now; lastly he assumes the deductions from these facts to apply to all the hundreds of occupations followed by the wage-workers of Great Britain. Had Mr. Giffen eliminated from his table four of the occupations mentioned in it, the advance he records in money wages (70 per cent) would have been but 52; subtracting from this 52 per cent the advance he concedes in rents, he would on this basis have left in these cases an advance in actual wages of only 12 per cent; he explains that rent has risen 150 per cent, but rent, he should have observed, is not the only addition to the expenses of the worker of to-day over those of the worker of fifty years ago—street-car fares, frequent necessary removals in seeking work, etc., must be added. Sir Thomas Brassey, who went more fully into the subject, found no such percentage in the advance of money wages as did Mr. Giffen; he found from zero to 20 per cent. Mr. Giffen's prices of commodities, which he quotes in proof of a declining cost of living, are wholesale prices, the relation of which to retail prices has greatly changed in fifty years, to the detriment of small city buyers; and while certain manufactured goods grow cheaper, the retail prices of nearly all food products, which enter into daily expenses, are, according to Mulhall, 10 to 25 per cent more than they were fifty years ago. All of Mr. Giffen's cumulative evidences of progress— the lessening of the death-rate, the increase in savings banks deposits, etc.—I deny, in so far as they are made to apply to the average wage worker. His point as to the shorter workday of the present time (which he regards as equal to a 20 per cent additional rise in wages) I answer further on. One example of my reasons for differing with Mr. Giffen's deductions I will cite: I hold the increase in servants' wages, generally quoted as illustrating the advance in all wages, to be no evidence whatever of such an advance, but merely to be the result of the leveling of wages in all ordinary occupations, consequent upon the common school education of the masses here and abroad, which has rendered the position of servant so distasteful that nearly all leave it who can. In several other common occupations, the apparent advance in wages has been only this leveling.

Implicit belief in Mr. Giffen being shaken, his many less well qualified imitators are to be doubted. It may require considerable hardihood to call in question what among the property-holding classes has become the whole drift of opinion as to a general rise in common wages. This, however, I emphatically do, especially with regard to the underlying inference that within the past fifty years society has gradually improved the conditions of the labor market— where the rates of wages are arrived at. In this point, whether labor offers itself in a free or a forced market, lies the core of the whole discussion. And this is the point commonly evaded by those who grow impatient when told how miserably poor the countless poorest are.

WORK AND WAGES IN AMERICA.

Turn, now, to this country: Have wages here risen or fallen? In a note on American wages, in the appendix to Putnam's edition of Mr. Giffen's book, the editor says the materials obtainable for a careful and scientific examination of the economic results in the past fifty years affecting the laborer are of "an extremely unsatisfactory nature." He points out, for instance, that the usefulness of the comparison of wages in the Tenth Report of the Massachusetts Bureau of Labor Statistics (1878) between wages in 1860 and 1878 is "somewhat impaired" because weekly and not yearly wages are given. Allowing for advance in the cost of living, irregularity of employment, etc., the labor commissioner made out for this State for that period a possible advance in wages of 10 per cent. (I will engage to find honest and capable opposing counsel who will figure out a loss of 10.) The editor says that Mr. John G. Carlisle obtained—from the census—the idea that in purchasing power wages in the cotton, woolen, and iron industries advanced 4 per cent between 1850 and 1860, declined 10 per cent between 1860 and 1870, and increased 18 per cent between 1870 and 1880. Hence a decline of 12 per cent between 1880 and 1890 would have put wages in America for these three leading occupations where they were forty years ago. The editor cautions the reader that the two sets of reports from American consuls in Europe (1878 and 1885) are of little value, since they do not take into account many modifying influences in various places. In fact, this "American note" stamps error on the figures in all the common official American sources of information, of to-day or of the past, on the subject of wages.

But, Mr. Atkinson? The would-be Mr. Giffen of this country. A few weeks ago the conservative "Christian Union" referred to Mr. Atkinson as neither profound nor accurate. The "Christian Union" was one of the last observers in the country to arrive at that estimate of this prolific writer and eccentric arithmetician. Mr. Atkinson's figures and diagrams, however, satisfactory to the wealth-retaining classes, are widely quoted in the daily papers, in spite of their self-contradictions.

When, a few years ago, Mr. Atkinson had just published a series of his peculiar tables on wages, Prof. E. J. James, of the University of Pennsylvania, publicly drew attention to their misleading and unreliable character. Prof. James further declared that, as to the wages question, the censuses previous to 1880 were "in the highest degree untrustworthy,"—a statement which may readily be credited by any one who has ever tackled, wrestled with, puzzled over, and finally been baffled by, the census reports. For instance, from our census Mulhall gives an increase of wages of 10 per cent for the Western States in the decade 1870–'80. The statement is preposterous, unless the salaries of bank presidents, railroad managers, and the like were reckoned in by the census-takers. In that decade wages fell in all the country between the Missouri River and the Pacific Ocean,—fell 30 to 60 per cent. Miners, teamsters, house builders, printers, tailors, clerks, telegraphers, cooks, servants—the whole range of ordinary occupations there—saw wages in those years slump. An equalizing process in wages for this country, consequent on railroad extension, was then going on there at a lively rate. So we may as well leave the census figures on wages to Mr. Atkinson.

Rather let us trust for light to common observation.

POVERTY GENERALLY INTENSIFIED IN THE PAST FORTY YEARS.

Prof. James suggests a general fact when he says: "I can remember when it was possible for a farm hand in Central

Illinois to save enough from his wages in a few years to buy and stock a thirty-acre farm."

In the New York "American," April 6, 1825, a correspondent, writing on "The Situation of the Working-Classes of our City," said: "I took a station at Catherine market, which is the great emporium for the mechanics and laborers on Saturday evening, to offer a joint and trimmings to any one who appeared to be in want. At the end of two hours I observed but one individual whose external appearance warranted my offering the boon. He answered (in reply to my application) that he received ten shillings per day wages, and that he had in his pocket five dollars of the week's earnings to buy his Sunday dinner. I counted upward of 870 men and women who passed me to buy at the market in two hours." What would be the experience of this humanitarian in New York to-day could he repair to the Catherine market neighborhood, or any other, east side or west, occupied by mechanics and laborers, in search of people whose external appearance might suggest need of a joint and trimmings?

Forty-five years ago, New York had not one tenement house; even the thrifty wood-sawyer could then own the cottage he lived in; Thackeray, after making acquaintances among the old-time Bowery boys, attributed their independence and manly qualities to high wages and plenty of work. In New England, good board in factory towns was then $1.25 a week. In the West, first-rate land was open to settlers. Mechanics and laborers commonly lived in the country or in small towns, often raising their own pigs, poultry, and garden produce, they and their families often obtaining extra work and wages in harvest time. What went on their table was pure and fresh—vegetables, fruits, berries, jams, the butchering; and in these commodities, at the lowest barter prices, they frequently took their pay.

To-day, New York has 40,000 tenement houses, with more than a million occupants. A tenement house is a narrow stable, three fifths of each of its superimposed rows of stalls dark, all of its air stable air, badly overworked. The feed of the beast of burden tied up in one of these stalls is the culled-off grades of meats and vegetables; his groceries are adulterated, Prof. Chandler says his cheap butter is filthy, while his jams are glucose, his poultry bone and blue skin, his sausage watersoaked offal, and his beer drugged and hopless. The horrors of old Five Points have not been done away with: they have simply been diffused over the city, with headquarters at Mulberry Bend. As to medical and dental attendance, what proportion of the tenement population is not yet pauperized? And how many New York workingmen own their own homes? Five years ago, I found in a trade in which wages stand about the highest that not 50 in the 5,000 workers in New York lived in their own homes, mortgaged or unmortgaged. Nearly every one of the 50 lived, as he must, in the suburbs. To-day, every city, every industrial center of America, has its slums, overcrowded, repellent, degraded. The poor tenant who travels about seeking a home in the murky back streets of this otherwise fair city, and then repairs for a breath of pure air to its outer zone of high-priced vacant lots, may find some excuse for the fervid Anarchist whose essay at his club was, " Why I Hate Brooklyn."

Our brief investigation of what large classes of facts we can readily get at has been profitable. Mr. Huxley has not exaggerated. To multitudes of the poverty-stricken, what can life be worth? Removal from city to country, or to any part of this new land, can offer them small hope.

But students of the social problem are not left to grope helplessly for truth among either foggy figures or what may be illusory facts. Economic science affords us certain well-tested principles to assist us in our conclusions. And every economist since the foundations of his science were laid has shown us the effect of a surplus of labor in the market on the price of labor. Every economist of the higher rank, too, has shown us that a surplus of labor, competing for work in a forced market, is an inevitable consequence of the monopoly of the land of a country. And therefore, to argue that any of the wage workers at all are growing better off must imply that a method has been at work somewhere which in some measure counteracts this fundamental economic law. Can any such method be named?

What is the trades-unionist's reply to Messrs. Giffen and Atkinson? The trades-unionist says: "You do not mean to ask us, because our unions have compelled employers to put up wages 20 per cent or so, to concede to society a progressive justice? You do not mean to quote to us as a social boon the better conditions for labor, when those better conditions simply mean the shorter hours enforced by the unions and the factory laws due primarily to union agitation? You do not mean to tell us that the unemployed hordes of to-day are twice as well off as the workers of fifty years ago? You do not mean to offer us as evidence of better government a slightly decreased pauperism in England due to the fact that the hundreds of thousands of united workers there have learned how to insure themselves—pay out-of-work benefits, take care of their sick, and bury their dead? You do not expect us forever to be deceived by statistics gathered from employers and swollen by returns of the salaries of managers, foremen, and other superintendents? You can not hope that the ambitious among us will continue to be deluded by the fable that the place of the apex can be taken by the whole base? You can not expect us to rest satisfied with the deprivations of last century's unfranchised English serfs or America's pioneers, when in the various branches of industry our own daily work (to lay no claim to that of the captains of industry) produces double, quadruple, in some cases twenty times as much, as did daily labor forty years ago? You can not mean to attribute our discontent to artificial desires while social conditions render impossible to us the satisfaction of the primary desires, not of civilized, but of savage, man: the desire for a certain to-morrow (humanly speaking), for self-mastership, for the results of our labor, for a roof of our own, for—no repetition can stale the words—the exercise of the full right to life, liberty, and the pursuit of happiness."

These claims and assertions of the trades-unionist are true. The claims are established and the assertions verified by accepted economists and well-known public observers.

EFFECT OF TRADES-UNIONS ON THE CONDITION OF WAGE EARNERS.

No improvement in the laborer's condition followed modern methods until trades-unions were set up. Says Prof. Nicholson: "The industrial revolution . . . took place at about the end of the last century." "For fifty years after the introduction of production on a large scale, the condition of the working classes was on the whole deplorable."[*] And of all that time Prof. James writes: "The workers were mercilessly exploited." The English trades-unions rose in the '30s and '40s. In 1845 Mr. Thornton was one of the first to record publicly that for some years the trades-unions had been putting up wages.

[*] "Wages," Encyclopædia Britannica.

Acts of Parliament to regulate factories, excepting two or three bills meant to prevent murder and the most shocking of inhumanities, never appeared on the statute books until the trades-unions had put England into constant agitation. The first general factory act was passed only in 1836.

In this country, labor statutes are the result of bids for labor union votes. The labor organizations support lobbies, and send up committees to demand, under threats to candidates, labor legislation; in labor affairs non-unionists have never sent up a committee, nor maintained a labor paper, nor swung a labor vote, nor boycotted a faithless representative, nor procured a labor law. The labor laws demanded by employers have been the conspiracy laws, by which union men are jailed. Legislators, of themselves, as statesmen, initiate no labor laws; as politicians, they promise, and compromise with, both sides, and when possible avoid committing themselves. The crew of critics, the writers for the press and the pulpiteers, speak for the immediate interests of their chief patrons, and dub their talk public opinion, and do nothing.

Improvements in industrial conditions have gone on just as the labor unions have enforced them. Says Joseph D. Weeks: "Labor has had to fight for every advantage it has gained." Says Prof. James: "The laborers have taken the matter into their own hands, and by their local, national, and international combinations are exercising, whether for weal or woe, a marked influence on the legislation of all civilized nations."[*] What help from society have the horrors of Homestead brought to labor? Who, excepting unionists, are to-day working by act to prevent another and worse Homestead? Where are all the philanthropists and scribblers of last fall that were to give us compulsory arbitration, cheap tenements, and what not for the workers, with absurd rights in the capitalist's plant or an impossible right to permanent employment? All are out of service now.

Much so-called labor legislation, however, has been sham, much of it invalid, some of it of evil effect. The labor organization of itself, as a striking machine, has been the real reliance of the members. Mr. William Trant[†] alleges that the improvements in wages and hours have been "solely and entirely" due to the unions. And further: "No action

---
[*] "Strikes and Lockouts," Cyclopædia of Political Science.   7
[†] "Trades-Unions," Kegan Paul, Trench & Co., London, 1884.

of the trades-unions has been crowned with such signal success as that taken to bring about the reduction of hours." Mr. Trant republishes Mr. Giffen's table, saying it is "worthy of note" that every occupation there named is among those having the "strongest unions" in England—unions which have shortened the workday. Mr. Giffen's audacity in illustrating the progress of the working classes by showing what privileges a few workers had wrenched from employers, and attributing the results in these cases to improved social conditions, is matchless. How bad his case must be! How willing to be deluded must be the classes whose mouthpiece he is! Had Mr. Giffen picked out fifteen non-union occupations, he might perhaps have found a reduction of wages of 100 per cent. Suppose he had selected different groups of sewing women!

We now see what the method is which has been at work counteracting the effects of the all-enveloping land monopoly. The monopoly of land has in some part been offset by a trades-union monopoly of labor.

All done, however, by the labor unions, through themselves or through the government, nothing has been done for labor's emancipation except to cut off inches from Legree's whip, to compel the masters to issue the slaves a little more rations, and in some trades to permit labor to nurse its strength that some time it may perhaps burst its bonds. In fact, all done, a terrible, a menacing, phenomenon is seen in every land—the unemployed. Secretary Evans, of the American Federation of Labor, recently told me that in the course of the year, in all the unions, a third of the men were more or less out of employment. Mr. Jos. R. Buchanan, who as economic and exchange editor of the American Press Association has the whole of this country under view, a month ago stated that in his opinion the number of the unemployed would-be workers in America was now two millions.

See what these facts signify. What chattel slavery ever produced a sweat-shop? No slaveowners would jeopardize their human property in a sweat-shop. Yet to-day, a legislative committee reports in Chicago alone nine hundred sweat-shops, with girls working in them sixty hours for seventy-five cents. In spite of all the labor laws on the statute books—to the avoidance of some of which sweat-shops in fact in part owe their being—all labor would be menaced by sweat-shop conditions were it not for the labor

Political Aspects of the Labor Problem. 349

organizations, which monopolize the more desirable labor. Says George W. Childs: "Were it not for the typographical union the printers of the country would see their wages reduced by a third." Says Mr. Gompers: "The union scale helps maintain non-union wages; the employers must bid against union market rates and bribe their men not to join the unions." Says Prof. Henry C. Adams: "The laborer is better off to-day than he was in 1830, but he was better off in the fourteenth century than he was in 1830." And Thorold Rogers has said the same. In centuries the laborer had not been worse off than in 1830. In other words, without the labor unions all the propertyless poor would still be worse off, materially, than were those in the Dark Ages. The first principles of economic justice are violated in the laws now as they were not then: the laborers were then accorded conditional rights in the soil.

THE UNIONIST'S REPLIES TO CRITICISMS.

Perhaps we may be further reconciled to the labor unionist if for a moment we listen to his replies to critics—those critics who crop up in press and pulpit during every recurring labor trouble, just as regularly as, when the hour strikes, the automatic figures move out and in around the Strasburg clock. The unionist greets these critics as dear familiar old enemies, and, knowing his catechism, he is as little affected by them as Father Time is by the clock manikins.

Says one critic: "I deeply sympathize with labor—but do trades-unions ever do any good?"

The unionist may explain union benefit features, the comforting shop rules, the union labor bureaus, etc.

Another critic: "I deeply sympathize with labor—but the trades-unions employ force?"

The unionist: "Force? How? We simply on occasions refuse to work. Violent labor disturbances, when there are any, commonly arise with non-unionists, who, untrained and excitable, at the last hour before a strike join the unionists and proceed to rioting. At Homestead, as now proved in court, the union officials actively opposed force. In England, the rise of the labor unions was characterized by a subsidence of riots and machine-breaking. But suppose we grant that quitting work, and maintaining the organization that will enable us to quit work, is force. What is to be done by us (who are forced by law not to earn our living by employing our faculties on the gratuitous utilities which are the inheritance of mankind), except to use counter-force to get the best use of what faculty the law leaves to us free?" But that is a thought beyond the depth of the sentimentalist.

Another critic: "I deeply sympathize with labor—but labor is misled by demagogues."

The unionist: "Where are the demagogues? Have you ever seen one, read a speech by one? The labor demagogue is the old-time aristocrat's myth. To the English Tory, every statesman in democratic America who appeals to the people is a demagogue."

Another critic: "I deeply (and so forth)—but, the walking delegate?"

The unionist, promptly: "In nine cases out of ten the walking delegate is chosen and stood by for his sense, courage, honesty, and uprightness. If the union is to avoid useless friction, the walking delegate must be a conciliator. He is a watchful servant of the union. No employer is ever subject to the whims of the walking delegate. Union laws prescribe the circumstances in which union men shall quit work: the delegate but announces when these circumstances arise."

Another critic: "I deeply sympathize with labor—but I believe in freedom, and the trades-unionist cruelly deprives the non-unionist of his freedom to labor."

The unionist: "An error. The non-unionist is free to work wherever he can get employment. And employers are free to employ whom they can. But unionists decline to work except with unionists. To do otherwise would be suicidal to the union."

The Trades-Union's Alleged Interference with Personal Freedom.

How plausibly the critics of organized labor play with the idea of freedom. In this free country, they say, employers should be free to hire any laborers they want, union or non-union, and non-union workers should be free to work for any employer. This means that these critics would not have union men to be free to stipulate the terms under which they shall sell their own labor. Here is a paradox— freedom at cross-purposes with freedom—and up to this paradox specious pleaders for the employing classes carry their thought through a series of discriminations, sometimes to this point just and admirable, leaving on their hearers' minds the impression that they are battling for freedom, while they either ignore the query they provoke as to the freedom of which the union men are to be deprived, or sophistically declare that such freedom is immoral and intolerable.] But no need to-day for any one to flounder in this paradox. It has been cleared away. It rests on flashing on the mind several times in rapid succession the idea of freedom in several conflicting applications. (The term freedom, used unrestrictively, is vague and indefinite. It is but the correlative of the term restraint.) It is applicable alike to things and to men. Its import is neither good nor evil, moral nor immoral, attractive nor repellent. Only when the word freedom is specifically applied can it impart to us a concrete idea and arouse in us a sentiment.) When we speak of a free country,—that is, a free government,—we refer to political freedom (one of the many applications of the abstract idea of freedom). Now, if the term political freedom stands for any principle which may rest on scientific definition and analysis, it signifies the absence of any statute laws excepting those providing for an equal freedom (and a corresponding equal restraint) for all men in the use of their faculties; and if one or many individuals should by law restrain one or many other individuals beyond the degree at which all may be equally free, such legal restraint would be destructive of the first principle of free government. In practice this principle of equal freedom permits any man or class of men, at any time, in the absence of legal contract, to withdraw their labor from the hire of other men; and if we revert to contract our principle leads us back to freedom of contract; and that in turn to the prerequisites for free contract, and these bring us to the original state of self-sovereignty in which man, being wholly free, may, to provide for his physical necessities, exercise his faculties (his powers) on nature. He who can not do this is not politically free; initial, basic freedom is not his. On the other hand, when the word free is used to describe the condition in which employers may be free to employ non-union laborers, and by law compel union laborers to work with the non-unionists, such condition plainly involves depriving the union men of their equal freedom with other men, since equal freedom would leave to them the right of free contract. And, again, when the freedom is demanded for non-union men to work for any employer who desires their services, the reply is that in the political sense all non-union men have that freedom now. And further, if it then be rejoined that union men should be deprived of the freedom that permits them to refuse to work with non-union men, because such freedom is immoral, the reply is that under a law providing for such a deprivation a free government would give place to a tyranny. The government would itself infringe the principle of equal freedom. Hence, from these deductions, it is clear that the strike (the right to cease work) and the boycott (the right to buy or not to buy) are elementary political rights under freedom. As to a freedom which may be immoral, what are morals and what must a government do to enforce morals? Morals are but social conventions, widely varying in different ages and countries, largely derived from fetich worshipers' fears, savage impulses, and conflicting religious dogmas, and only recently in any measure based upon philosophic inferences. What has logically followed legal enforcement of moral law has been the Inquisition, the established church, the blue laws, the suppression of thought. If it be averred that the refusal of union men to work with non-unionists is immoral, the reply is, first, that if so such immorality lies outside the jurisdiction of a free government, and, secondly, that probably the way to put an end to this and much other so-called immorality is to make the government really free; and a free government would recognize the political freedom which gives all men access to land. In this case, the strike and boycott could deprive no one of work or, consequently, of the necessaries of existence.

And so is disposed of the list of captious objections which form employing class cant. Unionists, doubtless, occasionally fall into errors, disgraces, and excesses; but to them all times are war times. Against them their enemies ceaselessly employ every weapon—force, class-made law, newspaper false-rumor, calumny, bribery, hypocrisy. What profession does not act toward the rich as counsel under fee?

INEFFICACY OF THE CONVENTIONAL SOLUTIONS OF THE LABOR PROBLEM.

There is at least one valid "but" to the labor organization: it has never yet gone to the root of social wrong.

Many other things has labor tried; many other things have been tried on labor.

The Christian religion has been tried, and—how many Christians has it given us? Self-help has been preached until self-help has come to signify help yourself and keep within the law. Poverty compels men to do hateful things—to perform almost superhuman labor, to toil at distasteful tasks, to run forever on like tireless wheels in a machine, to commit mean actions, to deceive in trade, to adulterate food, to overreach. Churchmen sometimes tell us that in all the commercial world—wholesale, retail, and the stock exchange—dishonesty is customary. It is so perhaps because, conditions being what they are, as Wilde phrased it in epigram: "It is finer to steal than to beg."

Co-operation, profit-sharing, arbitration, technical education—into these blind alleys fallacious, or false, teachers direct earnest but deluded followers. Co-operation! What is all business but co-operation? Unfetter labor first, and well-adjusted co-operation may then come. Profit-sharing! What this but a form of wages—and who pays more wages than market rates? Education! What to the poor avails education when the many are educated? Europe is overpacked with a learned proletariat. Arbitration! When did labor refuse to arbitrate? When did unorganized labor ever get a chance to arbitrate? With whom shall the unemployed arbitrate?

Charity has been tried until it is to-day denounced even in Christian journals, and for good reasons. In the "Dawn," an assistant of the Rev. Mr. Bliss has traced the evil effects of charity in Boston and described how the city's charity lodging-houses, reformatories, refuges, and homes have added fearfully to degraded poverty;—and the fact is true of every large city. Charity unfailingly perverts character. It especially harms the rich as a class; it is an anodyne to their sluggish conscience; it obscures to their eyes social wrongs; it makes them see in the one brazen pauper who exploits their purse the ten honest poor who would die first. The undiscriminating rich, in discussing the habitual and notorious frauds of the pauperized, grow more unfeeling and domineering and insultingly patronizing to those poor who are true men and women, and with a total misconception of the principle of evolution they assume themselves the morally fittest and the poor the morally degraded, an atrocious misconception which may have to be dislodged by force. Delegated charity, like all machine work, is soulless, cowardly, harsh. It puts into the hands of the charity societies a branding iron for the foreheads of the unfortunate, whose names they record, and whose frailties they pry into. The most precious boon men can ever confer on the world will be that social condition in which one may, with a clear conscience, kick the beggar from his doorstep and bid him go to work. Charity brings more beggars to your doorstep. Charity to the able-bodied is decisive evidence that society rests on the crime of preventing the able-bodied from employing their own faculties. Were it not for charity, men might agitate for justice, which gives to all the right to employ themselves on the resources of nature. Of charity to the able-bodied surely may be said what Pentecost said of all charity: "Better than charity, the streets strewn with the corpses of men starved to death."

Not Charity, but Justice.

All methods of social melioration range themselves under two headings: charity and justice. Hence around the globe to the unionists in every land has passed the watchword: "Not charity, but justice!" With this watchword goes the cry: "Workingmen of all countries, unite!" Away with every prejudice of race, country, or trade. (And the labor organizations of the world are uniting to eradicate social injustice.) International workingmen's congresses are now common, and in each country the labor unions promote social agitation. In Germany the labor unions have been the backbone of the Social Democracy. In England, the New Unionism is widely employing its vote. In France, the 1,300 unions that have sprung up since in 1884 the government ban was taken off trades-unions, are making radical political demands, already 60 communes, with several important cities, having, largely by union votes, passed under working-class rule. In Australia, the Labor parties are usually labor union parties. In the United States, in many industrial centers, the parties of genuine social reform, of anti-monopoly principles, which five years ago polled large votes, depended on the ballots of the labor unionists; the Knights of Labor are now assisting the new political party, and at their annual conventions last fall, for the first time, both the Knights and the American Federation of Labor, together representing one million men, or more, called for political action through direct legislation.

(Broadly, then, the indications are that the world is to-day on the eve of great political and economic changes, for the most part the direct results of the strength of the labor organizations. None of the pioneers of thought—the radical economists, the builders of Utopias, the poets of labor, the leaders in labor politics, the editors, the sociological societies—would have an effective following at hand without the labor organizations.)

Indications there are, also, that united labor will steadily employ its political strength for the full emancipation of all labor from the effects of every law which deprives the worker of any right whatever to which as a free man he should be entitled. The unionists are selfishly interested in all labor, down to the lowest stratum. This constrains them now to study, as is done by their press, all economic truth and to see the necessity of beginning social reform at the foundation,—with man's fundamental rights, with the abolition of legalized private monopoly.

Whether this is true of all who call loudly for social reform, is a question. Were their own peculiar wrongs righted, to many the world might be all that they wished it to be. Let us hope this is not the case with the leading element in the Populist party. Oppressed by every monopoly apart from that of the agricultural land, to a poor grade of which it has access in the West, this element is part of Mr. Huxley's host living close by the edge of the social swamp. It is in the woods wailing. If it shall recognize and strive for justice down to the foundations of society, the Populist party will become a part of the now world-wide labor movement. If it shall not, if it shall depend merely on temporary forms of relief for poor employing farmers, it will offer little to distinguish it in the eyes of radical social reformers from the older parties. In such case, what career awaits it?

In the field of radical action, present indications are of a considerable lowering of the barriers which have hitherto separated the various strict schools of social reform, accompanied by a union of all the schools in the tasks nearest at hand. With the tide of affairs the radical social reformers in general have in a large measure become Opportunists. Local work brings the adherents of the various schools together. Besides, all classes in society—excepting the spoils politician and the plutocrat, and their retainers—are interested in purifying government and simplifying its structure. Hence probably, from time to time, a union of many citizens supporting reforms which may be achieved through direct legislation. Thenceforward, by the same method, in the various communities, reform toward justice could proceed until the opinion of the majority in each community as to what is justice should be embodied in the law. And thenceforward reform for the majority itself in its conception of justice.

SUMMARY AND CONCLUSION.

If my words this evening have stood for truth, we have seen, if only in glances, that labor's strength lies largely in the labor organization; we have seen that that organization is in accord with political freedom; we have seen in the democratic labor unions the potency for economic revolution through political effort; we have seen reason for such revolution in the frightful condition of the huge lower stratum of wage labor, due to a surplus of labor in the market, resulting primarily from land monopoly—a denial of freedom; we have seen the uselessness of certain palliatives which are popular; we have seen a world-wide agitation which portends either a sweeping peaceful economic change, or blood; we have seen in direct legislation a method by which bloodshed may be averted.

ABSTRACT OF THE DISCUSSION.

MR. GEORGE E. WALDO:

Labor organizations may have done much for skilled laborers, but they have done practically nothing for other people. The wages of unskilled laborers, as the lecturer practically admits, have gone down. It must necessarily be so: skill secures the larger proportion. We can not evade this natural law by legislation. Our political institutions are not intended to benefit any class. They leave all free to help themselves. That is why labor is better off in this country than elsewhere. Poverty naturally attaches to indolence everywhere. The unfortunate, incompetent, and indolent suffer. The only way in which they can be taken care of is by charity. It is hard to find laws intended to benefit capital in our country. Acts incorporating banks, railroads, etc., are not passed for the benefit of the stockholders or the presidents, but because these enterprises are for the advantage of the whole people. True, the great managers become wealthy, but the wealth which they secure is of small account in proportion to the enormous wealth which is added to the country.

The trouble with the laborers is, as Mr. Dolge told us, that they do not save from their earnings. Those who are so inclined can always save something. We all know instances of poor boot-blacks and day-laborers who have become wealthy. Others have the same chance, if they had the same desires and self-control. Reformers want the nation to reform the people, and make all happy and good, by legislative act. We must stand with the individual man. Laws can not help him. Laws may be useful for the protection of children and the weak, but it is idle to look to legislation for a cure-all for our social ills.

The labor reformer asks that land be made free to all. Substantially, it is so now in this city. There is plenty of land for any one to work who desires to. The vacant lots of Brooklyn are free to-day to any one who will till them. In the West, the best land in the world is practically free, and no settler who has worked industriously has failed to better himself.

The Populists also ask for free silver. That is little better than free paper. Either is good as long as you can go to the bank and get gold for it. With free silver, gold will be driven out, and the silver dollar will bring only what it is worth—sixty or seventy cents. I can not see how this will benefit the laboring man. They want all the railroads and telegraphs in the hands of the Government. I am opposed to this on principle. It is un-republican and un-American. We want to be permitted to work out our own salvation, not to be cared for as children. "Sovereigns do not take tips," and the American industrial sovereign will spurn the socialistic panacea as a thinly-disguised form of that public charity which the lecturer repudiates in his behalf. No government has yet been able to carry on successfully and economically enterprises involving the expenditure of large sums of money. The postal business has been successful because no capital is required. As an evolutionist, I expect no Utopia. There will always be a world of work, with joy and sorrow, sunshine and shadow mixed every day in the year. Our duty is to learn self-control, economy, and a wise direction of our energies to the supply of our wants. What a man needs and strives for he can get by his own efforts, and it is best that he should so get it.

MR. ELLSWORTH WARNER:

I have observed that, if one wishes to convert the Ethical Association to his views, he must attempt to show that his conclusions are in the line of evolutionary law. At the risk of being called to order, I should like to refer to what I consider the "labor problem" is. It is one phase of those great social problems which always face a community. Society advances by a constantly recurring series of adjustments; and maladjustment is a necessary concomitant of readjustment. The more rapid the growth, the greater the number of maladjustments. All our troubles come from maladjustments which are the result of rapid progress. Evolution is always in the line of greater individual liberty. The human will is the principal factor in social evolution. Wills differ with varying intelligence of the people, and hence come these maladjustments. We are responsible for the condition of the slums and the injustice done to the laborer, to the extent that we make the social conditions. I expected the lecturer would refer to the recent decision of Judge Ricks respecting the rights of organized labor. Whatever view we may take of labor organizations, this decision indicates clearly that these questions are forcing themselves upon public notice and compelling the Government, in its judicial capacity, to act. Individualism is impossible. It is the educational influence of such events that counts. We perceive that government must interfere with the organization when a strike, set on foot by it, interferes with public business. Labor organizations have acted more on the defensive than on the aggressive, but what they have accomplished has been more in the way of educating the laborer than

Political Aspects of the Labor Problem. 359

of securing laws for his protection. I look forward confidently to a time when the interests of the capitalist and laborer will be harmonized, and strikes and lockouts will be no more. On a low plane, the labor problem is merely a question of wages; but in the larger view it involves sanitary and moral conditions as well.

DR. LEWIS G. JANES:

The recent action of the courts has been referred to. To the Spencerian evolutionist, the decisions of Judge Ricks and Judge Taft convey a very obvious moral. The interstate commerce laws were passed in the avowed interest of the laborer. These decisions show that the legal sword cuts both ways. The natural inference is that governmental interference is a dangerous and impolitic expedient. Government has no right to legislate for any class, or to consider any question except that of securing justice to all—the equal opportunity to exercise their faculties. Legislation should therefore be chiefly of a negative character, aiming to remove obstructions to free individual action.

MR. THADDEUS B. WAKEMAN:

I have come a hundred miles to hear this discussion, and I am amply repaid. The real trouble is, we have, under the law of evolution, reached a stage in which all former talk is meaningless and out of place and belongs to fifty years ago. This was illustrated by the first critic. He is a representative of a large class who think they know it all, but they have not kept step with recent events. We have reached a step where further advance in competitive methods is impossible; where in production and distribution there is no such thing as the individual as an independent factor, and you go on talking as if our social condition was the same as it was seventy-five years ago. There can be no more competition until nationalization makes it possible. You can not go into any business without a large capital and as a monopolist. Twenty-five thousand people practically control the production of the country; and where the people can no longer control those who control the necessaries, they become their slaves. All civilization now is capitalism; it wasn't so fifty years ago. The question is, whether we shall have freedom or be the slaves of capitalists. How are we to adjust ourselves to the new conditions under which evolution has brought us? Competition, individual freedom, must be obtained by bringing all great public functions under public control. A previous speaker said wisely that the human will is the chief factor in social evolution. The assumption that Bellamy's idea is to make all men equal is a mistake. There is to be no "dividing up," etc. It is the right and duty of each to see that every individual has the conditions of life and development guaranteed to him, else we shall never achieve the ultimate happiness of mankind. Evolution makes that the end. The type of the future society is the cigarmakers' union described by the lecturer. The members are freer than ever; they did not give up their liberty. The whole United States could work in the same way. Until the people own their masters, they will be slaves.

DR. ROBERT G. ECCLES:

We are not offered facts but feelings when Bellamyism is on the stand. I should like to have the last speaker show me one unfavorable change in the condition of things from fifty years ago. The fact is, the conditions are better. For every chance a man had a hundred years ago to progress in wealth, he now has a hundred. The conditions complained of are caused by this very advance. The world to-day has a population half as large again as it had a century ago. This proves the better condition of things, else how could production keep pace with the population? A hundred years ago men died of starvation and thousands more were killed in wars. We are now outgrowing these things. There will always be a top and a bottom to society as population increases. The poor you will always have with you. The contrast is greater to-day because the rich are richer; but the poor are also richer, absolutely, and have more of the comforts of life. The educational advantages are all the workingman has got out of the trades-unions. It is preposterous to say that they have advanced the rate of wages. I am reminded of the Irishman on shipboard who, frightened by the ghost stories of the sailors, pulled the blanket up over his head and uncovered his feet. He complained that the blanket was too short at one end and too long at the other. Though he cut a piece off the long end and sewed it on the short end, the blanket was still no longer. Capital is the total resource of society. If you cut off from one end and add to another, "sorry a bit longer" do you make it. The rich man can not eat his gold. He can do nothing with it but pay wages. The more money he has to pay for wages, the higher wages are.

MR. SULLIVAN said that, the hour being late, he would rather labor under what disadvantages might accrue from not replying to his critics at all than to take up the time of the audience with a reply.

THE PHILOSOPHY OF HISTORY

BY
EDWARD P. POWELL
AUTHOR OF OUR HEREDITY FROM GOD, LIBERTY AND LIFE, ETC.

COLLATERAL READINGS SUGGESTED:

Hegel's Philosophy of History; Lecky's The Political Value of History, and History of European Morals; Priestley's Lectures on History; Froude's Essay on the Philosophy of History; Crozier's Civilization and Progress; Early Chapters in Buckle's History of Civilization; Green's History of the English People; McMaster's History of the People of the United States; Fiske's *The Doctrine of Evolution: its Scope and Influence*, in Evolution in Science, Philosophy, and Art, and Historical Works; Droysen's The Principles of History, translated by President E. Benjamin Andrews; Dr. Janes's *Carlyle's Philosophy of History*, in Westminster Review, October, 1889.

THE PHILOSOPHY OF HISTORY.

BY EDWARD P. POWELL.

A. DEFINITION OF HISTORY.

I CAN not persuade myself at the outset that history is not the story of a certain thing, a unit, rather than, as Mr. Froude asserts, the incoherent drama of millions of men. It seems rather to be the story of man. We must conceive of humanity for once concretely, rather than of individuals abstractly. Each human being is a part of humanity, as each cell is an integer of the full organism, the body. But no cell, nor any member of the body, can be fully understood by itself. When I wish my boys to comprehend human language it seems to be quite the wrong thing to set them down first to the study of a dozen languages, all of which are only accidents of that germinal idea, language. On the contrary, I take them back to the earlier races of men, when the organs of articulation, if we can trust Mortillet and Hale, were not evolved. They must see the river drift men conversing as animals converse—by signs and inarticulate sounds. They must note the development, by effort, of frontal brain, and the correlated organic power of speech. They thus begin with an anatomical lesson. They must know man. Let them then move down the historic line of developing language, stopping what time is needful at the great ganglia of thought and of language-making. When Mr. Froude tells us he knows nothing of and cares nothing for what are called the laws of development—that he sees only a drama of humanity, played by successive actors—we reply, history has not been so careful of individuals, but it has wonderfully cared for humanity. It concerns itself with man's origin, man's organism, man's nature, man's proposings, man's evolution. The histories of races, nations, and individuals have their places subordinate to the story of man. The Philosophy of History is the ascertained inherent laws that run through the past, define the present, and forecast the future of man. These laws we call nature, as we speak of the natural laws that govern in the material universe.

B. History is an Evolution.

Civilization is the progress of historic evolution, where the organic tendencies are not arrested, or are not reversed toward degeneration. It is a definite process. (To become civilized has always required by all races essentially the same steps. Each has begun with very similar customs and ideas, and moved through similar stages of progress. Every civilizing race at some time was practically patriarchal (or matriarchal), as it was later in its career monarchical and feudal, on its way toward popular or constitutional government. That this should be so is no more strange than that we should all dress alike, eat alike, and have the same general customs. We are all of one physiological type, and can not widely diverge intellectually. The white, the negro, the Oriental, the Occidental, the Turanian, the Aryan, so far as they succeed in development at all, are sure to make very similar discoveries and inventions, to have very much the same social and political institutions, at corresponding stages of progress—even to have the same myths, games, proverbs, and nursery tales. The similarities of human stocks are far more striking than the divergencies.

C. History a Development of the Family.

I will not enter into a discussion of the diverse theories of the primitive state of man; but this is demonstrable, that all civilization has been in the line of those races that began with the family as an established institution, and all civilizing processes have been the unfolding of the family. We can not get back of the family, to begin history with the individual, because the beasts, antecedent to man, had already reached the family stage. We inherit from animal heredity eminently the family, and have added prolonged infancy, with a purpose to perpetuate it hereafter. Immortality, at its origin, was not a hope of perpetuated individual life, but of reunited family life. Family customs have been the basis of all codes of laws; family religion underlies all theologies and churches; family occupations were the germ of all our industries. In fact, I wish to emphasize not so much the accepted idea of the family origin of government, as that not one thing has ever been devised, and that nothing to-day exists in society or politics, that was not germinally in the original family.

(1) *The State and the Church.*

The earliest differentiation of the family was into Church and State. The patriarch was at first both priest and civil monarch. He governed the whole family, both the living and the dead. Natural economy at a very early age, in every race, seems to have given the care of the departed to a second head man, thus creating a dual government. It must be premised that no primitive people was ever capable of thinking annihilation. The dead were only conceived to have been transformed or exalted. Their needs were supposed to be still similar to those of the living. To serve the departed became fairly one half the obligation of the family. But the dead grew in numbers with great rapidity, and over to them passed heroes, sages, and the loved. The office of the priest grew in influence as that side of the family enlarged. The Church and the State, thus begun, have been collateral factors of all history. The power of the Church increases as belief in future life increases; it wanes as men grow skeptical of immortality. The key of all religion is belief in the persistence of the family beyond the dissolution of the body. So in that wonderful idea, the family, lies the germ of all religion and all morals, as well as of all politics and industries. It tended to lengthen infancy, it created a desire for continuance of love, it made immortality a necessity.

(2) *The Family and Ethics.*

The original family combated higher ethics by its very structure. The individual was barely recognized. Wife and children were property. By its coherence and completeness each family antagonized every other family. So the first problem for history to work out was an evolution of the family on such a line as to retain its integrity, and yet recognize the rights of individuals. The second problem has been to retain the integrity of the family and yet evolve a method of fellowship with other families. We shall see if these problems have been solved. Each original unit lived for itself alone; war was a natural state of society. Humanity was inconceivable by primitive man, as it consists purely in evolution. The patriarchal family allowed no brotherhood outside of kinship.

(3) *The First Stage of Family Development.*

The first stage of evolution of the family was adoption. The adoption of gods was as common as the adoption of the living. The coalescence of families necessitated the coalescence of the deceased members of the same families. In earlier periods of history nothing is more confusing than the pantheons.

(4) *Development of Clans and Tribes.*

It is not my specific province to enter into the disputes concerning early societies of mankind. The clan and the tribe arose by alliance and coalescence for mutual assistance. The Hebrews carried the idea of union as far as a federation of tribes. Jerusalem at one time came barely short of being the capital of a federated republic of tribes. It was the noblest political episode of ancient history. But no people also kept the family relation so vigorously dominant. This prevented the complete development of a nation, while it gave a mighty propulsion to religious ideas. The intact Jew family kept its intact Jew gods—except in periods of captivity—while other races fell into a promiscuity of worship that ended in pantheons, and then in skepticism. So it has come about that the Jewish race has given a religion to the world, while the Gentiles have always furnished a State for the Jewish Church. Greece developed the family into the city; the Athenian nation was a municipality. Alexander could conceive for his vast conquests only redivision. He could create cities like Alexandria, but not a nation. The Romans went further, and conceived of a world held subject to their municipality.

(5) *Migration of the Family.*

Meanwhile the family, which in the far East had built about itself a hedge or wall for protection, called in primitive language a tun, moved westward. It became itself nominally the tun, or town; and the land it occupied a township. By the exigencies of combat and struggle for existence it had become a co-operative association. The household commune became a village commune—that is, purely for economic purposes, the growing household fell apart into separate householding. About the North Seas the townships that were of kin had become clans of Saxons,

Jutes, Angles, and Danes. As such they passed over, about fifteen hundred years ago, into England. They conquered Britain as families, in the stage of towns. It is not necessary to dispute Concerning the origin of these Aryans, or whether all Aryans are such by descent or by adoption. Practically, civilization advancing westward has for ages been Aryan. Somewhere back of the Christian era, three to five thousand years before Jesus, out of some archæan white stock flowed the Aryan and the Shemitic.

(6) Arrested Development.

Meanwhile, line after line of family development had been either arrested or obliterated. War or famine had dropped races into savage degradation. Our own stock to-day could probably not carry forward its evolution under a burden of fifty years of continuous war. In China paternalism expanded enormously, and all China is to-day practically an extended patriarchate; paternalism is absolute. In Greece the family was arrested at the city. For many centuries in England territorial possession was too unstable to allow of a consolidated nation. King John for the first, about 1200, was termed king, not of the English, but of England.

(7) The Family in America.

American colonists were the Saxons and Jutes moving on. Whatever Dickens may condemn in the forcible moving on of London's poor by the police, Nature has ever moved the Aryan family westward. It came to New England as the tun and county; it went to Virginia as the parish and manor and county. The origin of government as a deliberate social compact so far had appeared nowhere. But for the first time in historic evolution it did crop out on the Mayflower. The *disjecta membra* of Puritan families drew up a basis of government, a compact, a constitution. Hereafter we shall see and hear much of constitutions. Mr. Fiske tersely makes the stages of nation-making to have been conquest without incorporation, conquest with incorporation but no representation, and incorporation with representation. England reached the latter stage of development. It remained for the United States to devise one new and extraordinary further development of the family. Its towns formed counties; its counties States. It now devised the federal union of 'States. Clearly here at last was a solution of the problem how to retain the original family unit intact, and yet allow of unlimited expansion. Practically, a monarchy, to be safe, must not cover too large a territory; practically, a republic, to be sound politically, must cover a large area. The fundamental discovery of the founders of our republic was not popular government, or popular suffrage, but that the tribal system could be reconstituted on a new basis of federal co-operation. The nearest approximation heretofore to this conception was not to be found in Greece, or in Holland, or in Switzerland, but, curiously enough, in the league of the Iroquois. Its founder, Hiawatha, distinctly defined it to be a union of independent tribes, each with its own government, and in its nature expansive enough to take in any and all other tribes that chose to join. With grand foresight he anticipated an American nation covering the same territory as is now occupied by ourselves. We did not invent the republic. More immediately the American republic and constitution are the direct outgrowth of English institutions; more remotely of the village moots of Friesland across the German Ocean; still more remotely of the primitive family.

The English family developed definite territorial sovereignty—a king and a parliament. The American family developed the town and county into States, and the States into a nation. England moved on the line of the governing classes; America on the line of the governed classes.

(8) *Our Double Heredity.*

But clearly, as our colonial life passed over into the federal union, we passed out of the sole and defined current of Anglicanism. During some centuries, while the Aryan family in England had moved on one line, bringing forth a representative Parliament, in France the same Aryanism had worked on a different line, bringing forth the rights of the individual. Our idea of town rights and States rights is English; our idea of the rights of man is more definitely from France. These two meet in American nationality. Our Revolution could not have occurred before Montesquieu, Voltaire, and Rousseau; or, if it had, it would not have ended in founding a federated union. The New Englanders were naturally federalists; the Virginians, feeling less of the town, were naturally individualists. French influence captured Henry and Jefferson and Madison, while

Adams and Otis and Ames and Hamilton held in view the ideal nature of the English social system. Our Declaration of Independence was English in grit and French in sentiment. Our Constitution is by no means an exact product of the unwritten Constitution of England. Our two great parties, strangely equal in numbers from the very beginning, have been the Teutonic and the Franco-Celtic ideas in generous conflict; the individualism of the latter and the concreteness of the former.

(9) *The Town and the Individual in American History.*

The most important fact of American history is that while the town retains its full force and importance as the evolutionary unit of the State and nation, the individual becomes the governmental unit. To sustain the integrity of the town and the sovereignty of the State is equally important with sustaining the rights of man. The nation is sovereign only within the limits of yielded privilege. Landon says: " It is a curious reflection that the United States Government began as nothing but a few sheets of paper lying in the drawer of the Continental Congress, with about 5,000 words written on them." Natural evolution has gone on inside the limitations of those sheets of paper, as it was intended it should. The States have moved forward with their original freedom. A few writers wholly overlook or deny this evolution of the nation, and make the township to exist as the city exists—by sufferance from a central will. This is to flout history. If the sovereign will can curtail local power it can abolish it altogether. This is the inevitable consequence of centralization. In the Orient the smaller communities exist only by the will of a despot; here the central power exists by sufferance of the people.

(10) *State Integrity.*

The wisdom of our Constitution framers was in what they refrained from doing. It was in not undertaking to override the States. Had they undertaken this the Constitution would never have been adopted. We have expanded from ocean to ocean by multiplying States. There is no reason why a federation of States, constituting a permanent Union, may not cover a continent. A few more years of natural evolution will bring this about. There is no more reason for custom houses between Ontario and New York than between New York and Massachusetts. The name United States is definite and exact. It is as appropriate to one hundred States as to thirteen or forty-four. No new State loses autonomy by fraternization. We may as well cover ten degrees of latitude as five. Each State retains its independence, yielding only a definite sum of powers for the common welfare. No one of our States alone could have retained its independence; certainly not equality of prosperity. The very basis of union is the agreement that there shall be no tariffs between the States. It is like the cells in the human body; not even the brain cells can exist alone and defiant. Rhode Island without union would be but a pocketful for a millionaire. It would long ago have ceased to exist but for the republic. So also the nation would long ago have fallen in pieces but for the States. The States abolished, as Hamilton hoped, and the nation would have no more meaning than a jellyfish. It would divide as readily as it agglomerated.

(11) *The Evolved Family.*

We thus have traced the kernel idea of associated humanity forward into American federalism. We have found the current in Europe dividing somewhere back of one thousand years ago, and reuniting somewhat over one hundred years ago. The family has passed by natural stages into the federated nation. The United States is, we see, also a stage and a pledge of internationalism. We are on the road to a recognition of universal kinship—a federated humanity. The charming idea of an "English-speaking fraternity" wrought out by Hosmer, is anticipated and surpassed by "the federation of the Americas" for industrial and commercial ends. The high seas meanwhile have become a free democracy covering two thirds of the globe.

The family in this process of evolution has accomplished two things: It has reached that ethical and political point where conflict is supplanted by federation; and it has found a method for recognizing and rendering sacred the rights of the individual. The two ethical defects of the primitive family are thus rectified. Unconsciously the aim of evolution has been to secure that family that can save each individual, and that can be cordially interested in the welfare of all other families. The ballot achieves the former end, as federalism accomplishes the latter. Laws are no longer made for the family, but for the person.

(12) *Rights of Man Presupposed in the Primitive Family.*

In the primitive family the individual was suppressed, but not wholly ignored. While the patriarch owned the family he never dreamed of being lord of custom. Sir Henry Maine says of Rungeet Singh, whose word was life or death to millions, that he probably never thought of enacting a law. Custom had the prompt recognition of tyrants and conquerors long after the patriarchate was developed into tribes and peoples. One of the earliest customs gave to male children a voice in the alienation of property. The land cultivated in common by village communities was marque land; and those who equally reapportioned it were "the men of mark." So the individual was recognized in the family and in the commune. From the first the substantial law of life was, as it is, that no man lives to himself as no man dies to himself. The suicide was a criminal because he owed the commune. Crime and sin are life-wasting; rightness and righteousness consist in saving life. Religion and law had one end—the ennoblement of life and living. In the animal family also, while the individual subordinates to the group, his rights exist. At times the family lives for the baby kid or the baby bird. The parents fight for it, as they toil for it and sing for it. But when migration begins the babe will be deserted for the family, even though it starve. Individual right to property is recognized by our domestic animals, so far as it is in actual possession or use. But when the art of accumulation has been developed, property is stored by all for all.

So we see that while Rousseau seized upon the rights of the individual, and Thomas Paine emphasized the rights of man at the critical hour of our nation-making, it was only the elaboration of an elemental idea contained in the ancient family. Our Declaration of Independence affirmed the equality of human beings on the basis of an appeal to Nature. Equity was prominent in the courts of Rome, followed by jurisprudence based on equity. Law of nations and law of Nature were recognized by Roman lawyers as identical. Jurisprudence has a strong distaste for looking forward; legal methods look backward. Jurists in Rome always assumed a former perfect state of man. Rousseau assumed the same premise, and strove to reconstruct the state of Nature. Jefferson applied legal equality before the judge to politics; that is, all were declared to be equal in making law as well as in obeying it.

(13) *The Evolved Individual.*

But it must be borne in mind that as the modern family is a vastly evolved family, so we are dealing with an evolved individual. The modern individual is a more imaginative, ethical, sensitive person. We feel the depths and heights as the primitive man could not—as even the mediæval man did not—as other races do not. The Chinese, says Dr. Parker, can endure unbound the severest ophthalmic surgery. Our self-consciousness has gone up as well as our consciousness; so also our consciousness of the "self higher than ourselves." Equality of culture approximates possibility. The lower classes rise to equal privileges in the State. The value of the Bible was in the equalization of men's hopes. Science does for us the same thing in greater degree. Universal institutions, such as a seventh day's rest, also help to keep us from a loss of equilibrium. Tyranny enforces uniformity; freedom seeks unity of aspiration and privilege.

(14) *Internationalism.*

The next stage of the evolved family must be international. The problem of the possible fellowship of nations is solved. Internationalism is demanded by commerce, by industries, by science, by enlarged ethics, by the forces steam and electricity. Our present difficulty in expanding our patriotism into philanthropy is a no greater task than has been laid on us at every period of evolution. But every stage of social progress persists; nothing is destroyed by evolution. The primitive family exists in its entirety. The evolved family depends for its safety on the integrity of the unevolved. The three foes of the family—celibacy, licentiousness, divorce—are equally foes of the State. So the township stands firm in the nation. Its importance was not exaggerated by Jefferson, nor its position emphasized too strongly by Freeman and Fiske. A State is a process of life. It can not ignore its past. The ideal to find is that of easiest readjustment to changed environments. No social adjustment is permanent. We have still to invent the family of man, in which God shall be the one All-Father.

The Philosophy of History. 373

(15) Further Evolution of the Individual.

The evolution of personal rights will also continue. Woman's rights are real rights; not pathetic appeals for unnatural privileges. She is an individual. We have found individualism to have reached this point; not only of equality before the law, but equality in creating custom and statute. Lawmaking to-day should rest freely where custom-making rested in the primitive family—that is, with intelligence and character. Women create customs, so should they affect statutes. Herbert Spencer's argument that legislation is unsuitable for women because of their comparative excitability would not only reduce lawmaking to men, but to a very few men—the least excitable. Tested by an oil-well discovery, the nonexcited remnant of community should be the voters, while the excited develop the business and hold the property. The argument carried out would make a Hollander a better qualified voter than a New Englander, and would disfranchise the French altogether. State burdens should rest on all; but Mr. Spencer refuses to permit lawmaking, like custom-making, to rest equally. Early suffrage in Massachusetts was allowed only by vote. Any one could be elected a freeman; any one might be rejected; while Connecticut required church membership. It by no means follows that suffrage is a universal right. Its natural basis is exactly the basis of custom-making—that is, intelligence; it is not a natural right coming from family membership, but a privilege for those who qualify themselves wisely to exercise it. A few able writers have of late advocated family suffrage as the true solution of the problem. To give the family vote to the father would be to restore the primitive family in form without its evolution. However, family suffrage might be based on a preliminary vote of the members of the household.

(16) Other Differentiations of the Family.

All of our industries, our schools, our trades, and our arts were originally of the household. Nor did they cease to be family affairs until a recent date. It is in the memory of some of us when an American household included nearly all that is now carried on by corporate institutions. We made our own lights and fuel; clipped, carded, spun, wove our own wool; cut and sewed our own garments; knit our stockings, hoods, and gloves; wove our own carpets; shod our horses and made our own shoes; raised our own meat as well as fruits and vegetables; and made our own sugar from the juice of our own trees. We bought little besides needles, pins, potash, and cutlery. Now the exigency of steam power has created great factories, to make each one its own specialty; and we at home are left, with narrowed industries and lessening enterprise, to buy what once we made. Since leaving us, each industry has demanded protection, while there is no protection, but increased prices, for the householder. The natural result has been to create a migration toward city life, and a reduction of our producing class from ninety-five per cent. of the population to sixty-five per cent. The herding instinct is on the increase, while the ganglia of society are gorged and congested, and degeneration is evident in more than one stratum of society. This is but a temporary phase of the family I do not doubt. Electricity is a distributive force, whereas steam was concentric; and it will rapidly tend to restore social equilibrium. But we have undoubtedly passed forever that condition of the family which was inclusive of the main arts and industries. The home of the future we can not forecast; its beauty and glory will depend on its adaptability to rapidly evolving social conditions. As the secular family has been compelled to yield up arts and industries, so the church family has been compelled to pass over education and medicine to the general public. From the earliest days the priest father was the educator and physician. Worship and instruction went together. The children were governed by the household; they were taught customs and rightness by the Church. In Europe the Church monastery slowly passed into the university, and the nunnery into the female seminary. Our common-school education has but recently discarded religious instruction; and many of our colleges still are traditionally the property of denominations of believers. We are now in the throe of an effort to formulate a code of teachable morals, apart from a canon of supernaturalism. The press is flooding us with the tentative results.

(17) *Our Industrial Problems.*

If I have suggested the right key to historic evolution, we may look for the solution of our industrial problems inside family lines. Co-operation in production and profit-sharing in distribution are distinctively ideas primitive to the family, but have undergone great development. While the anarchist looks for a subversion of historic evolution, the commune would be a restoration of the undeveloped family. All social reform must have its eyes in its forehead. To restore communistic land possession we must restore compulsory agriculture. The communism of the early family was adapted to the most perfect distribution, but not to the maximum of production. It required not only annual redivision of property, but continuous migration. As fast as one territory was exhausted another must be seized. This principle was inadequate to the subjection of a continent. The Danes and Jutes were, in fact, able to occupy only narrow strips of England. They were, as Mr. Green shows, held fast or turned about by swamps and forests. Those Europeans gained permanent possession of America who were best able to conquer not men, but land. Co-operation and profit-sharing are highly evolved conceptions of family unity of purpose, and seem to be the natural leading factors of any just and sound industrial reform. Certainly we have it demonstrated by history that, while charters and constitutions are of priceless value to restrain evil statute-making, laws will not compel or secure social industrial or political progress.

(18) *Lawmaking and its Dangers.*

Our great danger to-day is in the energy of legislation. No nation on earth enacts so many laws as the American. The average of new statutes per day is at least one hundred and fifty, besides the minor legislating of supervisors and municipal corporations. Those that may affect every citizen of the United States are certainly over one hundred new ones every twenty-four hours. We remain as ignorant as unborn babes of nearly all of these. The primitive Aryan grew laws; we deliberately manufacture them. (1) Came patriarchal authority; (2) family precedent; (3) codes of precedents, like the Ten Commandments and the Twelve Tables of Rome; (4) an aristocratic interregnum, such as feudalism in Europe; (5) pleading and contention; (6) monarchic legislation; (7) popular legislation. In our stage of development we are expending the most virile energy in devising new statutes. This Mr. Spencer terms "the new tyranny." The evil is not only in the enormous increase of new laws, but the perpetual annulling of those not yet seasoned. The range and sweep of these laws is also dangerous, while the drift is to enlarge the power of the State at every session of the lawmaking bodies. The instincts of the people are changed from a sensitiveness for local rights to a desire to multiply general legislative encroachments. A senator is held to be efficient in proportion to his activity in introducing new measures. Lawmaking may absorb far too much of the energy of a people. Statutes are not panaceas for ills that lie in the habits and natures of the people.

D. THE EVOLUTION OF THE CHURCH.

Incidentally, while tracing the evolution of the State, I have noted that of the Church. We must, however, go back to trace more carefully the collateral and alternately subordinate advance of these two differentiations of the primitive family. As the care of the living became statecraft, the care of the dead became priestcraft. The two crafts naturally collided in authority, and for most of the time the priest has held the advantage. His was the growing side of the family, and none ever left it. Sooner or later all heroes went over to him, and he was in communication with the chiefest of the patriarchs. He easily became inspired; as Sir Henry Maine reminds us, the earliest customs, as well as the later laws of all nations, were supposed to be inspirations. Evolution also went on among the dead, and heroes rose to be gods. To this day the Church feels the need, above all things, of affirming inspiration, and requiring our belief in the same. After the State grew its codes of law, there arose a conflict of canon law with code. We do not even yet find it easy to discard a distinction between sacred and profane literature, between divine authority and secular, between natural right and supernatural decree. Our modern heresy trials mean no more nor less than this: that the priestly class finds it difficult to withhold its books from investigation according to the natural laws of criticism. Biblical history must submit to historical tests. Supernatural episodes are no longer credited without demonstration. The Church has been an evolution, a process of life, precisely as the State has been. From the deceased family and the departed saints and heroes it has eliminated and evolved the idea of the Living Infinite God—the All-Purpose. The infinite anthropomorphic deity becomes the infinite interpenetrating Will in Nature. So it is that history is compelled to consider the gods and God, as well as man; religion as well as politics. Cope's Origin of the Fittest constructively follows Spencer's Survival of the Fittest. The family is the unit of both Church and State; one body, one blood, reaching toward the family of Humanity, enfolded in the love of our Father.

(1) *Conflict of Church and State.*

The conflict of the Church with secular ideas simply shows that the Church, by its origin, is more conservative than the State. Yet we must not forget its power for good. In some ways it has always been sure to touch the State helpfully. It was the Church that saved the Roman Empire from lapsing into barbarism. It was the Church that united Great Britain and made possible its national life. To Archbishop Leighton, equally with the Barons, we owe Magna Charta. The Church of Rome became the court of appeals for Europe, and we are bound to say that its authority was exercised, on the whole, for good. There was a vast utility in the Dei Gratia idea that mastered civilization for ages, and tempered both feudalism and absolutism. The priest brought the king to his knees. The State discovered new worlds, and the Church gave them away. But it was an arbiter for peace. The Church in America has been equally beneficent. Whatever the bigotry of Puritanism, its patriotism never flinched. But for the ministers of New England our Revolution would have failed, and our Constitution would, in 1789, have been rejected.

At no point in history does either State or Church quite disappear. They struggle with each other mightily, but the hierarchy is never quite triumphant. Most dangerous have been the eras when priest and king formed an alliance, by "God's grace," against the people. The Church has brought about our finest historic episodes; it has delayed, but it has ripened, our noblest fruits of progress. The papacy became arrested in its moral development because it must melt into the mold of the old decaying empire to save civilization from anarchy. But to-day the Pope is renewing the evolution of Christianity. Rome as a State is reborn, and the Church is free to expand as a Church. Our age has no more interesting feature than the assured fact that secular internationalism is to be mated by a cosmopolitan democratic creed and Church of humanity. Leo XIII is fulfilling the prophecy of Cavour.

(2) *The Church and the Home.*

It would be interesting, had I space, to more than note the parallel evolution of the house and the kirk. The house has ever been the castle of its owner: the Church ever the asylum of the endangered. Beginning with equal humility, each has reached the highest point of pride and beauty. The stone on which the first priest fed the departed became the pile of stones, more or less orderly; the stone tomb became the richer mausoleum, and finally a building large enough to cover both living and dead. This building grew till its airy spars rose to the skies in the pinnacles of the cathedral. On the other hand, the cave and the bark tent became a substantial house, and by stages the cottage and the mansion. The English 'All and the English Altar have with equal steps moved upward to the glory of Westminster and the social comforts of Lambeth.

E. HISTORY HAS BEEN REAL PROGRESS.

As in the organism that constituted life there are stages that the biologist does not hesitate to describe as progressive from lower to higher, so in the social organism. Mr. Froude, following sharply after Mr. Maudsley, denies this. He affirms there have never been finer specimens of womanhood than Nausicaa and Penelope; and among men that there are none now to surpass Socrates, Cicero, and St. Paul. He can see nothing in the increasing rights of individuals but decay of authority. As for any science of history, it is all "guesswork" with the historian. "Theories," he avers, "shift from generation to generation, and one ceases to believe any of them. I know nothing of, and I care nothing for, what are called laws of development, evolution, or devolution." He then quotes Carlyle, that "the history of mankind is the history of its great men." This extreme hero-worship is nothing novel. Aristotle gravely argued that the inferior should be slaves to the superior: a doctrine that always ends in a reign of brute force. The logic of force is the same in all ages; but, as Hood says, "I do wish our physical-force men would take a trip up the River Rhine— if it were only that they might see and reflect on these tumble-down castles. To my mind, every one of them is like a gravestone set up at the death and burial of brute force." If we had no other proof of progress this would be enough, that the advocates of "might makes right" have certainly lost control of both the social and political world. As for St. Paul and Jesus, the majority of the civilized men of that day joined in putting them to death, while such as Cicero, Socrates, and Seneca fared likewise or little better. The grandest poem of the ancient world concerns the rape of a wife and the sacking of a city in revenge.

(1) *Plausibility of the No-Progress Theory.*

There is a certain plausibility about the no-progress argument. One may discover delightful features at every stage of history. Evolution does not imply that we may congratulate none but ourselves. I can understand why the Cherokees resist the pressure to adopt statehood, take land in severalty, and give up tribal organization. Red Jacket sincerely loved forest life. I took a friend into a biological museum. " Really," said he, " why speak of this creature as higher than that? I deny what you call progress. I do not concede that this lancelet with its gristle, or this shark with its spine, is one whit ahead of its spineless predecessors; or that these modern birds are superior to the old saurians that were fish, bird, and mammal—all in one. The saurian had positive character: the strongest ruled. 'As those knights lie there' (he was quoting Mr. Froude), 'so they moved when they were alive; and when hard blows were going they had an ample share of them.' An amœba has its advantages. It can be now a stomach; and anon its stomach becomes legs. As for ourselves, we are too much differentiated. My arms once lost, I must go on forever, as best I can, without arms; but here is a creature you call very low down, yet it can grow a new leg in a few hours. There are certainly great disadvantages in not being able to molt our skins, or to hibernate in winter; as there would be great advantage in getting on without puzzling our brains about immortality, liberty, evolution, and progress. ' I see in biology only a stage on which the drama of life is played by successive actors.' "

(2) *Some Tokens of Progress.*

Not only long reaches of history but abbreviated segments show unmistakable gains in politics, ethics, and general sociology. It is not that we are more free, but that our freedom is more generous and more honest. There was good in slavery, in war, in celibacy, in the duello; but no reputable historian fails to recognize it as positive human progress to have outlived and worked out slavery and the duello and celibacy from the social system. No one dares to sneer at our hope to reach a stage of universal peace. That life is vastly more valuable because of the development of individualism, and because of science that teaches alike our infinite and our infinitesimal relations, is evident. Carlyle makes the anarchists say: " Our fathers had at least another life to look forward to, but with your intellect and your progress you have taken from us that consolation." But such consolation is needed only when religion is pessimistic for this world—as, unfortunately, all our orthodox religions have been. At last the growing creed is a creed of the life that is, and faith in the truths that are revealed by research; and progress of the upward-lookers. Athens with her Socrates lived by the labor of slaves and the tribute of allies; America has abolished slavery, and trusts in personal thrift and in educated tact.

(3) *Progress not Completeness.*

History describes a dream, a hope, an aspiration, rather than a complete real. But the realizations are quarter-mile stones on the road that man has trod. Goethe sang of the universe :

> " It must go on creating, changing,
> Through endless shapes forever ranging,
> And rest we only *seem* to see.
> The eternal lives through all revolving,
> For all must ever keep dissolving,
> Would it continue still to be."

If social organization is to move on forever, then the last thing to be desired is completeness. " The end of the older theology was perfection; of the older metaphysics, happiness; but the hope of evolution is eternal betterment. The glorious accumulation of moral power for the past century jeers at pessimism. It will be sad for our age if it long remain so alien to God that we despair because we are not yet altogether happy."

F. THE LAWS OF PROGRESS.

(1) *Power of Renewal.*

Comte, with a grand generalization, affirmed that the life of humanity, like that of an individual, rises from youth to old age. Maudsley and the English pessimists carry this idea to its logical conclusion—namely, that after a laborious rise, life and progress will speedily rush down into degeneration and death. Mr. Spencer allows that the future progress of civilization, under the never-ceasing pressure of increasing population, will be accompanied by an enhanced cost of individuation. The larger body of emotion required by the increased struggle for existence will require larger brain. The nerve system will pull harder on the muscular organism. Already the brain of civilized man is larger by nearly one third than that of the savage. This he believes will eventuate in lessening the reproductive faculty and checking increase of population. If this be true, the effect of the higher civilization, while it lengthens individual life, leaves the lower stocks the privilege of more rapid increase and the certainty of overrunning the more advanced—as has in fact occurred in all the past. When the eminent pomologist Van Mons undertook the creation of a finer stock of pears, he did not begin with the best sorts then existing, but went back to wilder varieties and secured a new start. Any line of evolution in fruit, he assumed, has after a while done its best and ended its progress. Then Nature makes a new beginning with fresh unexhausted material, to see if she can not go farther another time. Races are constantly seen in history to have touched their limit of development. Nature wastes no time in trying to force them; but she brings up new crude barbaric forces and sets them at work on the accumulations of their predecessors and expects them to go farther. She almost surely succeeds, for Greece surpassed Assyria, Rome surpassed Greece, and the Saxon races, on the break-up of Roman dominion, have made indubitable advance over the politics of the old mistress of the world. Our Puritan stock was new stock—men and women selected on the Van Mons principle. The culture of Europe was little drafted upon, and we did not fail to suffer in some directions because of the raw material of Virginia and Massachusetts. But the result was a group of men, both in the North and the South

of our colonies, capable of going a rifle's range ahead of
European thought and enterprise. The highest culture of
Europe would have been incapacitated by conservatism for
creating our federated Union and our popular government.
When Puritan blood began to flow thick, Nature overran it
with a new invoice of migrants. As early as 1640 "The
Simple Cobbler of Agawam" bemoaned that foreigners
were allowed to come so freely to America as to "crowd the
natives to the four corners of the earth." We lament the
inferiority of the present foreign influx. Apart from
criminals and the debauched, it is our constant salvation.
"Naturalization" is primitive "adoption," adapted to higher
stages of society. Immigration or migration of the common
and unexhausted stock has always been the primest necessity
for human advance. The populace must be renewed exactly as leaders must be. Not one of the great living leaders
but has sprung from below the peerage. Gustav Freytag
in The Lost Manuscript shows that a moral disease attacks
dynasties. Moral imbecility and insanity soon set in with
hereditary aristocracy. The same law applies to municipal
centers. Statistics show that the population of great cities,
without renewal from rural districts, collapses in moral and
physical energy within three generations.

(2) *Antagonism Essential to Progress.*

The better part of social, like that of organic evolution,
comes about by effort and use. War, so far from being an
unmitigated evil, is, in the lower stages of civilization, a
normal condition. We have even seen our own national
life accelerated by the struggle with slavery; and its accompaniments lust and brutality. The Thirty-Years' War in
the seventeenth century established in bloodshed the right
of private judgment. Federalism had to show its horns at
once. We began with a Secretary of War and a Secretary
of the Treasury; we added, as afterthoughts, a Secretary
of the Interior and a Secretary of Agriculture.

The first division of family power we have seen was into
Church and State—a conflict at once. The irritation of
these two forces, their mutual criticism, their struggle to
win the favor of the people, their mutual restraint in crises
of power, have been potent factors of human progress. The
value of religion has ever been not so much what it taught,
as its conflict with the secular powers; now to restrain, now

to propel. In the Roman Empire secular power dominated; in Palestine theocracy was supreme; the two were essential to the rise of Christianity.

The value of antagonism was recognized in the oldest and in the best literature. Homer and the Bible alike show us that valor and virtue were and may be synonymous. Moses and David and Ulysses, as well as Lincoln and General Jackson, called on the gods for patriotic purposes. Out of the grosser struggle rises the moral and intellectual. The æsthetic and the ethical struggle survive that of brute force.

Modern industrial strife must not be considered as an unmitigated evil, but as a wholesome effort for betterment. The first want of life is food; to this need have been added the very large number of wants which modern industrialism and commerce undertake to supply. Coalescence as well as conflict followed the demand for food and companionship. Bagehot makes persecution and imitation the chief factors of progress—an external and an internal potency. Primitive life was homogeneous, instinctive, methodic; it made few trials, and moved along the shores of archæan seas, feeding on mussels. But modern life has contested with every possible force, or hindrance, making tools of the Caliban of electricity and of steam, while free schools reduplicate the honest needs of the toilers. Ancient life made masses; modern life makes individuals. No one is a copy of his neighbor, and, above all, each despises the idea of lacking originality. Genius to do startling things we most admire. We must expect and must endure industrial conflict as part of the process of man-making.

Ethically, civilization is a battle with error. Mr. White finds science to have been constantly battled by supernaturalism. Ancient history, like ancient theology, created its causes. To reason was to antagonize the revelations of deities; to study Nature was profane. Credulity was a virtue. That this struggle should persist into later evolution is not surprising. "Monkeys can get on with what religions and philosophies they have without conflict, but man can not—until he has reasoned Reason's broadest demonstration, equal rights." All religions, all philosophies, all parties have sought to establish an eternal camp at some milestone of progress; and would have succeeded but for antagonists. So it is that reforms have been struggles, and have cost the world some of its sweetest lives.

Religion began as honor for family gods. Conflict of the

living involved at once conflict about the family ghosts. Patriotism was also family virtue. It involved hate of outsiders. Naturally followed slavery for this world, and hell for the next. We have at last developed beyond the secular need of slavery; we shall soon have outgrown the sacred need of hell. The battle between *Dei gratia* and *vox populi* is ending in that grand compromise, *vox populi, vox Dei*. Human brotherhood meets with Divine Fatherhood to construct the final family. The subtle force working for equity, for temperance, for brotherly kindness, has marvelously gained during the nineteenth century.

Conflict is not the finality; it is the means and not the end. The very principle of antagonistic forces involves the opposite principle of possible helpfulness. The differentiation of sex in Nature involved not only the long servitude of the female, but the origination of all that which is involved in those magnificent words mother, father, wife, and babe. The differencing of the vegetable from the animal kingdom involved not only antagonism, but everywhere also co-operation. Man alone has five hundred species of plants in alliance with his civilization.

The general course of progressive thought has been (1) an accumulation of knowledge of natural phenomena, with an attempt at referring the same to causes; (2) this effort ends in an agglomeration of myth and science, as theology; (3) a code of arbitrary morals and a creed of arbitrary belief follows; (4) another advance in knowledge attacks ritual and belief, ending after bitter strife in a reformation; (5) the new heresy, having established itself as orthodoxy, loses its plasticity, and is assailed in turn by later knowledge. By such stages of conflict all historic progress has proceeded. Evolution emphasizes the struggle, but it also emphasizes the gain thereby.

(3) *Progress Conditioned.*

We have to free ourselves of the fascinating notion that we have defined development by showing relations of physical environment. Buckle was tempted by his antagonism for reactionary creeds to emphasize too lightly moral causes of progress. He made climate convert the Pagans; and he held Christianity to be purely a matter of latitudes. Canon Taylor believes Africa, from its position, to belong legitimately to Mohammedanism. Draper says: " Each race follows a predestined course, determined by the configuration of the continent on which its lot is cast." His own pages do not fully confirm the theory. Mr. Lecky goes so far as to say that "the rivers that rise and fall with the winter's torrents or the summer's drought, the aspects of vegetation which pursue appointed changes through recurring seasons, do not reflect more faithfully or obey more explicitly external influences than do some great departments of the acts of men." It has been argued that Christianity owes its rise to the fact that the Roman Empire had put an end to a host of tribal and national autonomies, and created a universal government. But why did not some other one of the religions that thronged the Pantheon step out into power? It is much truer to facts to say that Christianity won its way as the religion of humanity and of higher morals. It was the best product of Aryan and Shemitic culture; not the chance product of a rustic and a few ignorant disciples. Mr. Fiske more justly makes progress contingent on both environment and popular purpose. He sees in all historic advance a decrease of egoism and an increase of altruism. Mr. Spencer makes progress depend on moral changes caused by the discipline of social life. Mr. Wallace defines progress as a capacity for acting in concert. This is a just definition, if we remember that only highly individuated minds can rise above petty prejudices, and grasp the social problems of their generation, so as to perceive that no man can live to himself, and no man die to himself. Only by the development of individuals can we secure international humanity. Home rule in Ireland is a personal question also in San Francisco; for justice established anywhere creates moral sentiment everywhere.

It is easy to multiply the ifs of progress. Mr. Bagehot affirms that one Australian tribe, could it have got rid of omen-searching, would have outstripped all others. As it was, the most alert noses whipped; and so Australian life remained on the dog-level. The native boys can run on all fours and track marauders as easily as a Scotch collie can track sheep. I have elsewhere shown that but for the development, contemporaneously with the human family, of the rose family and the cereal family, man could not have become a creature of progressive civilization. The rose family alone includes our pears, apples, peaches, plums, cherries, raspberries, strawberries, and blackberries. Mr. Shaler notes with much power the effect on civilization of glaciated soil, of snowy and arid mountains, of deforestization, as well as the influence of a single food product like the maize and the pumpkin Napoleon, in his St. Helena conversations with O'Meara, never tired of portraying the relations which England bore to the seas. Mahan, with immense power, shows The Influence of Sea Power on History. If England had been united with the continent by ever so narrow a neck of land, she would have been invaded by Bonaparte, and the nineteenth century would have had a vastly different story concerning the spread of English ideas and Saxon tongues.

Voltaire played with the chances of history. Gibbon liked a brilliant passage hinged on the possible. Pascal tells us that if Cleopatra's nose had been shorter the whole face of the world might have been changed. I should not lay half the emphasis that Mr. Creesy does on great battles. If Bunker Hill had gone wrong, it is easy to say but not to prove that the republic would not have been created. Such haps do not hinder the great currents of evolution. Mr. Lecky quotes Gibbon approvingly, that had Charles Martel been defeated at Tours, Mohammed would have displaced Jesus over most of Europe. We may more readily believe Mohammedanism would have been converted in Europe much as Christianity was, by the ethical and physical force of Northern tribes. German and English Christianity were, and could not be less than, Saxon emotions. There are gulf currents that absorb a thousand lesser currents; and warm and utilize the floating bergs of icy prejudices and narrow determinations.

This whole discussion, which has absorbed so much of the energy of historians for half a century, arose from and was necessitated by the rise of faith in law—law as above special Providences. The first escape from the supernatural interpretation of history was through Erasmus and the scholars of the sixteenth century, who brought the thought of Greece into the Western world and established the unity of art and literature. Geology and astronomy quickened the idea of irreversible law on earth and in the skies. Darwin showed us the unity of organic life, and Spencer elaborated the method of Nature in determining progress. Spencer is not only the synthetic formulator of science, but the father of the philosophy of history. The harmony of science and religion is coming about not by yielding the idea of a moral purpose in Nature, but by including purpose in Nature. Nature is itself purposive law. The theological party refused to find goodness in the natural, but demanded a supranatural Providence. This position fell of necessity into supplementary designs and afterthoughts. Buckle completed the rout of supralegalism. But the temporary arrogance that placed all the emphasis on physical environments has been reproved by physical science itself. Evolution is not only ethical, it is also devoutly religious. It affirms not only the moral in history, but the Divine in Nature.

The historic schools of our century may be summed up as (1) That of *Dei gratia*, or Divine supranatural Providence. (2) That of intuitional ought. Quashee *ought* to be a slave. In this school the arbitrary factor outside of Nature steps into the world of Nature. (3) The experiential. This school finds man to be the creature of circumstances; possibly moral, more probably physical. Here Mr. Buckle ranged himself. (4) The school of evolution; that of the organic growth of society. Here both the heredity and the environment are considered; and it is not denied that a universal purpose is involved in universal progress.

(4) *The Unconscious in Progress.*

In estimating human progress it is impossible to overlook the fact that instinct plays a great part. Biology shows us that in our individual organism and its functioning there is a constant packing away of purposive volitions as subconsciousness; that is, we do much the larger part of what we do automatically. This is a requirement in order to clear the way for advance steps of voluntary design. We digest, breathe, and perform most of our vital functions without a thought. We are assured that this tendency has ever gone on, and ever will go on. As we can perform complex quaternion problems where our ancestors could not count fifty, the future man will be able to perform our severest mental problems by intuition. So with society. We collectively inherit instincts which relieve us of much conscious effort. But where they are erroneous, instincts become the worst hindrances to progress. Much of our religion is instinct, because religion is backward-looking at its origin. Learned doctors of Berlin and amiable followers of the Russian Jesus engage with moral enthusiasm in Jew-baiting. It is a part of their instinctive race hatred. Negrophobia is another phase of the same inheritance. In secular affairs also we have our automatism. Before laws, the instincts of races were customs, for which they fiercely fought, and without which they perished. Civilize an Indian tribe and you obliterate it. Lawmaking in like manner is becoming an instinct with civilized races. Crane calls attention to the fact that the division of government into three departments—legislative, executive, and judicial—has been our Aryan peculiarity for thousands of years. Sunday is a popular instinct of all races. It would be impossible to create a Sunday by law; as surely is it impossible to enforce a special method of Sunday observance.

Our own age is establishing scientific and industrial instincts, for there are age heredities as well as race and family heredities. Our children are born with an intuitive propensity for tools, for invention, for engines, that does not come out of our family drift. It is the age in their begetting. So each age is marked by the creation of new instincts. Occasionally the ages concentrate their power in a few individuals and give us great leaders. You can not account for them as you do for others. The crowd does not recognize them as of themselves, and is likely to kill them as demons or worship them as gods. Luther, Napoleon, Darwin, were thus products of the activities of the ages—as well as Jesus and Socrates.

History must also estimate lapsed instincts. Such was the custom of the earlier Aryans in India to divide society into three groups. Before twenty all were under tutelage; from twenty till fifty all were persons of affairs, carrying on works or war; from fifty onward all retired, says Mr. Maine, to "forest life." This last group no longer labored, but prayed, and were cared for by the second group. Such a custom, being lost, has left modern society with the shame of old age neglected and helpless. We care for the young even more tenderly than did our ancestors; our next problem must be to pension old age.

Such a loss of social faculties is parallel to our functional losses as individuals. Our sense of smell, for instance, has lost the power which belongs to the Australian savage in common with the dog, while it is far keener for purposes of art and culture. Lower races migrate like animals; and only the most advanced have been able to establish a home instinct.

In general terms, we may say that civilization is the confirmation of purpose over drift. Our social instincts are very liable to become stubborn and non-progressive. We have religion inferior to our knowledge, and politics beneath our ideals in sociology. Parties boast of what they have done, and churches plant their flags over the beliefs of their ancestors. But periods of purposelessness are incontestably briefer than formerly.

Our ablest writers fail to consider mankind as having, at the very outset, a fair propulsion in the way of hereditary progress. Inheriting the family, the lengthening of infancy increased the power of the conjugal bond, and improved the art of architecture; pointing toward a more permanent home. The æsthetic arts, also to some extent inherited from animal life, naturally progressed in the way of adorning dwellings and persons. The art of defense grew apace to defend the home. Music, as with birds, was a home art, rarely used except for domestic purposes. Music at the outset was purely a refinement of animal language, the antecedent or perhaps earliest stage of articulation. Bagehot thinks we can trace the history of man back to a pre-economic age. In my judgment, no such age is indicated. It is possible only to consider the human family as born of a trend forward in animal life, and as inheriting that push to progress that had already turned the fore feet into hands and filled them with wit, while projecting forward the frontal brain for comparison and direction. Purposing preceded function in organic life; and in social life we must conceive man from the start as a moral power, moving down time by the milestones of articulation—the alphabet, the press, the telegraph. Progress is not an accident of latitude and scenery.

The earliest records are those of reforms. The Vedas, 2,500 years before Jesus, are a contention of rightness with evil. The Turanian stock shows marvelous achievement until development was arrested by a conceit of completeness. The Shemitic and Aryan races have moved on together, complementary irritants to progress, but mutually interdependent and helpful. I do not believe any author has yet conceived the power of the interaction of these two races to stimulate progress, if not even to prevent reaction and degeneration. The Australians, Tasmanians, and Eskimos made great gains in primitive art, and were checked either by isolation, climate, or war. Degeneration has been an item, but not the larger item, in the history of mankind. Conservatism, valuable as it is as a preservative art, is, however, backward-looking and tends to arrest of purpose. Churches have become museums of antique views; schools have ossified. The academies of Calcutta and Pekin and the University of Morocco have a contempt for modern life and thought. Evolution in organism advances, we know, by definite accumulations of definite variation in successive generations, antagonistic to any and all tendencies to retrogression. This is equally true of society. The earliest languages speak of men as divided into two classes—the upward-lookers and those who refuse to look before them.

But as there have always been periods of greater and of less speed in evolution, so there have been eras of special progress in special departments. While Greece stumbled in politics she went with swift certainty toward perfection in the fine arts. So it happens that we must go back 2,000 years for our models in sculpture and painting. Never has ethico-social and industrial progress been so rapid as with ourselves. Puritanism, which with Cromwell reacted locally toward absolutism, crumbled like a rock of shale, but in America it went straight forward toward civil and religious liberty. Human bondage, apparently never better intrenched than in 1850, in 1870 remained only in footprints. We shall not be able to build like the Egyptians, or lay such roads as the Romans, until we can do it by machinery. Men's lives are now too sacred. The grand dream that man is only in the making is upon us; and the belief that he will still be making æons of æons in the future we owe to Darwin and Spencer. Optimism is the first of political duties. Faith is the final generalization of all knowledge.

G. Writers of History.

(1) *Earlier Writers and Recent.*

History as written by the earlier races was not intended as a record of facts, but as the science of possible causations. That was the most admirable history which was the grandest dream. The pantheon of gods became vastly enriched with historic causes. The Great First Cause held his place as a historical necessity. It has been a later task of historical writing to show that all development is purely natural. Buckle's central word—one vastly needed to wholly clear the atmosphere—was "uniform sequences."

Herodotus, Plutarch, and Tacitus stand out as fathers of the better method. Mediæval history as well as modern, until very recently, was written for partisan purposes. Mitford wrote his History of Greece to defend English aristocracy; Grote followed with twelve volumes in the interest of democracy.

Macaulay said: "Facts are the mere doors of history; to secure the abstract truth of facts is the historian's duty." But, with excellent theory, no man failed worse in achievement. He used up all his energies on seventeen years of English life. Bancroft failed precisely in the same way, by spreading before us a vast elaboration of facts, embellished in high literary art. Bossuet foreshadowed the true method in his Universal History. Gibbon seized upon the idea of unity in history. He prepared the way for evolutionary method. The God in History of Bunsen was another superb preparatory work. He pointed the way to that undeniable purposiveness which we find in the orderly consecutiveness of human development. Mr. Green, while writing mainly of the people, does not fail to trace the laws that control progress. For popular instruction the work of Johnston and of Fiske surpasses all heretofore done in this country. For a general discussion of history I believe we have hardly surpassed the compressed and just chapters of Joseph Priestley in his Lectures on History, published just one hundred years ago. Parkman has succeeded in touching very near a golden mean between narrating the dramatic facts of history and suggesting the truths that they touch. Notably he has kept not only a simplicity of narration, but a childlike zest in story-telling that is the very genius of historical writing

(2) Definitions of History.

History has been defined to be the biography of great men, and following this idea we have writers who give us nothing of an age but Frederick or Cromwell. It is a definition too narrow for even the overriding genius of Napoleon. Following another line, historical writing lapses into a rise and growth of constitutions. The master pledges himself to write the history of the people. The rise of the laboratory method of investigation places history at last among the sciences. Our universities and colleges begin to recognize historical research as a superior element in education.

(3) Editors of History.

Hereafter the rough drafts of history—the cyclopædic—must be done co-operatively. The magnificent achievements of Winsor and Hubert Bancroft as editors recognize this need. Buckle undertook single-handed the work of a regiment. Literature holds no more pathetic passage than that in which he describes the discovery that his ambition has been vastly beyond his power of accomplishment. "Law," says Mr. Freeman, "has become a part of history." The same is true of archæology, folk lore, ethnology, sociology. The laboratory method of investigation may be applied to elaboration. The work of the editor is synthetic. We have lived in and through an age of mere analysis in science and of criticism in literature. The editor is not a mere collector. He does far more; he arranges and classifies facts to make them shed light on the reader and student.

(4) *Historical Dust.*

The real object of historical study is light. What we need to know is ourselves, not merely the men who have gone before us. Beware of loading down literature with local repetitions, mere trumpery outside your detached circle. There are cartloads of rubbish piled away in our libraries good for nothing but to be catalogued. We must learn in all directions to winnow. Bancroft fanned a good deal out of his volumes at their last editing. We can not afford time for huge volumes of commonplace facts concerning the Baxters and the Randolphs; nor do we need to know your town annals when they in no way step apart from the doings of a thousand other towns. There is little value in gorging the memory with facts merely because they occurred. The first of moral obligations is to try not to remember the useless. I know men with faculties who have spent their best energies on genealogies. A ton of such books is not worth one truth. They only show that at the other end of the line a useful man did live. Wendell Phillips says: "Tremble, my good friend, if your sixpenny neighbor keeps a journal. You shall go down to your children not in your fair lineaments and proportions, but with the smirks, elbows, and angles he sees you with." To unload history has become a prime obligation. We owe a chief debt to those who edit well for us.

H. IMPORTANCE OF THE STUDY OF HISTORY.

(1) *History Prophetic.*

Prophecy, prevision, and hence provision, is the dignity of man above all brutes. It constitutes our chief title to supremacy. We are socially great by two things: property—things pre-vided—and the use we make of it. That the power to forecast increases in us is certainly true. It is folly to say we do not to-day comprehend the nature of popular government—its limits, its dangers, as well as its advantages—better than one hundred years ago. And it is true that we are schooled by such knowledge to less selfishness and to greater patriotism. There is less danger of an Aaron Burr, because we all see more clearly the folly of treason or secession from federal union. It is true that men can and will go wrong; the problem is the ratio in which we learn and resolve to go right. Prevision in the longer reaches of history is of precisely the same nature as that prevision which we do not hesitate to exercise in our industrial affairs and in our political purposing. The same anticipative calculation covers the farmer's sowings, the parent's advice, the preacher's warnings, and the educator's instruction. That we are victims of an incoherent drama is happily a crotchet of men who have so often failed in prophecy that they deny that forecast is possible. The most doleful false prophecy of the nineteenth century was Mr. Froude's prognostication of the success of the Southern Confederacy in disintegrating the Republic. His final conclusion is natural, that "history can tell us little of the past and nothing of the future."

Mr. Lecky suggests that wisdom of the historic sort might make many a revolution turn out wholly otherwise. It is certain that our American Revolution, and the consequent nation-making, was presided over pre-eminently by the genius of history. Adams and Jefferson were constant in their appeals to the past. It is a curious fact that New Englanders are even yet instinctively Federalists and Virginians are instinctively Democrats. Stronger even than pecuniary gain is the bias that runs in our veins and shapes the arrangement of the cells of our brains. To understand the men and things of this generation we must understand those of the past; to foresee what men will become we must have a thorough knowledge of the present. The chief error of humanitarian socialists is neglect of history. They feel as widely as the world, but do not grasp the causes of evils, and hence fail of the remedy. A young man opened a correspondence with me from reading my articles in the St. Louis Globe-Democrat. It was shortly before the Anarchist uprising in Chicago. When the leaders of the movement were hung he wrote me from a small town in Georgia, saying: "I hope to live to shoot the judge, and avenge the death of those martyrs. I hate the flag and the laws that tolerate such tyranny." I had not suspected his views, but I wrote to him: "You are making a mistake. Study American history. It is your only antidote. Go back to John Adams and to Thomas Jefferson, and learn why our institutions are what they are, and the toilsome evolution of ages that crowns itself with our Federal Union." Some time later he wrote to me: "I have taken your advice; and now my wonder is that Americans dare let their children grow up without a more thorough understanding of their political and institutional life. I am now ready to die to sustain this marvelous fabric." It is, I assure you, no small pleasure to find in our best magazines the name of this same young man attached to articles of studious worth. History saved him.

(2) History expounds our Institutions.

The trend of historical writing is so strongly of late to the study of institutions that there is no just reason why any young American shall grow up ignorant of our political system. But it is important that he shall be able to distinguish the vital from the transitory. I have seen of late an arrogant attack on the right of the smaller States to be represented in the Senate equally with Illinois and New York. But the whole Federal system is possible only on the basis of equality of the States. The study of Bryce's American Commonwealth, supplemented by Fiske's Civil Government, should enter not only into school life, but family life.

(3) History broadens our Sympathies.

The study of history, by broadening our relations to men, serves like extended travel. While intensifying patriotism, it cures us of the serious error of hoping or aiming to convert all men to our views and customs, our creeds or our Constitution. Federalism is the true historic child, in that it brings into friendly co-operation diverse types of men and methods. The moral element of history is thus predominant. It enables us to get beyond partisanship. It shows us that true citizenship and true statesmanship consist in pure character, and that a healthy nation is, after

all, only a healthy family. It throws a search light also on the Church, showing us that religion originated as a family bond, and finds there the key of all its problems.

It is dawning upon the writers of American history that our institutions run as far back as our language for their roots. We can not study the history of the United States intelligently except as an evolution. So long as the study of history is held to be the overloading of the memory with royal genealogies or with superabundant facts of little personal application, it is an intellectual and moral detriment. But we are learning to study America as a life; its institutions as a natural growth; and, what is of equal importance, the inherent or coincident dangers to progress. Collateral systems are of almost equal importance. I know no study likely to teach American youth more of value than the development of federalism in Switzerland and Australia. Our own periodical literature has of late overflowed with crass plans for compulsory arbitration. Nowhere in the world has there been a thorough governmental study of the subject except in New South Wales. Switzerland has in her new Constitution important lessons for us in taxation, representation, and popular legislation.

(4) Questions that History must enlighten.

Arnold calls the art of government "the highest earthly work." This is peculiarly true of a republic where each voter is equal to a king. "History," says Goldwin Smith, " is a series of struggles to elevate the character of humanity in all its aspects—religious, intellectual, social, and political— sometimes rising in an agony of aspiration and exertion, frequently followed by lassitude and relapses, as great moral efforts are in the case of individuals." Dr. White with great emphasis says: "The demand of the nation for men trained in history, political and social science, can hardly be overestimated." Our congressmen should be, what perhaps they seldom are, men trained in questions of capital and labor, political economy, taxation, crime, pauperism, and the rise and growth of our institutions. The recklessness of legislating without information is a crime. It is only in the light of history that we can prevent the extremes of oscillation from centralization to local sovereignty, and the reverse. Since the war we have swung very far away from a true historic conception of State rights. Questions that crowd on us for immediate settlement, and that can be solved only in the light of historic investigation are the representation of the minority; suffrage based on intelligence; loss of suffrage for dishonor as citizens; proportionate taxation; referendum, or the reference of all laws to a vote of the people to be affected thereby; the rights of the Cabinet to appear on the floors of Congress in advocacy of measures proposed by the Executive Department; the rights of employers and of employed; an entire liberation of our punitory system from the principle of revenge; the pensioning of old age; the completion of the public-school system after the model designed by Franklin, Jefferson, and Washington, so that our schools shall not remain headless for lack of a national university; a civil service delivered from the incubus of pauperism; the complete and intelligent settlement of the money question so that our industries may be delivered from the baneful influence of indecision; public control of all poisons, including alcohol and drugs; the proper limits of paternalism in controlling industries, such as railroads, post offices, telegraphs, and common roads; the liberation of agriculture from legislation that meddles with markets and the establishment of postal savings banks. These questions must be solved by the slow process of evolution; nevertheless, not one of them but needs the white light of history. Madison averred that popular government without education in the principles of government would "be but the prologue to a farce or a tragedy, or both." It must be an education so high as to create a national sentiment of honor, something to counteract the debauching influence of a partisan civil service.

Our danger is from raw experiments, and overconfidence in the manifest destiny of the American people. Red tape is sometimes the best kind of tape. Conservative institutions serve the useful purpose of showing what has been done or attempted. Traveling in circles is a constant political danger. Our financial experiments especially incline to repeat old blunders. Our activity of legislation has crippled agriculture, multiplied sumptuary laws, made a muddle of municipal government; while taxation is fourfold the requirements of national development. Lincoln said, "We are making history very fast." True statesmanship allows a nation natural and therefore wholesome evolution.

Mr. Parkin, in his admirable work on Imperial Federation, says that national sentiment can be safe only when based on sound historical and industrial knowledge. "Above all is it true for a nation which has the great birthright of free popular institutions, which has traditions behind and prospects ahead fitted to fire the noblest and purest enthusiasm. It seems a lamentable thing for any British child to grow up without having felt the splendid inspiration to be drawn from the study of British history. The work of giving education upon the immediate problems of national life, begun at school, should be carried on at our colleges and universities." Our American schools need precisely this advice. We shall wreck our Federalism, if at all, on the rock of historic ignorance.

I have held only to the main current in my discourse, because compelled by the exigencies of the occasion. It would be quite as easy to spend the full time in enlarging on the difficulties of the historic science—to show how very much progress is, after all, no progress at all, only coming around to an old solution of a social difficulty—and at least very small gain made with enormous travail. I could with equal ease enlarge on the complexity of data that must be handled in historical study, involving politics, sociology, ethnology, theology, the consequence being that able men fail to agree in their estimates, and therefore the laws of historic progress are differently estimated. But, on the whole, while Buckle and Lecky and Fiske and Spencer and Taylor and Stephens and Bryce and Draper may disagree in the emphasis placed on special factors, they agree in the essential fact that progress there is, always has been, and always must be; they also agree substantially in the belief that a science of history is possible, and that the modern laboratory method will revolutionize historical synthesis as it has historic analysis. There is no reason for believing that while political economy is a recognized science, history, which furnishes the data for political science, must remain a chaos. Even psychology becomes a quantitative science, as physico-psychology; and takes its place calmly in the laboratory with scales and alembics.

I have implied, as I believe facts entirely warrant, that there is one main line of progress and evolution in history culminating politically and industrially in the Federal Union of evolved families which we term the United States—that right on down the ages there has been one main line of gains in civilization. In spite of hindrances of all sorts, and many checks, there has been no long stay of that human tendency onward and upward which, arising in Asia, passed by the milestones of the Orient, of Greece, of Rome, of the Saxon States, and now, borne forward with impetuous zeal for a full humanity, is rolling over this continent; has even touched Japan and China, and begun to convert the old fatherland of nations to higher ideas of the human family. Nor do I fail to see that the Australian States are in some respects improving on our American development. Not only empires but ideas move westward about the globe. The future, I as firmly believe we are warranted by the laws of history to hold, will be in all respects a gain, a constant evolution beyond the present. Humanity escaped the bestial life as slowly as the anthropoid escaped the animal organism. At three points, the frontal brain, the hands, and the organs of speech Nature lifted us; on these lines moves our historical evolution—intellectual, industrial, and social. There is not a hint in contemporaneous life that this progress will cease.

ABSTRACT OF THE DISCUSSION.

WILLIAM H. MAXWELL, PH. D.:

While I do not deny the possibility of a science of history, I have the temerity to doubt whether such a science has as yet been developed. I take it that those who speak of the philosophy of history use philosophy and science as synonymous terms, because the definition of the philosophy of history usually given embraces the chief marks by which we recognize a science to be a science. The philosophy of history, we are told, is the ascertainment of the laws that run through the past and forecast the future. In this definition the word *law* is the important word. What is meant by a *law* that runs through the past and that enables us to forecast the future ? Before we seek to determine whether there are such laws we must know exactly what such a law is. I take it that law in this connection means the same as law when used with regard to natural phenomena. In this sense Prof. Huxley defines "law" as " a rule which we have always found to hold good, and which we expect always will hold good." Mr. Spencer defines " law " as " an unchanging order." The Century Dictionary defines "law" in this sense as "a proposition which expresses the constant or regular order of certain phenomena, or the constant mode of action of a force: a general formula or rule to which all things, or all things or phenomena within the limits of a certain class or group, conform, precisely and without exception." The law of gravity, according to which alike the planets move in their courses and a feather is wafted downward from an eagle in its flight, is at once the best and most familiar example of such a law. The physical and biological sciences have given us so many of these laws that it is no longer difficult to determine their characteristics. A fact is not a law. An empirical formula, even though it satisfies a series of observations, if it does not explain all cases, is not a law. The first test of a law, then, is: Does it explain all the facts ? The second test is : Does it enable us to forecast the future ? In other words, given precisely the same conditions, will precisely the same effects follow ? The ascertainment of the laws of astronomy has enabled astronomers to foretell with perfect accuracy future movements among bodies of dimensions so large and removed from us by distances so great, that of them the mind can form no adequate conception. Have such universal laws dominating men's actions in this world been formulated? If they have not, then there is no science of history. Empirical formulas, remember, are not universal laws.

The evolution of a natural law will necessarily follow a certain order.

1. The ascertainment of facts and their classification.
2. The discovery that from certain antecedents certain consequences are sure to follow.
3. The forecast of the future.

The first question, then, which we must determine is: Have the facts in which the law is inherent, as the statue in the block of marble, been ascertained and classified?

Those who take the affirmative side of this question rest their argument in the main, if not exclusively, on the supposition that our own institutions are developed out of the family customs of the primitive Aryan race. Now, admitting for a moment that this hypothesis is correct, I have to remark, first, that the members of the so-called Aryan family, albeit the most powerful and progressive of the human race, constitute but a part of the people of this world. A theory which explains Aryan development throws no light, for instance, on the origin and fate of the Mound Builders. As little does it explain the wonderful phenomena of Egypt. As the traveler on the Nile gazes on the wonderful monuments of a civilization now wholly effaced, as he examines each new evidence of mental strength and physical force, the questions are forced upon him, "When and how did they learn to do these things?" and then, "How was such a people ever wiped out?" In the presence of these facts, evolution is silent. And when the same traveler sees depicted in the hieroglyphics six thousand years old precisely the same methods of irrigation, of navigation, of manufacture, which the natives around him are using to-day, he seeks in vain for an explanation. The first thing then which we are forced to note is that the so-called philosophy of history is not a science, because it does not explain, nor attempt to explain, all the facts.

But this is not all. Instead of analyzing and grouping facts, it starts out with a pure assumption—the assumption, namely, of an Aryan race, from which have descended to the Indo-European races not only kindred tongues but community of blood. I have no hesitation, however, in saying that, with the possible exception of Max Müller, no investigator of standing has now any confidence that such a distinct race ever existed. The evidence derived from language goes for very little in presence of well-known historical facts as to whole nations changing their mode of speech.

The very foundation, then, on which this particular science of history rests is but a vague conjecture unsupported by evidence.

Again, investigators are not by any means unanimous that in the primitive patriarchal family we find the promise and potency of our modern governmental system. They are not even agreed that the original family was patriarchal in its nature. There is some ground for the belief that it was not; and it is almost certain that various customs and laws, whose origin has often been attributed to the patriarchal family, could have arisen only in a community that was matriarchal or polyandric.

Judged, then, by the first test, there is as yet no science of history.

Now, as to the second test of a science. Given certain antecedents, do certain consequences surely follow? Man's highest nature cries aloud against such a supposition. Is man free to choose one of several lines of action placed before him? "If," to use Mr. Froude's words, " it is free to man to choose what he will do or not do, there is no adequate science of him. If there is a science of him, there is no free choice. Mankind are but an aggregate of individuals; history is but the record of individual action ; and what is true of the part is true of the whole." For my part, I prefer to believe that man is free to choose what he will do and what he will not do, at least within certain limits, and not that he always acts in obedience to an inexorable natural law.

The common saying, "History repeats itself," contains a gigantic falsehood. The same conditions never occur twice exactly alike. Each individual is different from every other; each generation is different in some degree from that which preceded it. From differing antecedents no process of logic has yet been discovered by which we can infer similar consequents.

Coming now to the third test—the forecasting of the future—we find the science of history on no firmer ground. Prophesying is sometimes easy after the event. But even in case of great religious and social movements we ask the science of history in vain for an explanation. The science of history has not restored to us the lost secret of the foundation of Rome. The professors of that science do not pretend that they can now explain the rise of Buddhism or the origin of Mohammedanism. It is doubtful whether any of them, with all their present skill and knowledge, had he been set on this earth one hundred years ago, could have foretold that the social instinct, after sleeping for thousands of years, would have suddenly waked to life and produced the kingdom of Italy and the unification of Germany. Nor will any one of them undertake to tell us now what changes in the map of Europe the instinct of Panslavism is yet destined to produce.

That certain empirical rules may be formulated I do not doubt. That much of what the evolution philosophers tell us in their sociological studies is true I am ready to affirm; but it is true only within very narrow limits, and gives but a shade of probability to our prognostications of the future. For my own part, I believe that the chief use of history as applied to present affairs is to supply the experience without which it is impossible to interpret the signs of the times and the significance of passing events. As a botanist can classify a new plant only when he is familiar with the species to which it belongs, so the man who would interpret social movements and governmental policies can do so only by determining the likeness to and the difference from similar events in the past. This, however, he may do without claiming the gift of prophecy.

But even this is not the chief use of history. That use is ethical. Mr. Froude has stated it in language which can not be changed except for the worse: "One lesson, and only one, history may be said to repeat with distinctness: that the world is built somehow on a moral foundation; that, in the long run, it is well with the good, and in the long run it is ill with the wicked. There are laws for man's digestion, and laws of the means by which his digestive organs are supplied with matter. But pass beyond them, and where are we? In a world where it would be as easy to calculate men's actions by laws as to measure the orbit of Neptune with a foot-rule, or weigh Sirius in a grocer's scale."

Mr. A. Emerson Palmer:

It seems to me that the question whether there is a philosophy of history is very much the same thing as the question whether there is a science of sociology. To argue such a question as that before this association, especially in view of the fact that one of its valuable publications consists of a book on sociology, containing not less than seventeen lectures, would appear to be a superfluity. Sociology is a new science, but the materials with which it deals are as old as society itself. It will not do to say as old as man himself, for we can scarcely conceive of primitive man as a social being. So is geology a comparatively recent science; but the materials with which it deals are as old as the emergence of the earth from the fire-mist.

He would be a bold man who should talk of the philosophy of history as a thing fully formulated and complete. No science that deals with man can be an exact science. But that there is a potential philosophy of history can not, I think, be denied by any rational mind. And it is certain that from the beginning of recorded history the materials for such a philosophy have been accumulating. Our perspective doubtless is not long enough to obtain a complete view or to enable us to draw inferences that are certain and invariable.

Macaulay has said that facts are the mere dross of history, but that I take to be a partial and incorrect view. Facts seem to me rather the scaffolding on which history must be supported; and if the scaffolding be removed the whole structure will fall in ruins. But of course the historian must be a good deal more than a mere annalist. It is only within a comparatively recent period that history has come to be written in a philosophic spirit.

Lord Bacon said that "it is the true office of history to represent the events themselves together with the counsels, and to leave the observations and conclusions thereupon to the liberty and faculty of every man's judgment." But, happily, this is not the principle on which our best and wisest histories have been written. If all men and women were Bacons, history written in that way might perhaps be all-sufficient. But most of us require more than a narration of "the events themselves together with the counsels," and feel quite unable to depend upon "the liberty and faculty " of our own judgment.

Carlyle said a far wiser word than that of Bacon when he spoke of history as the Life of Man, and described it as "what men did, thought, suffered, enjoyed; the form, especially the spirit, of their terrestrial existence, its outward enjoyment, its inward principle, *how* and *what* it was, *whence* it proceeded, and *whither* it was tending." Here we have the root of the whole matter. How different is history written on this principle from so much of the so-called history which consists of dates of battles, the coronation of kings, the rise and fall of dynasties, court intrigues, and the like! These things tell us nothing of the Life of Man, which is the chief thing of interest, and that which alone contains useful lessons for us.

Viewed as the Life of Man, it is too plain for argument that there are principles underlying the history of the race that should be diligently sought out and most carefully studied. Given the facts to find the principles: that is the duty of the philosophical historian.

Of course if we accept Napoleon's dictum—that history consists of fables agreed upon—we may easily deny that a philosophy of history exists or is possible. But with infinite patience the historian searches out the facts and verifies them, weighs and compares statement after statement, detects errors as by more than human insight, rejects much, and finally educes the life of the period with which he deals, the principles underlying it, and the lessons which it teaches for the present and the future. This is truly scientific work.

There is one point that I should like to emphasize. In thinking of history, we are apt to think of something remote—far off from us in time, if not in space. The fact is, nevertheless, that every day we are making history, or helping to make it. It seems to me that Emerson sounded a true note when he said: "I have no expectation that any man will read history aright who thinks that what was done in a remote age, by men whose names have resounded far, has any deeper sense than what he is doing to-day." Shall we not feel a keener sense of our responsibility as citizens and as members of society if we realize the fact that we ourselves are contributing something toward the sum total of that comprehensive philosophy of history which the future shall write?

"The more thou searchest the more thou shalt wonder," said a wise man of the ancient time. It is a saying that has not lost its meaning with the enlarged and enlarging stores of science, which has taken the universe for its field. But not only is our wonder increased with the widening horizon of knowledge, but likewise there is an increased recognition of the unity of man and the continuity of his history. It is because man was the same yesterday that he is to-day that we feel so vital an interest in those old Greeks and Hebrews and Romans. So with increased study of men and of man, the conception of a true philosophy of human history must become more and more vivid to our minds and vital in our lives; and we can not fail to perceive a sense of orderly development and of unity of purpose that inevitably leads up to the thought of

"One God, one law. one element,
And one far-off divine event
To which the whole creation moves."

Mr. Powell, in reply, said that he had no special comment to make on the indorsement of Mr. Froude's views of history, as he had taken pains to reply to such doctrines in the body of His lecture. If there is no science of history, then there can be no science covering any space of time; but the farmer plants on the contrary supposition, and the trader buys with a belief in ascertainable laws. Our parents advise us with a distinct understanding that age accumulates foresight. Is there no science of astronomy because comets sometimes break away from estimated courses? Is there no science of biology since the Challenger upset some of our established data and theories?

As for the Aryans, it is a crotchet that catches us occasionally to deny everything. Archbishop Whately took off this propensity by denying the existence of Napoleon Bonaparte. Others have enjoyed themselves very much in denying the historical existence of Homer, of Jesus, and of Abraham. The fact that several whole tribes went over to Aryanism in language and worship shows only the powerful genius of the Aryan cult. The real dispute is whence the Aryans emerged into history. Did they originate in Asia or in Europe ? It is nonsense for a company of ethical Aryan philosophers to deny the existence of their ancestors.

If there is no science in history, the savage is as well off as the civilized. We all are blind together, and sure, sooner or later, of the ditch. But let us go home with the conviction that pessimism is an evil above all evils, and optimism the chiefest of all virtues in a republic. With Mr. Maxwell's closing remarks Mr. Powell was in hearty sympathy.

INDEX.

INDEX.

ADAMS, PROF. HENRY C., on the condition of laboring men, 349.
Adams, Prof. Herbert B., on the Germanic origin of the New England town, 67, 68.
Adams, John, 369, 394.
Adams, Samuel, the man of the town meeting, 70.
Agriculture: natural preparation for, in the United States, 27, 30, 32, 38, 40, 49 ; prosperity of, in America, 100, 101, 103 ; as related to transportation, 123 ; woman's contribution to, 207 ; as related to the labor problem, 309–311 ; in England, 340 ; liberation of, from meddling legislation necessary, 396.
Alcohol: deleterious effects of, 280–295 ; effect of its moderate use, 283 ; its influence on the bodily tissues, 286 ; as a medicine, 287, 303 ; its food value discussed, 296, 302, 303.
Almsgiving no charity, 260–261.
America : its special indebtedness to Nature, 26 ; its geography, 29–32 ; its virgin soil, 32–33 ; its territorial size, 33–37 ; its physical characteristics, 37–41 ; its climate, 41–42 ; its natural scenery, 44–47 ; what it owes to the Old World, 55–82 ; its wars as affecting its civilization, 92–115 ; its interstate commerce, 119–144 ; its foreign commerce, 147–169 ; position of women in, 181–196, 202–223 ; prison systems in, 232–236 ; increase of crime in, 236–237 ; capital punishment in, 241–242, 251–252 ; public charities in, 264–276 ; inebriety in, 279–294 ; profit-sharing in, 319, 324–326 ; the labor problem in, 331–360 ; the family in, 367–372 ; lawmaking in, 375–376 ; Church and State in, 382–384.
American Commonwealth, 62, 63, 64, 65, 328.
American federation of labor, 354.
Anglophobia, irrationality of, 59.
Anglo-Saxons : their instinct for institutional organization, 6 ; their contributions to local self-government, 12–13 ; their conquest of America, 37–38 ; penal legislation adjusted to their criminal propensities in America, 240 ; their family organization in England and America, 366–376; their political sagacity, 381–382.
Arbitration, international, 106–107, 185 ; compulsory, between labor and capital, 353, 395.
Aristotle, on man as a political being, 6 : on slavery of the inferior, 378.
Arnold, Matthew, on the United States Senate, 60.
Aryan race : its origin, 7 ; its folk-moot and mark, 67 ; its family development, 364, 366, 367 ; its existence questioned, 400 ; affirmed, 404–405.
Asia : its contribution to the world's civilization, 80–81.
Atkinson, Edward, on the wages of American workingmen, 343, 345.
Atwater, Prof. W. O., on soil exhaustion, 164.
Australian ballot, 74.

BAGEHOT, WALTER, on the uses of conflict, 86, 87, 88–89 ; on indiscriminate charity, 268 ; on the conditions of progress, 385 ; on the evolution of man, 389.
Ballot, the secret, 73–74.
Bancroft, George, on the origin of our public-school system, 71–72.
Beckwith, Mrs. Emma, on the social and political status of women, 195–196.
Bellamy, Edward, his nationalism, 78, 359, 360.
Brockway, Z. R., on the new theory of crime and its punishment, 246–250 ; his system commended, 233 and *note*, 251–252, 291.
Bryce, Prof. James, on religious freedom in America, 61, 63 and *note* ; on the American Constitution, 64–65 ; on Montesquieu's Spirit of Laws, 65 ; on profit-sharing, 328 ; his American Commonwealth, 62, 63, 64, 65, 328, 394.

Bryson, Dr. Louise Fiske, on the social and political status of women, 194–195.
Buckle, Henry Thomas, on the influence of the physical environment, 8, 25; his social philosophy, 239; his historical method criticised, 384.

CABINET, the English, 66.
Campbell, Douglas, on the Puritan, 61; on religious toleration, 64; on the origin of our public-school system, 72; his book criticised, 79, 82.
Capital: its combination in American railways, 131–132, 136–137; its use in foreign trade, 161; its relation to labor, 310–322, 341–350, 359–360.
Capitalization of labor, 327.
Capital punishment, 228, 241–242, 251–252.
Carey, Henry C., his economic theories, 166.
Carlyle, Thomas, on the English prison system, 231; on talking, 298; his ideal hero, 336; his view of history, 378, 408.
Chadwick, Rev. John W., on America's debt to the Old World, 79–80; on the social and political status of woman, 173–193, 196.
Charities: evolution of, 255–276; utility of, 258–259; influence of religious sanctions on, 259–260; as administered by the Church, 260–261; by the State, 261–262; evils of State administration, 265–267; ethical aspects of the question, 268–270; as related to the labor problem, 353, 354.
China, its paternalism, 367.
Chinese, their exclusion from America, 13, 77.
Christianity: its unending prayer, 27; its view of the natural world, 46–47; its spread limited by the area of the Roman conquests, 87–88; its relation to war, 113; to commerce, 168; to the labor problem, 353; its new evolution, 377; its physical conditions, 384–385.
Church, the, in England and the United States, 62; its relation to charities, 260–261; evolution of, 376–377; its conflict with the State, 377–378; its relation to the home, 378.
Cities: competition between, as stimulating progress, 36; as related to commerce, 148, 162; the labor problem in, 344–346; in Africa: Carthage, 148, 162; Karnak, 229; in America: Albany, N. Y., 298, 299; Auburn, N. Y., 233; Baltimore, 236, 267, 270, 271; Boston, 35, 70, 95, 125, 190, 205, 206, 267, 271, 353; Brooklyn, 162, 221, 236 note, 252, 265, 274, 275, 307, 318, 345; Buffalo, 141; Charleston, 125; Chicago, 35, 41, 137, 298, 348; Cleveland, 137; Duluth, 40; Elmira, N. Y., 233 and note; 236 note, 246, 247, 250, 252, 303; Indianapolis, 184; Johnstown, 256; Memphis, 207; New Haven, 236, 237; New Orleans, 35, 97; New York, 35, 61, 125, 131, 137, 141, 160, 162, 176, 179, 184, 205, 209, 210, 236 note, 252, 266, 274, 300, 333, 335, 344, 345; Pawtucket, 100; Philadelphia, 206, 232, 267; Pittsburg, 125; Plymouth, 94, 95; Providence, 94, 100 note; Quebec, 79; Reading, 142; Salem, 45, 74; St. Louis, 393; San Francisco, 385; Sing Sing, 240; Washington, 186, 238, 267; in Asia: Calcutta, 160, 390; Jericho, 35; Jerusalem, 35, 366; Pekin, 390; Sidon, 148, 162; Tyre, 148, 162; Yokohama, 160; in Australia: Melbourne, 160; Sidney, 125; in Europe: Angoulême, 316; Athens, 35, 68; Berlin, 387; Berne, 106, 107; Brussels, 239; Derby, 68; Elberfeld, 271; Ghent, 230; Liverpool, 162; London, 107 note, 162, 188, 340, 367; Manchester, 237; Milan, 230; Oldham, 314; Paris, 238, 239, 316; Pentonville, 243; Queenstown, 232; Rome, 46, 68, 229, 238, 239, 242, 375, 377, 401; Sparta, 35; Tours, 386; Turin, 238; Whitby, 68.
Civil service reform, 16, 180.
Climate, as affecting American civilization, 41–42.
Collateral readings, 2, 22, 54, 84, 118, 146, 172, 198, 226, 254, 278, 306, 330, 362.
Columbus, Christopher, 23, 28, 30, 37, 55, 57–58, 194, 360.
Commerce: a great civilizing agent, 108; internal—developed by intelligent foresight, 120; as related to transportation, 121–127; enormous volume of, 127; beneficent effect of, on our civilization, 128; power of Congress over, 129; how developed by railways, 130; foreign, 147–169; beginnings of, 147; evolution of, 148; modern methods of, 149; governmental interference in, 150; of the United States, Mexico, and South America, 151–153; reciprocity in, 153–154; influence of, on American civilization, 155; ethical value of, 155–156.
Commons, House of, 66–67.
Communism, a primitive phase of social evolution, 375.
Comte, Auguste, his religion of humanity, 113, 114; his grand generalization, 380.
Confederation, 11.
Conflict, early uses of, 85; not a finality, 385.
Congress, 67; its power over interstate commerce, 128.
Constitution of the United States: its guarantee of religious freedom, 62; Hon. William E. Gladstone on, 64; Sir Henry Maine on, 65; State constitutions its model, 65; its control of interstate commerce, 129.
Contract system, in industrial evolution, 327–328.

Index. 411

Coombs, Hon. William J., on foreign commerce, 147-156, 169.
Co-operative production, 312-316 ; as related to socialism, |326 ; its origin in the family, 374-375.
Cope, Prof. Edward D., his Origin of the Fittest, 377.
Copernicus, 124.
Cosmopolitanism in government undesirable, 14.
Cost of our military establishment, 101-103.
Cowperthwait, Col. J. Howard, on interstate commerce, 143.
Crime : in England, 75 ; as related to war, 103-104 ; its primitive treatment, 227 ; its increase among women, 228-229 and *note* ; its rapid increase in America, 236-237 ; its rationale, 238-241 ; as affected by immigration, 236 and *note*, 240, 251.
Crothers, Dr. T. D., on the drink problem, 279-295.

DARWIN, CHARLES : on clover-raising, 28 ; his principle of the correlation of growth, 174 ; his Origin of Species, 239, 377 ; his study of facts, 240 ; R. W. Raymond's reference to him, 327 ; his demonstration of the unity of organic life, 386 ; himself a product of his age, 388.
Declaration of Independence : historical factors of, 369 ; its affirmation of human equality, 371.
De Garmo, Dr. Charles, on the nation's place in civilization, 3-15, 20.
Degeneration, in human history, 389.
De Montfort, Simon, 68-69.
Depew, Chauncey M., on the restriction of immigration, 76-77.
Direct legislation, in labor organizations, 337-338 ; by the people, 338, 396.
Dolge, Alfred, on the labor problem, 324-326.
Draper, Prof. John William, on the influence of the physical environment, 8, 384-385.
Drink problem, the, 279-304.

ECCLES, DR. ROBERT G., on the nation's place in civilization, 18-19 ; on foreign commerce, 158-161 ; on political aspects of the labor problem, 360.
Economic position of woman, 199-223.
Education : in the United States, 70-73, 264 ; of women, 201-202 ; of criminals, 250-251 ; of the poor in our cities, 267 ; as related to the labor problem, 341-342 ; as a remedy for social disorders, 353.
Eggleston, Dr. Edward, on the Pilgrims, 60.
Elmira Reformatory, 233 and *note*, 236 *note*, 246-250, 251-252, 291, 303.
Emerson, Ralph Waldo, quoted, 33, 89, 98, 245, 250.
England : America's debt to, 38, 58-70, 79 ; our wars with, 96-97 ; her commercial influence, 149 ; her commercial methods criticised, 164-165 ; woman suffrage in, 189 ; number of working women in, 207 ; penal reform in, 231-232, 242 ; decrease of crime in, 236 ; co-operative production in, 314-315 ; increase of poverty in, 338-342 ; influence of trades unions in, 346-348, 354 ; growth of the nation in, 367 ; Saxon influence in, 367, 375.
Environment, influence of, 8, 119 ; necessity of adjustment to, 372.
Ethics : of national life, 8, 10-11 ; as related to war, 97, 99, 109-110 ; of commercial intercourse, 155-156 ; of the criminal problem, 243-244, 250 ; of the charity problem, 268-269 ; of the labor problem, 354-356 ; of the family, 365.
Evolution : of the nation, 9-10 ; of American institutions, 55-78, 80 ; as affected by militancy, 109-150 ; by the railway problem, 139 ; by foreign commerce, 157-169 ; of woman, in society and industry, 199-223 ; of penal methods and institutions, 255-276 ; of the temperance problem, 299-300 ; of the wages system, 307 ; of profit-sharing, 310-320 ; as related to the labor problem, 358 ; of history, 364 ; of the family, 364-376 ; of the individual, 371-372, 373 ; of the Church, 376-378 ; its laws and conditions, 381-390.
Export duties, advocated by James A. Skilton, 167-168.

FACTORY system: as affecting woman's work, 204-205 ; as related to industrial evolution, 311-312 *et seq.*, 323, 326.
Family : its place in social evolution, 3, 6, 86 ; its relation to the nation, 11, 364-376 ; its primitive status, 200-201 ; as affected by woman's industrial position, 213-214, 215-216, 217, 218 ; its place in history, 364-376 ; its ethical status, 365 ; its development, 366 ; its migrations, 366-367 ; in America, 367-368 ; the evolved family, 370-371 ; as related to the individual, 370-372 ; differentiation of, 373-374.
Federalism, in America, 394.
Fiske, Prof. John, on Puritanism, 60 ; on early Indian wars, 93, 95 ; on nation-making, 367 ; on the township in America, 69-70, 372 ; on the conditions of progress, 385 ; his historical works commended, 391 ; his work on civil government, 394 ; on historical progress, 397.

Index.

Food : as related to racial types, 25 ; supply of, 27 ; as related to transportation, 123–125 ; degeneracy of, in America, 164 ; as related to the drink habit, 285 ; alcohol as related to, 287, 296, 303 ; of wage-laborers in our cities, 341.
Foreign commerce, 147–169.
Foster, Prof. Robert, on the evolution of charitable methods, 273–274.
France : why her hold on America was not permanent, 37–38 ; our indebtedness to her, 58,79–80 ; cost of its military establishment, 105 and *note ;* number of working women in, 207 ; penal reform in, 238 ; profit-sharing in, 316–317 ; administration of charities in, 262 ; labor unions in, 354 ; individual rights developed in, 368.
Franklin, Benjamin, 396, 397.
Freebooter, his relation to commerce, 162, 167, 168.
Freedom and determination as moral factors in social evolution, 9, 18.
Freedom, political ; its dependence on national government, 9–11, 15 ; its natural necessity in America, 34 ; its relation to trades-unionism, 350–352 ; of the individual, 371–372 ; threatened by excessive legislation, 375–376 ; its recent advances, 390.
Freeman, Prof. Edward A., on the derivation of American institutions, 61 ; on the New England town meeting, 67, 372 ; on law and history, 392.
Free trade : the evolutionary ideal of international relationships, 36–37 ; and protection, as adapted to special stages of social evolution, 36 *note ;* tendency toward, in eras of peace, 99–102 ; as related to our commercial interests, 152, 157, 158–169.
Froude, James Anthony, on the impossibility of a philosophy of history, 363, 378–379, 393, 399–402, 404–405.

Gates, Nelson J., on crime and its punishment, 245–246.
Geographical factors in American civilization, 29–32.
Geological factors in American civilization, 26–29.
George, Henry, on the Australian railway system, 142 ; on poverty, 276.
Germany : its nationality as affecting its governmental evolution, 14, 17 ; its influence on the New England township, 67–68, 366–367 ; cost of its military establishment, 105 and *note ;* its commercial relations with America, 155 ; condition of woman in, 195, 202, 207 ; its universities, 220 ; peasant proprietors in, 309 ; labor-unions in, 354 ; Jew baiting in, 367 ; unification of, 401.
Giffin, Robert, on the condition of the poor in England, 340–343, 345.
Gilman, Nicholas Paine, on the labor problem, 307–322, 328.
Gladstone, Hon. William E., his name for Americans, 58 ; on the American Constitution, 64.
Gorton, Samuel, his relation to the massacre of Miantonomo, 93.
Graham, J. Whidden, on interstate commerce, 142–143.
Greene, Prof. George Washington, on King Philip's War, 94.
Gunton, Prof. George, on the nation's place in civilization, 17–18 ; on the economic position of woman, 216–217 ; his lecture on the wage system, 307 ; on the labor problem, 323–324.

Hall, Bolton, on charity, 275.
Hamilton, Alexander, 65, 100, 369, 370.
Heredity, as related to crime, 239, 245 ; to the drink habit, 285 ; to the growth of American institutions, 368–369.
Hiawatha, his federal league, 368.
History, the philosophy of, 363–405 ; definition of, 363 ; on evolution, 364 ; a development of the family, 364–376 ; progress in, 381–390 ; writers of, 390–392 ; importance of its study, 392–398.
Holbrook, Dr. Martin L., on natural factors in American civilization, 49.
Holland : its influence on American institutions, 38 *note,* 61, 68, 71, 72–73, 75, 79, 81 ; its interest in international arbitration, 107 ; woman's position in, 202 ; its early improvement of penal institutions, 230 ; the federal idea in, 368 ; non-excitable character of its people, 373.
Hughes, Thomas, on co-operative production, 313.
Humanity, the religion of, 112–113.
Human selection, 256–257.
Huxley, Prof. Thomas H., on the functions of government, 18 ; on religious charities, 260 ; on social diseases and their remedies, 338–340, 345, 355 ; his definition of law, 399.

Iles, George, on the drink problem, 300–301.
Immigration : importance of, 49 ; problem of, 76–77 ; from militant nations, 106 ; as related to criminal statistics, 236 and *note,* 240, 251 ; its value to America, 382.
Indian, the American, his status when America was discovered, 29 ; his influence

on our colonial development, 38 ; injustice of our treatment of, 38 ; our wars with, 92-96, 112, 113 ; his development of the federal idea, 368 ; his tribal organization, 379 ; his decay under civilization, 388.
Individual, evolution of the, 372-373.
Individualism : dangers of excessive, 6-7, 19 ; the basic principle of the English character, 81 ; Wordsworth Donisthorpe's book on, 327 ; its impossibility in social adjustment affirmed, 358 ; its evolution in America, 369, 371-372, 373.
Industrialism : its conflict with militantism, 89-92, 99-102, 106, 108, 109-111 ; its evolution, 315-322 ; its problem in America, 374-375.
Inebriety : as related to charity, 265 ; prevalence of, 279-280 ; growth of, 280-281 ; as related to brain development, 281-282 ; to heredity, 283-284 ; influence of marriage on, 284 ; as related to defective nutrition, 285-286 ; its psychological factors, 287-288 ; scientific treatment of, 280-295.
Initiative and referendum, 337.
Instinctive selection, in effecting race improvement, 257-258.
Insurance for laborers, 325-326.
Internationalism, 372.
Interstate commerce, 119-144.
Intoxication : problem of, in the United States, 279-304 ; of laboring men, 335.
Inventions, by women, 220-221.

JANES, DR. LEWIS G., on Herbert Spencer's theory of the state, 19-20 ; on the treatment of the American aborigines, 51 ; on free trade and protection, 51 ; on war and progress, 85-111, 114-115 ; on interstate commerce, 143-144 ; on foreign commerce, 168-169 ; on the economic position of woman, 217-218 ; on the punishment of crime, 250-252 ; on the drink problem, 303-304 ; on the dangers of excessive legislation, 359.
Jefferson, Thomas, on the township and town meeting, 70, 372 ; French influence on, 368 ; on equality before the law, 372 ; his influence on our institutions, 394 ; on the public-school system, 396.
Jesus, his prayer for daily bread, 27 ; his martyrdom for man, 379 ; a product of the ages, 388.
Jones, Sir William, on the state, 5.

KENYON, ELLEN E., on the economic position of woman, 218-223.
Kimball, Rev. John C., on natural factors in American civilization, 23-48 ; his views criticised, 50-51, 95-96.
Knights of Labor, 337, 354.

LABOR : its productiveness in America, 33 ; evolution of, 90 ; woman's relation to, 174-176, 200-223 ; in penal institutions, 232-234, 236, 249-250 ; as related to the charity problem, 272 ; to the drink habit, 293-294 ; the problem of, 307-328 ; perpetual need of, 308-310 ; working on shares, 310-311 ; the factory system, 311-312 ; profit-sharing, 315-320 ; as related to civilization, 321-322 ; political aspects of its problem, 331-360.
Labor problem, 307-328 ; political aspects of the, 331-360.
Laissez-faire, 144, 237, 263.
Landesgemeinde, 67.
Land monopoly, as related to charity, 275, 276 ; as affecting the labor problem, 349, 352.
Law : natural origin of, 6 ; as related to freedom. 9-10, 19 ; origin of, in America, 61-62 ; as related to religious freedom, 63 and *note ;* Montesquieu's influence on, 65-66 ; as affecting the ballot, 74 ; Asiatic obedience to, 80 ; as regulating interstate commerce, 129-134 ; as related to foreign commerce, 150 ; how it should be executed, 241-242, 251-352 ; its effect on morals, 246 ; as related to labor organizations, 337-338 ; statute, as related to laws of Nature, 371 ; equality before, 372 ; proper basis of, 373 ; dangers of too much legislation, 375-376 ; canon law in conflict with code, 376 ; natural, and special providences, 386 ; lawmaking an instinct of civilized races, 388 ; a part of history, 392 ; proper qualifications for making, 395-398.
Lecky, W. E. H., on the physical conditions of human progress, 385 ; on the chances of history, 386 ; on the value of historical studies, 393.
Leibnitz, his monadology, 4.
Le Row, Caroline B., on the economic position of woman, 199-214.
Libel, the law of, in the United States, 73.
License system, 299, 303.
Lincoln, Abraham, 28, 185, 191, 383, 396.
Logan, Walter S., on foreign commerce, 157-158.
Lowell, James Russell, on our country, 23 ; on its discovery by Columbus, 57 ; on corporal punishment in schools, 73.
Luther, Martin, 71.

McKeen, James, on the evolution of penal methods and institutions, 227-244.
Madison, James, 65, 368, 396.
Magna Charta, 66.
Maine, Sir Henry Sumner, on the Constitution of the United States, 65 ; on law and custom, 371, 376 ; on the Aryans in India, 388.
Malthus, his economic theories, 166, 168.
Manufactures: growth of, 100, 101; in Switzerland, 108; woman's relation to, 204-207 ; as related to the labor problem, 311-312, 314-319, 323-326.
Marriage : legal protection of, 11 ; of city and country dwellers, 42 ; as affecting woman's industrial status, 175, 213, 215-216, 217-218, 220-223 ; as related to charities, 269 ; as related to inebriety, 283, 284-285, 294, 295 ; as related to family development, 364-374 ; evolution of, 384.
Maudsley, Dr. Henry, his pessimism, 381.
Maxwell, Dr. William H., on the philosophy of history, 399-402.
Mechanical view of the nation contested, 9-12, 25.
Merwin, Prof. Almon G., on the economic position of woman, 215-216.
Mexico, the Gulf of, as related to our civilization, 39-40 ; our war with, as related to our civilization, 97-98 ; our commerce with, 152-153.
Miantonomo, the massacre of, 93-94.
Militancy : its early uses, 85-87 ; when it becomes injurious, 88-89 ; as related to industrialism, 89-91 ; its history in America, 92-98 ; recent revival of, 99-100 ; its effect on our industries, 101-102 ; its cost, 102-103, 104-105 ; its relation to crime, 103-104 ; how it will cease, 109-110.
Monks, Prof. J. W., on the political aspects of the drink problem, 303-304.
Monopolies : of railroads, 131-132, 142, 144 ; of land, 275, 276, 349, 352 ; as related to the labor problem, 355, 359.
Montesquieu, his influence on American thought, 65, 368.
Motley, John Lothrop, on public schools in Holland, 72.
Müller, Prof. Max, on the Aryan race, 400.

Napoleon I : influence of his conquests, 88 ; his *laissez-faire* doctrine, 263 ; on England's relations to the seas, 386 ; on history, 403 ; his existence questioned, 404.
Napoleon III : the alleged popular character of his wars, 113, 115.
Nation, its place in civilization, 3-20 ; its place in social evolution, 91-92.
Natural factors in American civilization, 23-51.
Natural scenery as affecting human thought and life, 44-47.
Natural selection, in social evolution, 199-200 ; in race improvement, 255-256, 257-258.
New England, 32, 41, 42, 45, 60, 63, 64, 67, 68, 69, 70, 71, 72, 93, 205, 206, 309, 344, 367, 368, 377.

Opportunism, in social reform, 355.
Origin of American institutions, 60-62.
Origin of Species, 239.
Origin of the Fittest, 377.

Paine, Thomas : his religion of humanity, 113 ; on the rights of man, 371.
Palmer, A. Emerson, on what America owes to the Old World, 55-78, 81-82 ; on the philosophy of history, 402-404.
Parliament, 66, 67, 68.
Paternalism, 367.
Pauperism, necessity of a quarantine against, 76 ; its increase in America, 101 ; its scientific treatment, 255-276.
Peace, beneficent influence of, on our civilization, 100-101.
Penn, William, his treatment of the Indians, 51, 95.
Penology : primitive methods of, 227-228 ; evolution of, 228-229 ; improved science of, 229-233 ; reforms in, in America, 232-234.
Pension system : abuses of, condemned, 102-103, 114 ; for laboring men advocated, 325.
Philip, King, his war with the New England colonists, 93-95.
Philosophy of history, 363-405.
Physiography, as related to history, 8, 23-48.
Piracy, as related to commerce, 162, 167, 168.
Police idea of the state, 3-5, 14.
Political aspects of the labor problem, 331-360.
Political status of woman, 173-196.
Politics : how degraded in America, 78 ; international, 110 ; as affecting woman, 173-196 ; as related to penal institutions, 252 ; to public charity, 266 ; to the drink problem, 304 ; to the labor problem, 331-360.

Pooling, among railroads, 136.
Populist party, 355, 357.
Potts, William, on the nation's place in civilization, 16–17 ; on the labor problem, 326–327.
Poverty, intensification of, in recent years, 101, 343–346.
President of the United States, 66.
Priestley, Dr. Joseph, his lectures on history, 391.
Prisons, in Asia and Europe, 224–232 ; in America, 232–234.
Product-sharing in industrial evolution, 310–312.
Profit-sharing in industrial evolution, 315–322, 324, 327, 353, 374–375.
Progress : in human affairs, 379–380 ; its laws, 381–382 ; antagonism essential to, 382–384 ; its conditions, 384–387 ; the unconscious elements in, 387–390.
Prohibition, its efficacy as a cure for the drink evil discussed, 279, 290, 291, 296, 297–300, 301, 303–304.
Puritan, the, his influence on American institutions, 60 ; in Holland, 61–62 ; his intolerance, 93 ; his treatment of the Indians, 93–95.
Puritan spirit : its influence on American civilization, 60–62, 377 ; immigration as related to, 382 ; its triumph in America, 390.

QUAKERS, persecution of, in New England, 64 ; their relations with the Indians, 95, 112–113 ; their tendency to survive, 257.

RACE-HATRED, a hindrance to progress, 387.
Railways : as factors in interstate commerce, 130–131 ; their legal status, 131–132 ; as controlled by the Interstate Commerce Act, 132–133 ; later aspects of the railway problem, 134–138 ; the proposed remedies, 138–139 ; the method of evolution, 139–140.
Raymond, Dr. Rossiter W., on the labor problem, 327–338.
Reformatory, New York State, 233 and *note*, 236 *note*, 246–250, 251–252.
Religion and progress, 383–384.
Religious freedom, guaranteed by the United States Constitution, 62.
Revolutionary War, its effects on our civilization, 96–97.
Ricardo, his economic theories, 166, 168.
Richmond, Miss Mary E., on charity organization, 270–273.
Rights of man, their true foundation, 4–5, 365, 368 ; presupposed in the primitive family, 371–372.
Rogers, Prof. Thorold, on the condition of wage-earners, 349.
Rousseau, Jean Jacques, his theory of the social contract, 4 ; his influence on American ideas, 368 ; on the rights of the individual, 371.

SALOON, the, deleterious influence of, 286–287, 301, 304.
Saloon politics, evils of, 304.
Salvation Army, 268.
Sampson, Z. Sidney, on America's indebtedness to England, 81.
Schools : their value to the nation, 10 ; origin of the public, 71–73 ; their opportunities for educating women, 176–177, 201–202 ; their differentiation from public charities, 264–265 ; differentiation of, from the family, 373–374 ; from religious supervision, 374 ; importance of historical studies in, 397.
Shepard, Dr. Charles H., on the drink problem, 301–303.
Skilton, James A., on America's indebtedness to Asia, 80–81 ; on foreign commerce, 161–168.
Slavery : its influence on American civilization, 12, 28, 80 ; as cause of the Mexican War, 97-98 ; as related to the great rebellion, 98 ; its dependence on militantism, 100 ; its practical annihilation as an institution, 106 ; its existence in the East, 162 ; relation of the cotton-gin to, in America, 205 ; contrasted with the wage system, 307 ; as related to the sweat-shop system, 348 ; Aristotle's advocacy of, 378 ; its rapid extinction, 380, 390.
Social and political status of woman, 173–196.
Social Democracy in Germany, 354.
Social evils preventable under scientific treatment, 293.
Socialism: as related to trade organizations, 113, 312, 354 ; Herbert Spencer's opposition to, 115 ; as related to penal methods, 237–238 ; as distinguished from co-operation, 326 ; as related to capitalism, 359–360 ; modern tendencies toward, retrogressive, 375 ; its chief error, the neglect of history, 393.
Social Statics, 3, 19.
Spencer, Herbert, on the nature of government, 3, 17, 18, 19–20 ; on militant and industrial types of society, 89–91 ; on war, 110, 185 ; criticised by T. B. Wakeman, 112 ; defended by Dr. Janes, 114–115 ; on freedom in America, 163 ; economic tendencies of his philosophy, 166 ; on woman suffrage, 183, 184, 185 ; on prison ethics, 251 ; on legislation by women, 373 ; on the new tyranny, 375 ;

on the future progress of society, 381; on the conditions of progress, 385, 397; the father of the philosophy of history, 386; his definition of law, 399.
State rights, 12, 19, 395–396.
States: Arkansas, 63 *note*; California, 160; Colorado, 46; Connecticut, 51, 65, 71, 94, 96, 292, 373; Dakota, 309; Delaware, 63 *note*; Florida, 42, 160; Georgia, 394; Illinois, 69, 344, 394; Indiana, 264, 265; Kansas, 137; Kentucky, 28, 31; Maryland, 61, 63 *note*, 144, 185, 266, 270; Massachusetts, 51, 61, 63, 64, 70, 71, 74, 93, 94, 96, 186, 189, 190, 204, 207, 342, 370, 373, 381; Michigan, 267; Minnesota, 267; Nebraska, 265; New Jersey, 144; New York, 32, 38 *note*, 63, 71, 74, 81, 125, 131, 137, 179, 195, 206, 207, 209, 231 *note*, 233, 234, 250, 252 *note*, 264, 266, 344, 370, 394; Ohio, 126; Oregon, 160; Pennsylvania, 63 and *note*, 73, 74, 95, 96, 104, 124, 125, 126, 131, 158, 232, 241, 264, 343; Rhode Island, 74, 94, 95, 96, 100 and *note*, 370; Tennessee, 63 *note*, 207; Texas, 97, 141, 160; Utah Territory, 188; Vermont, 63 *note*, 103; Virginia, 63, 69, 70, 72, 143, 367, 381; Washington, 188; Wyoming, 188, 189, 195, 196.
State, theory of, 3–15; its evolution in America, 367–371.
Suffrage: in the town meeting, 69–70; its secrecy essential, 73–74; in Switzerland, 108; for women, advocated, 181–193, 209–210; in labor organizations, 336–338; the pledge of individual rights, 370–371.
Sullivan, J. W., on the political aspects of the labor problem, 331–356.
Sunday observance, 388.
Supreme Court: its place in our federal system, 66; the model for an international tribunal, 107.
Sweat-shop system, 348.
Switzerland, popular government in, 108–109, 337, 368, 395.

TARIFF: as related to American civilization, 36–37, 51, 99, 100 and *note*, 101; early economic advances little affected by, 100 and *note*; prohibited between the States, 143–144, 370; as affecting foreign commerce and American civilization, 150, 157–169; its artificial stimulation of the herding instinct, 374.
Tayler, Robert W., on interstate commerce, 119–140, 144; quoted by J. A. Skilton, 163.
Taylor, John A., on the drink problem, 296–298.
Temperance reform in America, 279, 304.
Territorial size, as related to our material and social development, 32–33.
Tobacco, injurious effects of, 302.
Town and individual in American history, 369.
Town meeting, its place in our political system, 67–70, 367, 369.
Trades unions: their militant organization, 99; their relation to the labor problem, 312, 333–356; their democratic methods, 336–338; their influence on the wage-earner, 346–349.
Trade winds and the St. Lawrence River, as affecting our national development, 37–39.
Transportation: economic philosophy of, 121–122; superiority of home consumption, 122; natural trend of, 123; primitive methods of, 123–124; evolution of, in the United States, 124–127; present problems of, 130–144.
Trusts: their place in our civilization, 47; their militant methods, 99; how they serve the people, 142, 161, 326.
Tungemot, 68.

UNFORESEEN consequences of human effort in historical evolution, 119–120.
Union for Christian Work, 274.
United States: their geology, 29; not visited by Columbus, 37; the term used synonymously with America, 55–57; relation of their institutions to Teutonic models, 68; their military establishment, 102–105; their internal commerce, 120; their railway system, 130–140; their foreign commerce, 148–169; woman suffrage in, 188–191; their evolution from the family, 367–371.
Utopia, 355, 358.

VEDAS, 389.
Verinder, Frederick, on the condition of rural laborers in England, 340.
Virgin soil, a bequest to our civilization, 32–33.
Volapük, 60.
Voltaire, his influence on American ideas, 368; his character as a historian, 386.

WAGES: system, as related to tariffs, 169; as affecting woman's industrial status, 205, 207, 208, 215–217; as related to the labor problem, 307, 310–312; modifications of, in industrial evolution, 312–315; as related to profit-sharing, 315–322, 323–324; Mr. Dolge's modification of, 324–326; as related to contract, 327–328; influence of trades-unions on, 333–342; in America, 342–343.

Wakeman, Thaddeus B., on war and progress, 112-113; on the political aspects of the labor problem, 359-360.
Waldo, George E., on the political aspects of the labor problem, 357-358.
Wallace, Alfred Russel, his definition of progress, 385.
War: and progress, 14, 85-115; its early uses, 85-88; when it becomes injurious, 88-89; the type of society created by it, 89-91; its effect on national development, 91-92; America's wars, 92-98; its effect on our industries, 101-102; its cost, 102-105; and crime, 103-104; how it will cease, 109-111; its relation to commerce, 156; conflict not a finality, 384.
Ward, Dr. Duren J. H., on natural factors of American civilization, 49-50.
Warner, Ellsworth, on the political aspects of the labor problem, 358-359.
Warner, Prof. Amos G., on the evolution of charities and charitable institutions, 255-269, 276.
Washington, George, his model of the public-school system, 396.
Welch, John C., on interstate commerce, 141-142.
What America owes to the Old World, 55-82.
Wheeler, E. J., on the drink problem, 298-300.
White, Hon. Andrew D., on science and supernaturalism, 383; on the importance of historical studies, 395.
Williams, Roger, his treatment of the American Indians, 38, 51, 93-95.
Wingate, Gen. George W., on war and progress, 113-114.
Woman: social and political status of, 173-196; her present condition, 173-174; her industrial opportunities, 174-176, 202-208; her higher education, 176-177, 201-202; her place in the professions, 178-179; her work in literature, 179-181; her claims to the suffrage, 175-193, 209-210; obstacles to her industrial progress, 207-209; her work as affecting the family and society, 213; as related to crime, 219 and note; as a lawmaker, 373.
Wright, Carroll D., on woman's industrial position, 204-205.

THE END.

www.ingramcontent.com/pod-product-compliance
Lightning Source LLC
Chambersburg PA
CBHW020545300426
44111CB00008B/803